THE
RADICAL
LEFT

Under the editorship of

RICHARD P. LONGAKER

University of California at Los Angeles

THE RADICAL LEFT
The Abuse of Discontent

Edited with introductions by
WILLIAM P. GERBERDING and
DUANE E. SMITH

HOUGHTON
MIFFLIN
COMPANY

BOSTON
NEW YORK   ATLANTA
GENEVA, ILLINOIS
DALLAS   PALO ALTO

ACKNOWLEDGMENTS:

Our major debt is to the other contributors to this volume. We thank them for their permission to reprint their articles.

We also wish to express our appreciation to those publishers who granted us permission to reprint their articles.

Frank Shelton, Political Science Editor at Houghton Mifflin, has been encouraging, patient, and persistent. Richard P. Longaker, our colleague and Political Science Advisory Editor for Houghton Mifflin, has been helpful beyond the call of duty. Lance Wickens, also of Houghton Mifflin, has made many helpful suggestions and criticisms. We thank them all.

We owe a special debt to Mrs. Douglas S. Hobbs who performed the time-consuming task of acquiring the permissions as well as various other editorial duties with generosity and in good spirits.

We are, of course, responsible not only for our own essays but also for the political perspective of this volume. None of the other authors should be held responsible for anything save his own article(s).

University of California
Los Angeles

William P. Gerberding
Duane E. Smith

Contents

THE RADICAL LEFT
The Abuse of Discontent

INTRODUCTION

THE EMERGENCE of a new radicalism of the Left in American politics is one of the most striking features of our recent history. Whatever its short or long-range significance may turn out to be, this new radicalism has received a good deal of attention from the mass media and has been hailed by many as a salutary, even saving, new dimension in American politics. Many of its admirers and many of its critics have adopted its own somewhat apocalyptic rhetorical style, and many impressionable people at home and abroad have come to believe that the United States is at or near an historic, perhaps revolutionary, turning point.

This book is a collection of essays and articles which take the new radicals seriously but look with a skeptical eye on their ideas, their activities, and their pretensions. The editors who made the selections have a point of view: they are sharply critical of the new radicalism. The selections are not, however, characterized by ideological uniformity. The commitments of the contributors range from the left to slightly right of center. The majority are probably clustered somewhere around the much-maligned middle. In any event, if one wanted to give a quiet cocktail party, undisturbed by the raucous sound of vigorous disagreements, one probably would not invite this particular group of people.

This collection is not designed to counter each and every criticism and prescription put forward by the new radicals. In general, our purposes are as follows:

1

1. to argue that traditional democratic politics have served this nation rather well on balance in terms of such criteria as freedom, justice, material well-being and playing an honorable and effective role in international affairs;

2. to argue the legitimacy and perhaps the superiority of a political system where interests tend to play as vital a role in politics as ideas (or ideals);

3. to suggest that proposals for change should be carefully examined lest their unanticipated consequences turn out to be worse than the problems allegedly being resolved;

4. to point out that the means employed by many of the new radicals are in violation of traditional libertarian norms and are a threat to the survival of those norms both by themselves and by virtue of the reactions they produce from hostile and at least potentially anti-democratic forces on the Right;

5. to suggest that an exclusive and fervent preoccupation with idealistic policies and objectives is by itself no substitute for—and, carried to extremes, is sometimes incompatible with—such positive political qualities as tolerance for dissent and disagreement, and appreciation of the uses of diversity and prudential judgment; and to suggest, moreover, that such single-mindedness sometimes carries within it the seeds of a dogmatic, crusading style of politics that seeks to rule or ruin;

6. to suggest that certain styles of politics, especially those with a revolutionary or utopian quality, are often more the consequence of their advocates' psychological disorders than they are an appropriate response to the shortcomings of the political system.

2

To describe the politics of the radical Left over the last decade or so is an extremely complicated enterprise. Ideologically, it runs the gamut from the vaguely New Left fringes of the otherwise quite "mainstream" movements that developed in support of the presidential candidacies of Senators Eugene McCarthy and Robert Kennedy all the way to the extreme views adopted by the Students for a Democratic Society (SDS), the Weathermen and some of the more alienated elements in the civil rights movement. The confusion was perhaps best illustrated by the events which took place at the Convention for a New Politics held in Chicago in 1967. (See Renata Adler's article in this volume, pp. 31–49.) Moreover, one cannot take refuge in a convenient phrase, such as the "New Politics." Initially possessing fairly radical connotations and serving as a sort of umbrella under which were clustered a variety of groups of varying degrees of militancy, the term was later associated with the presidential campaigns of Senators Kennedy and McCarthy. This later usage has now become generally accepted and most people currently associated with the "New Politics" are active in fairly traditional reformist party politics, especially, of course, in the Democratic party. The "New Politics" may owe some of its style and ideas to the new radicalism of the Left and clear distinctions are obviously impossible to draw, but this book is primarily about the radical Left.

One of the reasons for the difficulty of describing the contours of the new radicalism is the refusal of its adherents to spell out their ideological goals with any degree of precision. It is easy enough to perceive what it is about American society that they dislike, and in a few instances, a fairly clear response to the problem is evident. During its earliest phase, for example, the Free Speech Movement at Berkeley was an instance when the grievance was clearly defined and the solution was equally clear. This moment of clarity, it goes without saying, did not last, and the rebellion against restrictions on speech, restrictions which even many conservatives viewed as fatuous at best, was broadened to a general attack on the university as an institution. This attack included a revulsion against a multiplicity of alleged evils such as the bureaucratic character of the institution, the irrelevance of the curriculum, indifferent teaching, complicity with the military-industrial establishment, and so on. Oddly enough, this reluctance to define an exact ideological position is very typical of American political life and discussion. Americans, even those who have written about politics, have been notoriously fuzzy regarding ideological matters, to the eternal despair of European observers.

The radical Left can be viewed from various perspectives. Some observers, for example, see it simply as an aspect of the rebellion of the young against the authority, life styles, and values of their elders. While there is some reason for describing this development as yet another episode in the continuing generational warfare and for being tempted to dismiss it as a modern children's crusade, this is probably not the most fruitful approach. For one thing, while the new radicalism may be dominated by the young, it does have its adherents, and for that matter its heroes, who can no longer claim to be under the magic age of thirty.

Nevertheless, it is possible to discuss a series of events and certain general attitudes which are likely to be common to those who express a disenchantment, indeed an alienation from, American society and politics.

In 1960 the House Un-American Activities Committee held a series of hearings in San Francisco, an event signaling the emergence of various forms of protest which culminated in violence. Not the least important result of this affair was the fact that it probably enhanced the reputation of HUAC, nourishing the belief among the more susceptible that the nation was seriously menaced by an internal Communist conspiracy. A film of the events, made from the Committee's point of view, enjoyed considerable success at meetings of groups such as the D.A.R. This film was also widely distributed at government expense on college campuses, where its reception was scarcely that intended by the committee. In the eyes of the students, HUAC looked both ridiculous and menacing. In a symbolic sense, at least, this marked the beginning of the current period of radical protest, although it also has roots in the civil rights sit-ins which began in the South at roughly the same time.

The new mood was reinforced by a number of developments in the 1960s. Perhaps the most important of these were the "rediscovery" of poverty in affluent America, the increasing intensity and salience of the black revolt, the assassination of President Kennedy, and the war in Vietnam. Any one of these—or at least any one of the last three—contained enough symbolic and substantive significance to have proved disorienting to a population reawakened to politics. All together, they unleashed a sense of fury and frustration which fostered the radicalization of substantial numbers of people, especially younger people.

The dissenters of the alienated Left have focused their attention on a relatively few, easily identifiable, highly visible issues. The war in Vietnam and, more generally, the role of the United States in world affairs has been the most spectacular target, with the dissent having been marked by various dramatic forms of protest including violent civil disobedience. While there is little doubt that the war in Vietnam provided a powerful impetus for those movements which are characterized by some degree of alienation from American politics and society, it would be a mistake to assume that the end of the war will bring in its train an end to this style of political activity. In addition to the war, and potentially more explosive, are the problems of race and poverty in the United States. The failure of the political and economic system to respond with sufficient speed in resolving the racial and economic problems of the nation as well as its alleged insensitivity to public opinion in the conduct of the Vietnamese war gave rise to an attack upon the organization of the political system, a system which was condemned as irretrievably corrupt, unresponsive, and beyond repair.

Closely related to this disenchantment with American political institutions has been an attack upon the organization of quasi-public institutions. Thus far, the universities have borne the brunt of this attack, for the obvious reason that many of the activists of the left are either students or hangers-on in the major academic communities. Other organizations, however, are not immune, and a few forays have been made into the trade unions. Thus far, the unions have been rather more resistant than the universities, and a coalition between the students and the workers does not appear to be an imminent possibility. Indeed, class warfare between these two groups is far more likely.

The current protest has focused on these issues for the very good reason that they are important issues, reflecting some very important problems in American society. The moral and strategic wisdom of our original decision to fight in Vietnam and of the many related subsequent decisions is quite obviously questionable at best. Similarly, only the obtuse would deny that the plight of various minorities in the United States represents one of the most serious problems confronting the nation. As far as the political institutions of American life go, a concern with the extent to which they are functioning successfully not only is fairly widespread, it is a concern with a lengthy history.

3

It is not the issues, then, but the character of its response to them which distinguishes the radical Left from the other strands of American political life. While there are, to be sure, differences of degree as well as of emphasis between the members, say, of the SDS and the followers of Abbie Hoffman, certain general observations can be made about this response.

Perhaps the most important characteristic is an alienation from American society and politics. Many are convinced that America is afflicted with an excessive materialism, that the competitive ethic has run wild, that America has become an inhuman society. While some of the dissenters would deny it, there is a certain millenarian streak which can be seen in the politics of the new radicals, and this millenarianism emerges out of their alienation. It also contributes to the restless impatience which leads to the easy dismissal of virtually all of the existing institutions and practices of American life, and more specifically, of American political life.

What is most breathtaking about this dismissal is the refusal to suggest the sorts of institutions and practices which would replace those apparently so inadequate as to be beyond salvaging. There is, to be sure, much talk about giving power back to the people, "participatory democracy," and such, but there is very little discussion of the institutional means by which this would be accomplished. Indeed, it is considerably less than clear just what sort of power is going to be given to the people that they do not already have; relatedly, it is not at all clear who "the people" are in this cloudy scenario.

It is not unfair to conclude that the advocates of this approach to the political problems of the United States are possessed of an anti-institutional bias, a bias emerging from the conviction that institutions, whether of the government or of the university, are likely to be corrupt and oppressive. This view leads to a regrettable carelessness about institutions, an attitude that if they are destroyed, not very much is lost.

This anti-institutionalism is intimately bound up with their hostility to politics. This hostility can be seen not only in the fact that goals are often pursued outside of the ordinary political organizations, but also in the demonology of the new radicals. It is not easy to escape the suspicion that the revulsion against most political leaders results to a large extent from the fact that they are thought to be guilty of the corruptions, the compromises, the moral evasions, and the equivocations which many people are inclined to attribute to the politician. The millenarian is likely to be devoted to purity, and politics is admittedly not pure. Whether it is to be dismissed for that reason is another matter.

The rejection of the tradition of civilized discourse has been frequently noted, particularly among the more radical elements of the alienated Left, of which the Students for a Democratic Society is probably the most prominent example. This involves matters far more important than a propensity for obscenities, a propensity mildly irritating or mildly amusing, depending on one's mood. It involves the rejection of the kind of self-restraint freely accepted by civilized men and which is essential to the acceptance of the principles of free speech. It is interesting to note that whereas one of the classic battles waged by the student Left evolved over the issue of free speech, the concept of free speech is explicitly rejected by some members of the radical Left, most notably by Herbert Marcuse, a philosopher who enjoys a certain cachet among the young radicals.

Rather than being viewed as a means of discussion and communication, speech is frequently seen as simply another form of confrontation. Physical confrontation sometimes replaces verbal, all pretense at discussion and communication vanishes, politics is moved into the streets, and the result is action, emotion, participation of a sort. Violence is not uncommonly condoned and sometimes encouraged by many who have not given any serious thought to the consequences of its becoming a commonplace political technique. Those who express concern about the increasing use of violence as a tactic are either dismissed as timid liberals or malevolent fascists.

Closely related to this contemptuous dismissal of the tradition of civility and the casual acceptance of the techniques of violence is the emphasis on the doctrine of civil disobedience. Civil disobedience has ordinarily been viewed as acceptable only as a last resort for those whose moral sensibilities permit them no other course of action and who have exhausted the other paths of redress available to them. Now, however, it is readily engaged in on behalf of objectives which are sometimes dubious, and in circumstances in which the available remedies have scarcely been attempted, much less exhausted. Some people regard civil disobedience as an almost automatically justifiable response to any alleged injustice. For a small but highly visible group, it has become virtually a way of life, a sign of moral and political purity, to be persisted in until the arrival of the millennium.

The passion for civil disobedience is one aspect of the romantic attachment to action which is the final characteristic of the politics of the alienated Left. This devotion to action can fairly be described as romantic, since it is not necessarily action directed toward a specific goal. Quite to the contrary, there is a certain tendency to dismiss clearly defined goals as in some way corrupting the purity of action as action. From one point of view, action of any kind is seen as a confirmation of the fact that one is not simply the passive object of manipulation by big government, big business, or the big university. It is seen, finally, as an assertion of identity, of humanity. In light of this, the possibility that the results may be harmful is not thought to be very significant. Indeed, it is not so much results in the sense of objective changes in the external environment but rather the emotional satisfactions derived from being active which are sought.

These attributes of the radical Left raise serious doubts about its political and social criticism. These doubts are strikingly reinforced by some remarks of Edmund Burke written in 1791 regarding the French Revolution:

> Men are qualified for civil liberty in exact proportion to their disposition to put moral chains upon their own appetites; in proportion as their love of justice is above rapacity; in proportion as their soundness and sobriety of understanding is above their vanity and presumption; in proportion as they are more disposed to listen to the counsels of the wise and good, in preference to the flattery of knaves. Society cannot exist unless a controlling power upon will and appetite be placed somewhere, and the less of it there is within, the more there must be without. It is ordained in the eternal constitution of things, that men of intemperate minds cannot be free. Their passions forge their fetters.[1]

[1] *The Writings and Speeches of Edmund Burke,* Beaconsfield Edition, 12 vols. (New York, 1901), IV, 51–52.

PART I

The New Left

ONE OF THE WEAKNESSES of a moderate—and especially of a conservative—political posture is its tendency toward complacency and stagnation. Those who, like the editors of this book, are sensitive to the limitations on the efficacy of political action and who are likely to be fearful of the unanticipated consequences of precipitate change, tend to become too cautious, too protective of existing institutions and policies, and insufficiently concerned with the generation of helpfully innovative ideas and policies. It is in constantly prodding such complacency that political radicals can serve a useful, sometimes even a saving, purpose in a dynamic, adaptive political system. To some extent, the New Left has served the radical's historic purpose of raising fundamental questions that had lain unexamined for too long and stimulating action in areas where it was long overdue. It is too soon to try to assess and evaluate definitively the New Left's impact on the United States, and some of it will unquestionably be desirable.

It is not too soon, however, to suggest that much of the style and substance of New Left politics violates traditional democratic values. The most disturbing aspect is the wholesale rejection of even the best strains of American political thought and practice. The New Left apparently believes that American democracy as it has evolved over nearly two hundred years is irredeemably corrupt and intolerable. The catalogue of what radical rhetoricians call "bourgeois" values and ideas that must be summarily set aside includes virtually everything that most political liberals, moderates, and conservatives have generally regarded as little short of sacred: freedom of speech, tolerance of diversity and disagreement, non-violent change, and the legitimacy of democratic politics as it is practiced in the United States. These attitudes are expressed through intemperate rhetoric and coercive behavior and they are combined with a utopian faith in the saving utility of what is vaguely called "the revolution."

For our own part, we welcome this vagueness, this apparent infirmity of purpose and organization in the New Left. While some commentators have been critical of the New Left's failure to prescribe a distinct set of programs and remedies for the ills that beset American society, we are relieved by this shortcoming. If its analyses and actions are any guide, its long-range prescriptions would be absurd on paper and disastrous in practice.

American political history has had its share of extremist political movements. A few of them have been salutary, almost despite themselves; most have been a blot on our record. Happily, none of them has ever attracted anything like a majority of our generally rather sober citizenry. The following articles provide some insights into the latest manifestation of this recurring phenomenon.

The authors of these articles can, with one exception, be fairly characterized as liberals. The fourth—Howe—is an American socialist. They are all members of "The Establishment" in the sense that they are prominent and successful, even distinguished, in their fields of endeavor.

For the New Left, such a background renders their criticisms at best suspect, at worst fatally corrupted. But for anyone with an open mind, such *ad hominem* dismissals should not be persuasive. Their criticisms are not rooted in a complacent acceptance of the *status quo* or an automatically unsympathetic view of radical ideas and politics. They are thoughtful and experienced observers of good will, and their analyses merit sober consideration.

THE NEW
LEFT AND ITS
LIMITS

Nathan Glazer

For the last few years I have looked with increasing skepticism on the analyses and the actions of the radical Left in America. By the radical Left I mean those who believe there is something fundamentally and irredeemably wrong with our society, and who think the chief way of righting it lies in mobilizing the power of all the disadvantaged groups among us behind a drive for radical change, change going to the roots. My own skepticism in the face of so much passion and indeed accomplishment often troubles me, and it will certainly annoy radicals. They may say that to have been radical or liberal in one's youth, and to become relatively conservative in one's middle years, is so common an experience that it needs hardly any explanation at all. However, just as I would not explain the radical mood or outlook on psychological or temperamental grounds, so I would hope that radicals might suspend such easy judgments on my own outlook. There have been, after all, young conservatives and old radicals, even if not as many as the other way around. And just as I would accord the radical outlook full respect—as a perspective on the world that has its own rationale, its own roots, its own great thinkers, its own successes—so I would hope that radicals might for a while consider the point of view that is skeptical of their analyses, their programs, and their hopes.

Nathan Glazer, "The New Left and Its Limits," *Commentary* (July 1968), 31–39. Reprinted from *Commentary,* by permission; copyright © 1968 by the American Jewish Committee.

There are three principal areas in which the new radicalism expresses itself: the problem of the Vietnam war, and by extension the whole question of the role of the United States in world affairs, and in the development of the poorer countries; the problem of achieving equality for Negroes, which now centers in the crisis of the great urban ghettos; and the problem of higher education—in particular the role of youth in the administration of the campus and the shaping of the curriculum. In none of these three areas can we point to much to be happy about. I need not describe the sense of catastrophe that hangs over us whether we consider the war, or the black-white conflict. I would not apply so grand a term as catastrophe to the campus situation, and yet there is a growing sense of the triviality of much of mass higher education; and while I would hesitate to go so far as to say that the hearts and minds of our young people are being destroyed, I think the crisis in the universities is as serious in its own right for American youth as are Vietnam and race for the larger society.

In all three areas, radicalism, true to the term, wishes to go to the roots because, it says, what is wrong in each case is wrong at the roots. To find a half-million Americans in Vietnam, killing and being killed, burning villages and destroying crops, is sufficiently outrageous to make it plausible that there is a horror within the bowels of our society which has called these outer horrors forth. To find in the ghettos vast numbers of poverty-stricken people who have lost all faith in society, their fellow man, and their own power, who present a picture of disinheritance that no other advanced industrial society can show us; and to find on the other hand among many whites a ferocious hatred of these unfortunates that again no other advanced society can show us—this too is sufficient cause to assume that the roots are poisoned. To confront, finally, in the colleges and universities a host of petty demands and restrictions irrelevant to understanding and education, makes it easy enough to believe that something very basic is the operative cause.

Faced with these evils, and the general sense that something fundamental is wrong, the radical chooses between two broad general approaches to getting at the roots. One is the whole grand scheme of Marxism, in its various modern formulations. Capitalism is too old-fashioned a term to arouse much interest —it is now replaced by imperialism. Similarly, the increasing misery of the working class is replaced by the increasing misery of the underdeveloped world, and by that of our own "colonials" at home, the Negroes and other minority groups. The machine presumed to be at the heart of the misery has also been modernized, but fundamental to it still is the selfishness of a ruling class which cannot or will not give up its power and which therefore must be smashed. The mechanisms of a better society are still not studied much—they fall under the ban Marx and Engels imposed on utopianism and reformism. Thus the Communist country where the most serious effort to establish such mechanisms has been made, Yugoslavia, is of no great interest to today's radicals. They are more concerned with Cuba and China, which still maintain a pre-institutional—or a post-institutional?—revolutionary vigor, in which the thought and decisions of the central leader of the revolution are capable of overturning the new and barely established social structures every other day.

The most attractive aspect of the new radicalism is that it has developed a second and more popular approach to getting at the roots—more pragmatic and empirical, more humanist, less mechanical and dogmatic. This is the approach suggested in the Port Huron statement of 1962, a document characteristic of the early spirit of Students for a Democratic Society (SDS). But the candid and open stance of the New Left in its first phase of development—that something deep was wrong but no one quite knew precisely what it was or what would change it—could not be maintained forever as a basis for action. Thus an explanation began to emerge. The simple analysis of the Old Left, that capitalism or imperialism is at the root of the matter, was not very satisfactory, if only because it was too easy to point to the example of capitalist countries like Sweden and England on the one side and Communist ones like Soviet Russia and East Germany on the other to prove that no necessary causal relation exists between oppression and the institutions of capitalism. Referring to real experience—"where am *I* bugged?, where do *I* feel the pinch?"—the New Left began to decide that the problem lies not in the institutions of capitalism as such but rather in all types of fixed and formal institutions. The university administrator is not involved in the search for private profit, nor is the indifferent slum school teacher, the insensitive social worker, the hypocritical mayor, the technologically minded general. Rather—so goes the new argument—they are all small men trapped into serving big and powerful institutions that have grown hopelessly distant from immediate human needs and satisfactions. The institutions nevertheless draw on strong per-

sonal motivations to achieve their inhuman ends—the desire
for money and power and advancement, for security, for a
comfortable home-life in suburbia. In the view of the New Left,
the minor and more benign motivations of men emerge as
having greater potentialities for evil than the grander ones. It is
the man who wants to do his best for his wife and children,
keep up the mortgage and buy a new car—it is this man who
also releases the gas in the chambers and who makes the
napalm containers. He may even be a good union member and
vote Democratic.

WHEN ONE SEES INSTITUTIONS themselves as the source of
our present evils, and when one sees these institutions fed not
by the limited and distorted motivations of rampant capitalism,
but by such ancient and well-rooted human impulses as the
drives for comfort, security, and family, then one has forged an
analysis which is indeed powerful.

Nevertheless, the New Left has an answer—a conception of
democracy in which our traditional mix of civil liberties and
elected legislatures and officials is supplemented or supplanted
by new rights and new forms of democratic intervention in the
process of decision-making and administration. Thus attempts
have been made to establish such rights as those of the poor to
direct representation in the institutions that affect their lives,
to financial support with dignity, to legal counsel. These new
conceptions have already scored remarkable successes. We have
seen formerly unshakable Boards of Education begin to bow to
demands that only a year or two ago may have seemed extremist and irrational—for example, the demand for community
control of ghetto schools. We have seen "student power" in
higher education reach levels that were inconceivable four years
ago. To be sure, the forging of foreign policy still appears to lie
beyond the reach of New Left ideas. And yet is it? In recent
demonstrations we have seen revolutionary techniques employed that are justified less by resort to the traditional rhetoric
of revolution than by the argument that new forms of "representation" of minority points of view are required in a democratic polity.

The question of how enduring these new developments will
be still remains open, but it is clear that they already serve as
extremely effective weapons to advance the argument that something fundamental is wrong with American society. Of course,
the argument that something fundamental is wrong leads easily

to the conclusion that something grand and apocalyptic is required to set it straight. And indeed, the two positions reinforce each other: given the inclination toward some tremendous change, some tremendous flaw must be found to justify it (just as the reverse is true). But a powerful analysis of what is wrong with society may be too powerful. The radical Left explains what is wrong by the tendency of men to act within institutions which develop their own dynamic, and a dynamic which may become irrelevant or positively subversive of the ends they are set up to realize. As instances, they point to the tendency of educational institutions to act in such ways as to inhibit education, welfare institutions in such ways as to reduce competence, defense institutions in such ways as to increase the likelihood and the ferocity of war. When I say that this analysis may be too powerful, I mean to raise the question: what alternative is there to institutions designed to deal with problems, calling upon the most common and everyday motivations, and developing their own rigidities and blinders?

There is an answer on the New Left even to that—and the answer is to release man's natural creativity and spontaneity, whether through revolution, or through participatory democracy, or through the smashing of the old institutions, and to hope that these newly released forces will finally lead to the overcoming of ancient social dilemmas. For the New Left believes that man is good by nature, and corrupted by institutions; that the earth and its riches are sufficient to maintain all men in comfort and happiness, and that only human selfishness and blindness prevent the emergence of this ideal state. One can appeal to the early Marx, who is so popular today, and his vision of a society in which man can fish in the morning, work in the afternoon, and criticize the arts in the evening, just as he will, and entirely according to the rhythms of his own being. Some on the New Left believe that only a violent overthrow of the institutions of society can bring such a world to birth; others believe that a steady and determined and unyielding pressure on power elites and power holders, if applied long enough, ingeniously enough, unflinchingly enough, will force these groups to give up their power and their goods and to desist in their willful obstruction of those who wish to create a better and more beautiful world.

THERE ARE, in my opinion, three serious flaws in this position. The first is the assumption that the problems of bringing a better society into being are fundamentally problems of power. This has become a matter of gospel, and not only with the New Left. Yet the fact is that only certain basic problems can be settled, and even those only to a limited degree, by direct clashes between conflicting interests; and in advanced societies, the number of such problems grows progressively smaller and smaller. The natural history of social problems seems to involve an initial stage in which a selfish power monopoly must be defeated or overthrown. But clear evils to fight against are rapidly succeeded by increasingly ambiguous evils, whose causes and solutions are equally unclear. The minute we move to this later stage, we confront one important limitation of the radical perspective.

Let me be concrete. In the South not long ago, the resistance to equality for Negroes was centered in an irrational and inhuman racist ethos that denied to Negroes the most elementary rights of man in a democratic society, such as the right to a fair trial, to the security of life and property, and to the vote. The task of confronting these evils was simply to fight them, to organize to fight them, to insist that the Constitution be obeyed—even, if one was heroic enough, to die or risk death in the process.

But this was the initial stage of reform: equivalent in its moral clarity to earlier battles like those aimed at extending the franchise, banning child labor, establishing labor's right to organize, setting up systems of unemployment insurance and social security. After the principle has been established there comes a second stage, in which the problems are more complex, often more technical. It is in part for this reason that the administrators and the experts now take over, together with those whose interests are directly concerned, while the army of reformers moves off to issues in which the conflict between good and evil is still clear cut. This is precisely what happened after the victories of the civil-rights movement in the South and the shift of the movement to the North.

We are often very sympathetic to cynical explanations of human behavior, including our own, and we are thus attracted to the belief that when Southern whites only were affected by Negro demands, Northern whites could be staunchly militant in defense of Negro rights, but that when the Northerners themselves were affected, they fell silent or slunk off the battlefield. But something rather more important occurred as the battleground of the civil-rights movement shifted from the South to the North. In the South, the issues were civic equality and the vote; in the North, because both these goals had long been attained, the issues became employment and upgrading in jobs, income, education, housing. These are all highly complex matters that no simple law can settle. It cannot be decreed that Negroes and whites should have the same income regardless of their skills and education, or that they should have the same education regardless of their home backgrounds, or that they should have the same home backgrounds, regardless of their history, their culture, their experience.

Of course it is possible, even in this later stage of reform when the key element has ceased to be the obdurate political power of a selfish interest group, to insist that nothing has really changed. Thus, many who argue that it is "white racism" which is keeping the Negro down—an idea strongly encouraged by the Report of the National Advisory Commission on Civil Disorders—are in effect trying to cast the enormous problems of creating a true and widespread equality for American Negroes in the pattern of the heroic battles to change the cruel social structure of the South. Yet this interpretation flies in the face of the fact that racist attitudes have been in steady decline in this country for two decades. And if "white racism" refers to practices, it contradicts the reality that most of the major institutions in American life—government, big business, higher education, the foundations—have been engaged for years in a variety of efforts to increase and upgrade Negro participation in every area of American life. Paradoxically, "white racism" has become a rallying cry precisely at a moment when it has never been milder.

THE TRUTH IS THAT it is not white racism but the difficulty of the problems which has so far frustrated us in finding satisfying jobs for the hard-core unemployed, or improving education and housing in the ghettos and slums. Not even the enactment of such legislative proposals as are being put forward by the Poor People's March on Washington would by itself settle matters—as, in its time, the enactment of the right to collective bargaining did. If the government were to become the "employer of last resort," there would still be thorny questions concerning rates of pay (certainly minimal wages would no longer be a solution, as they were with WPA in the depression), civil-service protection for these workers, and policies for dealing with incompetence and absenteeism—for after all we are speaking of people who cannot get jobs or will not take those which are available in a fairly brisk labor market.

If we consider education, no reform has yet been proposed or envisaged that can reasonably promise better education for ghetto youth, though we can passionately support community control of schools as a measure which *might* at least help to affect the tricky factor of the child's motivation. And even when we speak of housing and neighborhoods, where simple physical facilities alone are important, we have no easy solutions—as becomes evident once the question is raised of how much happier the poor have proved to be in public housing projects than in slums. In none of these major areas is there a major reform that can promise what social security or the right to collective bargaining promised. This is only an index to the increasing complexity of our problems; themselves the result of the increasing sophistication of social demands— not *any* job, but a good and meaningful job with security and promise of advancement; not merely free education, but education with certain effects; not just a minimally adequate dwelling, but one located within a network of social supports that we can often scarcely divine, let alone set out to create.

Even the demands for a guaranteed annual income, or a negative income tax, or a family allowance—demands that are, it is clear enough, pressed because there is no rapid and easy path to equality through good jobs—raise further technical questions that will not be solved by the passionate insistence that Congress decree an end to poverty or that communities do away with white racism. The guaranteed annual income or negative income tax would have serious and undetermined effects on those who work for rates at or near the legal minimum. If such workers (maids, messenger boys, janitors, hotel employees, restaurant employees, etc.) are to retain any incentive to work, the guaranteed annual income or negative income tax return must be set below the minimum wage—at which point we are back to welfare and the painful issues it involves (who qualifies, for how much, etc.?). The family allowance is less problematic, but as generally proposed it is too small to permit the abolition of the welfare system; nor can we be happy over the inevitable support it entails for population growth at a time when for other good reasons we might want to discourage large families.

At the moment it is fashionable among radicals to ignore these details and to justify their indifference by an assault on the idea that work is necessary to society. But anyone who looks concretely at what human beings in this country want, and what radicals feel is the least they should have (good housing, good education, various social services, good health care, recreational opportunities, etc.), and then simply adds up what that requires in the way of material and human resources, would soon be disabused of the notion that we can ignore the effects of various social measures on the incentive to work. Quite characteristically, the radical wants it both ways—he wants services that are enormously costly in manpower, and he wants social measures that will encourage fewer people to work.

If the issues become thus complex, when there are no simple slogans to proclaim—or, when such slogans are proclaimed, there are no visible routes to their immediate realization—then understandably the fervor and commitment of many reformers and radicals fall off. This is in part what happened when the issue of civil rights for Negroes in the South was replaced by the issue of achieving effective equality for the Negro throughout the nation. We can trace much the same development in all the earlier areas of reform; indeed, the advancement of a society can almost be measured by the extent to which political issues are transformed into technical issues—when this happens it is generally a sign that the central power struggle is over. In Scandinavia and England the provision of good medical care, for example, has come to involve such questions as how many doctors and nurses are needed, how they should be trained, how they can be kept from going to America or induced to move to small towns and distant rural areas, what kind of hospitals should be built, etc. Of course, politics enters into all this, with parties taking positions according to their class composition, their history, and their ideology. Yet such differences are relatively marginal, and only one element of many—among which they are by no means the most important—going into the framing of solutions.

To my mind, there are fewer and fewer major areas of American domestic policy in which the old-fashioned conflict between interests representing clearly reactionary forces, and the interests of the society in general, still remains central. One is the continued Southern resistance to legislation aimed at bettering the lot of the Negro; another is the continued resistance of organized medicine to an adequate program of medical care. In most other areas, I would argue, complex technical issues have superseded the crude power struggle between the forces of reaction and the forces of progress. This is not to deny that self-serving interests still operate throughout the political sphere, but so long as care is taken to pay them off, they do not constitute serious roadblocks in the way of improving our society. The drive for security is a massive one—in farmers, in businessmen, in workers—and I am not sure that our special interests are so much stronger than their counterparts in other societies which manage their problems pretty well, or in any imaginable future society.

A SECOND ARGUMENT against the perspective of radical leftism follows from this general point in an industrially advanced society, whatever its background and history, social problems become more and more complex, more technical, and less political: Because change is continuous in such societies, no solution is ever complete or final, and consequently there is no alternative to bureaucracies, administrators, and experts. Of course, certain issues are on occasion structured so that solutions really can have a once-and-for-all character—in particular those issues which can be posed in strictly political or legal terms. Thus, the right to organize, when put into law and upheld by the courts, finally ended one great battle in American history. But most of the problems we face are not so simple and require continuous expert attention.

Consider, for example, public housing. No directly political measure, like a huge appropriation of money, could solve the problem of housing in this country; nor could the introduction of some new principle, like the once-new principle of public housing itself. For no matter what we might do on the political front, we would still have to decide what kind of housing to build, where to build it, in what size developments and at what scale; we would need to know the effect of setting different income limits, of excluding or not excluding those with criminal records, of accepting this proportion or that from the relief rolls; and we would have to determine the further effect of these and many other decisions on the balance of integration and segregation. There is no way of reaching such decisions from any large political position, radical or conservative: indeed, these questions (and they are increasingly becoming the ones that any advanced society must settle) make those very distinctions irrelevant. A few years ago I visited Warsaw and spoke to researchers in the field of housing and other social services.

The problems we spoke about, that troubled them, were not very different from those of anyone dealing with housing in New York or Chicago, or, I would hazard, in Stockholm and Moscow.

Public welfare is another example. In the 1930's the basic issue was raised: is the government responsible for providing subsistence to those unable to earn it themselves? And the answer, after a struggle, was given: yes. It was, as is common in this politically complex nation, not as good or sharp an answer as other nations have given, but in the more advanced states of the Union, at any rate, public services of a standard commensurate with that of Northwestern Europe were established for the widowed and orphaned and abandoned and aged and disabled. The battle was over; reformers and radicals rested, or moved off to other fields. Twenty years later they were back, in force, denouncing the social workers, organizing the clients against them. What had happened? Had welfare services deteriorated or been cut back? Quite the contrary. More was being spent on them and they were probably being run more efficiently. Yet where it had once seemed the achievement of a generous society that those without income were no longer required to beg or to depend on private charity, but now received as of right some minimal level of subsistence, it seemed to the society of twenty years later an outrage that they were maintained on a dignity-destroying dole, that they were not rehabilitated, turned into productive and self-respecting citizens. Let me suggest that it is much easier to give someone money than to turn him into a productive and self-respecting citizen. The first task is also a much easier one to place on the banners of a political movement or to write into legislation than the second.

Or consider the poverty program. Within Congress, Left and Right both agree that something should be done about poverty, and that training the unemployed or the not-yet employed is a good idea; in consequence we have now developed a large range of training programs, of varying kinds, under varying auspices. When any one of these programs comes up for renewal, the technical people running it will always argue that theirs is the most important and should be maintained or expanded, and will try to convince their friends in Congress. Now it is true that congressmen, faced with conflicting expert opinion and pressure from differing interests, will tend to fall back on old prejudices and old political commitments—the liberals will generally say, spend more, the conservatives, spend less. But the combat takes place in a surprisingly restricted area. It is not yet as restricted as the area of political combat in England and Sweden, but it is much narrower than it was in this country twenty years ago.

Admittedly the overall scale of expenditures on housing or welfare or work-training programs is still an important political question in America, but this is not really what many on the radical Left are concerned about. For even if we were to spend twice as much in each of these areas as we do now, things would not really change that much, and no one—least of all the radical Leftists themselves—would believe that the millennium awaited by the radical Left had arrived.[1] But as a matter of fact, even the scope of politics as regards the scale of expenditure is remarkably restricted. In all advanced countries, taxes are very high and not easily increased; similar proportions of the GNP are devoted to social welfare; and the increasing competition among equally worthy programs—health, education, welfare, work-training, scientific research, and the like—poses similarly perplexing decisions. We may come to a better understanding of these matters, but scarcely by following the assumptions and perspectives of the radical Left.

If, then, the need for reform and change is continuous, and depends on the expert knowledge of technicians continuously applied, there can be no alternative to institutionalization, the permanent bodies devoted to permanent problem areas, with all its consequences. I do not see how any sensible man can still think, as Lenin did in *State and Revolution,* that institutions and the state will wither away to the point where they can be run on a part-time and unspecialized basis by—in his term— cooks. Yet this is the vague, if not always expressed, hope of the New Left. Knowing that institutions corrupt, they hope to do away with them. One of the major grounds for my skepticism is my belief that, even though they corrupt, there is no chance of doing away with them.

I am aware, of course, of the common wisdom that to put education in the hands of the educators, housing in the hands of the professional housers, welfare in the hands of the social workers is to ensure that traditional practices will become

[1] New York City spends twice as much per child in its public schools as most other large cities do, yet these schools hardly serve as a model for the solution of the problems of urban education.

institutionalized, that reformers will be fought, and that difficulties will pile up and get worse. But the fact is that judicious, flexible, creative people are always in short supply. Not every problem can be placed in the hands of the best men in the society—though this often seems to be what we are asked to achieve when we are told that our doctors must be better, our teachers must be better, our social workers must be better. Where after all are we to find a place for the people in our society who are less than the most imaginative, the most energetic, the most effective? The great majority of men, whether or not they lead lives of quiet desperation, certainly hope to lead lives of minimal security and moderate gratification. While we take it for granted that this is a reasonable and humane objective for Vietnamese peasants or Indian city-dwellers, we consider it reprehensible that most American doctors, teachers, social workers, and the like are of the same sort. No doubt this common human tendency seems reprehensible when viewed in the context of the suffering we are called upon to alleviate. But what solution is there? As far as I can see, only the normal political one—when the problems become bad enough, and enough people get angry and protest, new programs are started, new men and new ideas flow in, and hopefully all this leads to a new level of achievement, itself to become institutionalized in its turn, and to require at some later time another infusion of ideas, money, and innovators from the outside.

THE NEW LEFT's main answer to the problem of institutionalization is participatory democracy, a concept derived from the Paris Commune in which, according to Marx's account, the people, permanently politicized, permanently in arms, met every day to settle their fate. This is a grand vision and one which makes it possible to argue that all established institutions, even if formally democratic, are actually undemocratic because they do not reflect the desires of the people at any given moment. I cannot imagine, however, how one can ever overcome the danger raised by a direct dependence on the people, permanently in session. For it inevitably means depending on that part of the people that is willing, for one reason or another, to stay permanently in session.

Participatory democracy is suited to truly revolutionary movements and moments—but only moments. No people as a whole has ever been ready to make a primary commitment to political action over a long period of time. Those who assert that formal democracy cannot be true democracy because many do not vote, many who vote do not know, the candidates do not reflect the full range of opinion and possibility, etc., ignore the fact that this limited interest on the part of most people most of the time is actually among the greatest defenses of democracy. It means, as Aaron Wildavsky has pointed out, that there are always enormous reserves to be mobilized whenever significant interests are affected. Wildavsky contends that one of the most critical resources in politics is time—time for talking, electioneering, canvassing— and the poor have as much of this resource as anyone else. Perhaps money decides only unimportant things, such as which of two not very different candidates will carry an election. But if important issues arise, reserves are available that can be brought into battle. Is it not such reserves that the organizers in the slums are now trying to mobilize? If they fail, as they sometimes do, it may be because they have not correctly diagnosed what is really troubling people in the slums, because they have been unable to convince them that the potential gains are worth their sacrifice of time and energy. And if issues are indeed becoming increasingly complex, it also becomes harder and harder to isolate and sloganize action that, if demanded and then taken, will result in a clear improvement of conditions.

IN RESPONSE to all these realities, we find new and astonishing doctrines coming into vogue. Herbert Marcuse, for example, attacks democracy and tolerance as themselves being barriers to the actions required for the overthrow of a monstrous society. In the past, even the Leninists, whatever their actual practices —the suppression of free speech and the murder of political opponents—usually tried to cover them up with such terms as "peoples' democracy" and with such justification as the paramount need to defend the revolution from the violence of others. But lip service to the virtues of democracy and tolerance are now, it seems, to be abandoned by radicals on the ground that democracy and tolerance only protect an evil society—protect it precisely because they can be displayed as its virtues! We have come to such twisted arguments as one recently given by an American professor against accepting a Fulbright fellowship: he agreed that he was free to attack American foreign policy abroad, but by so doing he would mislead his foreign audience into believing that the United States was a free society and worthy of support by men of good will.

In the universities, participatory democracy has now been

replaced by a new doctrine which decrees that when democratic procedures either do not exist (as indeed they do not in many sectors of many universities) or when a democratic system fails to respond to deeply felt needs (as with the Vietnam war) then it is quite legitimate to engage in disruption and disorder to bring about change. This argument has attracted the support of substantial minorities of students and even of faculties, though it has been less effective among the American people at large.

The new doctrine, which we see exemplified at Nanterre and Columbia, is a far cry from the ideals of participatory democracy, especially in the early days of the new Left when meetings were open to all, when discussions to gain consensus went on endlessly, when there was deep soul-searching about the morality of engaging in activity that provoked the violence of political opponents and police. Under the auspices of the new doctrine, the rights of the majority are held in derision, and political opponents are prevented from speaking or being heard. Tactics are worked out to strip authorities of dignity through staged confrontations, to arrange matters so that violence will erupt for the benefit of the press and television, to win over basically unsympathetic students who, owing to their commitment to fairmindedness, will almost always be "radicalized" by exposure to police intervention. In effect, we have moved from the ideal of the politicized masses with direct control over their fate—an unlikely form of organization in any case—to the quite cynical manipulation of the masses by those who themselves object to "formal" democracy and to the public order and tolerance that are its foundation. That small minorities are able to get so far with these tactics is attributable to two circumstances: first that they operate in an environment (the university) which is in fact undemocratic and which is also totally incapable of handling confrontation, disruption, and provocation; and second, that we have in the Vietnam war a case in which democratic processes most certainly do not work well, any more than they do in less explosive sectors of foreign policy in this country.

I think some good has and will come out of these tactics— university constitutions are being revised, and probably for the better—balanced by a good deal of evil. Alongside the wrong of university administrations which are unresponsive to faculty and student opinion, we now have the new wrong of groups of students who can impose their will on the university, regardless of what the majority of their colleagues and teachers want or think. Just recently, the students of Stanford University voted 70 per cent in favor of allowing the government agencies and Dow Chemical to recruit on campus—but on how many other campuses has policy been made by an aggressive minority, without a student vote to determine majority sentiment? The fact that our universities are not democratically organized has made it possible for small groups to instigate change and reform—and this is to the good. But the ultimate end of these changes and reforms will still have to be something on the order of formal democracy—universal suffrage, free discussion, free balloting, all of which seem remote from the affections of the passionate on the New Left. For when these democratic forms prevail, leftists can claim no greater rights than others, regardless of how strongly they feel they are right.

THROUGH THESE CHANGES IN attitude and tactics, an anti-institutional bias remains at the heart of the New Left position; and at the heart of my own critique of that position is my belief that there can be no substitute for institutions, even though they may become tired, bureaucratic, and corrupt. Yet no more, in my view, can there be any substitute for the organized and aroused people when the institutions become, as they ineluctably will, inadequate to their task. At that point, they must be supplemented or supplanted by new institutions, which will hopefully respond more sensitively to the needs of their clients. I think in the host of proposals and experiments of the past six or seven years there have been many good ones—but then they eventually will become part of the institutionalized system too. We now have neighborhood law firms, which some people around the poverty program saw as the guarantor of a determinedly antagonistic and suspicious attitude toward all institutions. But why? How can they escape becoming institutions themselves? They will have to recruit staff, set limits to their work load, accept some cases and reject others, arrive at a modus vivendi with the rest of the institutionalized world, give security to their employees. And would we want it otherwise? Do we want to devote, each of us, full time to every problem— welfare, education, housing, legal rights, and what have you— or are we prepared to accept the subdivisions of a complex society, leaving some of our resources in reserve, to be called out against the worst problems, the most serious scandals? One does feel rather like a Scrooge in insisting that spontaneity and feeling can never replace the institutions, with their bureaucrats, clerks, secretaries, forms, computers, regulations, and—hopefully—appeal boards. But there are to my mind more serious reasons than any I have yet suggested for thinking that this dream of the New Left must remain a limited one, and this brings me to the third major failing of the radical perspective. As I look to the future, I see that the expectation of more freedom, of more spontaneity, must be disappointed. Kenneth Boulding has pointed to three factors pushing us inexorably toward a more rather than a less organized society: one is the existence of the terribly destructive atomic weapons, the second is the growth of population, the third the exhaustion of natural resources. To these three might be added a fourth: the pollution of the environment.

The interesting thing about all these problems is that they take on roughly the same character in all advanced societies, and in each case the answer seems to come down to greater controls. Thus, once the atomic weapons emerge, there is no way of sweeping them under the rug. They are a reality, and to deal with them involves a species of considerations which makes the radical perspective all but entirely irrelevant. Perhaps I am wrong. Perhaps one can envisage the masses raging through the streets of Moscow and Washington demanding the absolute destruction of these horrible weapons, and with full faith in the good will of the other side. But even if we were to get this far, can anyone imagine the same thing happening in the streets of Peking, or Tel Aviv, or Cairo?

The population explosion—and I assume we are all frightened at the projections—constitutes a similar trap, for it means that the most basic of all forms of human spontaneity will have to be subjected to elaborate institutional controls if the world is ever to arrive at anything like the good life, or the good-as-possible life, that radicals so mistakenly tie to the overthrow of organized society. So too the gradual exhaustion of natural resources—which we are less concerned about today but which we will soon be forced to worry about constantly—sets another inexorable limit to the kind of society in which freedom is maximized and controls put at a minimum. As to environmental pollution, it is a more immediate concern, and one ironically linked to higher standards of living, in the form of insecticides, soaps, fertilizers, automobiles. Here too we can only foresee greater and more intrusive controls being imposed—not only in America but in all advanced countries, and not only under capitalism but under Communism (as a glance at the Russian response to these same problems quickly reveals). The radicals have offered no alternative to these imperatives, except the return to smaller communities, and lower standards of living. This I would regard as wholly consistent with their outlook, and one that makes sense in its own terms. Relatively few people, however, are willing to adopt it, and in the underdeveloped world it makes no sense at all.

MY DISCUSSION up to now has concentrated solely on domestic affairs. Perhaps many might agree that our domestic problems are complex, require continuous and expert attention, and in large measure transcend or make irrelevant traditional political distinctions. But what about Vietnam? It is on this issue, after all, that the radical Left now principally expresses itself. Does not Vietnam point to some horrible illness in the American system—a sick reliance on technology as the solution to all problems, an outrageous view of the American role and prerogatives in the world, a suppressed violence which will out in the most grisly forms, an inhumanly narrow view of other societies and other peoples? I would agree that just as domestic politics stops at the water's edge, so my analysis in large measure is relevant only to our domestic problems. Many people look at the war and conclude, as I said at the beginning, that the roots are poisoned, that radical change is needed. Many other people—and this is a constant in the history of radicalism—begin with the idea that the roots are poisoned, and take the war as proof of their original conviction. Like the Talmudic scholar in the old story, they once ran through the streets shouting, "I have an answer! Does anyone have a question?" But now Vietnam has given them a very good question, too.

Nevertheless, I cannot accept the idea that the fundamental character of American society, its political or economic life, is the prime cause of the horrors of Vietnam. In the end, I cannot help believing, the Vietnam war must be understood as the result of a series of monumental errors. The key point to me is this: *America would not have had to be very different from what it now is for some President to have gotten us out of Vietnam rather than deeper and deeper into it.* Was America so much different or so much better under Eisenhower than it has been under Johnson? And yet all it took was a simple decision by Eisenhower to keep us from intervening in Vietnam in 1954.

The Vietnam war does to my mind point to something basically wrong with the American political system, but it is less apocalyptic than the analyses of the radical Left suggest. I believe—along with Senator Fulbright—that foreign policy, which was relatively marginal for the United States until the late 1930's, has become, or has remained, too exclusively the province of the President and his closest advisers. Whereas in domestic affairs the President must answer constantly to Congress, he has become literally irresponsible in the area of foreign affairs, where he must answer only to the electorate and only once every four years. If he is stubborn or stupid or makes mistakes and insists on sticking with them—and his position as head of a political party gives him every incentive to do so—he can destroy the country before being called to account. Since, moreover, we are still relatively insulated in our day-to-day national life from the world outside, the President can deceive the people as to the extent of his errors in foreign affairs much more effectively than he can in domestic affairs. This is a very serious matter indeed and the United States may be fatally damaged before we find a way out. But I cannot easily reconcile my own understanding as to how we have come to this terrible position with the basic perspectives and criticisms of the New Left. Nor are those perspectives particularly helpful in figuring out what we can do to repair the political system against a defect of this character and magnitude.

ULTIMATELY, MY DISAGREEMENT with the Radical Left comes down to this: I see no Gordian knot to be cut at a single stroke, the cutting of which would justify the greatest efforts (as in the past it has seemed to justify great horrors). Nationalizing the means of production, as Socialist countries have discovered, is no all-embracing answer; nor is permanent mobilization of the people, which is in any case fantastically difficult to accomplish, and which, if it were to be accomplished, as it has for a time in China, would create a society that we would find repulsive; nor is the destruction of the upper classes—in the advanced countries at any rate, whatever value such destruction might yield in underdeveloped nations—for the upper classes now consist of the managers, the organizers, and the highly skilled professionals, whom we would inevitably have to re-create.

From the point of view of the heroisms of the past, it is a gray world we are entering, in which technicians and interest groups, neither of whom can be said to bear the banner of humanity in its noblest form, will be the determining forces. The best we can do is to ensure that as things go wrong—and they inevitably will—the people will have an opportunity to protest. They will rarely know, I am afraid, quite what to do to set things right, but their complaints and their occasional rebellious fury will be important "inputs," to use the dreary language of the future, in setting the matter right. The logic of the situation—the size of our population, the number of our organizations, the extent of our problems, the interrelations among the different parts of our society, the development of science and technology—all point to this outcome. Under the circumstances, even reform and its traditions become part of the system. How much protest do we need to keep the system straight and keep it correcting itself? At what point will protest wreck the institutions altogether and prevent them from functioning? The system is necessary; not this system exactly, but some system, and one which, given the external forces that govern our lives, will turn out to be not so significantly different.

I view radicalism as a great reservoir of energy which moves the establishment to pay attention to the most serious and urgent problems, and tells it when it has failed. To a more limited degree, it is also a reservoir of potential creativity—a reaching for new solutions and new approaches. What radicalism is not, and what it can no longer be, is the great sword of vengeance and correction which goes to the source of the distress and cuts it out. There is no longer a single source, and no longer a single sword.

LETTER FROM THE PALMER HOUSE

Renata Adler

The national New Politics Convention, which was held at the Palmer House in Chicago over the Labor Day weekend, began as a call from the National Conference for New Politics —an organization that has given financial support to radical candidates in various elections since early in 1966—for delegates from all radical and liberal groups opposed to the American involvement in Vietnam to unite on a course of political action for 1968. The convention presented, from the first, a travesty of radical politics at work. In the quality of its radical dissent, the no longer New Left—which had seemed in its youth somewhere midway between the plain frivolity of a college prank and the struggle of a generation out of apathy into social consciousness—now seemed a vulgar joke, contributing as much to serious national concern with the problems of war, racism, and poverty as a mean drunk to the workings of a fire brigade. Throughout the convention, delegates seemed constantly to emerge, wet-lipped and trembling from some crowded elevator, some torrent of abuse, some marathon misrepresentation of fact, some pointless totalitarian maneuver, or some terminal sophistry to pronounce themselves "radicalized." Being "radicalized" had, among alumni of earlier New Left conventions, two possible meanings: voting against one's principles

Renata Adler, "Letter from the Palmer House," *The New Yorker* (September 23, 1967), 56–88. Reprinted by permission; © 1967 *The New Yorker Magazine,* Inc.

31

with an expression of Machiavellian deviousness, or discussing one's politics as a most interesting turn in one's personal psychology. Among novices, being "radicalized" meant having been persuaded of something by radicals.

One of the reasons for the complete disintegration of the New Politics was the convention's persistent debasement of language. The word "revolution," for example, was used for every nuance of dissent. There were the electoral revolutionaries, who meant to change American foreign policy simply by voting the present Administration out. And there were the moral revolutionaries, like Dr. Martin Luther King, who sought to bring about certain kinds of social change by the pressure of non-violent civil disobedience. Closer to violence were the therapeutic-activity revolutionaries, former members of S.D.S. (Students for a Democratic Society), F.S.M. (the Free Speech Movement), and Vietnam Summer, who seemed to find in ceaseless local organizing—around any issue or tactic demonstrably certain of failure—a kind of personal release, which effective social action might deny them; and the aesthetic-analogy revolutionaries, who discussed riots as though they were folk songs or pieces of local theatre, subject to appraisal in literary terms ("authentic," "beautiful"). There were the historical, after-them-us syllogist revolutionaries, who applauded all riots as pre-revolutionary, an incitement to right-wing repression, which would, in turn, inevitably—presumably as it did in prewar Germany—bring on popular revolution and lasting peace; and the amphetamine revolutionaries, who seem to regard uncontrollable, permanent upheaval, on the model of the Red Guard's, as both a prescription for restoring personal vitality and the most vigorous expression of participatory democracy at work. Finally, there were some local criminals, who, despite the determination of the "radicalized" to view them as revolutionaries, pursued their isolated acts of mugging in the elevators and vandalism in the halls, and who, as a closing touch, stole three hundred dollars from the only people present who had defied a genuinely oppressive power structure at great risk and in the name of genuine new politics—the delegation of the Mississippi Freedom Democratic Party. It was obvious that the only way all these "revolutionaries" could find common ground—the only way Steve Newman, of the (Maoist) Progressive Labor Party, could agree in any detail with, say Dr. Benjamin Spock, of the baby book—was by jettisoning meaning from vocabulary. Within a short time, such a phrase as "bringing down the system" was used equally for the program of a citizen who sought to speed along by legal means the natural evolution of his country—which, he would readily concede, was already the noblest social experiment, on the largest scale, in history—and for the program of an arsonist committed to the country's literal destruction. When words are used so cheaply, experience becomes surreal; acts are unhinged from consequences and all sense of personal responsibility is lost. At the Palmer House, the word "genocide" began to be tossed about as though it could apply to acts of simple rudeness, and eventually speaker after speaker—from Arthur Waskow, of Washington's Institute for Policy Studies, in plenary session, to the Reverend William Sloane Coffin, Jr., Chaplain of Yale University, at table—could argue that a list of thirteen proposals submitted, along with an ultimatum, to the convention by what was called the Black Caucus should be endorsed without modification of any kind, regardless of the substance of the individual proposals, in a spirit of interracial unity. That this implied a paternalistic white racism that would startle a South African plantation owner seemed not to enter the minds of these speakers—or of the convention at large, which endorsed the list and delegated to the Black Caucus all authority for amending the proposals in the future. The list ranged from an accusation that blacks had been systematically excluded from "the decision-making process" of the convention (one of the convention's two chairmen, Julian Bond, the Georgia assemblyman, was a Negro, as were its keynote speaker, Dr. Martin Luther King, nine of the twenty-five members of its Steering Committee, and six of the twenty-four members of its executive board; moreover, no actual "decision-making" had taken place before the adoption of the thirteen Black Caucus proposals), through a condemnation of "the imperialistic Zionist war" (the Black Caucus itself subsequently reversed this condemnation, so the convention found itself in the position of having both endorsed a proposal and pre-endorsed, *carte blanche,* so to speak, its reversal), to demands for the formation of "white civilizing committees" to deal with "the beastlike character" of "all white communities . . . as exemplified by George Lincoln Rockwells and Lyndon Baines Johnsons," for "immediate reparation for the historic physical, sexual, mental, and economic exploitation of black people," and for support of all resolutions passed by the Black Power Conference in Newark. No white person could in good faith endorse the substance of all the proposals. Certainly many of the white people at the convention knew the statement about decision-making to be false, and many did not know what the resolutions of the Newark Black Power Conference were, since no official list was ever issued and it is not certain that any was ever drawn up. From the moment the ultimatum was accepted, the convention became a charade. To disregard substance in favor of a spirit of unity was to justify McCarthy's empty lists of names on account of the spirit of patriotism in which he waved them about. But the real white-racist presumption lay in thinking that a specious endorsement of inane proposals was an act of support for Negroes—or, for that matter, in thinking that most Negroes could endorse the resolutions. From the beginning of the convention, the "radicalized" whites had resolutely refused to deal with any competent or intelligent Negroes—any rational Negroes, as it turned out—as authentic blacks. Non-failed non-whites were simply regarded as sell-outs to the system, and ignored. The effect of this was to produce what can only be described as a new, young, guerrilla-talking Uncle Tom, to transact nitty-gritty politics with his radical white counterpart. The assembled revolutionaries (whose voting strength was determined on the basis of the number of "activists" they cared to claim at home) selected such Negroes, on the model of H. Rap Brown, to speak for the romantic, rioting, "authentic" children of the ghetto (for "the ten thousand activists in Newark," as John F. Maher, Jr., of the Cambridge Vietnam Summer, put it, in a meeting, "who were willing to die to change their way of life"), for the Black Caucus, for all the other Negroes at the convention, and for the nameless, faceless, personalityless black monolith that the American Negro has now—in the white-radical racist imagination—become. The tragedy is, of course, that no one speaks for the young rioters, since no leader has emerged from them yet; and Rap Brown seems merely to tag along rhetorically after them. The Black Caucus, which never consisted of more than fifty delegates, sometimes spoke for the majority of the Negro delegates to the convention and sometimes did not. Its composition changed often. It occasionally broke into groups or disbanded, and entry to it was often denied to some Negroes by goons at the door. By choosing to empower the Black Caucus to speak for the entire convention, the convention simultaneously abdicated in its favor and denied it respect. A radicalism whose one worthy aim had been "to give people more of a voice in the decisions that affect their lives" relinquished its own voice at once, and celebrated the birth of the New Politics by voting itself totalitarian.

TWO DAYS of pre-convention sessions—called, in the prospectus, "the pre-convention"—had started off quite differently, as a gentle convocation of kooks. The main factions of plotters and counter-plotters, traditional at New Left reunions, had not yet arrived to present their strategies. (The Socialist Workers Party, together with other Trotskyists, favored the establishment of a third party; in default of a permanent party, they were willing to settle for a temporary national ticket, with their own candidates for President and Vice-President. The "non-electoral local organizers"—like the S.D.S. and Vietnam Summer people who believe in organizing rent strikes, coöperatives, and demonstrations, rather than in the vote—came mainly for the purpose of blocking any national ticket and getting some money. The W.E.B. Du Bois Clubs and the Communist Party would have liked a national ticket, but in order to preserve unity and avoid alienating the non-electoral block they were willing to settle for local organizing and the option for a national ticket later on. Their position corresponded closely with the one taken by Mrs. Donna Allen, of the Women Strike for Peace. The California delegation—which was also known as the New Politics group, because its position corresponded most closely with the original position of the National Conference—favored leaving each state free to have a national ticket if it wanted one, and possibly maintaining the Conference as a nationwide hookup for the various national tickets of the states. The likely candidates for President and Vice-President in California were, respectively, Simon Casady—co-chairman of the convention, and a former head of the California Democratic Council, deposed for his opposition to the war in Vietnam—and Robert Scheer, managing editor of *Ramparts* and a former candidate for Representative from California. In default of local options for locally chosen candidates, the California group was willing to settle for a national ticket chosen by the convention. Democratic Councilman Theodore Weiss, of Manhattan, together with other Democrats, favored working through the regular parties for candidates opposed to the war in Vietnam. In default of that, they were willing to settle for a national King-Spock ticket. A Chicagoan named Arthur Rubin was running for President himself; his platform consisted of an explanation of "the generally misunderstood film 'Blow-Up' " and a map of the

universe "available in a variety of versions." A group called the
Student Mobilization Committee came to recruit demonstrators
to immobilize the Pentagon on October 21st. And some young
people came only to look for jobs with established radical
organizations.)

Within hours after registration, on the Tuesday evening
before Labor Day, other delegates, less firmly committed politically, were roaming the corridors of the Palmer House—a
huge, ornate, labyrinthine hotel, with a basement arcade, a sub-
basement arcade, gusty, arctic air-conditioning, and small tran-
sient-looking rooms. The obvious intention of these delegates in
coming early was to have truly sweeping reforms to offer for
consideration when the convention began. Nonpolitical guests
at the hotel that Tuesday seemed to view the delegates with
tolerant smiles, pointing them out in the lobby as "the student
convention." (On Wednesday, the hotel closed the swimming
pool "for repairs." By Thursday, the convention was being
described bitterly as "those draft-card burners." Saturday morning, the lady clerks at the newsstand were worriedly insisting
that the New York *Times* had not yet arrived: "I told you we
shouldn't have opened early, Bea. Here's one of them just won't
go *away.*" But by Sunday—the day before the convention ended
—things were fairly normal: players in a local bridge tourna-
ment regained their concentration, and Sandra Max and David
Wasserman, two apparently apolitical Chicagoans, were married
without incident in the Red Lacquer Ballroom, where a White
Radical Caucus had met the night before.)

Wednesday morning, after a welcoming speech by Co-Chairman Simon Casady, a kindly, bewildered-looking gray-haired
man, the pre-convention delegates split into committees: one for
Resolutions, one for Perspectives, and one for Structures. The
Black Caucus, which had been a tradition of radical conventions since the early days of S.N.C.C. (the Student Nonviolent Co-
ordinating Committee), was already in separate session. S.N.C.C.
itself (sometimes referred to as the Non-Student Violent Disinte-
grating Committee) is now—except as a source of publicity measured in column inches detrimental to the cause of civil rights—to
all intents and purposes, defunct. Somehow, it never quite re-
covered from the federal government's passage of the Civil
Rights Act of 1964 and the white radicals' defection to the more
fashionable causes of campus free speech and Vietnam protest.
The Black Caucus, however, remains, as though to preserve

in memory the idealistic, soul-searching band that S.N.C.C. once was.

The Structures Committee met on the third floor, in Private Dining Room 8—a tiny, dimly lit imitation-Romanesque chapel, featuring cloudy chandeliers, a false hearth, false timbers decorating the ceiling, old branching wall lamps, folding chairs, and a medieval bestiary, with false heraldic devices, painted on its walls. The committee spent the two days before the convention discussing whether it ought to present to the conference a proposal that the New Politics disband altogether and leave its delegates to their local organizing. (Many delegates, it turned out, had come to the convention committed to its dissolution.) The Perspectives Committee, which met in the Red Lacquer Ballroom, on the fourth floor, spent the pre-convention days deciding whether to propose to the convention that it endorse a permanent third party, that it choose a third-party ticket only for 1968, that it endorse no ticket or party or nationwide hookup of tickets, that it disband for non-electoral local organizing, or that it endorse a platform set up by a Subcommittee on Perspectives, which concerned Mexican-American relations, the Dominican intervention, the Greek regime, strip-mining in Appalachia, the inequities of the income tax, and a number of other issues over which there was considerable indignation.

The Committee on Resolutions, which met in the Wabash Parlor, on the third floor, was by far the most thorough and animated. Under the dual chairmanship of Steven Jonas, a bearded young man from New York's Medical Committee to End the War in Vietnam, and Bertram Garskof, a bearded psychology professor from Michigan State University (and a member of the convention's Steering Committee), the Committee on Resolutions immediately split into four sub-committees to revise the American political and social system from top to bottom. The four subcommittees all met in the same room, but each sent a courier to each of the others every fifteen minutes, to make sure there was no duplication of effort. By Wednesday noon, Resolutions had abolished the capitalist system. By evening, it had revised foreign policy in detail, solved the problems of the cities, deplored alimony, and endorsed sexual freedom for citizens under twenty-one. ("We'll pick up votes on that when the youth reaches voting age," someone said approvingly. Jonas, normally the kindest of chairmen, looked reproachful. "I was hoping we were above winning votes," he said. "I hoped we were working on principles.") By Thursday morning, it had legalized marijuana, pronounced heroin medically harmless, established more humane old-age homes, and resolved that "if police agencies would do their jobs, organized crime can be smashed." (Garskof proposed that all white police be removed at once from black communities. "But there are understanding white cops," someone protested. "Then let them work in Scarsdale," Garskof replied.) By Thursday afternoon, so many resolutions had been passed that the committee established a subcommittee to improve the literary style of all its previous resolutions. Then, perhaps dissatisfied because there was so little left to do, Garskof deplored the lack of black representation on the Steering Committee. Since he was on the Steering Committee himself and should have known better, it was odd that he should make such a complaint, but his beard—even in the context of new radicalism—was an eccentric one, running straight, dense, and furry back along the underside of his chin, never touching his jaws at all, and it is not unlikely that he was just trying to liven things up a little. In any case, two resolutions were immediately passed: one expressing grief over the separatism of the Black Caucus, and the other deploring the lack of black representation on the Steering Committee. Martin Peretz, an instructor in government at Harvard and a member of the convention's executive board, objected. "You are trying to railroad chaos through this convention," he said, and he deplored the committee's "militant ignorance." (Later, Peretz said to Todd Gitlin, of Chicago's JOIN Community Union, that he resented the implication that the Steering Committee had been "coöpted." "Don't let's get up tight about coöptation," Gitlin replied.) In any case, more than half the Committee on Resolutions ultimately walked out, to form a Whites in Support of the Black Caucus Caucus, and what turned out to be the major preoccupation of the convention—attitudes toward the Black Caucus—was established. From then on, there was so much talk of caucuses of one sort or another—the White Radical Caucus, the White Revolutionary Caucus, the Radical Alternatives Caucus, the Poor People's Caucus, the Women Strike for Peace Caucus, the Mobilization Caucus, the Labor Caucus, the California Caucus, the Anti-King-Spock Caucus—that delegates seemed to be not so much discussing a New Politics as croaking mating calls to one another from adjoining lily pads. On Thursday evening, the Black Caucus itself consisted mainly of local Chicago teen-agers and Black Nationalists, who ordered (and charged

to the convention) a lavish meal, and who advocated withdrawing from the New Politics Convention altogether, to join a Black
People's Convention to be held on the other side of town. The
Reverend Ralph Abernathy, of Dr. King's Southern Christian
Leadership Conference, however, briefly entered the group with
what he called "some of our folk," and persuaded the others to
remain—for a while, at least—with the still nominally integrated New Politics Convention.

THURSDAY NIGHT, in Chicago's Coliseum, a large, ugly stone
fortification on the South Side, the full convention met for the
first time. Julian Bond, the convention's co-chairman, was introduced by the moderator, Ossie Davis, as "a black terror in
tennis shoes." He spoke briefly and then left the Coliseum, and
he took no further part in the convention. Dick Gregory delivered one of his less effective monologues, in an apparent attempt
to unite the convention by offering an apologia for its more
extreme elements ("Every Jew in America over thirty years old
knows another Jew that hates niggers. Well, it's even, baby").
He remained with the convention another day and then left to
march for open housing in Milwaukee. And Dr. King delivered
his keynote speech, a long and, for him, rather flat peroration,
in a tired voice. As he spoke, some local Negro teen-agers
shouted threats and insults at him from the back of the room.
Negro members of the audience tried to quiet them down, but
within moments a few self-styled members of S.N.C.C. were
charging through the crowd whispering "Make way for Rap
Brown." (This never failed to produce an awed "Where? Where?"
from whatever white radicals were nearby.)

The Reverend Andrew Young, of the Southern Christian
Leadership Conference (a member of the convention's executive
board), turned to a white liberal lawyer with whom he had
worked on many campaigns in the South. "These cats don't
know the country has taken a swing to the right," he said. "I
wish the violence and riots had political significance, but they
don't."

"They just have political consequences," the lawyer said.

"Yeah. All bad," the Reverend Mr. Young said. He left the
convention that evening.

Some teen-agers marked a cardboard box "Contributions for
Our Black Brothers in Prison," and laughed loudly whenever
whites dropped money in it. Two photographers who attempted
to take pictures of these transactions were threatened ("You

gonna lose that camera"), and it was only the quiet appearance of Dick Gregory, who caught two boys in a rather firm, friendly grip around the neck from behind, that dispersed the teen-agers. "Why, here's Brother Dick Gregory," they said, and they walked away, laughing and slapping each other's palms.

Dr. King left the convention the following morning.

At the convention's first official plenary session, on Friday morning, at the Palmer House, Gary Weissman, the chairman of the plenary (he had been an officer of the National Student Association but had abandoned it for the S.D.S.), announced to the delegates, whom he addressed as "Brothers and Sisters," that "the purpose of this convention is to enable the delegates to do what they wish to do."

Arthur Waskow, of the Steering Committee, immediately introduced a motion for the democratization of the Steering Committee with "members of all regions and all caucuses, if they feel they are not represented."

Sidney Lens, of the Labor Caucus, said, "Brother Chairman, I would move that the proposal be amended to include on the Steering Committee fifty per cent of the black people, to represent the thousands and millions who for four hundred years . . ."

In one of the long speeches that ensued (there were references to "this convention, with all its beauty and power" and to "this Chicago palace, with the country looking on"), someone referred to Appalachia as being in "the South," and a delegate rose to denounce this symptom of insensitivity to the problems of Appalachia. Someone proposed an amendment to Lens's proposal, and he accepted it. The chairman pronounced this acceptance out of order. Lens disagreed. "Brother Chairman," he said, "I've been thirty years a labor bureaucrat, and if I don't know that I don't know anything."

Many delegates questioned whether the plenary should continue to meet unless the Black Caucus joined it.

Paul Booth, a former national secretary of S.D.S., rose and threatened, if the discussion went on much longer without a consensus, to move to table whatever motion was on the floor.

A Mrs. Warfield, a Negro woman from Rochester, rose to suggest that she lead a delegation to the Black Caucus, wherever it was currently being held, to express understanding of whatever its demands might currently be.

Someone denounced this proposal as out of order, but the chairman disagreed. "This body is free to be as parliamentary as it likes," he said.

"Perhaps we could use the old Steering Committee as adviser to the new Steering Committee," a delegate proposed, referring to the motion for more Negro representation on the Steering Committee.

"What is the criterion for being black?" someone asked. Since one of the delegates in the Black Caucus was Miss Grace Suzuki, this was not an altogether unreasonable question.

"It won't hurt the convention to send a delegation," Mrs. Warfield said, rather impatiently. "I'll be standing here, if anyone wants to approach me."

"I'll tell you who's black," another speaker began. "If you were with us in Detroit, if you were with us in Newark, and Watts, and Cincinnati . . ."

Mrs. Warfield began to lead her delegation—ten or eleven whites and four Negroes—out of the room.

The motion was put to a vote. "What will mean an aye vote and what will mean a no vote?" someone shouted. There was no answer.

The motion passed.

Someone proposed that the plenary adjourn until the Black Caucus had given its response to Mrs. Warfield, but the Chair ruled him out of order and shut off his microphone.

A delegate from Indiana rose to deplore the enlargement of the Steering Committee.

"You are debating a motion that has already passed—is that correct?" the chairman asked.

"That is correct," the delegate replied.

Mrs. Warfield's delegation never found the Black Caucus—or, rather, Mrs. Warfield left her delegation behind while she sought out all rooms that happened to have Negroes in them. "Don't discuss among yourselves," she said as she left. "There will only be so much confusion." The members of the delegation stayed on a staircase, adjuring one another not to talk, for fear of government agencies and the press. Mrs. Warfield returned to them briefly, to announce that she would continue her search. "Go back to the convention floor," she said. "Remember who you are —the committee to bring a black structure into this convention." Barry Jones, a Negro who had actually participated in the Black Caucus, kept repeating that the caucus had disbanded earlier in the day. The whites ignored him. "Darling, not in the presence of the press," a white woman said. Mr. Jones gave up.

Friday afternoon, in what had been described in the convention program as "a panel discussion of perspectives," a number of people delivered speeches. In the middle of a discourse by Manhattan Councilman Weiss, who argued, not altogether tastefully, that the regular Democratic Party might still give dissidents "a couple of shots at Lyndon Johnson—speaking figuratively, of course," Floyd McKissick, of CORE, preceded by five Negroes in a flying wedge, walked down an empty aisle to the platform. By the time Weiss had finished speaking, all the chairs on the platform were occupied, and he unceremoniously climbed off. McKissick, standing between two impassive, bearded, gum-chewing Negroes in fezzes and khaki jackets (one of whom performed a sort of ballet with his hands while McKissick was speaking), began his speech. In the two years since the Mississippi March and the advent of the Black Power slogan, McKissick has tried to remain in touch with radicals and liberals alike, keeping his public utterances wild and his private influence moderate. It is a strange course to take, and the effort has told on him. His rhetoric veers back and forth from center to extreme. His head bobs and his voice climbs octaves. He blinks continuously. In describing the destruction wrought by Molotov cocktails, his words to the white man were "Hell, man. You made this problem. You clean it up." He spoke of "the twin brothers, capitalism and racism," and he referred to all Negroes who had risen to positions of national influence not as "blacks" but, contemptuously, as "Negroes." Then he remarked that no good could come to the black people from the New Politics Convention (he subsequently withdrew CORE from the Conference entirely), and invited all whites to attend the Black People's Convention that night instead. (Later, apparently under pressure from members of the Black Caucus, he revoked the invitation.) Preceded by the flying wedge, he left. Robert Scheer then made a speech urging that the convention address itself to "the vicious nightmare" (boredom, wife hatred, alienation) of life in white America. Like many radicals, he managed to refer to the unarguable proposition that material affluence has not brought complete happiness, and to make the reference itself sound like an alternative offer. He seemed to imply that a revolution of the prosperous was imminent. Regarded by many as the Bobby Kennedy of the New Left (since the New Left bitterly opposes the real Bobby Kennedy), he was given a standing ovation. Another white radical, Robert Cook, formerly of the Yale S.D.S., now of the New Haven AIM (American Independent Movement), argued that whites should support Negro riots by diverting police to other areas during the looting and sniping in the ghetto. He was applauded, also.

That night, the White Revolutionary Caucus (which consisted mainly of pale, thin, bespectacled women and pale, torpid men, making plans for guerrilla warfare) barred Negroes from its meeting; the White Radical Caucus (which consisted mainly of members of S.D.S., Vietnam Summer, and other local-project organizations) plotted to sway the convention from a national ticket, in order to use the Conference mainly as a servicing facility for the local organizers; and the Black Caucus—despite a last-minute plea from McKissick, who made a brief appearance there—voted to submit its thirteen proposals, along with an ultimatum stating that if they were not passed by noon of the following day the Black Caucus would leave the convention. All through the night, in an orgy of confession about their childhood feelings toward Negroes, the whites on the Steering Committee considered the ultimatum. Ivanhoe Donaldson, a Negro member of S.N.C.C., argued that since the blacks at the convention were the only radicals really "in motion," no real white radicals should balk at the letter of their demands. There was a great deal of soul-searching by whites. ("I have thirty years of working for civil rights," a white liberal said. "At least, nobody can take that away from me." Whereupon, with some dime-store analysis of his motives, they took it away from him.) Martin Peretz walked out. The Steering Committee voted to submit the ultimatum to a "special plenary," to be called the following morning, and by dawn most of its members were ready to pronounce themselves "radicalized."

Casady announced to a crowded Grand Ballroom on Saturday morning that a session's declaring itself a plenary did not make it so and that he could not participate in an extra-legal plenary. Then he, too, walked out. (His walkout, with Peretz's of the preceding night, initiated a kind of daily ritual; the few responsible whites at the convention often found themselves walking out, only to walk right back in, and out again.) The front center section of the plenary was roped off and reserved for members of the Black Caucus, creating the impression, that if only some-one had thought to rope off the back of the buses in Birmingham and shout "Black Power!" the civil-rights movement would never have been necessary. Gary Weissman, who again presided, let the gathering "formally, duly convene itself as a plenary," and thereafter granted what he called "the indulgence of the

Chair" to all deviations from parliamentary procedure that were favorable to the ultimatum. A woman who pointed out that one of the resolutions endorsed "wars of liberation," though many at the convention were pacifists, was ruled out of order. Several members of the Steering Committee, in the first of what became a series of conspiratorial jags, spoke in favor of accepting the ultimatum. The white radicals argued that the thirteen proposals should be accepted, regardless of their content, which was pronounced "irrelevant." (White radicals were constantly consigning matters, and people, of substance to some limbo of irrelevance.) Sidney Lens, representing the Labor Caucus, favored "not proposing to split words or commas or periods." Everyone seemed determined to foster a black illusion that the only whites interested in political coöperation were those who would accept terms of complete capitulation. Robert Scheer, who got up to make a motion to go the "Zionist imperialism" resolution one better, was inadvertently shouted down. In a heated interchange with the chairman, Charles Samson, who at that point was spokesman for the Black Caucus, denied Scheer's right to speak at all. "All of a sudden this person pops up," Samson said, pointing at Scheer in absolute outrage, "and he wants to make an amendment." Several Negroes who wished to speak against the adoption of the proposals were hustled from the room by enforcers from the Black Caucus, and threatened and silenced outside. One of the enforcers who ushered several Negroes out was an African Nationalist from California who was rumored to be the United Nations Ambassador from Tanzania. The ultimatum was accepted, three to one, and the plenary closed after the chairman proposed, and declared adopted by acclamation, a resolution to send a congratulatory telegram to Ho Chi Minh on the occasion of the twenty-second anniversary of Vietnamese independence.

THAT AFTERNOON, the White Radical Caucus was troubled. Its coup against a third ticket and in favor of local organizing had never got off the ground, and, as one member after another pointed out, the Israel resolution would scare off liberal money, and the bad press that the morning's developments would receive might scare off everyone else. No one mentioned the possibility that the resolutions might be substantively wrong—only the possibility that they might alienate support. Several members of the caucus proposed that the white local organizers withdraw from the convention and form an organization of their own. Todd Gitlin pointed out that "the convention might still rise from its ash," that, in any case, most members of the White Radical Caucus had voted for the resolutions, and that it might be worthwhile staying around to "neutralize" the convention. Eric Mann, a white organizer from Newark, and one of the few radicals present who never cast a disingenuous vote, suggested that the organizers remain at the convention to paralyze it by keeping the others from endorsing a national ticket and "from doing all the screwy things they want to do."

Saturday evening, the plenary voted down the proposal to form a permanent third party. Again, a delegate proposed that the plenary adjourn until the Black Caucus, which had again withdrawn into itself, was present, but his proposal was not accepted. The Black Caucus itself was in a state of shock. The advocates of withdrawal from the convention, who had rammed the thirteen proposals through the caucus in the first place, had been certain that the plenary would turn the proposals down, leaving the blacks with an excuse to move to the Black People's Convention on the other side of town. Now they walked out anyway, leaving the Black Caucus to the moderates. Claude Lightfoot, of the Communist Party (rated as moderate by the radical left), and several members of the Du Bois Clubs, also Communist, soon took over, to give the Black Caucus some direction.

The White Radical Caucus, meanwhile, was in session on another floor, still plotting whether to sway the convention from the idea of putting up even a temporary third ticket or to leave the convention. Theodore Steege, a white member of the Ann Arbor S.D.S., announced that the Black Caucus had come to a new conclusion: Since the white delegates had been willing to accept the Black Caucus ultimatum, the Black Caucus knew that it was not dealing with real radicals; it would therefore either withdraw from the convention or consider supporting a third-ticket proposal and withdrawing support from the local organizers. The only Negro present—who later turned out not to have been a participant in the convention at all—shouted from the back of the room that this information was false. His word was accepted. A delegate from the Third Ticket Caucus appeared before the White Radical Caucus to offer what came to be known as the California Compromise. The California people, mainly the staff of *Ramparts*, wanted to be free to put up a ticket of their own, and the proposed compromise was for all states to be free to put up local and national third tickets if they

liked but for the convention to go on record as mainly supporting non-electoral organizing. The White Radical Caucus adopted
the California Compromise.

The delegates at Saturday night's plenary, however, did not
understand the California Compromise. In fact, most of them
had never heard of it. A little old woman got up to say that she
never liked to make an important decision without "sleeping
and praying," that she disapproved of all the "intrigue," and
that she hoped no vote would be taken before morning. She was
applauded. A hippie wearing a headband and a card reading
"Free"—one of two hippies who showed up at the convention
—tried to speak and was denied the microphone. Before the
California Compromise could be introduced, a vote was taken
and the third ticket was defeated by two votes. A Negro appeared
and announced that the Black Caucus was once again being
excluded from the decision-making process and that it would
announce the method of its participation in the morning. A
motion to postpone all decisions until then was defeated. Delegates from the White Radical Caucus and the Third Ticket
Caucus agreed privately to reintroduce the California Compromise the following day.

Sunday afternoon, Rap Brown was scheduled to speak to the
plenary, but, at the insistence of James Forman, who was once
the executive secretary of S.N.C.C. and is now its international-
affairs director, he agreed to speak to the Black Caucus instead.
Forman, however, addressed the plenary session—originally
announced as a Black Liberation Panel—for several hours, in
the course of which he "passed" whatever resolutions he chose
(although it was not a voting plenary); denied the microphone
to anybody else; declared himself "dictator" at one point and
then, when Peretz and some other whites at last walked out,
dismissed the whole thing, rather unconvincingly, as a joke;
and made a proposal that both calumnied the genuine plight of
the poor and may puzzle genuine revolutionaries in other
countries for years to come. As an act of revolution, he suggested
a boycott of 1968 General Motors cars. He was given several
standing ovations, and by the end of his harangue most people
present agreed with the amphetamine radicals that although
he might not have said anything either true or important, he
had "really turned them on." (Bertram Garskof declared himself
honored, at this point, to be part of "the white tail on the real
movement.")

In the late afternoon, before the evening plenary, the Black Caucus made its new demands known: the plenary was to be regarded as merely another committee of the convention, and the Black Caucus was to be granted fifty per cent of the total convention vote. The White Radicals, who had been thinking of nothing but their conspiratorial compromise, were bewildered. Only one of them, in their caucus, spoke against the new demands. "I know it's all irrelevant and meaningless," David Simpson, of the University of Georgia S.D.S., said. "I'm just not going to vote for it, because it's such a sick thing. I just don't want to be part of such a sick thing."

In the California group, Simon Casady said to Warren Hinckle, executive editor of *Ramparts*, "I guess what they're asking is to let them hold our wallet, and we might as well let them."

"Especially since there's nothing in it," Hinckle said.

At the Third Party Caucus, rhetoric had lapsed into the style of another age. "We have preserved the unity of this convention," a delegate of the Socialist Workers Party was saying, "to present an alternative to the American people." "Hear! Hear!" the delegates replied.

At that evening's plenary, where the Black Caucus demand for half the convention's vote was introduced, Communist Party and Du Bois Club members rose one after another to endorse "our black brothers'" position. What had happened, it turned out, was that while the white radicals were planning their local-organizing coup, and then settling for the California Compromise, the Communist Party and the Du Bois Clubs had temporarily, for whatever it might be worth to them, taken over the Black Caucus, and, through it, the entire convention—an achievement roughly comparable to embezzling a sieveful of smog. By inducing the Black Caucus to make the demand at all, the Communists had turned blacks against whites: if the white radicals voted for it, they lost their power over any further decisions of the New Politics (including the power to paralyze a third ticket); if against, they lost Negro cooperation. "Radicalized," they voted for. ("Masochistic Fascists," the Reverend James Bevel, a Negro veteran of innumerable civil-rights campaigns, called them later on.) In the plenary, any Negro who walked up to a microphone to speak—even *for* the new demand—was approached by two tall young members of the Black Caucus and persuaded to sit down again. The demand was accepted, and a pink card representing half the convention's votes was given to Carlos Russell, a poverty worker from Brooklyn, who was now the Black Caucus chairman.

From this moment on, the Black Caucus showed itself to be more intelligent, more sensible, and more independent than any other group at the convention, and than the convention as a whole. To begin with, after a unity speech by Russell, the Black Caucus adjourned the plenary. Then, as white petitioners from the White Radical Caucus, the Third Ticket Caucus, the newly formed Israel Caucus, and even the pre-convention Resolutions Committee and the Progressive Labor Party cooled their heels in an anteroom, and delegates from SANE and Women Strike for Peace (who had either abstained or voted for) wandered about in the ranks of the "radicalized," the Black Caucus—in a surge of good feeling—let any Negro in who cared to come. As a result, the Black Caucus may have had the first genuine discussion of the entire convention. When William Higgs, a white associate of the radical National Lawyers Guild, who was out in the corridor, cast about in his mind for the name of some Negro he might know inside the caucus, and finally succeeded in summoning one—a woman delegate from the Mississippi Freedom Democratic Party—he failed to persuade her that a national third ticket would really help her much in Mississippi. ("I see what you mean, Bill," she said when she came out into the hall, "but I can't help thinking I need all the energy I got for the local issues.") And Steve Newman, of the Progressive Labor Party, who now threw in his lot with the local organizers, and against the conservative, third-ticket-strategy Communists (since Maoists believe in revolution by non-electoral means), never got a chance to talk to anyone at all. By the time the plenary reconvened, at midnight, the Black Caucus had endorsed a proposal by the Communist Party's Claude Lightfoot: local organizing, with a third-ticket decision to be deferred. But, in another surge of fellow-feeling, the spokesman for the Black Caucus—having heard the White Radical Caucus's point of view through an intermediary, Ivanhoe Donaldson—phrased his proposal as though it were the California Compromise. No one protested. Everyone was baffled. And it passed.

MONDAY MORNING, Arthur Waskow, of the Institute for Policy Studies and of the Steering Committee, tried to dissuade a woman from the Women's Rights Caucus from introducing a proposal that women be granted fifty-one per cent of the vote at the plenary. "You're not thinking politically," he said. "It will sound like a joke. A parody. I think you're completely insensitive to the politics of this convention." The White Radical Caucus was in session once again. Eric Mann said he thought that they would have to reckon with the possibility that most of the money except the Communist Party money would now withdraw from the Conference but that there was no point in being too fussy about where money for local organizing was coming from. In the two half-black, half-white committees—one for organizing, one for the third ticket—that would be set up in that afternoon's plenary, he went on, Scheer's people could be counted on to see to it that the Communist Party did not run away with the third ticket. And the white half of the local organizers could be turned into a white S.N.C.C. Then the plotting began again, in the intimate, nearly inaudible voices that are part of the white-radical mystique: "people already in motion," "implement specific programs at the local level," "relate," "in that bag," "where they're at," "doing their thing," "power structure," "coalesce with," "crystal-clear," "relevant," "beautiful." It seemed that some awful rhetorical cycle was coming to a close. A radical movement born out of a corruption of the vocabulary of civil rights—preëmpting the terms that belonged to a truly oppressed minority and applying them to the situation of some bored children committed to choosing what intellectual morsels they liked from the buffet of life at a middle-class educational institution in California—now luxuriated in the cool political vocabulary, while the urban civil-rights movement, having nearly abandoned its access to the power structure, thrashed about in local paroxysms of self-destruction. Both had become so simplistically opposed to order of any kind that society may become simplistic and repressive in dealing with them. There just may be no romance in moving forward at the pace that keeping two ideas in one's head at the same time implies; at least, there have been no heroes of the radical center yet. But the New Politics, black and white, seems to have turned from a political or moral force into an incendiary spectacle, a sterile, mindless, violence-enamoured form of play. In the final plenary, the Black Caucus, in addition to reversing its Israel resolution, managed to pass a few resolutions opposing Vietnam and the draft, and to appoint the two committees to recommend things for the New Politics, if there should be any, to do in the future.

A WORD ABOUT "BOURGEOIS CIVIL LIBERTIES"

Irving Howe

Objection after objection has been made that by obstructing (Dow Chemical) recruiters, we have been denying others— the recruiter and those who wish to see him—the right of free speech and assembly. In a sense, this is true. . . . The institutions our resistance has desanctified and delegitima- tized, as a result of our action against their oppression of others, have lost all authority and hence all respect. As such they have only raw, coercive power. Since they are with- out legitimacy in our eyes, they are without rights. . . . Our critique argues that the social order we are rebelling against is totalitarian, manipulative, repressive, and anti-democratic.

These lines, under the heading "Resistance and Bourgeois Civil Liberties," come from Interorganizational Secretary of SDS Carl Davidson and appear in *New Left Notes,* November 13, 1967. Because they reflect the thinking of some people in the American Left, I should like to raise a few questions, and if Mr. Davidson cares to reply, space will be available to him.

Precisely what are *bourgeois* civil liberties? One thinks of civil liberties as including provisions of the Bill of Rights for freedom of speech, press, assemblage, etc. That these are some- times violated by the bourgeois state or falsely linked with

Irving Howe, "A Word About Bourgeois Civil Liberties," *Dissent* (January–February 1968), 10–11. Reprinted by permission; © 1968 *Dissent.*

bourgeois ideology, is true. Yet to say that does not answer the question: in what way are civil liberties *themselves* "bourgeois?"

Would Mr. Davidson offer some examples of *non*bourgeois civil liberties? The main kinds of nonbourgeois society in the world today are primitive and Communist. In the former there are few civil liberties, in the latter none.

A historical examination would show that civil liberties have often been won through the struggle of labor unions, socialist movements, and liberal intellectuals, and sometimes in opposition to the bourgeoisie. Radicals have traditionally held this conquest to be precious as one that should be preserved and extended in a socialist society. It has further been our view that we should fight the hardest and the most consistently for civil liberties, first because we value them in principle and second because any trend to whittle them away would probably hurt us the most. If it is intolerable that a majority should deny the civil liberties of a minority, it is madness for a tiny minority to deny the civil liberties of a majority. But if no more is involved than *bourgeois* civil liberties which we can discard upon need, then, Mr. Davidson, they may not be so important?

"The institutions," he writes, have "lost all authority and hence all respect." Being "without legitimacy in our eyes, they are without rights." Very well; but "lost all authority" *for whom*? For a majority of the American people? Or even of American students? Who has appointed SDS the judge of whether the institutions of this country retain their authority and rights? Suppose it could be shown that 98 per cent of the people continue to respect those institutions—would Mr. Davidson still persist in "abolishing" their authority and rights? And if so, might he not be guilty of elitism, that is, of substituting his own judgments and decisions for those of the people?

SDS declares itself in favor of "participatory democracy." At certain universities—Columbia, UCLA—there have been referenda among the students on allowing Dow Chemical recruiters to appear on campus, and by a decisive majority the students voted in favor of so allowing them. Will SDS, in the name of participatory (or any other kind of) democracy, abide by the voice of the majority or will it continue advocating the forcible obstruction of recruiters? Mind: the issue is not whether SDS holds demonstrations against Dow Chemical, since no one can in principle be opposed to that. The issue is whether SDS will try forcibly to prevent recruiters from saying their wretched little piece, even though the majority of students favors allowing them to. And if so, how will SDS reconcile that stand with "participatory democracy"? Or are only right-thinking folk allowed to participate in "participatory democracy"?

If Mr. Davidson declares "the institutions" to be stripped of authority and rights, by what moral and/or political standards does he then propose to denounce them when they violate the civil liberties they claim to uphold? We are all outraged by General Hershey's proposal to draft antiwar students as a punitive measure. Our outrage rests on the assumption that he is violating due process and common standards of decency—procedures and standards "the institutions" claim to value. But if we no longer recognize their authority or rights, how then can we claim the protection of their rules?

If Mr. Davidson declares "the institutions" to have no further authority and rights, could he suggest on which *principled* basis —that is, more than an outcry that people of correct opinion are being hurt—he would argue against "the institutions" if and when these proceed to suppress *him*? And if he believes that SDS as a private organization has the moral authority to abolish the "rights" of "the institutions," on what grounds will he argue if other private organizations—say, the American Legion or the Birch Society—proceed on their own to abolish the "rights" of SDS? I know on what grounds Norman Thomas and Roger Baldwin would oppose the suppression of SDS by government or its persecution by enemy organizations; but on what grounds would Mr. Davidson?

These questions were faced by the Communists when they said that civil liberties were convenient under capitalism but could be disposed of once they took power. The results, as we all know, were disastrous. No one—even if, like myself, he felt obliged to defend the civil liberties of Communists as a matter of principle—could take seriously their claim to care about freedom. Does Mr. Davidson see any danger that people of good will might draw similar conclusions about him?

Mr. Davidson declares the U.S. is "totalitarian." Could he then explain how it happens that SDS manages to pour out of its Chicago office—and through the postal system of this very "totalitarian" country—large quantities of material denouncing the society? How it happens that SDS can hold demonstrations urging people to defect from the army and declaring the President to be a murderer? Might not the ability to do these things be taken as evidence that the U.S., whatever its many and grave faults, is not quite "totalitarian"?

A theory is now being advanced in New Left circles that we live in the U.S. under "liberal fascism." It is something to conjure with. In what ways does *liberal* fascism" differ from "*fascist fascism*"? In that the rights of organization and protest, action and speech so brutally destroyed by the latter, remain essentially operative under the former? In that Mr. Davidson and others of his persuasion, who under "fascist fascism" might well have been transformed into lampshades had they so much as uttered a peep of discontent, are, I am happy to say, continuing to shout their denunciation of the appalling Vietnam War under "liberal fascism"?

I would earnestly plead with Mr. Davidson and his friends that they look into the dismal story of an earlier but similar theory, advanced some 35 years ago under the label of "social fascism" in the Communist movement.

Finally, a friendly offer. I am prepared to read any book proposed by Mr. Davidson, if he will promise to read Lenin's "*Left Wing*" *Communism: An Infantile Disorder*. Perhaps we can then each report on our reading and thereby contribute to a dialogue on the Left.

NEW LEFT, NEW RIGHT

Irving Kristol

An old friend, who lives in California and is active in the Democratic party there, visited New York recently. We spent a lot of time together, and I found him to be in troubled spirits. California politics, he confessed, was beginning to slip beyond his comprehension. First, there had been the whole Berkeley business—and while specifically campus turmoil seems to have subsided, at least temporarily, it is also true that the "New Left", using Berkeley as a base, was now trying to move into the Democratic party in a significant way. Then there was the victory of Ronald Reagan in the Republican primary, and the discovery of the pollsters that he seemed to have an excellent chance against Governor Brown in November. This was a particular shock, since the Democrats had always felt—and earlier polls appeared to have confirmed their sentiments—that Reagan, as an "extremist," would have the least chance of election among potential Republican candidates. My friend didn't understand what precisely was bugging the militants of the New Left or why the citizens of California should show so keen an interest in Ronald Reagan. Neither this New Left nor this New Right seemed to have anything like a coherent program. Governor Brown's moderately liberal administration ought, by all rational analysis, to have been perfectly in tune with the consensus of political opinion in that prosperous and progressive state. Yet things weren't working out as one might have expected.

Irving Kristol, "New left, new right," *The Public Interest* (Summer 1966), 3–7. © 1966 by National Affairs, Inc.

One has the suspicion that, in this respect as in others, California may be the pacesetter for the nation. As Peter Drucker points out in an article elsewhere in this issue, the politics of consensus, so ingeniously engineered by Lyndon Johnson, is essentially a politics of transition from an older "interest group" conception of political behavior—in which so-called "gut issues" and "bread-and-butter" issues predominate—to one in which the issues are less tangible, less measurable, less amenable to the arithmetic of compromise. The tantalizing question is just what shape these new issues will take, and in what directions they will lead us.

Not that "gut issues" are likely to disappear. People always have taken, and always will take, the liveliest interest in obtaining their "fair" share of the nation's income and wealth. It is even possible that, with increasing affluence, there will be increasingly bitter argument over who gets what, when, and how. Given more to quarrel about, men are not likely to quarrel less: there is no sign that our industrial relations are sinking into apathy under the soothing pressure of accumulated fringe benefits. But what does seem to be evident is that this kind of class struggle—and it is unquestionably a class struggle, though merely over money, not power—is not going to serve as a focus for American politics. True, there are some in the New Left and the New Right who *think* it will, and talk as if it will—one still hears angry mutterings about "exploitation" and "socialism" from the two sides, as they contemplate the inevitably sordid business of parcelling out the nation's bounty. But this only proves what one would expect: that not everything is new on the New Left and Right. After all, walking backwards into the future has always been the most common form of political locomotion.

But what *will* be new about the "new politics"? As Mr. Drucker suggests, it is probable that foreign policy will play a more central and controversial role than ever before; the New Left gives more than a little evidence to support that proposition. It is also probable that the tensions involved in integrating the Negro into American society will give rise to significant electoral issues; there can be little doubt that at least some of Mr. Reagan's support comes from those who, while not racist in any traditional sense, are nevertheless fed up with the difficulties of coping with this historic and seemingly intractable problem. But beyond and beneath such specific urgencies, there appears to be a general and diffuse uneasiness, all the more powerful, and all the more dangerous, for being so stammeringly inarticulate. This uneasiness reveals itself in the astonishing frequency with which one phrase above all turns up in our current political rhetoric. The New Left uses it; the New Right uses it; President Johnson uses it; *everyone* uses it—though no one seems to know quite what it means. That phrase is: "the quality of American life."

At its most trivial—and the Administration is most especially tempted toward this interpretation—the phrase is taken to mean that the people of the United States should be enjoying more and better symphony orchestras, more and better art museums, more and better repertory theaters. The only thing to be said in favor of this meaning is that there is no conceivable harm in our acquiring all these cultural benefits. Against it, one can say that it is vulgarly simple-minded, and therefore ultimately misleading. People are not set into political motion by such matters; and the truly interesting fact about this new anxiety over "the quality of American life" is that it has so much *political* energy.

At its most portentous—and both the New Left and New Right have a high quotient of portentousness—the phrase is given an apocalyptic significance (and the convenient aspect of apocalyptic thinking is that it never gets bad marks for being vague and imprecise). For the New Left, the "quality of American life" is being strained by the massive organized complexity of our society, in which the individual becomes an anonymous unit and in which his personal authenticity, his singular "existential" dimension, is accorded no official recognition. The New Right, oddly enough, makes its complaint in not too dissimilar terms: the self-reliant individual is losing control over his own destiny, and over the destiny of his children too. A keen sense of personal impotence, an acute sense of personal frustration, is the watermark beneath the manifestoes of both Left and Right. Both feel that "things are in the saddle," that American life is something they cannot get a friendly grip on, that whatever is happening, it is happening *to* them, that they are the objects, not the subjects, of contemporary history. Were the word not so fashionable as to be a bore, one could say that it is "alienation" that is most distinctive of the "new politics."

Now, IT IS EASY to poke gentle or cruel fun at the fuzzy misconceptions about the actualities of American life, and the romantic notions about America's past or possible future, that characterize the lamentations now rising to the political heavens. One can, for instance, point out that these same people who find America so inhospitable are, in material terms, making out very well thank you, and much, much better than ever before. One can also legitimately assert—and Alvin Schorr's article, in this issue, does this splendidly—that the facts of American life, past and present, bear little or no correspondence to the popular image of them. One can impatiently demand, what has been notably lacking: specific proposals for the reform and improvement of whatever it is that is bothersome. One can, and I think one should, do all of these things. But I think it would be a grave error to do *only* these things. It is the part of prudent statesmanship to affirm that no real discontent can be reduced to imaginary causes. On this, as on so many political matters, Edmund Burke said the wisest word:

> To complain of the age we live in, to murmur at the present possessors of power, to lament the past, to conceive extravagant hopes of the future, are the common dispositions of the greatest part of mankind . . . Such complaints and humors have existed in all times; yet as all times have not been alike, true political sagacity manifests itself in distinguishing that complaint which only characterizes the general infirmity of human nature, from those which are symptoms of the particular distemperature of our own air and season.

As to the causes of "the particular distemperature of our own air and season," I am both too modest and too ignorant to offer a ready and forceful explanation. But I should like to hazard a weak guess of a general nature in the hope that others will be provoked into stronger and more cogent analysis.

It seems to me that America is experiencing what can only be called, even after all discounting of the melodramatic glibness of the phrase, a "crisis in values." The crisis—which is, of course, to be observed in many other Western nations as well— is twofold. First, a great many areas of human life and behavior, whose governance falls under the rule of custom, tradition, and conventional belief, have become affected with vast and unwelcome uncertainty. This is not a recent development; it has been observed, experienced, and commented upon for more than a century now, and is everywhere accepted as a distinguishing feature of "the modern era." But it is only relatively recently that the mass of the people have become directly and personally involved in it. Habits of thought and action persist long after they have been intellectually and morally undermined. Today, the shock waves are beginning to upset and challenge the most ordinary decencies and civilities. People do not know what they ought to think about relations between the sexes, about relations between parents and children, about relations between the citizen and his government. For some individuals, this uncertainty is seen as a creative opportunity—the old ways have decayed and new, more suitable ones are in the process of being contrived. Perhaps it is so. But the fact remains that ordinary people—by which I mean most of us—find this state of affairs almost intolerably exacerbating. It is easy to snicker, as popular humor now does, at the typical father trying, and hopelessly failing, to give guidance to his daughter about the regulation of her sexual life. Yet this father, even though he may join the snickering at himself, is all too likely to feel deep down that he has been unmanned by some kind of nebulous conspiracy, and that older certainties are to be preferred to a newer sophistication that is primarily destructive. I suspect that a great many such fathers in California find Ronald Reagan's rhetorical emphasis on the traditional virtues quite appealing—it is, in its own oblique way, a "gut issue." As for the youngsters, the evidence of Berkeley would seem to indicate that, whatever benefits the new freedoms might confer, contentment is not one of them.

But in addition to this personal crisis in values, there is an institutional one. Not only do people not quite know what to believe about private and public proprieties; they don't know where to turn for answers they could accept as authoritative, in however mild and attenuated a form. The value-creating and value-sustaining institutions in American life have traditionally been the family, the church, and the school. Events of the past decades have deprived these institutions of their authority over morals (and even over manners)—without, however, providing alternative authorities. The mass media by their very nature can only mimic the existing confusion. The universities might logically be considered as new centers of moral and spiritual authority, and perhaps they will eventually become such. At the moment, however, they are themselves probably the most crisis-ridden institutions in the nation, and are having the greatest difficulty defining their own reason for being.

Where does that leave us? With a great many questions and no answers? Not quite. For if there are no answers, properly speaking, there are nevertheless things to be said. I would myself venture to say two things, the first of which I am ready to be dogmatic about, the second of which I concede to be speculative.

First, on all the evidence, *the one worst way to cope with this crisis in values is through organized political-ideological action.* Most of the hysteria, much of the stupidity, and a good part of the bestiality of the twentieth century have arisen from efforts to do precisely this. Not only do such efforts fail; they fail in the costliest fashion. And if modern history can be said to teach anything, it is that, intolerable as the crisis in values may be, it invariably turns out to be far less intolerable than any kind of "final solution" imposed by direct political action.

Secondly—*and nevertheless*—there is no way of removing this issue from politics. A great many people would like to think that the New Left and the New Right are passing eddies on the mainstream of American politics, and that after a while we shall all happily return to politics-as-usual, bickering amicably over who gets what, when, and how. I do not believe this will happen. And I am not even sure that I would like to see it happen. Though I approve, on the whole, of the various programs for a Great Society, I too am full of doubt about their potentialities for a good life in a good society. There are a great many things wrong with the way we live now, and I have little faith that they will automatically right themselves. Above all, I cannot persuade myself that a democracy whose notions of public and private virtue are slowly being emptied of their substance can sustain itself. Democracy, after all, means self-government; and such self-government is, in the long run, utterly impossible without adequate self-definition, self-certainty, self-control. All of modern life and modern culture have combined to make the self a question to itself. I regard it as utopian to expect that people will not turn to politics for answers. And I regard it as certain that they will take vicious answers rather than none at all.

Is this not playing with fire? Of course it is. But that, I do think, is what "the great game of politics" is going to be like, in the period ahead of us. It will be anything but amusing; indeed, it could well be the most dangerous game of all.

PART II

Intellectuals and Politics

THE RELATIONSHIP of intellectuals to politics has always been a touchy one. This has been so, at least in part, because the values of the intellectual and the values of the politician almost invariably collide. For the intellectual, consistency, logical rigor, a commitment to the search for truth are the highest values. The world of the politician is a world of compromise, a world in which logic is not always of the highest priority, and truth is subordinate to the search for the general good. It may be said that compromise is of the essence of political life and that intellectuals, more, perhaps, than other men, are peculiarly incapable of compromise.

This conflict can, of course, be resolved by removing oneself from politics and cultivating one's own garden. This was the option taken by Thoreau, for example, who observed of political life, "practically I have never recognized that it concerns me at all."[1] Not all intellectuals, however, find the life of detachment or removal a satisfactory one. Indeed, it is far more common to discover a certain resentment at being excluded from the

[1] *The Writings of Henry David Thoreau* (Boston, 1894), IV, 480–481.

centers of power, a resentment intensified by the conviction that as intellectuals, they possess very special claims for occupying those positions monopolized by lesser men. This resentment becomes most dramatic when manifested within the framework of democratic politics. The intellectual who professes a commitment to the politics of democracy is frequently confronted with a personal crisis which borders on schizophrenia: publicly committed to the politics of democracy, he harbors within his soul the dream of the philosopher-king.

Given these circumstances, it is not surprising that a man whose thought is characterized by the highest degree of intellectual rigor when dealing, say, with the problems of physics, comes undone when he enters the political arena. Consequently, when we consider the demands of the intellectual for a role in the political arena, it is useful to remember Kant's caveat: "It is not to be expected that kings philosophize or that philosophers become kings, nor is it desirable, because the possession of power corrupts the free judgment of reason inevitably."[2] One is tempted to add that not only the possession of power, but the desire for power, "corrupts the free judgment of reason absolutely." And if politics corrupts philosophy, we must at least consider the possibility that the converse is equally true.

The authors of the following articles on the role of the intellectual in political life include a well-known playwright, two professors, a psychoanalyst, and an author and editor. They are by most definitions of the term intellectuals. They can hardly be accused of anti-intellectualism nor are they guilty of any particular hostility to intellectuals. One of the most valuable qualities of the intellectual, a quality which often results from intellectual pursuits, is skepticism. This skepticism which so frequently is seen when the intellectual turns his attention to the activities of others is, perhaps, discovered less frequently in the intellectual's attitude toward himself. The writers of these essays suggest that the actions and attitudes of the intellectual should be subjected to the same careful scrutiny as are those of other members of society. If one ought to remain skeptical about the claims of politicians, for example, so one ought to retain a similar skepticism about the claims of intellectuals.

Indeed, it is possible that one's skepticism ought to be intensified, for the man who views himself as an intellectual seems

[2] Immanuel Kant, "Eternal Peace," in *The Philosophy of Kant,* ed. and tr. by C. J. Friedrich (New York, 1949), 456.

to be particularly prone to the ancient Greek sin of *hubris*. It is very probably this vulnerability that contributes to the dubious reputation of the intellectual among those who have not cloaked themselves in the mantle of the intellectual. It is not necessary fully to agree with Tibor Szamuely's claim that the Anglo-Saxon nations have been well advised in "keeping intellectuals away from power and . . . [in] not paying any attention to their political views." One must agree, however, that like all the other elements of society, the claims of the intellectual are not to be uncritically accepted at face value, that his thought and actions are not above critical analysis, and that his status as an intellectual may equip him to deal with certain orders of problems very successfully at the same time as it renders him less capable than other men of making sound judgments about other sorts of issues. The performance of a significant segment of the intellectual community in discussing the political problems of the past ten years leads inexorably to the conclusion that politics is not the most natural habitat for the intellectual. The politician whom he scorns not infrequently shows more humanity, more modesty, a greater willingness to learn, and a greater commitment to the reasoned solutions of difficult problems. This in itself should make one hesitate before succumbing to the blandishments of those intellectuals who offer themselves as our saviors.

INTELLECTUALS AND JUST CAUSES

Tibor Szamuely

The western intellectuals' approach to the political developments of the last few years has been distinguished, it seems to me, by two essential qualities. One is the apparent alignment of the most vocal section of the intellectual community with what is broadly termed "the Left." There exists today a rigid set of orthodox progressive ideas, a kind of portable intellectual medicine-chest lined with dozens of neatly labelled ideological nostrums for every occasion: Abortion, Aden, Advertising, Afro-Asia, Big Business, Birth Control, Catholic Church, Censorship, Colonialism, etc., etc. . . . through the whole litany, down to UN, Unilateralism, Viet Nam, War-toys, Wilson, Yemen, Zambia and Zionism. One always knows beforehand, with infinite boredom, just what the progressive intellectual's position is going to be on any conceivable issue. This is one of the reasons why the Middle East crisis, like the Hungarian Revolution before it, was so important: it overturned the medicine chest, smashing the pre-packed panaceas, wreaking havoc among the certitudes.

The other striking—and paradoxical—aspect of the "progressive" intellectuals' involvement in politics is the fundamentally *non-intellectual* nature of their commitment. However sincere

Tibor Szamuely, "Intellectuals and Just Causes," *Encounter* (September 1967), 13–14. This article was a contribution to a symposium entitled "Intellectuals and Just Causes" published in *Encounter,* September 1967. Mr. Szamuely's article appeared on pp. 13–14. Reprinted by permission of the author.

and deep-felt, it is almost invariably an *emotional* attitude, owing very little, if anything, to the processes of reasoning and study that one usually associates with the word "intellectual." (Perhaps this is why actors and actresses have suddenly become so prominent in various "intellectual" political manifestations.) It is, for instance, practically impossible to carry on a rational argument about Viet Nam, to hear a case against US policy made in coherent, analytical, factual terms. What one gets is a confused mélange of overwrought emotive phrases: "people are being killed there," "the Americans have no right to be in Asia," "white men are killing coloured people," and so on.

Or take another example: the words "fascist" and "fascism" have now lost any meaning they originally possessed, and have become no more than emotive expressions, applied indiscriminately to any politician, policy, or régime of which the Left happens to disapprove. Today the "progressive" intellectual appears to have absolved himself from having to argue his case, from collecting the facts, mustering the evidence, demolishing his opponent point by point—things at which genuine radical intellectuals like Marx used to excel. All this has been done away with now: it is quite sufficient to cry "Fascist!"—and a great emotional groundswell of instant images and lurid associations will effectively drown out any timid voices asking for proof of the accusation. Curiously enough, the very same scholar who feels no compunction about hurling the charge of "fascism" at any political opponent in sight would never dream of using similar methods in his professional teaching or research work. That is quite different: there he scrupulously adheres to the highest standards of evidence and analysis. Intellectual standards are renounced in favour of emotions only when it comes to involvement in the political issues of the day.

It was not always thus. Thirty years ago the progressive intellectual would swear by Marxism—which, whatever one can say about it, was certainly a rational system of thought. But since then life has consisted of one disappointment after another: the patent failure of the collectivist economy, as against the achievements of capitalism in raising living standards; the stubborn refusal of Communist totalitarianism to become democratic; the appalling and increasingly hopeless mess in Afro-Asia. Every traditional pillar of the progressive *Weltanschauung* has crumbled to dust. A choice had to be made: either one looked the facts in the face and made an agonising re-appraisal, or one firmly shut one's eyes to reality. It is, I believe, this desperate escape from an unpalatable reality into a never-never world of imaginary heroes (Lumumba, Nyerere, Castro, *et al.*) and mythical villains (LBJ and a host of lesser demons), of nonexistent causes and artificial emotions, that characterises the "progressive" approach to politics. Facts and realities—whether of Soviet labour camps, East European political trials, African massacres, or Indian misrule—are not allowed to intrude into this cosy world of make-believe. Secure under the protection of US firepower—and knowing this, and hating himself for knowing it —the intellectual cries out for more stories of American atrocities. No horrendous anti-Western tales are too incredible to be disbelieved, no facts about Communism or the Third World sufficiently well-documented to be accepted. The liberal intelligentsia has replaced reason by faith, rational judgements by visceral reactions.

But what, one may ask, is there wrong with being guided by emotion in politics? A great deal. For one thing, these emotions are hardly the noble humanitarian ideals they are made out to be. Compassion for human suffering? Then how can they cast a blind eye on the continuing slaughter of tens of thousands in the Yemen, Indonesia, Nigeria, the Congo, Sudan, and a great many other places. Devotion to democracy and human rights? Then how can they be seeking out every possible extenuating circumstance in favour of unreconstructed Communist totalitarianism and "progressive" dictatorships in the Third World. Hatred of war and violence? Then how explain the martial postures over the Middle East, to say nothing of the open admiration for the Viet Cong and other "freedom fighters"?

Orwell exposed this stance years ago:

> There is a minority of intellectual pacifists whose real though unadmitted motive appears to be hatred of Western democracy and admiration for totalitarianism. . . . If one looks closely at the writings of the younger intellectual pacifists, one finds that they do not by any means express impartial disapproval but are directed almost entirely against Britain and the United States. Moreover they do not as a rule condemn violence as such, but only violence used in defence of the Western countries.

All this is as true today as it was then.

The real mainspring of intellectual emotionalism seems to be a strange compound of irrational guilt, self-hatred, anti-Americanism, wishful thinking, power-worship, and arrogance. A considerable element of hypocrisy comes into it as well. "We all, of course, abhor dictatorship and violence," they proclaim, "but in those remote, underdeveloped places there seems to be no other solution—and besides, the poor fellows wouldn't really know the difference anyway. . . ." It is very easy for the Anglo-Saxon intellectual to scoff at democracy and to gloss over such things as censorship, secret police, or concentration camps—fortunately, he knows of them only by hearsay. One could even formulate the following proposition as a general law of politics: the extent of progressive feeling among the intellectuals of any given country is in direct proportion to the distance between that country and the nearest totalitarian dictatorship.

I am afraid that our emotional intelligentsia is perpetrating an imposture upon society. Intellectuals demand special consideration for their views *qua* intellectuals—because theirs are trained minds, capable of intense mental concentration, possessing a fund of specialist knowledge, used to analysing the facts and establishing the truth in a detached spirit of scientific inquiry. This is why, they argue, governments should pay the greatest attention to their opinions. And it is under these false pretences that attempts are made to palm off on an unsuspecting public a jumble of tortured emotional attitudes dressed up as a reasoned, cogent, and substantiated intellectual case.

The Anglo-Saxon nations have a long tradition of keeping intellectuals away from power and of not paying any attention to their political views. On present form there seems to be every justification for upholding it in the future.

INTELLECTUALS AND JUST CAUSES

John Osborne

The last time I involved myself in any political demonstration was in 1961, when, with a great many other writers or hang-around writers, I "sat down" in Trafalgar Square. I fully expected to go to gaol but mercifully didn't, although I was looking forward at the time to a legitimate reason for not being able to write. In fact, I was lovingly carried off into a van by eight—I think—kindly constables who called me "sir." (All those I saw manhandled asked for what they got. And they wanted it.) Apart from being reviled and libelled by the *Sunday Express*, I was fined forty shillings and went home for a good soak in the bath with a severe headache. I don't regret having done this. At the time it had a kind of national poetic logic that certain of us should make this particular gesture. My sense of timing rarely lets me down and I know I was right at the time. However, I resolved then that I should never engage in this kind of concerted affair again unless some unforeseeable situation should arise. It revealed itself to my simple spirit that there is a certain kind of militant animal which seeks out and exploits political crises for reasons of personal aggrandisement and creative frustration. There is an odour of psychopathic self-right-

John Osborne, "Intellectuals and Just Causes," *Encounter* (September 1967), 3–4. This article was a contribution to a symposium entitled "Intellectuals and Just Causes" published in *Encounter,* September 1967. Mr. Osborne's article appeared on pp. 3–5. Reprinted by permission of HAROLD OBER ASSOCIATES INCORPORATED. Copyright © 1967 by John Osborne.

eousness about many of the hardy annual protesters which I find ludicrous and distasteful. I have long ago refused to sign those glib and predictable letters to the *Times,* including the one during the recent Israeli crisis when so many of these cause-happy activists leapt to the telephone and their pens.

The same principle applies to the Viet Nam War, the very name of which has become a synonym for left-wing sanctimony. I have not been able to come to a clear resolution over this or many other political dilemmas. I do know that I see little to choose between Communist police terrorism and shoddy American power politics. Except that I find the latter minimally less repugnant. We really do live in a very wicked world. I believe that writers should express their position about this as well as they can and in the country in which they have elected to live. Writers are often more thoughtful than the rest of the community and occasionally more literate. However, they should speak modestly as gifted or admired individuals and not as part of a privileged pressure group with access to revealed truths. The presumption and sentimentality of many of my fellow craftsmen is frequently appalling. May God gag all actresses forever. Unless they are divine and the ones who are just shut up. Consequently I sign letters no longer, friends who were never friends call me blimp. To hell with them. It is harder than they will ever know. I certainly don't give money. Not to subsidise ungifted people who organise these junkets. Better even to spend it on a subscription to ENCOUNTER. No, not for all those school teachers and pedants and readers of the *Guardian* and the *Observer.* Perhaps to *Horse and Hound* and a girl to read it with.

PROTEST AND REVOLUTION AGAINST WESTERN SOCIETIES

Robert Waelder

Since [the French Revolution] has made the impression of striving more for a renovation of mankind than merely for a reform of France, it has kindled a passion such as even the most violent political revolutions have heretofore not been able to produce. It started a proselytizing campaign and brought propaganda into the world. In this way, it eventually assumed a religious character which astonished contemporaries. Even more, it became itself a kind of religion, an imperfect religion, to be sure . . . but one which nonetheless has flooded the world with its fighters, its apostles and its martyrs. . . .

      Alexis de Tocqueville, *L'ancien régime et la révolution.*

At a time . . . when, with the spread of education and communications, the realisation and impatience of suffering [are] visibly and rapidly growing. . . .

      Translated from Jacob Burckhardt, *Weltgeschichtliche Betrachtungen* (1868) by James Hastings Nichols (ed.), in *Force and Freedom,* 1943.

Congenitally ordained to prey upon his fellows, interminably tempted and interminably deceived, man . . . is not, at any rate, fitted for happiness by his natural estate: to this

Robert Waelder, "Protest and Revolution against Western Societies," in *The Revolution in World Politics,* ed. Morton A. Kaplan (New York: John Wiley & Sons, Inc., 1962), pp. 3–27.

day, the whole creation groaneth and travaileth still. There have been times in which this state of affairs was taken more or less for granted. When it appeared that nothing but a conspiracy between privilege and superstition was blocking the way to the infinite perfectibility of the human race, and when the advance of science and the accumulation of wealth promised an endless progress of material welfare, the torrential forces of *temporal* hope broke out. But Time is an infernal ironist; and the invariable rebuffs inflicted upon the appetites, the ambitions and the aspirations of man could not fail to call out in desperate response the full resources of his natural ferocity; for man was not made to stand indefinitely on his hind feet.

Etienne Mantoux, *The Carthaginian Peace*, 1945.

We are living in the fifth act of the French Revolution.
Felix Somary, *Erinnerungen aus meinem Leben*, 1955.

The modern movements of protest and revolution against traditional Western society can be seen as part of a world-wide revolutionary process that has gone on for almost 200 years exploding first in one place and then in another, interrupted at times by periods of quiet and restoration, gaining momentum, at first slowly and then rapidly, and now encompassing the entire globe. Its main characteristics are a passionate desire for *change,* with little regard for the needs of conservation and consolidation, and impatience with slow, gradual change; a kind of *evangelical* moral *fervor* for the poor, in earthly goods or in spirit; the twin phenomena of protest against the existing intranational and international stratification, in the form of *socialism* and *nationalism,* respectively, with both movements occasionally hostile and occasionally cooperative. *Hatred for* private *property* and for the frankly acquisitive pursuits of men is characteristic of socialism and often of nationalism, too. Everything receives a particular flavor through the *alienation of the intellectuals,* from whose ranks the political leaders of modern times usually come, from their societies.

The Western Movements

THE PROGRESSIVE BIAS. Modern bias is strongly in favor of change, and it often favors quick and violent change over slow and non-violent evolution. "Progress" always is, and "revolution" usually is, a laudatory term. Even changes that involve no physical violence are called revolutions to give them added prestige; we speak of the urban, the scientific, the industrial revolution, of revolutions in style or taste.

This bias is a relatively new phenomenon. Throughout most of human history, heavy opprobrium was attached to any deviation from the traditional order of things. To be *cupidus rerum novarum* was a serious accusation in ancient Rome. The middle ages held to the concept of a closed world. As late as in the mid-fifteenth century, the humanist Lorenzo Valla still considered "the physician who tries out new and experimental medicines on the sick rather than the time-tested ones to be contemptible," like "the sailor who prefers to hold an uncharted course to one upon which others safely sail their ships and cargoes." Only forty years later, Columbus began his voyage to uncharted sea.

With some interludes of consolidation and restoration, the world has been changing with increasing velocity since, and public opinion has come to identify change with life, conservation with stagnation and death.

But the question of conservation versus innovation need not be a matter of *weltanschauung*, of principle and ideology. Civilization needs conservation, just as the cultivated soil needs it, as a protection against the return of the jungle and against corrosion; there are many historical examples of regression, of the loss of achievements already gained. But in quiet times and, in particular, in times in which living conditions have been steadily improving, people take for granted what they have and do not consider the possibility that it could be in jeopardy.

Equally, civilization needs innovation if it is to fulfill human aspirations. And in modern, industrialized societies, the end, or the mere slowing down, of economic progress would mean a major calamity because a large part of the people depend, directly or indirectly, on the investment sector of the economy. Whether, in any particular case, we should, or should not, embark on innovation, could be decided on an appraisal of the merits of the case, that is, on the chances and probable costs, material and otherwise, of the innovation. There is no basis for any generalized statement about the optimal relation of conservation and innovation and no likelihood that the same formula will apply in all places and at all times.

There is also the question, not of great immediate importance but possibly crucial in the long run, of how long this constant change at a necessarily accelerating pace can be maintained without progressive interference with the balance of nature and without reaching the limits of natural resources or the possibilities of human adjustment to perpetually changing conditions. Previous speculations about the limits of technology, or the limits of mankind, have proved highly premature, but that does not mean that such limits will not eventually make themselves felt.

However that may be, it is interesting to notice that the attitude toward "progress," which is a question of ideology in political and social matters, has been thoroughly de-ideologized in areas in which great advances toward rationality have been made, as in medicine. There was a time when the application, or non-application, of surgery was a matter of principle. Physicians foreswore the use of the knife in the Hippocratic Oath; surgery was practiced by another, not always fully respected, profession. Today the determination of medical treatment is no longer a matter of ideology; physicians are not divided into conservatives, always advocating conservative treatment, and liberals, always in favor of radical treatment. It is universally recognized that surgery is indicated in some cases and contraindicated in others. There is still a place for temperamental differences between doctors, but it is a marginal one. Perhaps there will be a day when the question of conservation and innovation in public affairs will be equally free from ideology, or prejudice, and nobody will profess himself in favor or against innovation just as a matter of principle.

THE EVANGELICAL FERVOR. The Western world has, in the last 200 years, been the scene of a kind of messianic, albeit secular, fervor. It has found expression in many documents and manifestoes, as in the American Declaration of Independence, the French Declaration of the Rights of Man, and others down to the Atlantic Charter and more recent documents. The moral climate that these declarations indicate has led to an improvement in the living conditions of countless common people beyond the boldest hopes of the reformers of earlier generations. But it has also had some other consequences: "Moral fervor," as Michael Polanyi put it, "in our lifetime has outreached itself by its inordinate aspirations and has heaped on mankind the disasters that have befallen us."[1]

The moral demands "outreached" themselves and became "inordinate" when self-criticism, or criticism of one's own government and society, and the attempt at a sympathetic understanding of an opponent's point of view were carried to the point where people could see only the mote in the eye of their own society and never the beam in the eye of its enemies. It is the kind of attitude which Bernard Shaw must have had in mind when he let the tailor Androcles, just about to be thrown into the circus, express his compassion for the poor lions. But although such attitudes make sense in the faithful Christian who is confidently looking forward to eternal life, they are more difficult to understand in their contemporary, secularized version.

The overreaching of moral demands is shown by the fact that no allowance is made by the moralist critics for the pursuit of national interest, including mere self-preservation. The United States is requested, in her dealings with other nations, to follow what is said to be "the right." She is requested to have complete disregard for the consequences which such a course would have for American interest in a world where not everybody is motivated by such exclusive dedication. Yet, self-preservation and the pursuit of one's interest are common to all living creatures who can neglect them only at their peril. Morality sets definite limits to the degree to which, and to the ways in which, interests may be pursued, and it sets up obligations to others. But a morality which plainly condemns the consideration of interest as such is not compatible with survival.[2]

[1] *Beyond Nihilism* (London: Cambridge University Press, 1960), p. 1.

[2] American leaders have often encouraged such unreasonable demands by claiming that the United States is guided in crucial decisions by high moral purpose only; e.g., that we resent Castro's attempt to revolutionize Latin America not as a threat to us but because it threatens our Latin neighbors; or that we engage in aid to underdeveloped countries only because we recognize it as a duty. Such claims are believed by no one and resented by all, as moralizing always is. And it seems to produce in people the irresistible urge to debunk these claims by subjecting them to ever more exacting tests until the breaking point has been reached at which the United States can go no further in jeopardizing its vital interests.

The United States should instead assume a more realistic attitude and make more modest moral claims which can be, and have been, lived up to: that, like everybody else, we defend our vital interests

How moral aspirations can outreach themselves can be seen, for example, in the attitude of extreme liberalism to crime and the criminal. The lawbreaker has from time immemorial been fair game for human sadism; people openly and unashamedly enjoyed watching wilfully produced human agony at public executions. The fact that the victims were criminals, hence, supposedly "got their just deserts," quieted whatever stirrings of conscience the spectators might otherwise have felt. In the last two centuries, the more conspicuous expressions of sadism have gradually been taken out of law and law enforcement—a development for which every humane person will feel grateful.

But the process has been carried further to the point where the lawbreaker appears to be fully exonerated as a victim of circumstance—"more sinned against than sinning"—and society is seen as responsible. The judges, the government, the upper classes, and even the victim himself[3] appear as the real culprits, and the plea of conditioning by circumstance is never entered on their behalf.

The position is logically untenable. If all behavior is determinded to the exclusion of all culpability and responsibility, neither the lawbreaker nor society can be called to account; neither exhortation nor condemnation makes any sense whatever. If, on the other hand, there is sense in attaching blame to society for its acts of commission or omission, the same ought

---

but that, in so doing, we always keep a decent respect for the vital interests of others and seek for a formula that combines them both.

It should be added, however, that the neglect of considerations of national interest, characteristic of liberal attitudes to international problems in the United States is not always due to exaggerated moral demands but sometimes merely to the fact that the possibility of a national catastrophe is not realized. The long period of unearned security which the American people have enjoyed because of their geographical remoteness from other centers of power, the balance of power in Eurasia, and the role of sea power—facts which have either disappeared or been downgraded in recent years—have made the people take security for granted; this feeling, together with anti-European resentment and the complacency produced by American successes, had created an atmosphere in which "power politics" was looked upon as something wicked, and the concept of national interest as a fraud.

[3] Shortly after the First World War, a novel by the Austrian writer Franz Werfel was published under the title: *Not the Slayer but the Slain One Is Guilty.*

to apply to the lawbreaker, too. The fact that, in this modern view, the lawbreaker is treated on the assumption of complete determinism, while society is treated on the assumption of freedom of choice, merely reflects the will to condemn society.

The basis for this paradoxical moral attitude is the belief, first made popular by Rousseau—and quite fundamental to one branch of liberal thought—that man is good by nature, considerate and kindly to his fellow men. If he behaves towards others in a selfish, callous, brutal, or even deliberately cruel manner, such behavior must be due, in its entirety, to environmental influences, perhaps to grave provocation and unbearable pressures to which he was subjected. He would assume, therefore, the kind attitude germane to his nature if these pressures were removed. Hence, if, for example, a man has slain another man, the *cause* must be sought in the environment, in society. And cause is, in human affairs, invariably equated with *guilt*,[4] no matter how much men may fancy themselves to be determinists.

In a social and international context this means that if groups or nations resort to violence, it *must* be due to grievances that all would consider legitimate; and such behavior could be remedied, and could only be remedied, by redressing these grievances. Thus, when the Germans embraced a rabid nationalism thirty years ago, it must have been due, entirely, to injustices from the peace of Versailles. "We must give justice to Germany," exclaimed Ramsay Macdonald in the League of Nations Assembly immediately after Hitler's seizure of power. Even the late Adolf Hitler himself, we hear in a recent re-interpretation of history,[5] never aimed at the domination of Europe by force. He had, in fact, no long-term goals at all but was merely pushed to what he did, step by step, by Western unreasonableness.

Or, if the leaders of the Soviet Union face the West with uncompromising hostility, it *cannot* be due to tenets of Bolshevism which antedate any contact with the West; it *must* be a response to Western unfriendliness. Perhaps it is a response to the brief and half-hearted intervention in the Russian Civil War; perhaps it is due to the more recent American demand (in 1945) to have Argentina included in the United Nations; or perhaps it is a response to suspicions aroused by the appointment, by the Brit-

[4] The Greek *aitia*, e.g., that lives in our word, etiology, has the original meaning of guilt; the negative form *anaitios* means "innocent."

[5] A. J. P. Taylor, *The Origins of the Second World War* (London: Hamish Hamilton, 1961).

ish government, of a diplomat of not sufficiently high standing for negotiations in Moscow. Similarly, Castro's relentless hostility to the United States, shown from the day of his ascension to power, *must* be due to a lack of understanding on the part of the United States for the aspirations of the Cuban people for a better life. And if the facts glaringly contradict these assumptions, the facts must be selected and rearranged until they seem to fit—because the basic assumptions *must* be true.

As Polanyi has suggested, the evangelical fervor of Western Liberalism should also be seen as a new edition of the ethics of the Gospel (and of prophetic Judaism). The moral prescriptions of the Gospel, the demand to offer the other cheek, with total self-abnegation, can hardly be practiced for any length of time except by people who live under at least partially sheltered conditions—as in monastic orders—so that the harsher necessities of life are performed by others less burdened by scruples or subject to a different code.

It has therefore been suggested that the prescriptions of the Gospels were never meant to govern the daily lives of continuing communities but that they constituted an *Interimsethik,* a set of moral rules for the waiting time, before the final consummation of history and the coming of the Kingdom of God which was then thought to be imminent.

However that may be, the Church interposed herself between man and the text of the Gospels. It was the function of the Roman Church to direct the messianic expectation away from daily life into an afterlife or a very distant future so to preserve a realistic attitude to the world around us. In this way the Church arrived at a synthesis of hope and realism, of the Don Quixote and the Sancho Panza in us—albeit a synthesis heavily weighted towards immobilism. The compromise became untenable once the possibility of secular improvement had been demonstrated.

The decline of the Churches and of any kind of supranaturalism seems to have led to a revival of messianism in its original form: the expectation of a consummation of history, in the immediate future, that will establish the realm of justice and happiness for all men of "good will."[6]

[6] For the messianic social beliefs cp.: J. L. Talmon, *The Origin of Totalitarian Democracy* (New York: Praeger, 1951), 1st ed. *Utopianism and Politics* (London: Conservative Political Center, 1957). *Political Messianism: The Romantic Phase* (New York: Praeger, 1960). Norman Cohn, *The Pursuit of the Millennium* (London: Secker and Warburg, 1957).

While this, presumably, is the origin of the immense moral fervor for the "disinherited of the earth" in our time, it is an open question in each individual case to what degree fervor is due to genuine moral passions that have been carried to extreme, even suicidal, conclusions, and to what degree it is due to envy of, or spite for, the establishment in one's own society. Both motivations may, in fact, operate in the same person although only the first, idealistic one is likely to appear in a man's conscious self-interpretation. The fact that moral fervor for the oppressed may sometimes be fed by unconscious hatred of the establishment may explain the frequent indifference of the moral critic towards oppression and injustice, however severe, when it is practiced by the enemies of his society.

But despite their self-damaging implications, these attitudes, whatever their origin, would still not constitute any real danger to the vital interests of Western societies were it not for the peculiar present constellation of forces. One school of thought in the messianic tradition, of particular determination and ruthlessness, has in our time succeeded in establishing complete power over the Eurasian heartland (to use Sir Halford Mackinder's excellent expression). Its leaders believe dogmatically in a modern version of Manichaeism according to which their own side represents both the morally good and the wave of the future, while our way of life is both irredeemably evil and irreversibly decaying. They not only believe that our downfall is preordained by inexorable laws of history, but so far have held it to be their task to carry out, or at least to help along, the "verdict of history." It is for this reason that the moral passions of Western liberals have often become, in effect, though probably not in conscious intent, an aid to an adversary who frankly rejects the very values for the minor infractions of which they are daily castigating Western society.

At the same time when Nebuchadnezzar threatened the existence of the Jewish kingdom, the prophet Jeremiah urged the people not to resist but to accept servitude to Babylon as a divine punishment for their sins. Like him, and other ancient prophets, many contemporary doctrinaire-liberals profess to believe that our peril is due to our sins and would disappear if we would practice strict morality in all our actions. But although the assumption of a relation between sin and misfortune makes sense for the ancient Hebrews, who believed that God punishes His people for their misconduct, it is less understandable in modern liberal atheists or agnostics who do not think that the moral law determines the course of events. But beliefs can endure long after the rationale for holding them has withered away.

In one important point, however, there is a striking difference between Jeremiah and his contemporary successors: Jeremiah was fully aware of what was in store for the people at the hand of their Babylonian masters; many of his contemporary followers tell us that Nebuchadnezzar does not really exist but that he is merely an hallucination of the State Department.

THE STRUGGLE AGAINST THE "ESTABLISHMENT"—DOMESTIC AND INTERNATIONAL. The protest against the status quo appears as protest against the pecking order of our society and the promotion of the demands of the lower strata at the expense of the higher ones. As has been emphazised before, protest that does not come from the lower orders themselves may be due either to identification with, and compassion for them, or to hatred of the higher ones.

The demands for justice for all men have grown ever stronger in the Western world since the eighteenth century. Justice, at first interpreted as equality of opportunity, is more and more becoming to mean equality of station; and, as Alexis de Tocqueville foresaw, "the hatred that men bear to privilege increases in proportion as privileges become fewer and less considerable, so that democratic passions would seem to burn more fiercely just when they have least fuel . . ." because in a world in which there are no great differences, the still existing inequalities are all the more unacceptable.[7] Thus, the anti-colonial passions in Asia and Africa have become more inflamed at the very time that more than nine-tenths of the Western colonial empires have become emancipated.

Nationalism, on the other hand, creates a feeling of solidarity along ethnic rather than class lines. It was, at times, welded to the political and social revolt as in the French Revolution, whereas at other times the two movements have been bitterly opposed to each other. Nationalism has been universalist as well as parochial, integrative as well as divisive. It was the former when it strove towards the unity of groups conceived as "nations" that had hitherto been divided into smaller traditional, mostly dynastic, political units as the unification of Italy and Germany. It was disintegrative and divisive when it broke up traditional multinational structures such as the Habsburg mon-

[7] *Democracy in America*, Vol. 2, Book 4, Chap. 3.

archy, or pursued its national aspirations without regard for the aspirations, or indeed the very existence, of other nations. In the latter aspect of nationalism, naive egotism, an attitude which in individuals or groups precedes moral development, has been elevated to a sacred duty, and the innocent selfishness of the primitive has thus been transformed into an evil of civilization, namely, the use of morality for immoral ends.

Not infrequently, nationalism has begun as an integrative force and has shown the latter characteristics only after it had realized some of its fundamental aspirations; this was the case of the German development from the nationalism of the Liberals of 1848 over the militaristic nationalism of the Treitschke generation (which still paid at least lip service to Christianity), to the paroxysmal nationalism of a Hitler who knew no law except "the interest of the German people."[8]

Nationalism has, therefore, been called a demonic force. There are examples of a nation turning away from nationalism in disillusionment after it has led the nation into disaster (as happened in France and, more recently, in Germany); but there are no examples of a successful appeasement of undefeated nationalism.

Nationalism sometimes sponsors the aspirations of groups at the lower level of the pyramid of power or wealth, and sometimes the aspirations of groups which are relatively high up on an international scale. In the latter case, it has a double face: It is a rebellion against those who occupy the top positions, but it is at the same time oppressive toward the lower echelons.

---

[8] It is unmistakable, however, that the germs of the later barbarism existed from the beginning. Sir Lewis Namier, e.g., said about Mazzini, whom he called "a man outstanding for spiritual integrity" and "a sincere lover of liberty," ". . . the moral fervor, purity of purpose and religious sincerity which pervade his writings—words of faith and action rather than of thought—were apt to conceal from contemporaries how deficient his teachings were in substance correlated to every-day reality, and what dangerous germs they contained. National self-glorification and claims to moral superiority were of their core: which entails a measure of depreciation of other peoples, and is not conducive to international comity." *Avenues of History* (London: Hamish Hamilton, 1952), p. 29.

The Austrian poet Franz Grillparzer, a somewhat older contemporary of Mazzini, said around 1848 that the development went "from humanitarianism over nationalism into bestialism."

That was the case of nationalism in industrially advanced countries like modern Germany and Japan; they struggled against the "have" nations—above all England and the United States—who, they claimed, had appropriated the best things on earth at a time when the "younger" nations had not yet appeared on the scene. There was either a demand for colonies, as in Germany and Italy, or an attempt to conquer adjacent territories populated by less advanced peoples—the Ukraine, parts of China —with a view to colonizing them and enslaving the inhabitants. This aspect gives nationalism its peculiar and ambiguous character, at once "revolutionary" and "counter-revolutionary."

But where nationalism takes hold of a poor and underdeveloped people, as in Latin America at the present time, the national and the social revolution may run parallel for some time as is demonstrated by the Cuban revolution, or by some of Mao Tse-tung's revisions of orthodox Marxist doctrine, allowing for a temporary coalition with the "national bourgeoise." This places the "struggle against imperialism," that is, the international revolution, ahead of the domestic class struggle.

Whether an individual is more attracted by Socialism (which, under present conditions, means Marxist Socialism and, most probably, Communism) or by nationalism, seems to depend on many circumstances—historical, situational, personal. Among them is also the response of the personality to Marxism's and nationalism's basic attitudes toward life, their implicit *weltanschauung:* The latter is expressed most clearly in their respective doctrines regarding determinism and freedom.

Marxism is strongly determinist and sees the world moving along inexorable laws of history. Men may accelerate or smooth the course of events by correct action or delay it and make it harsher by error and futile resistance, but they cannot change necessity. *Fata volentem ducunt, nolentem trahunt.*

Nationalism, on the other hand, is indeterminist; the future belongs to him who seizes it. Different temperaments are attracted or repelled by these two philosophies.

THE ANTI-CAPITALIST BIAS. The impact of the socialist idea has been cataclysmic. Its strength is probably due, in the main, to a combination of an egalitarian moral fervor with a particular, superficially persuasive interpretation of the non-egalitarian realities, namely the doctrine that the businessman acting under the profit motive is a social parasite who fulfills no social function but who has, through the possession of the means of production, interposed himself between the worker and his tools. He has, thus, been able to extract a heavy tribute from the "toilers"—not unlike the medieval robber barons who extracted river tolls from travelling merchants. This interpretation seems convincing to all but the very few who have either personal experience or theoretical training in economic matters.

This means that the problem of economic rationality, that is, the problem of an optimal employment of scarce resources, is little understood. The problem is difficult enough if only one goal is pursued, in which case we usually speak of a question of strategy rather than of economics. However, it receives a new dimension of complexity if there is a multiplicity of goals, each of which can be pursued only at the expense of some others, as in the promotion of general welfare.

It is the justification of a market, or capitalist, economy that it creates a field in which all players are constantly rewarded by an extension, or punished by a contraction, of their operating range, according to the results of their management in terms of consumers' preferences.

It cannot be taken for granted that consumers' preferences should always be the ultimate determinant of action; in fact, virtually everybody agrees that there must be at least some exceptions from the sovereign and irresponsible rule of the consumer (as in the control of the traffic in narcotics or in building and zoning regulations). Furthermore, even if consumers' preferences are accepted as the ultimate frame of reference, it cannot be taken for granted that a market economy is necessarily the only possible, or the best, solution of the problem of economic rationality. The capitalist system can, therefore, become subject to legitimate criticism on either of these two grounds: because it caters to desires which, in the view of the critic, are not worth indulging in, or because its function of selecting the most economic among the possible alternatives of action might possibly be achieved better by some other mechanism.

But capitalism has only extremely rarely been attacked on any such ground. It has been attacked for more than a century not by people who wished to substitute their solution of the problem of economic rationality for the solution of the market, but by people who are unaware of the very existence of the problem. For them the only economic problems are technological; one produces what is needed, it is as simple as that, and except for the engineer's task, the job of management, as Lenin put it, "can be reduced . . . to simple operations of registration, filing and checking."[9]

Unaware of the problem of economic rationality, the Marxists did not understand what hit them (and everyone else) when socialized industries, supposedly freed from the burden of having to produce "surplus value" for the capitalists, did not have that surplus value available for distribution among the wage earners as one had to expect according to the theory. Nor did they later understand how the "exploited" worker in privately owned industry can receive higher wages than his "liberated" opposite number in socialist countries. Even today observers report that leading men in Eastern Germany, looking at the prosperity of Western Germany and West Berlin, do not consider the possibility that something might be wrong with their economic system: The system, they are satisfied, is superior to capitalism, and it must be due to accidental factors such as bottlenecks if the people have not yet reaped the benefits of socialism.[10] Just the same, they are eager to get rid of capitalist Berlin and thereby of the case that visibly contradicts their theories.

It is this inability on the part of most people, including most intellectuals, in particular, to understand the nature of the economic problem that gives the socialist ideology its virtually irresistible appeal. The arguments which the defender of a market economy can put forward are simply beyond the understanding of those who have neither theoretical instruction nor practical experience in economic matters. They are, in any case, suspect of being self-serving if they are advanced by people with vested interests in the preservation of capitalism; and if advanced by others who are conspicuously lacking in such interests, they can be equally discounted as coming from "lackeys" of capitalism.

The problem of economic rationality is often not understood

[9] *State and Revolution.* Coll. Works, Vol. 21.

[10] There is evidence, however, that some economists in Communist countries have become aware of the problem in recent years. Their insight has been acted upon in Yugoslavia through decentralization and the establishment of a market of sorts. There have also been stirrings in this direction among economists in the Soviet Union and particularly in Poland. But they are still viewed with suspicion by the Communist party who fears the impact of any undermining of the labor theory of value. See Gregory Grossman, *Value and Plan* (Berkeley and Los Angeles: University of California Press, 1960).

even by men of very high intelligence. We are accustomed to speak of intelligence as though it were a unitary quality which, as much or as little as there is, can be applied with equal success to all areas of reality. Psychometrics, with its I.Q. measurements, has contributed to this conception.

Yet there is much evidence that an individual can operate on a high intellectual level in one area of reality and on a very low one in another. Theoretical intelligence capable of understanding how things are—in itself but a name for a whole group of abilities, each related to a particular area or aspect of reality— is different from economic intelligence that is quick in realizing how available things could be put to best advantage; from political or military intelligence that grasps the value of everything for a struggle for power; from social intelligence that knows how to make friends and influence people; or from the erotic intelligence of a Casanova.

Several types of higher intelligence are rarely found together in the same person. Lenin was one of the greatest, perhaps the greatest, revolutionary strategists of all times. He sensed like nobody else the points of weakness in existing societies and invented strategies for establishing footholds of power, for enlarging them, and for winning and keeping total power. Even his closest collaborators did not fully understand him for a long time. But the same Lenin was unable to grasp the problem of an optimal allocation of resources to competing goals and the dependence of human welfare on a solution of this problem; he thought economic management was a matter of accounting and statistics.

Andrew Carnegie, an economic genius of the first magnitude, had no understanding for matters of power or ideology. When he set up the Carnegie Endowment for International Peace, he wondered what role the Foundation could play once it would have succeeded in abolishing wars. He told his trustees that it would then be their task to decide on what ills the Foundation should focus next.

In the mid-1930's when civilized men were appalled at the prospect of another war, and one that would involve the bombing of civilians, to boot, a prominent English mathematician is reported to have pointed out that, of course, one would not actually drop any bombs, but in dealing with Hitler it might be necessary to behave for a while as though one would. It does not seem to have occurred to this outstanding man that one cannot bluff a determined adversary while putting one's card on the table.

The failure to understand the problem of rational allocation of resources and its crucial importance for human welfare may also be seen in another light, namely, as the consequence of *utopian* thinking. Human values are in some degree contradictory, that is one can often realize one value only at the expense of another; liberty and equality or, more generally, individual expression and social order, economic progress and security, income and leisure, are examples of such dichotomies. Decision involves a choice in favor of one value against another or, rather, the determination of an optimal point beyond which any further approach toward the realization of one value would cost too dearly in terms of the other. Because of these contradictions among the things which men hold dear, complete human fulfillment is not possible.

The utopian mind, however, does not accept this kind of reasoning. The utopian refuses to believe that there could be any inherent limits to human fulfillment; the very suggestion, he suspects, is a ruse to protect special privilege. In the good society, all men can be completely fulfilled in their individual aspirations, and society can yet be harmonious, without conflict; as Marx had put it: The free development of each is the prerequisite of the free development of all.

It is a kind of preordained harmony; the skeptics, of course, think that this is merely another way of saying that one can have one's cake and eat it, too.

If one believes that all human aspirations are in natural harmony with each other and with the interests of society, and of the whole of mankind—a harmony only so far disturbed and impeded by the "class structure"—one will, of course, not believe that decisions involve choices between irreconcilable values; for if one believed the latter, one would not have accepted the former.

But if the problem of rational allocation is not understood, the system of *private enterprise appears to have no raison d'être* but to be *merely* a form of *privilege,* at once immoral, and inexpedient.

This belief, somewhat weakened in the West but holding full sway everywhere else, that government operation of the economy is both morally indicated and practically sensible, while business management is both evil and stupid, appears to be the main reason for the fundamental goodwill enjoyed by the Soviet Union and the widespread distrust of the United States. It is for this reason, I submit, that over so large a part of the world, a light view is taken of Communist aggressive moves, while the West is severely castigated for even moderate acts of self-assertion: Communism stands in the minds of countless people for something fundamentally "progressive," while the West stands for an obsolete system of privilege. Without such fundamental aversion, it would be difficult to understand why a large section of world opinion condemns as aggressiveness in the West what it hails as strength in the East and ridicules as weakness in the West what it applauds as manifestation of peaceful intentions in the East.

To the enormous amount of goodwill which the Soviet Union has enjoyed as the land of Socialism must also be attributed the paralysis of American foreign policy at the end of the Second World War. The Soviet Union established her stranglehold over Eastern Central Europe then, at a time when the balance of physical strength greatly favored the United States and effective resistance would have been possible at small risk. But a vigorous policy toward the Soviet Union would have been vetoed by a substantial part of Western public opinion.

THE ALIENATION OF THE INTELLECTUALS. The intellectuals of the West, as a rule, are not fully identified with their societies. They stand aloof, and while they may feel enthusiastic about some "ideal" society, they are often indifferent or hostile to their society as it actually is.[11]

[11] A characteristic example for the attitude of many Western intellectuals appears in a psychological study of scientists; the author, a noted psychologist, points out that "scientists are very good citizens" and declares: "The scientists involved in espionage have been very few, indeed, and misguided as they may have been, they have acted on principle and not for personal gain." Anne Roe, *The Making of a Scientist* (New York: Dodd, Mead & Co., 1952), p. 240. Thus, the author is not sure whether she condemns espionage against the United States at all ("misguided as they *may* have been . . .") and, in any case, does not take a grave view of the matter as long as it was done for ideological reasons and not for monetary gain. It would be rash to conclude, however, that intellectuals of liberal persuasion advocate a *general* tolerance for all ideologies, as was done by John Stuart Mill; as a rule, they make no allowance for ideologies of the Right. But the ideologies of the Left are regarded as "idealistic," and action based on them is excused, or only mildly rebuked,

To some degree, this has been so in all societies in which intellectuals have enjoyed the freedom of expression. Since the days of the Sophists, they have been in the habit of questioning and challenging the values and the assumptions that were taken for granted in their societies. Some intellectuals, on the other hand, have followed the example of that dissident Sophist, Socrates, who used his intellectual powers not only to challenge current beliefs, but also to give the essential values of his civilization a new, presumably better foundation.

Intellect tends to question and thereby to undermine dogma and tradition.[12] The act of understanding, said the historian of science Charles Coulston Gillispie, is an act of alienation.[13] Psychoanalytic theory suggests a kind of primary antagonism of the ego against the id, that is, of the rational, goal-directed part of us against the impulsive and automatic parts. Alienation is an aspect of emancipation. It is the hostility of *Geist* to life of which there has been so much talk in German philosophy.

In principle this is unavoidable. It is rooted in the very nature of freedom because freedom is destructive as well as creative; the very viability of a free society depends on whether or not it can take advantage of the creative energies unleashed by freedom while keeping its destructive aspects within limits.

But this does not explain the degree of the estrangement or the bitterness with which many Western intellectuals look upon the society which has provided them with a degree of personal security and with opportunities of development not enjoyed at any other time or place. Is this a reaction to freedom which, for the inner-directed, vital like air, is deeply frustrating to the other-directed who need guidance? Is it the very consequence of the emancipation from drudgery and of the newly won leisure which makes people ask beyond life's necessities or luxuries for

---

whatever its consequences. No question is asked whether these ideologies may not also be fed from emotional sources not necessarily praiseworthy such as, e.g., lust for power or intellectual conceit.

[12] Cp. the following remark by Frank H. Knight: ". . . the 'liberation of the mind' seems to have released a tendency to acute discontent, criticism, fault-finding that was there all along but held in check by the harsh discipline of pre-liberal culture—or possibly new conditions have caused it to develop with astonishing speed as a culture trait." Frank H. Knight, *Intelligence and Democratic Action* (Cambridge: Harvard University Press, 1960), p. 144.

[13] *The Edge of Objectivity* (Princeton: Princeton University Press, 1960), p. 84.

a meaning in life while they are yet not able to find it for them-selves? Is it the constant increase in possible fulfillments and the simple fact that in such situations aspirations always grow a little faster than fulfillments? Or is it the attitude of those who have been conditioned in their childhood to expect immediate fulfillment of every wish, who have accordingly failed to acquire any tolerance toward frustration, and who go to pieces, bundles of despair and fury, whenever they meet with even the slightest frustration as is, after all, not forever avoidable? Somewhere along these lines an explanation must be sought for a phenome-non like the "angry young men," for the bitter hatred of their society by members of a generation who, perhaps as the first in history, "never ate their bread with tears."

It must be added, however, that the destructive criticism of Western societies comes only rarely from those intellectuals who have special training or experience in the areas which are par-ticularly relevant for socio-political problems; they come rarely from historians, economists, political scientists, professional diplomats, etc.

This, obviously, does not mean that historians, economists, or political scientists are miraculously free from the disintegrative potentialities of the intellect; but it suggests that in the field in which one has sound knowledge and with which one is in con-stant contact, such potentialities are likely to manifest them-selves mostly in the form of *creative* destruction, as a restructur-ing of the field[14] with creative value. But without such knowl-edge, the destructiveness of the intellect has full sway.

What then appears as antagonism of the intellectual to his society must, therefore, be attributed not only to the alienation inherent in the life of the intellect, but also to the naive and arrogant confidence of individuals with higher education. They feel competent not only in matters within the areas of their training and experience, but on any subject of public interest—a pretension to which taxi drivers or plumbers are far less prone.

The fact that the intellectuals of the type of Protagoras are the perpetual debunkers of their society would not change the balance of forces in the world if all societies were equally ex-posed to such pressures. But if this is not the case, if some societies are shielded against the consequences of intellectual skepticism and debunking as is largely the case in present totali-

[14] The expression is taken from M. Wertheimer, *Productive Think-ing* (New York: Harper Brothers, 1945).

tarian societies, the pressures which intellectuals exert where they are in a position to do so may have the effect of influencing the balance of power in favor of those societies in which they are not in such a position—in favor of monolithic Sparta, against free Athens.

The Anti-Colonial Revolution

THE SETTING OF THE STAGE. "Western culture," said C. C. Gillispie, "is set off from those of Asia, Africa and the world of Antiquity by two fundamental factors. From one of these it emerged: its religious chrysalis was Christianity, investing history with the promise of fulfillment of a sort. The other it produced: the most dynamic, distinctive and influential creation of the Western world is a progressive science of nature. Only there, in the technical realm, indeed, does the favorite Western idea hold any demonstrable meaning."[15]

These two characteristics contain the germs of the history of contact between Western culture and other cultures. The achievements in the *rational* analysis and control of man's environment gave Western culture an easy superiority over other people's, provoking them, at first, to futile resistance or to surrender—both exemplified in Caesar's story of the two Aedui brothers, Divitiacus and Dumnorix—and later stimulating identification, envy, and emulation. The *moral and metaphysical* beliefs of the West in an ultimate historical consummation, seen in modern times in the picture of continuous progress, on the other hand, manifested itself at first in missionary activities, both by religious and non-religious bodies, to bring the message of Western creeds to alien cultures; soon there were also men who espoused the cause of the natives against Western rulers. To the leaders of non-Western peoples, finally, Western moral beliefs gave the spiritual weapons with which to ask for a redress of their grievances.

TWO TYPES OF GROUP ANTAGONISM. Group antagonisms take different forms according to whether they are directed against more advanced, or against less advanced, groups. "Advancement," in this context, should be understood as advancement in terms of *alloplastic adjustment*, that is, in terms of man's ability

[15] Charles Coulston Gillispie, *op. cit.*, p. 8.

to control his environment and to find suitable means for advancing his ends in relation to his environment. It does *not* mean a higher degree of *autoplastic adjustment* (as the ability to bear frustration and suffering with equanimity or the wisdom of an Epicurus, a Buddha, or a Confucius); nor does it mean *moral* superiority. Least of all, of course, can it be taken as superiority in ultimate human values, or superiority before God —matters about which this writer has no knowledge.

Advancement, in the preceding sense, of greater control of the environment implies a lengthening of the road from impulse to action, that is, a larger measure of self-control in significant areas of human behavior. Under conditions of relatively fair competition, it is reflected by a person's place in the social hierarchies of power, wealth, income, and status. The relative advancement of a group in social interaction with other groups is manifested by the proportional participation of the group in the occupational hierarchy, inasmuch as occupations are open to them. A group is more advanced if fewer of its members are engaged in unskilled or semi-skilled labor than would correspond to their number, and if it has more than its proportional share in leading occupations—administration, spiritual leadership, science, education, arts. The Jews, for example, were a more advanced group in medieval Europe or, in modern times, in Central and Eastern Europe and in Arab lands; so were the Greeks and the Armenians in the Turkish Empire; the Jainas in India; the French in Algeria; so are whites in general as compared to Negroes in Africa, America, or Arabia; so is, on the whole, the West in the global community of men.

The antagonism which the more advanced group feels toward the less advanced one, such as the feelings of American Southerners toward the Negro, is quite different from the antagonism of a less advanced group toward a more advanced one, as in the case of the attitude of African Negroes toward the white settler or Algerian Moslems toward European settlers.

The less advanced group is not resented as such by their more advanced neighbors; rather, it is welcome to perform menial labor and, in some cases, has been imported for that very purpose. As long as their members "know their place," there is no opposition against them in the more advanced group; many people of the latter group may even have a personal affection of sorts for them. It is only if the members of the less advanced group step beyond the limits either of the general rules of conduct prevailing in the society, or of the social conventions regulating their social position, that they arouse resentment. In the cases in which the less advanced group is also believed to be closer to savagery and to an unbridled expression of sexuality, they arouse fear and horror, too.

A group that is more advanced than its environment provokes a different kind of antagonism. Its members usually behave with arrogance, and even if they should not do so, the simple fact of their superiority, difficult to hide, is felt as an insult. One then watches them carefully for any signs of weakness, for flaws; once these flaws are found, as needs they will, they are seized upon by the less advanced group and exploited to the full. Anti-American sentiment, and anti-Western sentiment in general, belong to this category; it is remarkable how closely current accusations against the West resemble the accusations against the Jews that run through the history of anti-Semitism.

While outbreaks of violence against backward groups rarely go beyond actions that should "teach them a lesson," so that they may assume again the humble station to which the more advanced group would like to confine them, the hostility against a more advanced group has no built-in limitations and may go all the way to effect their physical elimination.

These easily observable differences have been obfuscated by catch phrases such as "minority groups" (as though the relative place of groups in the pecking order were determined by their quantitative strength) or by pseudo-scientific investigations of prejudice in which the outcome of the research was implicit in the design of the experiments. For example, anti-Semitism and anti-Negro sentiment in the United States have been grouped together as sentiments or prejudices against "minority groups," although they differ radically in motivation and goal. Anti-Semitism has never been willing to tolerate the Jews, even if they were to behave deferentially toward Gentiles and take their meals in the kitchen; and anti-Negro sentiment has never aimed at eliminating the Negroes from the land through expulsion or harsher measures. The analogy to anti-Semitism can be found not in the anti-Negro sentiment of whites but rather in the violent forms of anti-white sentiment among Black Muslims.

Both responses to the phenomenon of difference in development are natural and therefore, in some measure, unavoidable. They represent a conflict of interest which only time can heal through elimination of the developmental difference and which in the meantime, charity can do much to mitigate. To ideologize this conflict by seeing it in Manichean terms as a struggle between good and evil can only inflame it and may make it insoluble except for the solutions unmitigated violence provides.

CONDITIONS OF REVOLUTION. Thus, in the contact between groups at different levels of development, the more advanced group is motivated by a fear of being pulled down from the levels already reached, while the less advanced group reacts to a blow to their pride.

But it does not react on any large scale unless and until the gap between the two groups is narrowed sufficiently so that a comparison between them is possible.

There is still a further step from resentment to action. For a long time the enormous superiority of Western power discouraged any thought of resistance until, in the Second World War, Western prestige was severely damaged through the defeats suffered at the hands of Germany and Japan. A revolutionary situation existed once the sense of grievance was ignited by the hope of success.

Revolutions do not seem to break out where men are most downtrodden, but rather where conditions have begun to improve.[16] As long as the prevailing conditions, no matter how bad, are stable they are taken for granted. Men *adjust* to them as one adjusts to the climate, to incurable disease, or to death. But once the possibility of improvement has been realized, conditions never improve fast enough to keep pace with rising aspirations.

This is closely analogous to a well-known psychiatric phenomenon and may be a manifestation of the same *biological truth:* The danger of suicide in severe depressions is great not at the height of the depression but rather at the time *when the depression has begun to lift.*

But the tremendous momentum which the anti-colonial revolution has gained in recent years is due, above all, to extraneous

[16] For example, see the following statements by contemporary scholars: ". . . it is not the backward countries which need revolutions. Being backward, Spain had not yet developed those internal strains which made France, with all its enlightenment, a social volcano." H. R. Trevor-Roper, "The Spanish Enlightenment," *Historical Essays* (London: Macmillan, 1957), p. 271.

"Paradoxically as it may seem, colonial nationalism is far less the response to oppression than to the widening horizons opened up by progressive colonial governments." Rupert Emerson, *From Empire to Nation* (Cambridge: Harvard University Press, 1960), p. 45.

circumstances: Namely, the Soviet Union, with all her might, has been backing up and encouraging the most radical anti-Western groups anywhere on earth. Under these conditions, a premium has been placed on the most radical revolutionary action.

So far this refers to events in Asia, Africa and Latin America. But the revolution may yet spill over United States boundaries; revolutions of American Negroes, Chinese in Hawaii, or Mexicans in the Southwest will not be out of the question if the Western position further disintegrates.

In a recent article on the social life of baboons,[17] the authors, two biologists, stated: "In troops where the rank order is clearly defined, fighting is rare" and "fighting [sc. over a female] may take place if the dominance order is not clearly established among the males." One may say that fighting between humans, individuals and groups, may break out *if power relationships are unclear,* or liable to different interpretations. As long as power relationships are unambiguous, and so interpreted by all, there is likely to be peace. The existing power distribution is the basis for the legal order; when the pecking order is not universally recognized, either because power relationships have changed and human thinking has not kept up with the change, or because different people interpret them differently, fighting may break out until a new pecking order has been established and recognized. This will result in a new legal order.

The Predicament of the West

THE AMERICAN RESPONSE. The anti-colonial revolution has assumed, or tends to assume, an anti-American stance, except in those countries or groups who feel themselves under pressure from the Soviet bloc or from a country or group that enjoys Communist support.

This development should have surprised no one. The United States has been on top of the world politically and economically for quite some time; with only about 7 per cent of the world's population, the United States has close to one-half of the world's capital. Its situation among the nations is comparable to that of the wealthiest landowner in a district where most people are

[17] S. L. Washburn and I. De Vore, "The Social Life of Baboons," *Scientific American,* Vol. 204, No. 6 (June 1961), p. 70.

destitute, at a time when the social order is no longer taken for granted.[18]

The new development came as a surprise to many, however, partly because revolutions were thought of as strictly national affairs and were not considered as part of a concerted international action, and partly because it was widely assumed that revolutions were reactions to oppression and injustice. The record of the United States as a neighbor and as a member of the international community, although not entirely spotless, compared very favorably with that of any other nation. Many a nation owes much to American generosity. It was overlooked, however, that there are reasons other than oppression and injustice, in the ordinary sense, as these words are understood in the West, why people may feel bitter against those more fortunately placed, and that they will feel little difficulty in interpreting their resentment and their aspirations, whatever they may be, as manifestations of a demand for justice.

There is tragic irony in the present situation in which the American people find themselves at the receiving end of a world-wide populist revolution, as Americans have seen themselves for generations as the avant garde of such movements against oligarchy-ridden Europe. For a long time this country has been a leader of populist and nationalist revolutions all over the world, busily undermining traditional political structures and the balance of power anywhere on earth in the name of the principle of self-determination until quite recently.[19] All this was

[18] Despite its wealth, the United States could maintain its role as the leader of populism in the world as long as American borders were wide open to immigration and everybody was invited to share in the advantages of the American situation. But once the immigration laws had set up "no trespassing" signs around the American real estate, the American people became a privileged nation. No amount of public relations artistry can erase this fact from world consciousness.

[19] One fairly recent example: When the Central Powers, Germany and Austria-Hungary, recognized their defeat in October, 1918 and appealed to President Wilson to mediate an armistice and peace on the basis of his fourteen points, the President requested, as a prerequisite of his mediation, from Germany that "the power of the king of Prussia" be curtailed, and in the case of Austria-Hungary he took the position that it was up to the various national groups of the Monarchy to decide what concessions to their aspirations by the central government would be satisfactory to them. He thus gave *carte blanche* to the nationalist governments in the Monarchy. In

with the expectation that the emancipation would appease rather than appetize the colonial peoples, and that they would behave with the moderation shown by the American colonists in the late eighteenth century with an emphasis on prosperity rather than on military power—assumptions for which there was no basis whatsoever.

There are many Americans even today who believe that the anti-American turn of the nationalist and populist revolutions in the "underdeveloped" countries was not a necessary phenomenon but merely the consequence of political mistakes which might have been avoided; perhaps the United States had "supported" dictators who were later overthrown, or failed to put pressure on friendly governments in favor of land reform, or failed to help one-crop countries out of their precarious situation by using American financial strength for a stabilization of world market prices of this commodity, etc. We had permitted ourselves, so it has been said, to be lined up on the wrong side, against the "aspirations of the common people," in the role of the Holy Alliance. If, so the argument runs, Americans only could fearlessly take up again the banner of the populist revolution, all would be well. One wise observer commented on this more than ten years ago: "A people with the highest standard of living in the world tries desperately to remain the leader of the Left."[20] The unsolved contradictions between the needs of

---

this way, Wilson enforced the overthrow of the Hohenzollern monarchy and the dismemberment of the Austro-Hungarian State. This led, in the first case, to the establishment of the unpopular Weimar republic, soon to be overthrown by the disastrous Hitler movement; and, in the second case, to the creation of a power vacuum in Central Europe, soon to suck in, at first, German, and then, Russian, power.

[20] F. Somary, "From Portsmouth to Korea. The Balance Sheet of American Foreign Policy," unpublished memorandum, 1950. Published German translation: *Neue Schweizer Rundschau,* December 29, 1950.

I can see no chance of the United States regaining its former international position except, *perhaps,* if the American people were willing to repeal the immigration laws and to open the country to countless millions of immigrants from Latin America, Asia, and Africa—a move that would play havoc with American standards of living and with the free institutions and the Western character of the nation. If, however, the American people wish to defend these goods, as every nation would, it would be better to acknowledge the realities of the situation.

self-preservation which urged the greatest possible conservation of the essentials of the old international order of Western dominance, on the one hand, and the ideological bias in favor of revolution, on the other, was, and I submit still is, at the bottom of the ineffectiveness of American foreign policy.

There are four possible reactions to revolution on the part of those who feel threatened by it. It is the *conservative* response to try to stem the revolutionary tide. The *Bonapartist* (or fascist) solution consists in the setting up of a counterrevolutionary totalitarianism which steals some of the revolutionary thunder and uses the same terror methods as the revolution. There is the *me-too* policy of trying to join the revolution and march with its legions, preferably in its spearhead. Finally, one may attempt to placate the revolutionary forces by inaugurating *reforms,* in the hope of thus weakening the revolutionary élan. These are, of course, marginal types (*Idealtypen*) of political behavior and, in practice, a policy may lie somewhere in between these sharply defined categories and show characteristics of more than one.

The conservative answer is historically represented most brilliantly by Clemens von Metternich; in our days, Winston Churchill tried it within the narrow limits of his power. It is widely asserted today, particularly in this country and in Britain, that such a policy would, in the present world, be doomed to failure. This may well be so, but it is questionable to what degree this assessment is based on a dispassionate analysis of the forces involved and to what degree on the progressive bias, which is part of the protest attitude itself. There are antirevolutionary forces everywhere in the world, and the current revolution, like every other revolution, cannot go on forever; a point must be reached where people can no longer adjust sufficiently fast to the constantly accelerating pace of events. One can hardly state *a priori* that a policy of digging in, defending crucial positions, and waiting for the next swing of the pendulum to occur is necessarily doomed to failure. But it runs strongly against the progressive stream of Western thinking.

The Bonapartist solution is quite alien to American traditions. But a policy of trying to stay ahead of the revolution has been repeatedly followed by the United States, although the pressures of national interest have made its *consistent* application impossible. The advocates of this policy believe that if the United States sides with Arabs against England, France, and Israel; with Algerian Moslems against France; with Indonesia against the Netherlands; or with African nationalists against Portugal, the African and Asian nationalists will appreciate these American attitudes and will in some way show their appreciation; to the very least, according to this theory, they will be less hostile than they would otherwise have been. Others, however, believe that this is an unwarranted extrapolation of political experience in a democracy from the domestic to the international scene. Only under conditions in which physical violence is effectively excluded, as is the case within a well-established legal order, so these critics think, is the accumulation of goodwill the royal road to power and influence. In international relations, however, particularly in the present conditions of extreme lawlessness in which nearly every nation faces grave perils, goodwill is of limited value. They believe, furthermore, that for Asian, African, and Latin American intellectuals, the United States is the arch imperialist power, not because of what it does but because of what it *is*, namely, it *is* the world's richest capitalist nation. It is believed, too, that manifestations of benevolence are not likely to alter the course of unfriendly nations, except adversely, by convincing them that the United States is already in so desperate straits that it can be abused with impunity; but that unfriendly nations may, nevertheless, at any moment, change over to the Western side if they feel threatened by Communist powers and *if* they believe that the United States can render them effective assistance.

The last answer to the challenge of revolution, finally, that of reformism, has been the main United States policy all during the crisis; support for a liberal policy of reform everywhere has been further emphasized by the present administration.

It is the basic idea of this American policy to try to convince the world that the American "Revolution," rather than the French and Russian Revolutions, holds the message for their present aspirations. It aspires to win a major part of the people of "underdeveloped" countries for a program of meliorism, financed by the United States, in preference over revolution— a repetition of the Roosevelt New Deal on a world scale. Success or failure of this policy is still hidden in the future, but it is clear that it is undertaken under conditions far less auspicious than those under which the New Deal was launched. A rich man of moderate temperament like Franklin Roosevelt was acceptable to the lower income groups of America as their leader, but that does not mean that rich and moderately tempered America will be acceptable as leader to the *descamisados* and African hut dwellers or to the students in Bogota and Rangoon, particularly while the Soviet world offers its full support for more radical alternatives. The United States can only offer help toward an improvement of living conditions, which must needs be slow, at the price of domestic tranquillity. At the same time, the more radical alternative promises, in addition to the immediate confiscation and distribution of accumulated consumers' goods (including durable goods such as luxurious homes or beaches), the excitement of revolution, with ample opportunities for the squaring of old accounts and for sadistic gratifications. While the embourgeoisement of the poor is more satisfactory in the long run, the expropriation of the rich suggests itself to human impatience as so much quicker and easier. It is the ancient cry: *panem et circenses.*

STRENGTH AND WEAKNESS IN THE WESTERN POSITION. The weaknesses of the Western position are patently obvious; they appear to be rooted in the following facts:

1. The contact of the poor with the rich, together with the progressive breakdown of caste barriers, has brought about constant comparison by the poor of their condition with that of the rich, and with it a sense of suffering, resentment, and envy. These sentiments can hardly be appeased by the prospect of slow improvement because, for a great part of the road at least, impatience *increases* as actual differences diminish and the goal is closer in sight.

2. Under these circumstances, utopian ideas seem entirely plausible to all but a few. Their plausibility rests in the failure of most people to understand the economic problem of rational choice, and in the naive belief that all problems can be easily solved once the authorities have set themselves to them. Furthermore, a democratic party is in a poor position to compete with a totalitarian movement because the democratic party cannot make utopian promises with impunity; a totalitarian movement is under no such restraint; it does not have to worry about redeeming its promises, because on the day of their maturing it has long achieved unchallengeable power.

3. Finally, there is, for Americans, an inner difficulty: The current revolutions strive for goals that Americans have traditionally upheld such as the right of self-determination of all nations, large or small, of all groups whose leaders declare them to be nations. Many of the declarations of nationalist leaders

today might have been bodily lifted from speeches of American leaders in the past.

In particular, the following beliefs, widely held in this country, tend to weaken it in the present struggle:

(a) The egalitarian illusion: the assumption that all branches of the human family have been equipped with equal genetic endowment, and that actual differences of performance, therefore, can be due only to differences in opportunity; lack of achievement of some is therefore the responsibility of the more successful ones.

(b) The democratic illusion: the belief that self-government is always workable and indeed the best possible government, regardless of the level of education and information, and that there is something sacred about the principle, "one man, one vote," or its present international application: "one sovereign unit, one vote."

(c) The materialist prejudice: the belief that people are always motivated by economic interest and by a correct evaluation of their economic interest, to boot. A revolution in, say, Asia, must therefore be due to a clamor for land reform denied by the American-supported government, or similar conditions; facts at variance with this theory simply cannot be true.

(d) The sentimentalist illusion: the belief that relations between nations are governed not by the demands of self-interest as interpreted by them but by emotions such as likes and dislikes for another people or admiration or disparagement for its domestic achievement.

(e) The rationalist and moralist illusions: the belief that the establishment of law need not have a basis in a community existing in the minds of men and in physical power, but that law can be based on an appeal to conscience alone, and that the social contract can create an effective community.

(f) The distorted view of revolution: the belief that revolution always is made by those at the bottom of the social pyramid and is caused by oppression and injustice of the regime in power. The very fact of the revolution appears then as *prima facie* evidence for the injustice of the regime;[21] and it is felt that unjust rule must eventually lead to revolution.

[21] How unreal this assumption is will be seen when we translate it from the vertical, intranational, to the horizontal context, i.e., from the civil to international war: Who would entertain the notion that the fact that one nation has taken up arms against another is sufficient evidence for the justice of its cause?

The fact that a substantial part of articulate public opinion holds some, or all, of these propositions to be true greatly interferes with a realistic evaluation of the situation.

But there is also one point of strength for the West in its competition with Communism for the allegiance of the remainder of mankind: While the West, in the present climate of opinion, appears to be outclassed in the propaganda battle—as was the Habsburg Monarchy in its final struggle for survival in the midst of revolutionary forces, and for similar reasons—there is also one strong card in the Western hand, and much will depend on whether it will be played with skill (as it has hardly been so far). The strength of the Soviets consists in the fact that the Socialist *idea,* which they incarnate, has an enormous appeal to the intellectuals and, to a lesser degree, to the poor; but it is their weakness that the Socialist *reality* is quite unattractive. No amount of argument and of good deeds is likely to convince liberal opinion in this country or abroad, or the masses in backward lands who have become aware of the possibility of a better life, that a capitalist country could do any right except by retreating and surrendering; but neither persuasion nor good deeds are necessary to convince, say, the East Germans.

Among men, as well as in animal and plant life, favorable living conditions bring about a proliferation of life, and whatever people may think ideologically, the direction of their migrations indicates the differences of living conditions. Where migration has been possible at all, as in Berlin and Hong Kong, it has been going from socialism to "capitalism."

It is the Western system, not the Soviet and the various other government-operated systems, that has actually worked better for the satisfaction of human needs and of the aspirations of people in their private lives. The strength of Socialism lies in the plausibility of its *arguments* and *promises;* the strength of the West lies in its *actual deliveries.* But the latter take a long time before they tell their story—long, not only because much experience must have accumulated before much inference can be drawn from it, but also because few people will revise satisfactory theories on account of inconvenient facts; most people will not notice such facts or will explain them away in some fashion. Also, governments unfriendly to the West can easily suppress such facts. It therefore takes at least the coming of age of another generation before there is any chance that widely accepted theories might be revised.

THE CRUCIAL PROBLEM IN THE STRUGGLE. The fundamental fact in the struggle between a pluralist society and a totalitarian system is the permanent *reversibility* of every victory of the former and the *irreversibility* of a victory of the latter. Whenever an attempt by totalitarians at seizing power has failed, the totalitarian movement, or the totalitarian countries that back it up, remains in a position to repeat that attempt tomorrow, the day after tomorrow, and forever after. Whenever totalitarians have seized power in a country, the result is irreversible (except for outside intervention such as overthrew Mussolini and Hitler), because totalitarians destroy every focus of possible resistance after a seizure of power. They must set up, as Lenin put it, a government that nobody will ever overthrow. This has been greatly facilitated in more recent times by modern technology, which has made possible an effective monopoly of the tools of coercion and communications such as has not existed for a long time and perhaps has never existed to quite the same degree.[22]

These ground rules put Western societies at a grave disadvantage. Nevertheless, they need not necessarily lead to catastrophe as long as the likelihood of a totalitarian take-over is as small as one chance in twenty, because the time that would have to pass until a totalitarian take-over became probable is sufficiently long that unforeseen events may upset all calculations. But, if the totalitarian chance is fairly good, perhaps one chance out of three, totalitarian victory becomes very probable within a relatively brief period of time. Eventual victory, by Communism or totalitarian movements allied to it, over most of the "underdeveloped" world appears, therefore, likely, unless

[22] In the eighteenth and nineteenth centuries, the main weapon of regular armies was the rifle; and rifles could be owned and operated by civilians, too. They could be hidden in backyards or smuggled across frontiers. Hence, the advantage of a governmental force over rebellious citizens was narrowed down to the advantages of superior training and discipline; these were real, but not necessarily decisive advantages, and men of courage had a chance against regular security forces. This was, therefore, the age of minute men, barricades, and expanding democracy; it was in this period that the word was coined that one could do everything with bayonets except sit on them. But tanks and bombing planes cannot be hidden under the floor, nor operated without a large visible organization. *Present technology* therefore *favors absolute State power.*

the West can effect a change in the ground rules and make a Communist take-over a reversible event.

It may be that Communism, though with its prestige greatly increased, may yet have less easy sailing in many countries than it had in Russia, China, and Cuba, because the middle classes, the peasants, and unionized labor may be less naive as to what is going to happen. But within the reach of Soviet power, effective resistance against a Communist regime already established is nevertheless an inauspicious enterprise, as events in Eastern Germany and Hungary have shown.

It may be different in countries which are not within easy reach of the Red Army and its air transport and which lie in the shadow of Western sea power. The latter has recently been shown as of little effectiveness in the case of a left-handed support for a small force of invading exiles, but it may yet be effective in enforcing a hands-off policy against a foreign, Hungary-style intervention to crush a local uprising. In this way, perhaps, Alfred Thayer Mahan's concept of the influence of sea power upon history may not yet be entirely obsolete. It may be one of the present-day possibilities of sea power and, therefore, one of the chances of the "world island" (Mackinder), which so largely depends on sea power for its survival, to keep revolutionary results reversible within a certain radius from its power center and, thereby, give trial and error a chance to work itself out.

From this point of view, the establishment of Communist States distant from the Soviet center of power contains, in addition to all too obvious dangers for the West, some possibilities for it, too. If conditions are reversible, Communist propaganda might be defeated in a certain area by the only effective argument there is—by a demonstration of Communism in action.

We, therefore, may question whether it is in the best interest of the United States to continue the policy of containment and to try its utmost to deny Communism access to Latin America and Africa. This policy is straining American resources to the utmost; it greatly antagonizes many people in these countries, as people do not like being told by others what they should do in their own best interest, which they prefer to judge for themselves; and it has not been conspicuous for its success of late. One may wonder whether it would not be preferable for the United States to take more of a back seat and, with the exception of the strategically most sensitive spots, to allow events to take their course. Under such circumstances, one must assume that Communist governments will be set up in some countries in these continents (as they probably will be anyhow); but it is also likely that some other countries will pursue a vigorous anti-Communist course and look to the United States for help. The United States would then not be in the thankless role of a proponent of an unpopular policy and an easy prey for blackmail but would be in the strong position of a power whose help is eagerly sought. In this way, a kind of equilibrium may be established in these continents which, though fraught with dangers for the West, may yet be one that can be lived with and upheld with less strain than is incumbent upon the present attempt of holding an umbrella over these continents and all their people—the willing, the disinterested, and the hostile alike. As time passes, Communism may find itself in these transoceanic outposts confronted with difficulties similar to those it faces in Eastern Europe, albeit without the possibility of easy military intervention.

The obstacle against the adoption of such a policy may lie not only in its undeniable perils, but also in the reluctance of the American people to part with universalist moral schemes and to have recourse to the despised strategies of "power politics."

IDEOLOGY AND CIVILITY: ON THE POLITICS OF THE INTELLECTUAL

Edward Shils

An ideological outlook encircled and invaded public life in the Western countries during the 19th century, and in the 20th century it threatened to achieve universal dominion. The intellectual classes which concerned themselves with politics were particularly affected. The intensity of the attack has varied from country to country. It has been least severe in the United States and Great Britain; in France, Germany, Italy, and Russia, it possessed an overwhelming power. Wherever it became sufficiently strong, it paralyzed the free dialectic of intellectual life, introducing standards irrelevant to discovery and creation, and in politics it constricted or broke the flexible consensus necessary for a free and spontaneous order. It appeared in a variety of manifestations, each alleging itself to be unique. Italian Fascism, German National Socialism, Russian Bolshevism, French and Italian Communism, the *Action Française,* the British Union of Fascists—and their fledgling American kinsman, "McCarthyism," which died in infancy—have all, however, been members of the same family. They have all sought to conduct politics on an ideological plane.

What are the articles of faith of ideological politics? First

Edward Shils, "Ideology and Civility: On the Politics of the Intellectual," *The Sewanee Review* (July–September 1958), 450–480. Reprinted from the Sewanee Review by permission; © 1958 The University of the South. This essay originally appeared as a review of *The Opium of the Intellectuals* by Raymond Aron and *The Pursuit of the Millennium* by Norman Cohn.

and above all, the assumption that politics should be conducted from the standpoint of a coherent, comprehensive set of beliefs which must override every other consideration. These beliefs attribute supreme significance to one group or class—the nation, the ethnic folk, the proletariat—and the leader and the party as the true representative of these residences of all virtue, and they correspondingly view as the seat and source of all evil a foreign power, an ethnic group like the Jews, or the bourgeois class. Ideological politics have not been merely the politics of a dualistic faith which confines itself to the political sphere. The centrality of this belief has required that it radiate into every sphere of life—that it replace religion, that it provide aesthetic criteria, that it rule over scientific research and philosophic thought, that it regulate sexual and family life.

It has been the belief of those who practice politics ideologically that they alone have the truth about the right ordering of life—of life as a whole, and not just of political life. From this has followed a deep distrust of the traditional institutions—family, church, economic organizations, and schools—and the institutional system through which politics have been conventionally carried on in modern society. Ideological politics have required, therefore, a distrust of politicians[1] and of the system of parties through which they work. Insofar as ideological politics have been carried on by organizations calling themselves

[1] The hostile attitude towards politicians, towards the "parliamentary talking shop," with its unprincipled compromise of interests, and the petty quality of personnel of civil politics is a continuing theme of the ideologist. Hitler said that politicians were "people whose only real principle was unprincipledness, coupled with an insolent and pushing officiousness and shamelessly developed mendacity" (*Mein Kampf*, München, 1941 [583rd-587th ed.] p. 72). "Parliament itself is given up to talk for the special purpose of fooling the 'common people' " (Lenin, *State and Revolution*, in *Towards the Seizure of Power*, Book II [*Collected Works*, Vol. XXI], New York, 1932, p. 186). At the other pole of intellectual sophistication, Mr. Edmund Wilson, during his own ideological phase, once wrote, "Our society has . . . produced in its specialized professional politicians one of the most obnoxious groups which has ever disgraced human history—a group that seems unique in having managed to be corrupt, uncultivated, and incompetent all at once" (*New Republic*, January 14, 1931, reprinted in *The Shores of Light*, London, 1952, p. 529). The anti-political literature of the ideological intellectual is vast: Hilaire Belloc and G. K. Chesterton, *The Party System*, London, 1911, is representative.

political parties, it has only been because that term has become conventional for organizations actively concerned with politics. It has not signified that their proponents were ready to participate constitutionally in the political system. Extra-constitutionality has been inherent in their conceptions and aspirations, even when their procedures have seemed to lie within the constitution—and by constitution, we mean not just the written constitution, laws, and judicial decisions, but the moral presuppositions of these. Ideological politics have taken up a platform outside the "system." In their agitation, ideological politicians have sought to withdraw the loyalty of the population from the "system" and to destroy it, replacing it by a new order. This new order would have none of the evils which make up the existing system; the new order would be fully infused with the ideological belief which alone can provide salvation.

Ideological politics are alienative politics. They are the politics of those who shun the central institutional system of the prevailing society. Ideological politicians feel no affinity with such institutions, and they participate in them for purposes very different from those who have preceded them in the conduct of these institutions.[2]

For the ideological politician, membership in a parliamentary body or the acceptance of office involves only an opportunity to overthrow and destroy the system rather than to work within it and improve it.[3]

[2] Mr. Aneurin Bevan, who has within him, together with other gifts, a powerful ideological strain, has written of the radical's entry into the House of Commons: "Here he is, a tribune of the people, coming to make his voice heard in the seats of power . . . The first thing he should bear in mind is that these were not his ancestors. His ancestors had no part in the past, the accumulated dust of which now muffles his own footfalls. His forefathers were tending sheep or plowing the land, or serving the statesmen whose names he sees written on the walls around him, and whose portraits look down upon him in the long corridors . . . In him, his people are here for the first time and the history he will make will not be merely an episode in the story he is now reading. It must be wholly different, as different as the social status he now brings with him" (*In Place of Fear*, New York, 1952, p. 6).

[3] Cf. Leon Trotsky, *Whither England?*, New York, 1925, pp. 111–112; "We Communists are by no means disposed to advise the . . . proletariat to turn its back on Parliament . . . The question . . . is not whether it is worthwhile to use the Parliamentary method at all, but . . . is it possible to use Parliament, created by Capitalism, in

Ideological politics are the politics of "friend-foe,"[4] "we-they," "who-whom."[5] Those who are not on the side of the ideological politician are, according to the ideologist, against him.

Thus, moral separatism arises from the sharp, stable, and unbridgeable dualism of ideological politics which makes the most radical and uncompromising distinction between good and evil, left and right, national and unnational, American and un-American. Admixtures are intolerable, and where they exist they are denied as unreal, misleading, or unstable.[6]

Ideological politics have been obsessed with totality. They have been obsessed with futurity. They have believed that sound politics require a doctrine which comprehends every event in the universe, not only in space but in time. To live from year to year and to keep afloat, to solve the problems of the year and of the decade are not enough for ideological politics. Ideological politicians must see their actions in the context of the totality of history. They must see themselves moving towards a culmination of history, either a new epoch, totally new in every important respect, or bringing to a glorious fulfillment a condition which has long been lost from human life. Whether totally without precedent or a renewal of the long lost, the ultimate stage will be something unique in history.[7] Everything else is a waiting and a preparation for that remote event.

---

the interests of its own growth and preservation, as a lever for the overthrow of capitalism."

[4] Carl Schmitt, *Der Begriff des Politischen*, München, Leipzig, 1932, pp. 14 ff.

[5] Striking evidence of the separatism of ideological politics may be found in N. Leites, *The Study of Bolshevism*, Glencoe, Illinois, 1953, pp. 291–309, 384–390, 430–442.

[6] Cf. Aron, Ch. I, "The Myth of the Left," pp. 3–34. The deep-rootedness of the mythology of left and right among intellectuals of the Marxist tradition, and its penetration even into allegedly scientific research in sociology and social psychology are treated in my essay, "Authoritarianism 'Left' and 'Right'," in Richard Christie and Marie Jahoda, *Studies in the "Authoritarian Personality,"* Glencoe, Illinois, 1954, pp. 24–49.

[7] The Communist Manifesto declared that in place of a class society with its classes and class antagonisms, there would be a new free society "in which the free development of each is the condition for the free development of all." In the first edition, this was regarded by its authors as an entirely unique condition: "The history of all hitherto existing society" being "the history of class struggles." In 1888, Engels added a footnote which corrected this view, saying

2

What are the grounds for thinking that the age of ideological politics is passing? How can we summon the naïveté to think such a thing, when the world is frozen into a menacing division engendered and maintained by Bolshevik ideas, when the Communist Parties of France and Italy are among the largest in their countries, when in the Middle East, in Africa and Asia passionate nationalist and ethnic ideologies continuously encroach on rational judgment and reasonable moral action.

Yet the expectation is not simply frivolously optimistic. The very heart which has sustained ideological politics among intellectuals over the past century is gradually losing its strength. Marxism is decomposing. The mythology of Bolshevik Marxism, the true nature of which was seen at first only by Bertrand Russell, Waldemar Gurian, and a handful of European Social Democrats and liberals, began its own self-deflation in the mid-1930's, at the moment of its maximum appeal to the world's intellectuals. The Moscow Trials were the first major step in the breakdown of the Communist claim that in the Soviet Union the ultimate stage of human history, the true realm of freedom, was being entered upon. The Berlin uprising of June 17, 1953 was a step further. The realm of harmony through which mankind would transcend its conflict-ridden history was unveiled as a phantasm when Russian tanks shot down German workingmen in the streets of Berlin. According to Marxism, there could only be harmony between Socialist societies bound together by the solidarity of the proletariat, but the Soviet Union showed no compunction about suppressing the East German workers by force. The eagerness with which Hungarian and Polish intellectuals greeted their prospective emancipation from a compulsory Marxism and the Russian repression of the Hungarian Revolution of 1956 also contributed to the demythologizing of Marxism.

"all written history" was the history of class conflict. There had been a prehistorical period of communally owned property which was free of class conflict. Communism would thus be a renewal on a higher plane of what had been lost since the beginning of history. (Marx and Engels, *Historisch-kritische Gesamtausgabe*, Erste Abt., Bd. 6, Moscow/Leningrad, 1933, pp. 525–526; p. 546.)

Political events alone have not discredited Marxism. Perhaps more important is its sheer unresponsiveness to the multiplicity of life itself. People still have a need to believe, but Marxism cannot satisfy it. Its formulae are too simple, and it offers nothing to those who are attempting to establish their intellectual individuality in the face of large-scale organizations and their accompanying professional specialization. The humanitarian element in Marxism—its alleged concern for the poor— can have no appeal when there are still many very poor people in Communist countries, and the poor in capitalist countries can now be seen not to be poor, not to be miserable, not to be noble —but to be as comfortable and as vulgar as, if not more vulgar than, the middle classes. Marxist utopianism has lost its power of conviction—the world is too tired and even, in this respect, too wise to be aroused by promises of a future which might be spurious and which would not be much different from the present. Journals like *Dissent* in the United States and the *Universities and Left Review* in the United Kingdom are valiant and touching efforts to save something of the ideological heritage. But they show how much ideological politics are now on the defensive, and how uncertain they are of the validity of their position. They know that their myth has faded, and that with good grounds, the intellectual spirit of the times is running against them. In every sphere of intellectual life, in economic theory, in history, and in sociology, Marxism has lost its power to attract because it is too simplistic, too threadbare intellectually and morally, and too often just wrong or irrelevant to the problems of the contemporary mind.[8] The emergence of the social sciences as major subjects of university research and teaching—even though they have their serious limitations and even though they sometimes bear a Marxist imprint—constitutes a major factor in the tarnishing of Marxism.

Nationalism too has lost its doctrinal grip on the intellectuals of the West. Its deeper, primordial hold is very strong, but it does not reach into the plane where it could provide a principle for political judgment and action, and even less does it provide a criterion for regulating other spheres of life. In the 20th century among Western intellectuals doctrinal nationalism has

[8] Even Professor Merleau-Ponty, against whose ingenious efforts to fuse existentialism and early Marxism Professor Aron directs an unsparingly detailed and devastating criticism, has lost some of his confidence in Marxism in the past few years.

never been long preponderant, although in France among the followers of Maurras and Barrès there has been a persistent and virulent minority. In Germany, it for a time suffocated reason, and in Italy under Fascism it found many willing proponents. Now, however, it is dormant. It might be said that it is at its lowest ebb in Europe and America since the Risorgimento and the movement for the unification of the Reich. The hideous example of National Socialism, the terrible national intoxication, and the monstrous deeds committed in the name of the nation have for the time being at least exhausted the ideological passions of the German people—intellectuals and laity. The fatigue and waste of the past World Wars, and the ominous possibility of an even worse war to come add themselves to all the other elements in the constitution of the intellectual outlook to render nationalistic enthusiasm one of the least attractive of all the available alternatives of the present time.

The ideals of the European Enlightenment have quietly reasserted their validity without arousing intellectuals to passion on their behalf. It was from the ideals of bourgeois liberalism that they had turned away in the great long wave of political enthusiasm which the Russian Revolution of 1917 had raised to a flood. Now that they have come back to these ideals, they have come back soberly, circumspectly, and with moderation. They do not yet even acknowledge that they have come back to them.[9] The mildness of religious faith in the Western countries, no less than the relaxation of nationalist passion to an unspoken patriotism, and the desire that national sovereignty should give ground to effective control of nuclear weapons seem to provide plausible grounds for an affirmative answer to the question as to whether we are at the end of the ideological age.

Moreover, the asperities of the debate between socialism and capitalism seem to be fading. The achievements of the American and Western European economies since the war, together with the political equivocality of centrally planned economies, the failures of economic planning in the Soviet satellite states, the re-introduction of the principles of the market economy

[9] Indeed, in the counterattack on ideological politics, recent writers like Professor J. L. Talmon (*The Origins of Totalitarian Democracy*, London, 1952) have not spared the French writers of the 18th century in their effort to trace totalitarianism to its most remote origins and to extirpate it. This view is not, however, shared by Professor Aron, *op. cit.*, p. 35.

into their economies by some of the Communist states, and the modest and by no means glamorous achievements of national-ized industries in England and France, have cooled the fires of a century-long dispute between the proponents of socialism and the advocates of capitalism.

The more valid aspirations of the older humanitarian ele-ments which were absorbed into Marxism have been more or less fulfilled in capitalist countries. The socialist and communist countries have neither realized their more grandiose ideals at all nor achieved their more reasonable aspirations any better than the capitalistic countries.

The Negro problem in the United States of course arouses passions, but no doctrines, no principles offer an apparently easy way out. The "woman question" has settled down to being a perennial headache, curable by no enunciation or espousal of clear and unambiguous principles. The ideology of egalitar-ianism has left the fundamental precipitate of moral egalitarian-ism from which it originally arose, but as a universally appli-cable principle it has lost its glamor. It seems almost as if what was sound in the older ideologies has been realized and what was unsound has demonstrated its unsoundness so ob-viously that enthusiasm can no longer be summoned.

Of course, ideological politics, Marxist, Islamic, Arabic, Hindu, Pan-African, and other, still exist in the new states out-side the West in a vehement, irreconcilable form and often with great influence. But many in the West who sympathize with the desires and deplore the excesses are inclined to believe that they too will pass when the new states in which they flourish become more settled and mature. Looking back from the stand-point of a newly-achieved moderation, Western intellectuals view the ideological politics of Asia and Africa, and particularly nationalism and tribalism, as a sort of measles which afflicts a people in its childhood, but to which adults are practically immune.

There seems to be no alternative ideology for the intellectuals to turn to now, nothing to absorb all their devotion, nothing to inflame their capacity for faith and their aspirations toward perfection. The conservative revival, though genuine, is moder-ate. People take Burke in their stride. They have become "natural Burkeans" without making a noise about it. The *Na-tional Review*, despite its clamor, is isolated and unnoticed, and the effort to create a "conservative ideology" which would stand for more than moderation, reasonableness, and prudence has not been successful.[10]

There seem to be no more grounds for ideological politics. Thus, it appears reasonable to think that the age of ideological politics is gradually coming to its end.

Does the present lull give us reason to believe that the tempests are now behind us and that we are now entering upon a pacific sea? An inspection of the traditions which have formed the outlook of the modern intellectual in the West and in the new countries is not entirely reassuring.

3

One of the grounds for believing that the age of ideological politics is ending is its modernity.

Professor Aron inclines towards the view that ideological politics originated in the French Revolution.[11] There is much truth to this contention. Ideological politics did indeed come into the forum of public life only at the end of the 18th century in an outburst not hitherto experienced by the human race.

The reason for this relatively recent appearance of ideological politics on a grand scale is not far to seek. Until recent centuries politics were not public. In the aristocratic republics and in the ancient city democracies, politics did not engage the attention of the mass of the population. Politics were the concern of rulers and of those who aspired to become rulers. The aspiration was, however, spread over a relatively small section of the population. Tribal, feudal, and dynastic interests, which were uppermost in the political life of societies before modern times, did not nourish the ideological outlook. There was, moreover, no intellectual class as a major factor in politics. Where the educated were taken into the civil service, as in China, in ancient Rome, and in the European Middle Ages, the bureaucratic *ethos* and personal dependence on the prince, to say nothing of the type of education preparatory for the civil service career, discouraged the emergence of an ideological orientation.

---

[10] Cf. Irving Kristol, "Old Truths and the New Conservatism," *The Yale Review*, Spring 1958, pp. 365–373.

[11] Aron, p. 42. The same view is put forward by Professor D. W. Brogan in his most interesting essay, "Was the French Revolution a Mistake?", *Cambridge Journal*, Vol. I, No. 1 (October 1947), pp. 43–55.

The intrigues of court politics did not foster the success of the ideologically minded man. There was no class of independent professional literary men and journalists, free of patrons and of the need to remain on the right side of the authorities.

The violent political struggles of the Greek city-states and of the last decades of the Roman Republic, even where they involved the bitterest class antagonisms, did not become ideological. They were fought on behalf of "interests." The notions of "justice" and of the "good social order" did not enter into them except peripherally.

The ideological orientation toward life existed, of course, as it must exist wherever human society exists. It passed judgment on all things, and so it passed judgment on political things. It censured the existing political order as a realm of iniquity, and counselled and predicted its destruction. This ideological attitude toward politics did not, however, enter the sphere of political activity, because the kinds of persons who espoused it or came under its influence were not admitted into the circles which discussed and decided on succession to political office and on the actions of governments.

As long as politics were not an instrument of justice or of the realization of the right social order and were concerned with the mere maintenance of order, the conservation of the power of dynasties and classes which already had or sought it, there was no room for ideological politics. Those who practiced politics were not susceptible to them, except on rare occasions, and they found no following even where great individual personalities were moved by ideological—above all, religious—considerations.

The invention of printing and the possibility arising therefrom of diffusing arguments to a wider public, the Protestant belief that the Bible and not the priesthood is the vehicle of the sacred, the Protestant belief that each man must make his own proper contact with the sacred by his study of the Bible, and the slow and gradual rising of the mass of European populations from their torpor—all of these had much to do with the creation of the necessary conditions for ideological politics. The crucial element, however, was the creation of a class of intellectuals no longer dependent exclusively on patronage or inheritance for their livelihood.

The body of intellectuals which came into existence in the 16th century was a new phenomenon in world history. It consisted of men whose sensibility, intelligence, and imagination carried them beyond the standards and requirements of everyday life; they were no longer forced inevitably to depend on church or state or princely, aristocratic, or mercantile patronage for their existence. Their capacity for loyalty thus liberated, they were endowed with the freedom to attach themselves to symbols beyond those embodied in existing ecclesiastical and governmental institutions. The steady growth in the scale and importance of this stratum of the population in modern European societies is perhaps the decisive factor in the "ideologization" which, on its better side, has been called the "spiritualization of politics." The intellectuals—who before the development of specialized technical training were co-terminous with the educated classes—have lived in a permanent tension between earthly power and the ideal, which derives from their nature as intellectuals. They have not, however, created from within themselves the imagery and passion of ideological politics. The numerous traditions which they have developed, e.g., the romantic tradition, the scientific tradition, the bohemian tradition, important though they have been in disposing intellectuals towards ideological politics, would scarcely have been sufficient to give to such politics their extraordinary attraction and compellingness.

Ideological politics are rooted in an ideological tradition which lives in our midst through invisible radiations coming down from the depths of our Western past. They are sustained by our Judaic-Christian culture, by passions which are part of our souls, and by the nature of society.

The millenarian tradition which is the oldest source of the ideological outlook is an ever-present potentiality in Christian teaching and experience; it is usually maintained, for most people, most of the time, in a state of latency. It has a living existence in the life of the Protestant sects and in the records of the saints of every Christian society. Even where religious belief has become attenuated or has evaporated, the millenarian expectations and judgments have persisted in an aromatic tradition which, on occasion, becomes crystallized in a sensitive and receptive person. Religious *enthusiasm,* as the late Ronald Knox[12] showed with such compassionate understanding and as Professor Cohn, writing from a very different point of view, has corroborated, has never been absent from Western civilization. As early as pre-Exilic times, Jewish prophets foretold the cata-

---

[12] *Enthusiasm: A Chapter in the History of Religion, with Special Reference to the XVII and XVIII Centuries,* Oxford, 1950.

clysmic end of time and the world as we know it, a Day of Wrath and a Last Judgment, when sinners, individual and corporate, would be cast down, and a regenerated Israel would populate Palestine and a second Eden.

The expectations of a Last Judgment on a sinful temporal order took a deep root in the early Christian communities. The tradition did not die out as the Church settled down to live on as an institution. Manichaeism, with its basic distinctions between light and darkness and its conception of the universe as a field of irreconcilable struggle between the forces of light and the forces of darkness, found hospitality in the Christian circles where this chiliastic tradition persisted. No church, indeed, no established institution, could survive if its members expected an imminent end of the world and its subsequent replacement by the Kingdom of God. It was to meet this view that Saint Augustine elaborated his conception of the Church itself as the Kingdom of God on earth. But for those with a great sensitivity to the sacred, and without Saint Augustine's powerful and disciplined intellect, no living church could ever represent the Kingdom of God. Insofar as it refused to preach the proximate realization of the Kingdom of God, it rendered itself subject to their most anguished and harshest criticism.

Professor Cohn, who is not concerned either to support the Marxist view that millenarian sectarianism was merely the ideology of a class conflict expressed in a religious idiom or to espouse the anti-Marxist view which argues that millenarianism was solely an expression of a hypersensitive and perhaps disordered religiosity, is at his best when he shows how it fused with the animosities of class, of ethnic hatreds, and of phantasies of national glory. The hatred-filled phantasies of princes, lords, wealthy merchants, the Pope, Jews, Turks, Italians, Saracens were amalgamated with the frightful images of Satan and the Antichrist. In its meandering and tragic history, full of misery, persecution and violence, rabid and deluded yearnings, false Messiahs, deranged visions, persecutions, and pitched battles, a single complex theme runs unbrokenly. This is the central theme of the ideological orientation towards existence.

The ideological outlook is preoccupied with the evil of the world as it exists; it believes in the immiscibility of good and evil. It distinguishes sharply between the children of light and the children of darkness. It believes that no earthly action can ameliorate or attenuate evil. It exhibits a violent hatred of the existing cosmic order, and especially of its earthly beneficiaries, governmental, economic, and ecclesiastical authorities, indeed, of authorities of any kind. It regards authority as an agent of evil and as a compromise with evil.

The mass of mankind lives in constant temptation and seduction by evil; the petty concerns of daily work and commerce, attachment to family, loyalty to friends, and the quest of private advantage are all inextricably involved with evil. Those who take upon themselves to rule the world as it is are either corrupt in their very nature to begin with, or become so through their contact with authority, which is diabolical by nature.

The ideological outlook expressed by millenarianism asserts, however, that the reign of evil on the earth is of finite duration. There will come a moment when time and history as we know them shall come to an end. The present period of history will be undone by a cosmic act of judgment which will do justice to the wronged and virtuous by elevating them to eternal bliss, and equal justice to the powerful and wicked by degrading and destroying them for all time to come. The order which will be ushered in by the cosmic last judgment will be a new realm of perfect harmony and peace, in which all men will live in accordance with the ultimate criteria of justice and mutual love. No conflict will mar their existence; there will be no scarcity to degrade and cramp them.

To usher in this glorious epoch requires heroism on the part of the small number of consecrated persons who live strictly in accordance with the dictates of the highest judgment. Heroism is required, above all, to give witness to the truth of the standards which ultimately will come to prevail and to inaugurate this totally new phase of existence.

Despite its extraordinary persistence, the millenarian tradition has been no ordinary tradition transmitted by the elders of a society to their next generation. Its reception is not the ordinary reception of tradition as something given, but a search and a yearning. There is no evidence of continuity of the movement of this tradition from person to person, and it is not commonly taught in any society. It is a phenomenon of the sinks and corners of society, and it creates groups which, in a state of inflammation, are remarkably shortlived as compared with the long history of the Churches. The tradition, however, has a long and continuous history.[13] From the Near Eastern seedbed of en-

---

[13] Cf. LeRoy Edwin Froom, *The Prophetic Faith of Our Fathers: The Historical Development of Prophetic Interpretation* (Review and

thusiastic religiosity, millenarian Christian sectarianism spread from the Near East into Southeastern Europe and North Africa, from Bulgaria into Northern Italy, from Northern Italy into Southern France, from Southern France into the Low Countries, from the Low Countries into Germany and Central Europe and then into England. Yet the mechanism of its transmission remains a mystery. There is some evidence of personal links of the founders and spreaders of particular variants of millenarianism, but this does not explain why the soil was so fertile for their labors.

Similarly, although the inner affinities of millenarianism and modern revolutionary politics are now perfectly obvious,[14] the lines of filiation are more difficult to trace. The German Marxists' discovery of their own ancestry in the Anabaptists of Münster, in the Levellers and the Diggers of the English Civil War,[15] is an acknowledgment of the affinity, but is not evidence of a directly received influence.[16]

Herald, Washington, D.C., 1948), Vols. I-IV; Steven Runciman, *The Medieval Manichee: A Study of the Christian Dualist Heresy,* Cambridge, 1947; Dmitri Obolensky, *The Bogomils: A Study in Balkan Neo-Manichaeism,* Cambridge, 1948; Knox, *op. cit.;* I should like also to call attention to a very sympathetic article by Miss Storm Jameson: "The Dualist Tradition," *Times Literary Supplement,* 6 August 1954.

[14] Aron, Ch. IX, "The Intellectuals in Search of a Religion," pp. 264–294; Erich Voegelin, *Die politische Religionen,* Stockholm, 1939, pp. 39–42; Fritz Gerlich, *Der Kommunismus als Lehre vom tausendjährgen Reich,* München, 1920, esp. pp. 17–78.

[15] Cf. Friedrich Engels, *The Peasant War in Germany,* New York, 1926; Karl Kautsky, *Communism in Central Europe in the Time of the Reformation,* London, 1897; Edward Bernstein, *Cromwell and Communism: Socialism and Democracy in the Great English Civil Revolution,* London, 1930; Ernst Bloch, *Thomas Münzer als Theologe der Revolution,* München, 1921.

[16] The German working class movements of the 1840's and British working class radicalism did, it is true, thrive in areas which had been the scenes of Protestant sectarianism from the 16th to the 18th centuries. It is a plausible hypothesis that the ideological traditions of sectarian life made for a receptivity to revolutionary and radical ideas by virtue of their correspondences; in turn, aided by theorists more deeply dyed by the revolutionary traditions of the French Revolution and the Hegelian (and ultimately Christian) idea of history, the tradition of religious enthusiasm was transformed into an apparently secular heroic doctrine of ideological politics.

Perhaps the continuity of the millenarian outlook through many different situations arises not from a continuously handed down tradition but from the recurrent attachment to its sources —the Book of Daniel, the Book of Revelations, the Sybilline Books, and the Johannine prophecy, which are available on the edge of our culture to all those who have a need for them. To these, time and again, persons with a yearning for the end of earthly justice and the transcendence of time in a new and purer realm, resplendent with harmony and love, have turned. In the past century, they have not had to go back to the original sources. Through the heirs of these sources, their transformations into the doctrines of contemporary ideological politics have been available in an idiom more acceptable to the contemporary mind.

Now, if this is no ordinary tradition, transmitted in the way ordinary traditions are transmitted, why then does it persist as such a recurrent theme in Western history? The answer must be sought in Christianity, which contains among its manifold potentialities the ever-present promise of a Second Coming and the unchanging imminence of the ultimate catastrophe which precedes the second coming of a Messiah. Although the central institutions of modern societies, out of the very necessities of their continuing existence and the nature of the human beings who live in them, preclude the widespread practice and observance of the ideological orientation, there are always some persons in these societies to whom the ideological orientation has an especial appeal. It is always there for those who have the ideological need to be in saving contact with the ultimate. Every society has its outcasts, its wretched, and its damned, who cannot fit into the routine requirements of social life at any level of authority and achievement. Max Weber said that salvationary religions are most commonly found among declining strata of handicraftsmen and small enterprisers. This proposition is capable of generalization. Those who are constricted, who find life as it is lived too hard, are prone to the acceptance of the ideological outlook on life. A society in which the lot of the many becomes more constricted, in which they feel more deserted and more uncared for as a result of the failure of their rulers, will encourage this proneness to seek realization.[17]

[17] Bengt Sundkler, *Bantu Prophets in South Africa*, London, 1948; Georges Balandier, *Sociologie actuelle de l'Afrique noire*, Paris, 1955, pp. 417–486; and Peter Worsley, *The Trumpet Shall Sound: A Study*

Naturally, not all those who live in a broken and disadvantaged condition are drawn equally by the magnet of the ideological orientation. Special personal qualities are required.[18] It takes a hyper-sensitivity to ultimate standards, to the sacred, and this is a quality which, although rare in all populations, is found in some measure at all times and particularly at times of crisis. There are human beings who, by personal constitution, are sensitive to the ultimate grounds of existence, just as there are human beings with a need for and a capacity for abstract reasoning, for understanding the mysteries of the universe in accordance with the powers of their reason. Some become mystics, some become scientists, others philosophers. Others who are filled with the sense of injustice and of grievance against the earthly order in its various manifestations, political and ecclesiastical, as well as familial and sexual, reach out

---

of 'Cargo' Cults in Melanesia, London, 1957, show the connection between salvationary, messianic religion and the deprivations arising from the disruption of traditional institutions.

[18] Professor Cohn declares that paranoid tendencies are a necessary condition for the expansion of millenarianism. His view is supported not only by the content of millenarian imagery and aspirations which his book so richly describes, but by contemporary experience of millenarian groups, religious and political. He does not claim that all members of such groups must be paranoid, but that the leaders must be such. ". . . there are always very large numbers of people who are prone to see life in black and white, who feel a deep need for perfect saviours to adore and wicked enemies to hate; people . . . who without being paranoiac yet have a strong tendency towards paranoid states of mind. At a time when such tendencies are being encouraged by external circumstances, the appearance of a messianic leader preaching the doctrine of the final struggle and the coming of the new age can produce remarkable results—and that irrespective of whether the leader is a sincere fanatic or an imposter or a mixture of both. Those who are first attracted will mostly be people who seek a sanction for the emotional needs generated by their own unconscious conflicts . . . these first followers, precisely because they are true believers, can endow their new movement with such confidence, energy and ruthlessness that it will attract into its wake vast multitudes of people who are themselves not at all paranoid but simply harassed, hungry or "frightened" (pp. 311–312). There is much truth in this well-balanced picture, but it seems to me that he omits the religious or ideological sensitivity—the sensitivity to remote things —which is not necessarily connected with paranoia, any more than imagination or curiosity is connected with it.

toward and seek fusion with the symbols of apocalyptic fulfillment. That is why the ideological orientation so frequently draws
to itself madmen full of hatred and fear—the paranoids who
play such an important role in Professor Cohn's interpretation.
Ideological sensitivity, even if it did not draw on the accumulated hatred and aggressiveness of its followers, would be separatist and in tension with the "world" of normal traditional
society. Its utopianism and its quest for perfect harmony would
put it at odds with the world of conflicting interests, half-meas-
ures, and self-seeking. The addition of the hatred and fear of
those who feel injured and neglected adds a highly combustible
fuel to its fire. For this reason, the ideological outlook is full
of the imagery of violence and destruction, and its practice is
often crowded with actual acts of brutality and a heartless asceticism, while preaching a message of an ultimate condition of
love and peace enveloping all human beings.[19]

Ideological politics have their nerve in this need to be in contact with the sacred. They live from grievance and the feeling
of injustice, and no conceivable society can attain the condition
in which everyone could be permanently free from grievance
and the feeling of injustice, any more than any society could
live up to the standards affirmed by the most saintly prophets
and maddest zealots of the apocalypse.

The tendency of intellectuals in modern Western countries,
and latterly in Asian and African countries, to incline toward
ideological politics does not, however, derive only from this permanent feature of the Judaic-Christian religious culture, which
affects even those who do not accept its explicit articles of
faith.[20] As intellectuals, they also live in the flowing stream of
other traditions which are particular to them as intellectuals.

It is probably not an accident that most of the traditions of

[19] One need only read the pacifist press to see how the preaching
of peace and love is combined with a pleasure in the contemplation
of maimed bodies and universal destruction. Mazzini once wrote,
"I am inclined to love men at a distance . . . contact makes me hate
them." Bolton King, *Life of Mazzini*, London (Everyman edition),
1912, p. 55.

[20] Is it entirely an accident that Communism in India has achieved
its greatest success so far in an area where previously Christian
missionary education had reached a larger proportion of the population than in other parts of India? It is not intended, however, to explain Indian leftism solely by an ultimate derivation from a secularized Christian outlook.

the modern intellectuals seem to dispose them towards an ideological outlook. It seems to be almost given by their attachment to symbols which transcend everyday life and its responsibilities. Some of these traditions have arisen as effluvial by-products of specific intellectual activities, as, for example, scientism has arisen from scientific research and analysis. Others, like the tradition of bohemianism, have arisen from the age and mode of life of persons whose inclinations drive them towards an effort to be independent of traditions and conventions and on whom their devotion to the symbols of artistic and literary creation, and the restricted market for the sale of their creations, enforces material poverty and uncertainty. And still others, like the tradition of Romanticism, are the complex products of a profound movement of the human spirit, so intricate and multifarious that it seems almost inexplicable.

Let us consider some of these traditions of the intellectuals, with regard to their contact with the ideological outlook and their inherent disposition towards ideological politics. Let us consider scientism first. Scientism entails the denial of the truth of tradition. It asserts that life, if it is to be lived on the highest plane, should be lived in accordance with "scientific principles," and that these principles should be achieved by the rigorously rational examination of actual experience, systematically confronted through the elaborate and orderly scrutiny and experiment which constitute scientific research. It regards the generally accepted traditions of society as impediments to the attainment of these principles, which are ultimately the principles immanent in the universe. As such, therefore, scientism constitutes a vigorous criticism of traditional and institutional life, and a refusal to accept authority on any grounds except those of scientific principle. It holds before mankind the ideal of a society in which scientists, and administrators and politicians guided by scientists, will rule and in which the ordinary citizens will hold no beliefs and perform no actions which are not sanctioned by scientific principles.[21] This rejection of the prevailing order, and

[21] Cf. F. A. Hayek, *The Counter-Revolution of Science*, Glencoe, Illinois, 1952, which provides the best account of one of the most important sources of scientism, that which derives from Descartes and which reaches its fullest elaboration in the work of St. Simon and Comte. B. F. Skinner, *Walden II*, New York, 1948, is an extreme contemporary statement of the scientific position, to which there are numerous approximations, not the least the Marxist. Marxist scientism is best represented by Professor J. D. Bernal, who has written,

its central institutions and traditions, and the appreciation of an ideal order governed by the ultimate principles of science obviously possess close affinities with certain features of the millenarian outlook. The hostility towards the barrier which received tradition raises between the human being and the ultimate principles of the universe, the dispraise of the authority of institutions, and the vision of an ideal order (infused by and conducted in accordance with the ultimate principles of universal existence) are only a few of the lines of affinity which link these two traditions. It is therefore not difficult to understand how the acceptance of the scientistic tradition can prepare the way to the acceptance of a secularized millenarianism and thus lead on to ideological politics.

Romanticism too flows in the same direction, feeding into and swelling the sea of ideological politics. Romanticism too views any existing order as repugnant because it mediates, compromises, and deforms the ideal. The ideal of romanticism is the spontaneous and direct expression of the essential nature of the individual and the collectivity. Both the individualistic and the collectivistic variants of the Romantic tradition placed great emphasis on the direct and full experience of the ultimate value of individual creativity or of the spirit of the community (folk or national or local). Like the millenarian outlook, Romanticism regards immediate experience of the sacred as a touchstone of the good. Whatever is mediated by calculation or contrivance, by organization or compromise is antithetical to it. That is why modern large-scale society as it has emerged since the end of the 18th century is abhorrent to those who live in the tradition of Romanticism. Civil society, which allows so much space for private concerns, and which permits neither the single individual nor the total community the complete realization of their essential potentialities, is seen by Romanticism as a system of arbitrary repression, in contrast with some ideal realm of freedom and fulfillment. Civil society

---

"Science has put in our power the means of transforming human life to a degree at least as great as those provided by the technical developments of the origin of civilization but the change differs in one crucial respect in that they can be consciously undertaken. What we can see straight away is the possibility of the removal of most of the hindrances to full human and social life that exist in our civilization." "Science and Civilization," in C. Day Lewis, *The Mind in Chains,* London, 1937, pp. 194–195.

requires compromise and reasonableness, prudent self-restraint, and responsibility, and these are all deviations from the unqualifiedness and spontaneity which Romanticism demands of all action. Romanticism is, as a result, at war with civil society.

The influence of Romanticism on the outlook of intellectuals runs far beyond those circles who knowingly acknowledge its sovereignty over them. It has become universally pervasive. It is a major determinant of the attitude of the intellectuals towards politics and the authority of institutions. And different though it is in content from the frightful and dazzling visions of millenarianism, they both work to the same end—the rejection of the existing order in the name of a pattern of existence more infused with the sacred.

In their spiritual genealogy, the traditions of bohemianism and populism are closely related to Romanticism. Bohemianism had an older history before it developed an *ethos* of its own. The restless scholars of the medieval universities[22] and the homeless minstrels and minnesingers who lived from begging, thieving, and the hope of selling their artistic wares were the ancestors of the modern bohemian. They were footloose; they were not incorporated into the routines and responsibilities which filled most of the medieval European social structure. They would not accept the burdens of family and vocation, and sought only to serve their own creative impulse and pleasure.

The development of printing and the appearance of a body of writers trying to maintain themselves from the sale of their written product added a substantial body of persons in Western Europe whose uncertain existence and whose intellectual sensitivity forced them into an irregular course of life. Bohemian practice and bohemian *ethos* were well under way in London and Paris before the beginning of the 19th century. The widened range of education and the increased reading public, fed by the romantic idea of the creative man, the lonely genius who knows no law, made the café intellectual, the bohemian writer and artist into a major figure of life in all the great capitals of the Western countries. Paris was the center of this life, but London, Berlin, Munich, St. Petersburg, Rome, and

[22] Miss Helen Waddell, describing these forerunners of bohemianism, quoted the Council of Salzburg: "They go alone in public naked, lie in bake-ovens, frequent taverns, games, harlots, earn their bread by their vices and cling with inveterate obstinacy to their sect, so that no hope of their amendment remaineth." *Wandering Scholars* (7th ed.), London, 1942, p. 188.

New York all had their bohemias. The traditions of the French revolutions of 1789, 1830, 1848, and the commune of 1871, and the tradition of anarchism, doctrinal and practical, found a warm reception in the Parisian bohemia, and with varying degrees of attenuation and adaptation to national political traditions, they found acceptance in the bohemias of the other countries as well. Antinomianism—moral, aesthetic, and political—was at home there, and the political police kept their eyes peeled for revolutionaries in bohemian intellectual circles. Bohemians were at war with society,[23] some on well-thought-out grounds, seeking a free life less encumbered by traditional standards, others out of an incoherent and impulsive aggressiveness against any sort of authority, cultural or institutional, and an inability to live in a settled routine of work or life. There were many points at which bohemianism and millenarianism diverged. Bohemianism was usually against the Church as well as against Christianity; millenarianism was Christian and only hostile to the authority of the Church. Bohemianism was usually opposed to asceticism; millenarianism was often ascetic. They had in common, however, their repugnance for *mere* tradition and for the constituted authorities who were associated with it.

Populism—the belief in the wisdom and the supreme moral value of the ordinary man of the lower classes—is a new phenomenon. In some respects it was a creation of Romanticism, but it was also an outgrowth of the moral egalitarianism of the Christian sects and of life at the peripheries of Western culture. By its praise of the uneducated and the humble, it places itself in opposition to the great and mighty of the earth; it denies their cultural creativity while imputing true creativity to the lower classes. Populism charges academic science and scholarship with a preoccupation with bloodless symbols unconnected with the essence of life. When it becomes political, populism asserts that the standards of the ordinary people should prevail against the standards represented by the authoritative institutions of society—the State, the Law, the Church, the Universities. Thus the populistic tradition, too, like the other traditions cited, expresses a deep alienation from traditional culture and from the society ruled through civil politics and the equilibrium of power.

[23] Baudelaire once wrote, "Usefulness to the community always seemed to me a most hideous thing in man." *The Essence of Laughter and other Essays, Journals and Letters* (Edited by Peter Quennell), N.Y., 1956, p. 178.

Populism and millenarianism share many significant features. Both repudiate the official traditions of learning, millenarianism declaring that the prevailing interpretation of sacred texts falsifies their true meaning, and populism charging the learned with the transfiguration of authority and with enmity towards the truth expressed in the popular will. Both oppose the mediation of contact with the highest values, by authoritative institutions, by priests, professors, and parliamentarians. Both are against the cold-blooded and impersonal rules of institutions; both are responsive to charisma. The conceptions of the people and of the proletariat easily merge, as do those of people and nation, and so populism can turn without difficulty into an ideological political orientation.

These are not the only traditions of the modern intellectual, but most of the others have the same tendency. Of course, these traditions are not accepted equally by all intellectuals. They are most widely accepted among men of letters and academic scholars and scientists. Nonetheless, although an increasing proportion of intellectuals in the broader sense, i.e., persons who have passed through colleges and universities, are engaged in practical tasks in administration and technology which curb their ideological predispositions, the atmosphere in which they acquire their qualifications, and the traditions which adhere to their professions, give to many of them some impulsion in this direction. The impetus to an ideological outlook inherent in the very constitution of intellectual activities would probably not be enough to account for the upsurge of ideological politics of the past century and a half. It has required the confluence of numerous traditions and their common confrontation with the situation of modern society to release the flood.

4

Traditions seldom die. They recede very slowly, yielding before new traditions which replace them by incorporating elements of their predecessors and assimilating them to new elements. The new traditions can grow only by attachment to older traditions which they expand and elaborate.

It seems excessively sanguine, therefore, for us to congratulate ourselves on the end of the ideological age. We would be more realistic to speak of its subsidence, rather than of its end. Old traditions, such as millenarianism, deep in the marrow of our intellectual bones, traditions such as Romanticism, which are at the very heart of the modern age, are not likely to disappear so soon after the fury and the disillusionment of the first fifty years of this century.

What we may legitimately hope for in the coming decades is a condition of quiescence of ideological politics and of the ideological disposition from which it springs. This quiescence can be sustained only if an effective alternative is available. Civil politics are this alternative.

Civil politics are based on civility, which is the virtue of the citizen,[24] of the man who shares responsibly in his own self-government, either as a governor or as one of the governed. Civility is compatible with other attachments to class, to religion, to profession, but it regulates them out of respect for the common good.

Civil politics do not stir the passions; they do not reveal man at the more easily apprehensible extremes of heroism and saintliness. They involve the prudent exercise of authority, which tries to foresee the consequences of that exercise while appreciating the undeterminable limitations of human powers and the uncertainties of foresight. The civil politician must be aware of the vague line between the exercise of authority and the manipulation of human beings as objects outside his moral realm. He must shun that line and yet on occasion go over it, realizing the moral costs of such crossing over and the difficulties and the necessity of crossing back into the domain of legitimacy. He must maintain a sense of affinity with his society and share with his fellow citizens their membership in a single transpersonal entity, while bearing in mind their unresponsiveness to the ideal and their incapacity to sustain a continuous and intense relationship with the sacred. He must maintain this sense of substantial affinity while being aware of their lesser willingness to be responsible for the common good and while keeping his own feeling of responsibility for it alive and taut.

[24] Civility has meant more than good manners, and it is an impoverishment of our vocabulary as well as a sign of the impoverishment of our thought on political matters that this word has been allowed to dwindle to the point where it has come to refer to good manners in face-to-face relationships. Two recent books by eminent British writers—*Traditions of Civility*, by Sir Ernest Barker, Cambridge, 1948; *Good Behaviour: Being a Study of Certain Types of Civility*, by Sir Harold Nicolson, London, 1955—show no awareness of the older meaning of the term.

The difficulties of civil political conduct are great in democracies. Their large size and the impossibility of direct contact between politicians and their constituents are strains on the sense of moral affinity which, lacking the support of personal relationships, must be self-sustaining. Civility was rare in aristocratic societies, partly because aristocratic virtue—the virtue of the warrior—and civil virtue—the virtue of the citizen—are so far apart in their inner constitutions and particularly because aristocratic systems by their nature restrict man's development of the empathic sense of affinity. Liberal democratic regimes place great burdens on the civil sense because they permit open conflict and acknowledge and thus encourage partisanship. The common good is always hard to define, but it is rendered even harder when it must gratify and reconcile opposing interests and simultaneously attempt to guard values for which no strong partisan contends, but which, nonetheless, are essential to a good society. The politician must be partisan himself, while civility requires a partial transcendence of partisanship, as well as an emphathic appreciation of the other parties within the circle of the civil political order. Partisanship must be carried on with the simultaneous perception of the civil and moral order which embraces both one's opponents and one's allies.

Civil politics—which are by no means identical with democratic politics—are especially difficult in contemporary society. The complex tasks which governments undertake and which nearly everyone thinks they should undertake, make so great the amount of material that a politician who devotes himself to the matter must master, and so many the obligations to which he must attend, that reflection is deprived of the quiet and leisure which it needs to mature. The complexity of the tasks renders easy understanding of them beyond the power of most of the citizenry and encourages a depreciatory attitude towards the capacities of the electorate, thus inhibiting the vitality of the sense of affinity between citizens and leaders that is essential to civil politics. The deep and increasing penetration of populism in all countries results in a greater pressure on the politician for the immediate satisfaction of class and sectional ends. The development of techniques of mass communication and of chemical, surgical, and psychological modes of controlling human behavior presents continuous temptations to the politician to respond to the incessant demands by manipulation. Not that he always by any means yields or that the techniques would be successful if applied, but the mere existence of the putative possibilities creates an atmosphere which impedes the cultivation and practice of civility.

Civil politics entail judging things on their own merits—hard enough in any case where the merits and demerits in any complex issue are so obscure and intertwined—and they also require respect for tradition. Civility requires respect for tradition because the sense of affinity on which it rests is not momentary only but reaches into the past and future. As to the past, civil politics appreciate the factual reality of past achievements as well as the human quality of those who, by virtue of having once been alive, command our respect for their names and the things they valued; as to the future, civil politics see the unity, in essence, of the present generation and those which are to follow, not just in a biological sense, but in the order of value as well. The population of a civil polity is in its fundamental being a continuous procession of those living in the present, preceded by those who have lived, shading off into the obscurity of time past, and to be followed by those who have still to live, shading off into the even more shadowy obscurity of time still unelapsed.

The traditional consciousness is not, however, one which encourages the direct contemplation of the merits and demerits of things as they are. The utilitarian mind usually has little patience with the pastness of things and is even disposed to assume that the mere fact of having been appropriate to the past is a disqualification for relevance to the present and future. Yet both the need for continuity—i.e., the maintenance of affinity with the past—and the need to draw on the benefits of the intelligence and artfulness exercised in the past, render imperative an appreciation of tradition.

Above all, civil politics require an understanding of the complexity of virtue, that no virtue stands alone, that every virtuous act costs something in terms of other virtuous acts, that virtues are intertwined with evils, and that no theoretical system of a hierarchy of virtues is ever realizable in practice. It has been a major fault of ideological politics that they made the mistake of thinking that a coherent, systematic doctrine could guide conduct unfailingly along a straight line which made no compromise with evil. Ideological politics believed that the more strictly one adhered to a virtue, the more intensely one was attached to it, and the more completely one fulfilled it, the better would be one's actions.

This was the basis of the idea of the political spectrum which ran from the pole of virtue—be it left or right—to the other pole, the extreme and complete negation of virtue. The realism and circumspection of civil politics cannot accommodate such a simplification.

Practicing politicians do indeed manage to avoid the excesses which are inevitable in such simplifications. As Professor Aron shows, French politicians in the 19th and 20th centuries, in one of the countries of the most extreme ideological politics among intellectuals, have in practice usually not been dominated by this distinction between "left" and "right."[25] Indeed, this has been one of the reasons why French intellectuals have been so alienated from the political practice of their country.

The practice of politics imposes some measure of civility, but it also stirs the temptation of demagogy and offers the easy solution of satisfying the most clamorous sectional interests. If intellectuals could settle down to a more reasonable political outlook, their concern for the more general and for what transcends the immediate advantages of particular "interests" would infuse a most precious ingredient into political life.

5

Is it plausible to expect intellectuals to renounce their attachments to anti-political traditions in which they have lived for centuries? Can it be expected that intellectuals will be drawn down from the heights of the ultimate ideal so that they could, while still remaining intellectuals, tolerate the burden imposed by the vicissitudes of maintaining themselves as politicians who have invested their future in the unpredictabilities of politics, and by the task of keeping a society going? Can intellectuals be brought to appreciate politics which are concerned to keep society on a steady course, as much concerned to keep it from becoming worse as to make it better? Can they be expected to affirm a political practice which provides no final solution and which does not promise to bring society or the human race to a resting point of perfect fulfillment?

[25] The avoidance of ideological politics is not synonymous with the practice of civil politics. Politics practiced in accordance with the prevailing constellation of interests is a third alternative, and it is one which is most commonly pursued by politicians. If the "interests" are intractable, then the civil order can be as badly damaged as it would be by ideological politics.

The civil politics which must replace ideological politics in the affections of the intellectuals have many competitive disadvantages. Their traditions are fewer and frailer. Cicero, who preached and tried to practice the virtues of civil politics, has been called an opportunist, and his assassination by the side with which he compromised has been regarded as evidence of his failure as a politician. Tacitus spoke on behalf of civility through his censure of its degradation in the Empire.[26] Clarendon's civil wisdom was put on paper in the rueful melancholy of exile and with the distrust of power which is the destiny of the disappointed and disregarded counsellor to princes. The fate of More and Raleigh and the disillusionment of the humanists who sought to guide the conduct of princes have left bitter memories of the tribulations of the intellectual in politics. On the other side, the image of politics reflected by those "advisors to princes" whose names stand out in our minds, Machiavelli above all, Halifax, et al., have given an appearance of justice to the condemnation of politics which the intellectual, devoted to the ideal of his calling, has often expressed.

The intellectual who seeks the path of civil politics has little to cheer and fortify him in his quest. He has many of his own prejudices to overcome—the whole complex of the traditions of ideological politics, and, in America, his traditional aversion for the politics of the porkbarrel and the patronage lists, and his image of the 42nd Ward Young Men's Democratic Club, with its smokers and its belching boorishness, and of the harsh selfishness of the Union League Clubs.[27] He has no feeling of standing in a great intellectual tradition. There is no equivalent civil tradition to counterpose to the subterranean pervasiveness of the

[26] "So corrupted, indeed, debased was that age by sycophancy that not only the foremost citizens who were forced to save their grandeur by servility but every ex-consul, most of the ex-praetors and a host of inferior senators would rise in eager rivalry to propose shameful and preposterous motions. Tradition says that Tiberius as often as he left the Senate House used to exclaim in Greek, 'How ready these men are to be slaves'" (*Annals,* Book III, Section 65).

[27] This is by no means confined to capitalistic America or to bourgeois politicians. Ferdinand Lassalle once said, "I have a real horror of workers' delegations where I always hear the same speeches and have to shake hard, hot and moist hands" (David Footman, *The Primrose Path,* London, 1946, p. 183). The intellectuals' attitude toward politicians, regardless of their class, is epitomized in: "I met Murder on the way. He had a mask like Castlereagh."

millenarian tradition, to provide an atmosphere in which he can breathe. He has the memory of Woodrow Wilson and Thomas Masaryk, Disraeli and Gladstone, and Guizot, to set alongside the far more numerous intellectuals approving of bomb-throwing and assassination, themselves engaged in wire-pulling and plotting, impatient and contemptuous of the political profession.

If civil politics depend on an acceptance of the limitations of human powers, their establishment in the second half of the present century will not be rendered easier by scientific developments. The advances in physiology, biochemistry, neurology, applied mathematics, cybernetics, and the foolish propaganda made by some of the enthusiasts of psychology and the social sciences, can hardly induce a feeling of modesty in man, nor can they be expected to promote that fellow-feeling necessary to civil politics.

Nor, for that matter, can the specialization of education which accompanies this scientific progress bring much support. Quite the opposite. It is not that the humanistic education of the past has provided much of a bulwark against the ideological outlook. Extreme specialization, however, adds a further strain to the weak sense of affinity. It is true that extreme specialization which reduces the contact of the intellectual with the broad range of traditions of the intellectual life of the past also restricts this relationship with many of the ideological elements in the traditions of the intellectuals. In many fields, however, and particularly in those of increasing importance, it exposes him more fully to the scientistic tradition. Thus, while it increases his matter-of-factness, it also increases his pride, his contempt for the past, and his confidence in the boundless superiority of the future, and these are not so congenial to civility.

If ideological politics thrive in conditions of danger, what are we to think of the chances of civil politics in an age in which peace is maintained by a conscious fear of cataclysmic destruction by nuclear weapons? These awful possibilities cannot avoid stirring up latent apocalyptic images and expectations. These real dangers make the sober, moderate, small-scale measures of civil politics appear excessively puny alongside the monstrous tasks which nuclear weapons impose on governments.

It should not be thought that civil politics can be stifled only by ideological politics, or that millenarianism is the decisive determinant of radical alienation. Radical transformations in society can be undertaken without millenarian impulsion. Western and Oriental antiquity have known revolutions without ideologies. Every social order, even the most just, will have some victims, and every population will contain antinomian personalities. These alone instigate tendencies towards a sort of proto-ideological politics, even when there are no ideological traditions living in the open or under the surface.

Finally, civil politics are not the only alternative to ideological politics for the intellectuals. They have in some instances entered upon political careers like professional politicians, given up their intellectual concerns and attachments, and devoted themselves to the conventional round of vote-getting, interest representation, self-preservation, and self-advancement. They could yield to the customary temptations of the vain and ego-centric, demagogy, flattery, and opportunism. They could, in short, conform to their own prevailing image of normal political life.

This, however, is not likely. What is far more likely is with-drawal—angry withdrawal or sad and serene withdrawal. The traditions of withdrawal among the intellectuals are among the profoundest in our intellectual inheritance. One can be anti-political without being ideological. This was the dominant trend among American intellectuals from the Jacksonian Revolution until the Russian Revolution; and it is unfortunately, despite the charges of conformity, of "other-directedness," and of being "organization men," still the prevalent current among American intellectuals today. The valiant effort to embrace "Our Country and Our Culture" is not a resounding success as far as civil politics are concerned.[28] The repudiation of ideological politics has not led to the espousal or practice of civil politics. The life of American society is affirmed, but its political life and the civil element in its political life are not.

The situation in Great Britain is not very different. Great Britain has a better record of civil politics than any other country in the world, and its intellectuals have their proper share in that record. What is the situation today? The post-war idyll has ended in disenchantment. "Butskellism" is in retreat. The "angry young men" are on the rampage. Even the most amiable Mr. Kingsley Amis, who says that he is, when he has to choose, a Labour Party man, cannot take politics seriously. His heart is not in it.[29] He, like those with whom his name is coupled, is

[28] Cf. Newton Arvin, et al., *America and the Intellectual* (Partisan Review Series No. 4), New York, 1953.

[29] *Socialism and the Intellectuals,* Fabian Tract 304, London, 1957.

distrustful of the "professional espouser of causes." The humiliation of the Suez fiasco and the danger of the hydrogen bomb
have seriously damaged the British intellectuals' capacity for
civil politics. Even a sober, responsible intellectual of long and
honorable political experience, Mr. Christopher Hollis, tells his
fellow intellectuals that the main task before the British electorate
is to discredit the two major political parties, even though
he expects no serious "Liberal revival."[30] Mr. John Osborne, who
has no such background of experience of political responsibility,
is far harsher in his anti-politics. "I can't go on laughing at the
idiots who rule our lives. . . . They are no longer funny because
they are not merely dangerous, they are murderers . . . they are
stupid, insensitive, unimaginative beyond hope, uncreative, and
murderous."[31]

6

Can the intellectuals re-educate themselves to a civil state of
mind? Can they keep the traditions of ideological politics quies-
cent while they modify their own outlook? Can they take advantage of the present lull in ideological politics in the West
and develop and fortify the incipient impulses of civility which
the harsh experiences of the past half-century stirred into movement?

One condition of the success of this effort at self-"civilization"
is that we should not think that we can or should completely
extirpate the ideological heritage. There are valuable elements
in that inheritance which are worthy of conservation in any
political outlook which lays claim to our respect. The demand
for moral equality, the distrust of authority and of the institutions which it conducts for its own continuance, the insistence
on justice, and the call to a heroic existence, even the belief in
the earthly paradise and the realm of freedom, all have some
validity in them. To deny them will only lay civil politics open
to the charge—not unjustified—of being philistine politics in
the worst sense, without feeling or sympathy, unimaginative,
timorously clinging to what already exists. The ideological ele-

[30] "What Shall we do Next Time?" *The Spectator* (No. 6765),
February 21, 1958, pp. 225–226.
[31] "They Call It Cricket," in Tom Maschler (ed.), *Declaration*,
London, 1957, p. 67.

ment in our intellectual classes will not die out so easily and so soon that its successors will be able to escape unscathed while conducting politics which, while called civil, are merely concerned with the maintenance of order and keeping things as they are.[32]

These impulses in the human heart will not be disregarded. The fact that they have been forced to an extreme and cast into the framework of unrealizable hopes does not mean that they are in themselves immoral. The discredit into which their doctrinaire proponents have deservedly fallen should not be extended to them. Life would be poorer without them, and a political system which sought to proceed entirely without them or entirely against them would find the most sensitive spirits of its society once more drawn up in embittered and irreconcilable opposition.

It has not been the substantive values sought by ideological politics which have done such damage. Rather it has been the rigidity, the exclusiveness, and the extremity with which particular values have been sought. There is nothing evil about loyalty to one's community, national or ethnic or cultural, nor is there anything wicked in the appreciation of equality or the devotion to any particular ideal. What is so malign is the elevation of one value, such as equality or national or ethnic solidarity, to supremacy over all others, and the insistence on its exclusive dominion in every sphere of life.[33]

Civil politics therefore will have a better chance to obtain more enduring devotion among intellectuals if their proponents do not disavow all continuity whatsoever with the substantive values of ideological politics. Correspondingly, their chances for success will be enhanced if the prudence they extol is exercised

---

[32] One of the dangers of the New Conservatism is that it fails to see that civil politics are as eager for improvement as they are ready to conserve what has come down from the past. Cf. Charles Parkin, *The Moral Basis of Burke's Philosophy,* Cambridge, 1956, Ch. VI, pp. 109–130; also Mr. Kristol's perspicacious essay in the *Yale Review,* mentioned earlier.

[33] Few writers have made this criticism of ideological politics, while retaining a compassionate sympathy for their ideals, as well as Conrad. Natalie Haldin says at the end of *Under Western Eyes,* "I must own to you that I shall never give up looking forward to the day when all discord shall be silenced . . . and the weary men united at last . . . feel saddened by their victory, because so many ideas have perished for the triumph of one. . . ."

in finding a just balance among the contending values rather than in merely seeking self-maintenance, which will degenerate into unprincipled opportunism.

A complete disavowal of every line of affinity between civility and ideology will not only be false in fact but would turn civility into an ideology. Civility would become an ideology of pure politics concerned with no substantive values except the acquisition and retention of power and the maintenance of public order and with absolutely no other interest. Civility would take upon itself the onus of the very same moral separatism for which it criticizes ideological politics, if it denied its affinity with the substantive values which the ideological outlook holds and distorts.

7

How can intellectuals retain those elements of Romanticism which prize spontaneity and genuineness of expression, and which aid the cultivation of individuality, while curbing their expansiveness? By excessive demands for individuality and the consequent exaggeration of the restrictions which institutional life imposes on it, Romanticism will discredit any social order and turn the intellectuals against it and arouse the custodians of order against the intellectuals. The "imperialism" which the late Baron Ernst Seillière bemoaned in so many volumes can disrupt any social order, and above all a liberal order. A way must be found to retain many of the values of Romanticism while restricting their expansiveness.

A renewal of the old idea, fundamental to modern liberalism, of a separation of the spheres is needed. It can, of course, be realized only very incompletely; economic life cannot be completely independent of government and politics and *vice versa;* religion and politics cannot be completely separated; culture and politics cannot be completely separated. Nonetheless, while acknowledging and accepting their necessary collaboration and affinity, it is very important that the guardians, practical and intellectual, of each of the spheres should be aware of the desirability, in principle, of their separateness. This would be a bulwark against the romantic—and ideological—insistence on the universal application of a single set of standards. The separation of the different spheres of life would not please those ideological politicians and intellectuals who seek complete consistency. Without it, however, civility would be extinguished and our best intellectual traditions would be frustrated.

It should be quite possible in practice to realize a far-reaching separation of the spheres while maintaining their overlaps and affinities. This is in fact done to a large extent in societies of the West, however imperfectly and unprincipledly. The real difficulty is to bring about the intellectual's acceptance of it as a reasonable policy. There is not such a completely unbridgeable antinomy between individuality and institutions as Romanticism insists—although there must inevitably be some tension. The intellectual's distrust of the ongoing life in the spheres outside his own arises from the defects in his sense of affinity.

The nature of the sense of affinity which binds the members of a society together is a mystery. It seems somehow connected with the empathic capacities of the individual—not just his empathy for persons whom he encounters in concrete form, in person, or through written or plastic symbols, but for classes of persons who must necessarily remain anonymous. Up to a certain point, it goes hand in hand with individuality, and societies which do not know individuality also live without a sense of civil affinity. It is shrivelled and shrunken by fear, and when it is restricted, it is in its turn conducive to fear of one's fellow men. If somehow the intellectuals could be got over their almost primordial terror of and fascination by authority, which, they fear, crushes their individuality, the movement for civility would make a tremendous advance.

Modern Western societies have witnessed a diminution in the moral distance separating the higher and the lower classes. This has in part been a result of the changes in the distribution of national income which have raised the lower strata and diminished the upper strata, so that standards of life are now very much nearer to each other than they have ever been before, however considerable the differences remain, and should, to some extent, still remain. But more significant, I think, is the change in the civil consciousness which has taken place in Western societies. This is in some measure a result of the inner development of the potentialities of the Protestant idea—the same complex of ideas and sentiments which has aggravated the millenarian disposition. The notion that every man has a spark of divinity in him, that all men participate in a common substance—sacred in the last analysis but civil in its concrete and mediated forms—has grown out of the conjunction of the modern national state and Christian protestantism. From this conjunction grew the idea of the citizen, and from it our modern idea of the civil order as a stratum of being in which all the members of a state participate.

The modest flowering of civility in the modern world is a new thing in history. Pericles' Funeral Oration foreshadowed its program. The great Roman forerunners were, however grandiose, no more than adumbrations of a human possibility, rather than indications of a well-functioning civility in ancient times. The growth of civility has been halting and very imperfect. Its growth has been attended by an exacerbation of ideology—and the two seem in the modern epoch to have some obscure and intricate interdependence. Yet it does seem that with the spread of individuality—imperfect now and never perfectly realizable —in the wider reaches of the population, the sense of civil affinity has increased its scope and power among the lower strata, who previously existed as objects of authority and economic power but did not dwell within the same moral and civil domain as their rulers. There is now in all strata, on the average, a higher civil sense than earlier phases of Western society have ever manifested—and this despite class conflicts and ideological separatism and irreconcilability. Even ethnic barriers seem slowly to be yielding to the rising tide of civility. Is it too much to hope that the intellectuals, who have provided such illustrious antecedents in the true "civilization" of politics, will themselves come more fully into this process, and thus, by one of the great continental drifts of history, bring the age of ideology to an end?

ANTI-
AMERICANISM
IN AMERICA

Midge Decter

I have a gloomy premonition . . . that we will soon look
back on this troubled moment as a golden time of freedom
and license to act and speculate. One feels the steely sinews
of the tiger, an ascetic, "moral," and authoritarian reign of
piety and iron.

> Robert Lowell in a *Partisan Review* symposium.

It is no insignificant trait of contemporary history that in its
rhythm of assigning epochs, the decade seems to have replaced
the century. Who among Americans, and particularly among
American intellectuals, cannot pithily characterize the 'twenties,
the 'thirties, the 'fifties? Each of them is now from our vantage
point seen to have had its own unmistakable social flavor: its
own politics, its own sense of life, its own dictates of public
and private comportment, its own literature. (Only the 'forties
have been scanted in these characteristics, given over as they
were to the war and its immediate aftermath and thus to the
strains of what was past and what was coming.)

History, to be sure, cannot be so tidy as to mete itself out in
ten-year measures. The decade to which we have affixed his
name, for instance, did not find Dwight D. Eisenhower in the
White House until two years after its inception. Similarly with

Midge Decter, "Anti-Americanism in America," *Harper's Magazine*
(April 1968), 39–48. Copyright © 1968, by Harper's Magazine, Inc.
Reprinted from the April, 1968 issue of Harper's Magazine by per-
mission of the author.

the 'thirties, which in some important sense can be said to have
been over in 1937 or '38. Still, there is more than mere con-
venience in describing certain patterns of American life and
thought in these terms. They do, after all, reflect the rhythm, if
not the exact chronology, of our spiritual development. In any
case, everyone knows what one means by them: The 'twenties
were the time—the 18th Amendment to the Constitution notwithstanding—of the explosive, exuberant, and sure-minded
throwing off of American provincialism and small-town puritan-
ism. The 'thirties were the time of a new, grown-up membership
in the society of the Old World—a participation in the crises of
what looked then to be its detumescence, a tuning-in to its
intellectual currents, and finally a bloody and costly sharing in
its salvation. And the 'fifties were the years when America self-
consciously assumed the role of the world's major conservative
power, with everything that such a position implies—including
an internal atmosphere ridden with, on the one hand, high and
righteous self-definition and, on the other, with a spirit of the
most dulling prudence and caution.

An American adult of today, then, has in his ordinary lifetime virtually spanned ages. His mind and imagination have
been confronted with the demand that they make room for,
accommodate themselves to, five traditional lifetimes' worth of
issues, movements, countermovements, revolutions, consolida-
tions, and counterreactions. His life-style—the expression of his
sense of social relations, his values, his aspirations—has been
assaulted not only by a technology that continually renders itself and the issues it creates obsolete but by shifts in basic
fashion that are, to say the least, unnerving in their rapidity. He
sees himself separated by experience and attitude not only, as
his modernity has prepared him to be, from his children, but
even from those five years younger than he. He struggles to
incorporate a new system of thought which, somewhere, a new
vanguard has already set itself up to discredit.

An exemplary serious and educated American has without
yet becoming an old man had something like the following
spiritual odyssey. He has, with the writers of the 'twenties,
thrown off the repressions and hypocrisies of the traditional
bourgeoisie. He has accepted the liberations and burdens of
Freudianism. He has, with or without any of the party affilia-
tions that might follow therefrom, taken over the Marxian
critique of capitalism and the class society, and, again regardless
of party affiliation, on the other side been profoundly influenced

by conservative warnings about the depradations against culture of the newly empowered masses. He has discovered the possibilities for totalitarianism—implicit in Marxism, explicit in Leninism—in the attempt at a radical reordering of society. Following on this, he has come to acknowledge the evolution of American capitalism into a variant system no longer comprehended in the categories of its traditional critics and, moreover, to grant its superiority to other economic systems as a means at least for the release of wealth. He has, largely through the agency of the Nazi episode in Europe, discovered in the heart of man an evil no mere social programming can hope to bring totally under control, much less eradicate. And he has discovered in turn that the preoccupation with such evil can be dangerously allied to complacency about those ills and enequities in the life of society that can in fact be remedied. Most recently . . . but of now later.

Taken all together, these ideas may sound like the very recipe for human "wisdom"—each view set off by another which softens, modifies, modulates it, and the whole, a balanced and "stable" amalgam. They have not, however, *been* taken all together, but rather come into intellectual power in a series over four decades, each of them for a time supplying the central impulse to a new movement of thought. Nor in the end would the wisdom resulting from the judicious combination of ideas and the critiques of ideas probably be worth very much. If the description of his odyssey makes the exemplary intellectual[1] sound, with desperate injustice, a little foolish, it must be remembered that such views as he has incorporated are not purchasable by choice but are the hard-won coin of experience and the effort to make sense out of that experience.

Ideas are powerful things, requiring not a studied contemplation but an action, even if it is only an inner action. Their acquisition obligates a man in some way to change his life, even if it is only his inner life. They demand to be stood for. They dictate where a man must concentrate his vision. They determine his moral and intellectual priorities. They provide him with allies and make him enemies. In short, ideas impose an

---

[1] Terms such as these are as necessary as they are questionable, and require their user to stop and state his case: by "intellectual" I mean quite simply a man whose life is committed to the direction of his thought. In his *The Steps of the Pentagon* Norman Mailer describes such a man as one deeply limited by the inexorable "logic-of-the-next-step." So be it.

interest in their ultimate fate which goes far beyond the realm
of the merely reasonable.

This is what accounts for the rabbit-like rate at which new
cultural "generations" are produced in America. For a "generation" under these conditions represents not a new batch of the
young who have come of age but a new preoccupation which
has found its style and its rhetoric. (It is also what accounts for
the fact that many Europeans, and particularly for some reason
Englishmen, find American intellectual life to be so full of brute
vitality by comparison with their own: the arguments they witness among us are often battles in which men are fighting for
their lives.)

In any case, to have taken part in what Lionel Trilling once
called "the life of the mind" has been a peculiarly double experience: energizing and enervating, offering promise and
promising despair. Each succeeding decade has come to an end
with its own record of disillusion and bewilderment. Each new
decade has begun with its own hinted promise of a revised and
corrected, perhaps this time eternal, vision.

Of course, simple stylishness has also played its part in these
dizzying shifts of attitude and preoccupation: vogues in thought
serve momentarily to brighten the life much as vogues in dress.
The point was once brilliantly illuminated by the historian R.
A. Nisbet when he observed that one of the most underrated
social forces in history is plain boredom. And how could even the
most dedicated intellectual community resist the hunger for
the new that stalks American society in general and the insatia-
ble media of mass communication in particular? But whatever
the motive behind one's submission to them, ideas about the
world, as we have noted, are consequential. Even slogans, whose
original purpose—take two leading slogans of the 'sixties,
"Black Power" and "The War on Poverty"—is only to call people
out of some impasse (or solace them while they remain there),
can often turn the course of events.

2

And what of the 'sixties—which will soon be drawing to a
close? What was their promise, and what will prove to have been
their disillusion? Naturally, in one way it is too soon to talk of
the 'sixties; something of their drama remains yet to be played
out. Nevertheless, certain things are already clear. The first of

these is that the 'sixties will—like the 'thirties, though in a rather different sense from them—be seen as a turbulent, a "radical," decade. And the second is that it will be known as the decade of the Vietnam war—despite the fact that consciousness of the war did not become keen or central until the decade was nearly halfway over and despite the possibility, remote as it seems at the moment, that it may end in peace.

Both of these characterizations would have seemed astonishing in 1960; for the decade, to begin at the beginning, opened not with the threat of ugly tension and war but on the contrary, with the promise of a new series of triumphs for American liberal democracy. This promise was one which had lain dormant through the years of war and Cold War, years in which the system was seen to be hanging on by its fingernails and was accounted well merely to have remained intact. A new sense of possibility was, now, not so much to be released as to explode— with all the energy of one of those historic revelations about what might be attainable if people only willed it to be.

The revelation was communicated in the main from two very different sources and in two very different ways. First, intelligibly, from the political reordering implied in the strategy of massive nonviolent protest which had recently been adopted by the civil-rights movement. And second, mystically, through the personality of John F. Kennedy. The meaning of the grand surge of protest that began with the Montgomery bus boycott—and that was obviously, despite whatever horrors along the way, going to make its effect—lay in the assurance that there was after all a simple, noble, and *aesthetically pleasing* way to bring to an end the age-old scandal of American society. (Criminally callow as this response seems today, what it most reflected was a longing to throw off that sense of social complexity which had since the onset of the Cold War hung like a dead weight over all our imaginings of the future.)

The effect of Kennedy himself is considerably more difficult to define. It had to do with his youth, his beauty, his—odious word—style, his being unlike our—even more odious word— image of a politician. Norman Mailer, for instance, in a long essay describing the Democratic convention that nominated Kennedy, spoke of the quality of cold liberation that came off the man and predicted what did in some way happen, that Kennedy's candidacy and election would help to release a host of energies and impulses long storing up in the psychic underground. Just how this release came about must be a question

for future historians of American culture to decide. The point
is that Kennedy's presence in the White House did in fact have
such an effect—almost without regard to his policies or record.
(Just as his assassination three years later set off a widespread
feeling of personal desolation that went much deeper than simply shock at the murder of the President.)

Meanwhile, that process in U.S.-Soviet relations which had
been converting Containment to Coexistence and Coexistence
into something called "the thaw"—however chancy or reversible
it might prove to be—had begun to still some of the anxiety
that seemed earlier to condition all of life. And perhaps even
more important than the abatement of anxiety it afforded, the
coming to an end of the Cold War left space in the political
thought that it had been so totally occupying for other and
fresher problems. Americans suddenly "discovered" that some
forty million of their number were still living in great poverty.
It was rumored that in a number of universities students were
no longer apathetically figuring the angles—as they had done in
the decade preceding—but were returning to the passionate
study of modern history, social justice, and Marx. The demand
for nuclear disarmament was receiving a growing, and grow-
ingly respectful, hearing, at least in the major cities and possibly
even in Washington. Popular entertainment, on stage, in films,
and on the printed page, was being touched by a healing and
invigorating new impiety. Books were being written, and widely
read, which helped to explain why the 'fifties, after all on the
whole a comparatively peaceful and comfortable time, had left
so many people feeling so bad, their lives so confined and
narrow, their young so cynical or delinquent.

The triumphs for liberal democracy that seemed forthcoming
in the early 'sixties were not, to be sure, millennial ones—and
perhaps not even material ones. They consisted largely in things
of the spirit: public tones and postures, the terms and modes
of public debate, the nature of the issues debated, the simple
willingness to acknowledge the existence of serious national
problems, the eagerness to pursue new thoughts and the hospitality bestowed upon those who thought them, a banishing of
priggishness from high places, a new tolerance and even sympathy for the liberties needfully taken by the arts and by artists
—in short, those things of the spirit which enlightened Americans, no matter how hard-nosed the times teach them to be,
never really lose their abiding faith in. Combined with the proper
legislation—not then, as it was usually not, given much search-

ing attention—and the necessary adjustment of our posture toward the rest of the world—to some extent being undertaken by the Kennedy Administration—the new spirit would be moving us a step or two anyway in the direction where the millennium might one day be discovered. Or if not the millennium, then at least the possibility for a reasonably stable world, a reasonably just society in the United States, and a reasonably attractive quality to life.

A great sigh of relief went up among the intellectuals (though that it did so would no doubt now be hotly denied by the majority of them) at the fact that they were, and once more in good conscience could be, liberals. The term "liberal" was not one that many people were to use. In the 'fifties it had come to be something of a dirty word: one generally used it with reference to oneself only in irony and reserved it in its uninverted sense for others who displayed either an unwonted simplemindedness or an unthinking loyalty to old cant. Insofar as it had been known truly to apply to one, liberalism represented a compromise with one's anxious quiescence parading under the banner of the Tragic: it meant a highly articulate, sophisticated, and well-documented accommodation to things as they were. Thus the word was to have little currency in the new prevailing atmosphere; people much preferred "radical." Nevertheless, the early 'sixties were in fact a moment when intellectuals could and did dream of influencing the taste for change being expressed by their government and by the society around them. This moment had arrived, moreover—it is a crucial point— within a system still operating by the most ordinary give-and-take of American politics. It had arrived without apocalypse, without even the help of most intellectuals in bringing it, and without appearing to threaten those comforts the society had already provided. The Negro, it then seemed, might at last be integrated without any fundamental overhauling of that system; the poor might at last be led out of poverty, the peace of the world at least minimally guaranteed, the educational system revamped, etc., etc.—all through the workings of a new spirit of willingness and the application of new and as yet untried ideas ("new ideas" was a favorite commodity of the Kennedy Administration and it sought experts to provide them in every field). Even the notion that an advanced technological society like ours might simply do away with money as the medium for the distribution of life's necessities was advanced by a social thinker or two without any reference to the inevitability of political upheaval. It was the imagination that was to be radical; the system would be plastic enough to incorporate it. The new active liberals had the comfort once more of knowing what there was to care about and, somewhat more vaguely, what it was they wished to advocate. People were beginning to have fun, and congratulated themselves.

3

Some seven or eight years have now gone by since the days described above. Their joyousness has been intentionally exaggerated (without a mention of the Berlin Wall or Bay of Pigs or a survey of the New Frontier's actual record on the issues of civil rights and poverty) because people who are committed to the shaping force of their ideas tend more than others to gloss over the texture of past experience—difficult in any case to keep hold of in the torrential rush of decades. *Of course* not everyone who expressed himself in that period was expressing enthusiasm unbounded. Of course such new political vitality as there was was braced by a hard-won and not so foolishly to be surrendered skepticism. Nevertheless, something of all this there was—I speak here not of the words alone but of the music, and the music said things are better for earnest men, better than they have been in a long long time.

During seven years, then—five, really—the atmosphere in the universities and centers of culture has sharply turned from a new wave of liberal enthusiasm to a storm of reckless, nihilistic, and profoundly despairing radicalism. All the things that had seemed most hopeful at the beginning of the decade have become precisely the sorest spots in this new radical sensibility.

The desire for a relaxation of American moral fervor against some abstraction called "Communism" has been completely reversed into a powerful moral fervor against some abstraction called "imperialism" or "capitalism" (read, America); and many of the people who most vociferously gave voice to the first now burn their ritual candles at the shrine of the second. The demand that the Negro be given his rightful place in the centers of white society has been muffled under a raucous cry of doom to that society; and many of the same people who applauded that demand and seconded it now applaud and second the longing for destruction that supplanted it. The poor whose release from the ugliness of poverty was to be the first order of social business are now exhorted by those who lead their cause to make a subversive value of their poverty; and many of the people who once sought to offer them some greater share of the nation's wealth now seek to support their subversion of the values needed to create that wealth. The cities that were to provide the centers for America's new forays into a more graceful and vivacious life now teeter at the edge of destruction as viable political and administrative entities—and at the edge, some of them, of destruction period; and many of the people who had been the most eager to take part in the social experimentation they promised to yield are now the most eager to pronounce them hopeless. Hallucinogenic drugs have powered and ratified a new youth culture that dictates disengagement from all forms of social and intellectual discipline, a settlement into creature existence, and a total, exclusive submission to the realm of self; and many of the people who once cheered the emergence of a serious, active, and disciplined youth—particularly after the disengaged and self-full 'fifties—now sympathize with the claims of that culture and, with a reckless disloyalty to the standards once imposed on their own intellectual formation, support its products.

Nothing serves better to illustrate the tone and feel of this shift than the career of Stokely Carmichael. That the man who had once been a leader in a serious, determined, and day-by-day attack on the unequal status of the Southern Negro—an attack whose nonviolence was the mark not of weakness but precisely of its determination to succeed once and for all—should now be spending his days making futile desperado announcements of a coming retaliatory terror against white society seems to sum up a great deal about the current decade. Future generations may one day blandly find in this career merely a symptom of the inevitable dynamics of the Negro Revolution caught at midpoint. For after winning what there was to be won, or very nearly so, in the way of Constitutional redress, the Negro's condition as a powerless minority was logically to require the transfer of his demands from integration to "black power." In the lofty and distant view which the future, looking back, so properly arrogates to itself, there will not necessarily be much attention paid to the violent language and behavior through which the Negro first set out to add his weight to the balance of American urban politics. Nor may the rioting in Northern urban ghettos be recorded as anything more than "incidents" in a certain process of political and social reorganization. Nor, certainly, may the use of the Vietnam war as the justification for the declaration of absolute, worldwide racial enmity—as Carmichael and his colleagues and sympathizers now use it— appear as anything other than the taking advantage of a certain historical coincidence to sharpen the pride and group consciousness of American Negroes. For many of his contemporaries, however, most particularly for those who share with him a coming of age in the 'sixties, Stokely Carmichael embodies something very large and real in their own current sense of life. He has become the very personification of their sudden total and implacable hatred for American society.

As a public spokesman, of course, Carmichael has to some extent been the victim of his listeners; and in this, too, he is peculiarly representative of the time. For they have not resisted him, have not even demanded that he make sense. They ask only that he speak to their mood, like people in search of entertainment. If and when he fails to thrill them, he will simply be abandoned, like so many before him, to the escalations of his own spirit. The role of "box office," like that of boredom, is one that modern social critics would do well to ponder.

But if the fate of civil-rights militancy illustrates the change in temper most dramatically, that is only because it is the most definable and containable of the present welter of public issues. The course from hope to despair has been run at exactly the same pace, and by exactly the same plotting of curve, in the realms of foreign policy, domestic politics, and the arts. The new position of "despair"[2] proceeds from one axiom: the American system has come to evil, it must in one way or another be undermined at its foundations.

The corollaries of this axiom are several, and stand in a complicated relation to one another. The first corollary is that any and all of America's difficulties abroad are of her own making and are thus amenable to her own unilateral unmaking. Supplying documentation for this view is a whole new enterprise in historiography—undertaken by such historians as William Appleman Williams, Staughton Lynd, Gar Alperovitz—which seeks to revise our theories about the onset of the Cold War and the

---

[2] I use quotation marks not because the despair is not real but because it is a despair of adopted posture rather than individual feeling; unlike personal despair, which counsels resignation and silence, it has brought with it a veritable whirlwind of energy, action, sociability, and noisemaking.

assignment of responsibility for it. The engine driving this enterprise and supplying its tone is the notion that by the end of World War II the United States had become the world's leading imperial power, in the face of whose possibly blind but inevitable will to aggrandizement the Soviet Union had to move to protect itself. Such a notion is, of course, not new, only the application to a more recent history of the theory of "capitalist encirclement" advanced in defense of the Soviet Union in the 'thirties. Many of these historians' most ardent students had not even been born in the 'thirties, however, and by one of those quirks of the American educational system—which appears to teach its students to maintain a proper skepticism only toward the experience and earned wisdom of their elders—they seem not to recognize behind all this merely the reversion to an older formula of Good and Evil than the one their mentors would have them discredit. In practice, the application of this attitude means that while, for instance, in demonstrating one's opposition to the Vietnam war one does not necessarily wish to march under the flag of the Vietcong, neither does one wish to be intolerant of, or make open quarrel with, those who do. One might not necessarily wish to give aid and comfort to one's country's enemies, but it is after all only by virtue of her own lust for power and profit that she *has* enemies.

Another corollary is that any and all of America's domestic difficulties are the result of the ill will of white society. In practice, then, while one might not necessarily wish for the *Schadenfreude* of the anarchic destruction of our cities, neither does one have the heart to make open quarrel with those who do. One need not necessarily favor the terrorization of one's innocent fellow citizens—white *and* black—but after all, no one of white skin, and no one of black skin willing to remain at peace in this society, is by one's own theoretical lights quite innocent.

Nor need one—in the realm of culture—take complete satisfaction from the evidence in one's own party of a growing illiteracy and a complacent disregard for all the hard work, hard thought, and hard spiritual discipline contained within the Western cultural tradition. But neither would one wish to oppose the spiritual freedom claimed by those who do make a principle of such disregard; to do so would not only be "square" but in some sense to affirm and perpetuate a curse on all mankind. For after all, that tradition has been placed in the keeping of heavy-handed and pusillanimous academic bureaucrats and has been made to serve the purposes of an evil status quo.

4

What has happened to create so nearly seismic a reversal of spirit? Much of the answer can be covered in three words: the Vietnam war. To put the matter very flatly, the government of the United States has become involved in a military venture which to the vast majority of the educated, enlightened, liberal community of Americans seems at the very least senseless and at the worst evil. Implied by these three words, however, is a problem far greater and more thorough-going than a merely bitterly unpopular government policy. Any military venture of the United States, to be sure, would in these days be fearfully opposed by that community; the existence of a vast nuclear weaponry throughout the world has, as Hans J. Morgenthau many years ago predicted it would, virtually ruled out the waging of war as a means for settling foreign disputes or securing new arrangements of international power.

The Vietnam war bespeaks a much greater failure than the failure to—or even a foolhardy unconcern to—keep the peace. Coming as it did hard on the heels of a new belief that our foreign policy would at last replace the mechanical reflex ideology of the Cold War with a flexible system of response to individual local problems, Johnson's escalation in Vietnam exposed the fact that the governing establishment in this country placed no credit whatsoever in that belief. Our "commitment" to the Republic of Vietnam could still be thought of as one of a complicated left-over tangle of holding actions and alliances; our direct and relatively large-scale intervention in a civil war—even in countering an intervention made on behalf of the other side—spelled out America's continuing determination to let no further inch of ground fall to the Communists. The same determination was evinced in our intervention in the Dominican Republic, but left by itself the Dominican adventure might still have seemed only an ugly blunder.

There was, then, to be no new American foreign policy, only a new enemy—and an increasingly desperate application of all the old justifications for dealing with him. What had appeared to be a genuine new adjustment of attitude could now be seen to have depended entirely on the fact that for three years our foreign dealings had been in the hands of a man with a penchant for traditional civilized diplomacy and a talent for operating without a full-blown policy. The "new look" under Kennedy had been Kennedy's alone, personal to him and, as it turned out, to only a few of his advisers; it had not been established in government beyond his person. Now, under Johnson, America was once more to return to being (or if you will, remain), in the accent of the late John Foster Dulles, "anti-Communist." In a sense, it was to be more purely anti-Communist than in the 'fifties, since the demise of a centrally controlled worldwide Communist conspiracy now made it less easy for government spokesmen to maintain their former confusion between the containment of a single hostile power, Russia, and the defeat of a hateful political order, Communism. Not that the attempt has not been made to identify this new holding back of the tide of Asian Communism with the containment of an aggressively expanding China. But in a world which has learned to discount the myth of the Communist monolith—and which is anyway apt, in the face of all the evidence, to remain somewhat skeptical of the picture of China ready and able to swallow all of Southeast Asia country by country—the analogy will not wash.

Thus though Johnson has personally borne the brunt of the blame for the mess in Vietnam, some opponents of the war, with considerable justice, find Johnson himself to be only the perfect representative of a larger, and as they would have it, reactionary ruling class. Enough talk of "aggressive Communism"—particularly in a period of hot, and unpopular, warfare —must sooner or later, it seems, breed its own corresponding talk of "aggressive capitalism." In any case, while a continuing sterility in foreign policy, as under Eisenhower, creates a feeling of acute frustration, the dashing of a promise for better things such as Johnson was responsible for creates a far deeper response for demoralization.

Beyond the war itself and what it means for the state of American foreign policy, this mood of demoralization has been even further deepened by the almost diabolical lack of public candor with which the citizenry has been treated on this subject. We have very nearly attained to that Orwellian nightmare in which "peace" means "war," "victory" means "defeat," and "consensus" means "individual will." If Johnson has at least an arguable case—and even some of his opponents might still be willing to believe he does—he behaves as if he does not. Senators who dissent from his policy, we are told, no longer have access to his person. Persuasion of the opposition consists almost exclusively of references to public-opinion polls which show them to be in a minority, or pronouncements, such as that given in a newspaper interview by John Roche, a member of the White House staff, to the effect that the President's opponents are isolated and unimportant people. Reports on the progress of the war consist almost exclusively of daily tallies of the enemy dead. And behind all of this there is an atmosphere emanating from Washington of ever-increasing petulance and bad temper —frequently, in this psychologically oriented age, taken to be the mark of an uneasy conscience.

Americans have of course—and with little benefit to the commonweal—had long training in taking for granted the disparity between government statement and government intention. Had not the Eisenhower Administration assured us that it would not rest content with the mere containment of Soviet power but would seek to do everything within its means to assist in bringing to Eastern Europe full democratic liberation? The majority of Americans were obviously quite content not to have to believe it. Did not both Nixon and Kennedy make stirring martial gestures in the direction of Cuba during their respective Presidential campaigns? Again, people instinctively understood the game and did not take them at face value. Any keeping of separate public and private accounts by the government is bound to leave its citizenry with some measure of anxiety followed by, or intermixed with, a certain creeping cynicism. Yet it makes a considerable difference whether official dishonesty is one which speaks belligerently for the sake of remaining pacific—as was the case under Eisenhower—or whether it is—as with Johnson —one which speaks the love of peace for the purpose of intensifying war. Dullesian hypocrisy about the aims of American policy in Eastern Europe buried us beneath a load of distorting language that often made it next to impossible to discuss, or think about, the problem at hand. Johnsonian hypocrisy about the aims of American policy in Vietnam, tied as it is to the destruction of a country and the killing of its civilian population on the most questionable of military and political grounds, has served to call into question—particularly among the young —the very legitimacy of government authority.

5

"It is enough," Franz Kafka once wrote in his diary, "that the arrow fits the wound it makes." In a very large measure the opposition to the war has come to reflect, and be reflected by, Johnson's conduct of it. In this sense, perhaps, the disaffection that goes so far as to wish a defeat upon one's own country is well deserved by the arrogance that dares pursue its own privately defined terms of victory. In any case, the radical, despairing nihilism that has ballooned among us in the past few years shares a number of spiritual and intellectual characteristics with the present atmosphere in the White House. Notably among these are an unthinking dependence on political formulas expressed in moral terms, a refusal to make certain necessary distinctions, a lack of candor, a shutting off of genuine debate, and an almost personal demand for loyalty, for the closing of ranks.

It would be silly, of course, to lay the entire current disaffection among the community of the enlightened at the door of Lyndon Johnson—or even of the war itself. Some of what accounts for that community's disgust with the state and nature of American society has to do with frustrations that were inevitable, particularly given the high, innocent expectation with which it greeted the early 'sixties. The single most important of these expectations, in fact, was not thwarted but on the contrary raised to fever pitch precisely by Lyndon Johnson: the expectation that there would be full-scale, orderly redress to the American Negro for his unthinkable treatment at the hands of his fellow Americans. Only the most insanely doctrinaire of his opponents would even at this heated point underrate Johnson's role as the foremost civil-rights President in history. The frustration arose from the fact that the Negro wanted and needed two contradictory things (contradictory, at least, within the particular legal and social tradition of the United States): individual rights and dignity on the one hand and group power on the other; and he could no longer wait patiently for the attainment of either. White society was prepared to give him, as an individual, the former. But the latter, because it would cost people something in the way of the diminution of their own power, was not to be given. Power was something that would have to be wrested. The problem very quickly became a grave one for the Negroes—and in a sense even graver for their white sympathizers—because the moral justice and urgency of their cause blinded most of their leaders to the fact that they were pursuing two separate and contradictory ends which would require two separate and distinguishable programs of action. Thus long before he was ready for it—which is to say, long before he had forged for himself the necessary community structure to serve him as a base—the Negro had to confront the resistance of the already structured communities into whose network of power he would have to make some incursion. The experience of the resistance, and of his unpreparedness for it, understandably left him in a rage. His white sympathizers, who had dealt only, and guiltily, in terms of morality and so had refused themselves the right to make any cool judgment of his political behavior, were then split into groups willing to share his rage or frightened by it. Having failed on both sides to understand the mechanism of power in which they had involved themselves, angry Negroes and angry white liberals and radicals fell back for an explanation of the new difficulty on a theory of American society as hopelessly and irremediably racist. This theory was perhaps as inevitable as the frustration that gave rise to it. Other things being equal, it would have to surrender some of its simplicity to the exigencies of a day-to-day struggle in which not all would be defeat and not all victory.

But other things did not remain equal—the country was engaged in a war which these same activists deemed to be an unjust one. And not only engaged in this war, but engaged in it beneath the clouds of an official temper which left very little open to the spirit of public consultation or influence. So the war, while it did not create the frustration of the civil-rights movement, helped to harden that frustration into the atmosphere of a beleaguered camp, and provided real fuel for the idea that "orderly political process" was a snare and a delusion for the complacent.

The same can be said for the sense of futility that now surrounds the war on poverty. The poor, too, were caught in a contradiction—very nearly the same one—and in this case without even the élan or drive which supports people who are making a fight for themselves. But the realization that even so little money as had been spent on the poor could not now be spared from the requirements of that other, realer, war once again hardened ordinary frustration into unheeding bitterness.

And so partly fairly, partly not, all the issues that had roused a spirit of opposition—mainly war and poverty and equality for Negroes, but not only these—were fused into one; and in that fusion much of the opposition—enough of it to leave an ineradi-

cable imprint on the entire culture of this decade—was fun-
neled into a single piously articulated attitude of anti-Americanism.

It is this attitude, and not adherence to any particular school
or schools of radical political ideology, that earns one ad-
mittance to that precinct of the intellectual community called
the New Left. It is this attitude, and not the chronological accident of one's birth date, that entitles one to claim membership
in that exclusive and intimidating generation Under Thirty.
It is this attitude, and not a commitment to the free adventure
of the mind, that now accredits one as a truly free spirit beyond
the taint of having sold one's soul for pleasure or profit.

Thus we have, within twenty short years, come full circle.
The word "evil" hangs heavy in the language of intellectual
discussion just as it came to do in the years after World War
II. Then it was applied to the Soviet Union, now to the United
States, but the refusal to countenance political complexity that
it bespeaks remains the same. Now, as then, dissent from the
prevailing currents of fashionable opinion is adjudged to constitute moral failure and places the dissenter beyond the pale
of argument. It is astonishing—and more than astonishing—
appalling—to realize that the developments of two decades, in
a rapidly changing world, have not deterred many of America's
most intelligent, most serious, most talented people from their
appointed round.

6

With all due respect, then, to the trials and frustrations of the
'sixties, the response of the intellectual community to those
trials and frustrations has been both disastrous in itself and a
depressing omen for the future.

At precisely a time when the values for which this community believes itself to stand—the enlargement of intellectual
possibility and the devotion to standards of excellence—are
being most threatened from the outside, it has responded only
in kind, by threatening them further from the inside.

When a historian like Staughton Lynd proclaims Hanoi to be
the model for the achievement of freedom by small nations, he
is perverting both the use of his intellectual discipline and his
mandate as a thinking man.

When the organizers of a movement to withhold federal

income tax in protest against the war draw up a statement which identifies the United States with Nazi Germany, they are, while pretending to appeal to the moral cause, perverting that sense.

When Susan Sontag, wishing to express her horror at the fruits of modern technology, launches an attack upon the Faustian spirit of the whole of Western Civilization ending with the observation that "the white race . . . [is] the cancer of humanity," she undermines the very ground on which she herself is entitled to speak or write.

When Andrew Kopkind, a highly talented young journalist, finds in the fascist tactics wielded by a group of Negroes at a conference of radicals a necessary—finally even a hopeful—experience, he reveals a carelessness toward the virtues of freedom that a writer may indulge in only at his peril.

When Robert Brustein, dean of the Yale drama school, indiscriminately and in a tone of deepest self-gratulation lends his sponsorship to any and all works of art whose intention is subversive, he is in fact subverting nothing so much as that artistic integrity to which he professes devotion.

The examples could multiply. They abound in the liberal weeklies, in the highly influential *New York Review of Books,* in some of the quarterlies, and are to be heard from the platform of every forum, symposium, teach-in, and round table on peace.

What is sorriest about this present climate is that it witnesses another betrayal for which yet another high price is sure to be exacted—in disillusionment and bitterness and violent reaction. An intellectual temper which has not the patience to sort out the illegitimate from the legitimate cannot long sustain itself. We learned this from the 'fifties; it will be this decade's lesson, too. The 'seventies will very likely bring a turning back —a turning back from the value of all social passion as well as from the futility of violence. And may we not expect that the disillusion of tomorrow will become the hard, cold, oppressive philosophy of day after tomorrow?

PART III

Students and the University

UNIVERSITIES HAVE traditionally been viewed, particularly from the outside, as oases of tranquility within which the faculty and students engage in a variety of pursuits which, while no doubt important, are essentially removed from the concerns of the outside world. This view of the university has never been fully accurate. Indeed, it involves a serious distortion both of what goes on within the university and the relationship between the university and the world of which it is a part.

Part of the historical mission of the university has doubtless been the disinterested search for truth, a search conducted regardless of its immediate practical value or its consequences for received opinions and practices. It has ordinarily been thought that this search is best carried on in a semi-monastic atmosphere, in which the scholar is not distracted by the practical concerns of the world lying beyond the college gate and is, moreover, protected from inappropriate interferences from that world when his research threatens the established order of things. This has not, however, been the only function of the university. It has had, in addition, the task of educating the young and providing professional training for those men who would perform tasks deemed necessary by society. In the six-teenth century, this meant the training of clerics and lawyers. In the twentieth, it has meant the training of scientists, bureau-crats, and others.

Consequently, while it is clear that the university has always had one foot planted firmly in the world of scholarship, the other has been very much in the practical world. And the world of scholarship, in spite of the ideal of the disinterested pursuit of knowledge, has not always been completely detached from the world of affairs.

Thus, while the ivory tower image may have had a certain utility from time to time, it has virtually never been an accurate description of the reality of the university and its relationship to the world around it. Consequently, the university community has usually been extremely ambivalent in its attitude to the outside world: at one and the same time seeking to influence the affairs of the greater world and claiming the protection of academic solitude.

Having said all this, we must still admit that the events of the recent past, although not completely unprecedented, do present us with problems of a very different order from those raised by the long-standing town and gown issue. And this is so because the university has become the center upon which have converged the various forces and issues which have shaken American society. Those who are dissatisfied with the shape and temper of that society have attempted to transform the university into an instrument for radical, indeed, revolu-tionary, social change. Why this has been so must remain, at least for the moment, in the realm of speculation. It seems likely, however, that the university is seen as a microcosm of American society as a whole. If that society is racist, so is the university. If the politics of the society is corrupt, at least some elements in the university have contributed to that cor-ruption. If American foreign policy is immoral, that policy has been, in part, designed and implemented by members of the academic community. The universities are, in short, seen as accomplices of a corrupt society and at the same time sharing many of the flaws of that society. Hence, if the average citizen is denied a meaningful participatory role in the decision-making processes of his society, so the average citizen as student is also denied such a role in the functioning of the university.

The university has, then, partly by accident and partly by design, become a major factor in modern American society.

This is probably unavoidable and not entirely undesirable. We cannot, and should not, seek to return to the comforts of the cloister, a condition which never really existed in the first place. The problem is how the university can maintain the integrity of its intellectual commitments and at the same time respond to the needs and demands of the society of which it is a part. One of the disturbing features of the current crisis is that it is precisely those intellectual commitments which are under attack. We are, of course, accustomed to such attacks from the right, but they are now emanating from the left. To reform its own shortcomings, to maintain itself as a place of scholarship, and to remain responsive to the changing needs of society while preserving the traditional values of civility, honesty, and generosity of spirit are the tasks which the university now confronts. The fate of the university may very well depend upon its success in confronting this challenge.

The authors of the following articles include the former Dean of the Faculty at Harvard University, three professors, and a journalist and editor. All of them are committed to the integrity of the university and the intellectual enterprise in which it is engaged. It is significant that had these articles been written fifteen or twenty years ago, the focus of concern would have been quite different from what it is in these essays. The danger to the university would have been viewed as mainly external, issuing primarily from the reactionary, know-nothing elements of the community. In contrast, each of these pieces centers on the student revolt, and although it would be foolish to suggest that the external danger no longer exists, the primary threat is now internal. None of the authors is blind to the shortcomings of the university or to its failure to provide a consistently good education for the young at the same time that it conducts its historical quest for knowledge. Neither are they unsympathetic to the students' complaints about these failures. But legitimate student criticism, at least in some circles, has been transformed into what one of the authors has accurately described as a drive to destruction. One of the most disturbing features of this campaign is its manifest willingness to abandon the traditional virtues associated with a university, of which the most important is a belief in the value and efficacy of reasoned inquiry. Indeed, this inquiry is often scorned and treated with derision. The emphasis is on sheer brute power rather than rationality. In major universities, violations of academic freedom by students have become so commonplace as scarcely to warrant notice. In short, the threat to the university and its academic freedom has become more complex. And the know-nothings are no longer to be found exclusively in the bizarre precincts of rightist political activity.

A FOOLPROOF SCENARIO FOR STUDENT REVOLTS

John R. Searle

In several years of fighting for, fighting against and simply observing student revolts in the United States and Europe, I have been struck by certain recurring patterns of action and internationally common styles in the rhetoric of confrontation. Leaving out student revolts in Turkey, Czechoslovakia and Spain —all of which have rather special features—and confining ourselves to the U.S. and the advanced industrial democracies of Western Europe, it seems to me to be possible to discern certain family resemblances in the successful campus rebellions. In general, successful student revolts in these countries tend to occur in three identifiable phases or stages.

The Creation of the Issue

In the beginning, the revolt always has—at least in the mythology of local administrations—the same two features: there is only "a very small minority" of troublemakers, and "they have no legitimate grievances." These conditions, I have found in visits to campuses all over the U.S. and Western Europe, are, by common administrative consent, universal. They are also the reasons why "it won't happen here"; that is, they

John R. Searle, "A Foolproof Scenario for Student Revolts," *The New York Times Magazine* (December 29, 1968), 4–12, 14, 15. © 1968 by the New York Times Company. Reprinted by permission.

are always the reasons why "this campus won't become another Berkeley" or, lately, "another Columbia." I have discovered, incidentally, that a legitimate grievance is defined as one in which the students win. If you win, it turns out that your grievance was legitimate all along; if you lose, then alas for you, you had no legitimate grievance.

"The small minority with no legitimate grievance" starts out by selecting an issue. Curiously, almost any old issue will do. At Berkeley it concerned the campus rules on political activity; at Columbia it was the location of a gym; at Nanterre, a protest at the offices of T.W.A. and the Chase Manhattan Bank; at Essex it was a visit by a representative of the Ministry of Defense, and many places have used recruiters from the Dow Chemical Company and other variations on the theme of the war in Vietnam.

Almost any issue will do, provided it has two crucial features: (1) It must be an issue that can be somehow related to a Sacred Topic. In the United States, the Sacred Topics are the First Amendment, race and the war in Vietnam—in that order, though I belive that in the last year race has been pulling ahead of the First Amendment. (In France, *la révolution* is itself a Sacred Topic.) If the issue can be related to a Sacred Topic, then the majority of the students, even though they would not do anything about it themselves, will at least be sympathetic to the demonstrators' position in the early stages. (2) The issue has to be one on which the university authorities cannot give in. The authorities must initially refuse your demands. If you win, you have lost. If the authorities give in to your demands there is nothing for it but to pick another issue and start all over.

The demand, therefore, has to be presented in the maximally confrontationalist style. This usually requires a demonstration of some sort, and sit-ins are not uncommon at this stage, though a "mass meeting" or march to present your demands will often do as well. The number of people in Stage One is usually small, but they serve to "educate" the campus, to "dramatize" the issue. It is a good idea, though not always necessary in Stage One, to violate as many campus rules or civil laws as you possibly can, in as visible a manner as you possibly can, during the initial presentation of your demands. In other words, you should challenge the authorities to take disciplinary action against you, and generally they will oblige by suspending a few of your leaders.

Stage One closes when the administration rejects your demands, admonishes you to better behavior in the future and, if possible, brings some of your leaders to university discipline for rule violations in the demonstrations. Berkeley 1964 and Paris 1968 are the models of a well-managed Stage One. At Berkeley, one of the weaknesses in the issue of Eldridge Cleaver's invitation to lecture in an accredited course on racism is that university discipline has never been effectively tied to the substantive question, as it was in 1964. True, the regents, in ruling that Cleaver could give only one lecture in a course for university credit rather than the 10 for which he'd been invited, did "censure" several faculty members, but no students were involved in rule violations in Stage One, and it has subsequently proved very difficult, in spite of hard rule-violating efforts in Stage Two, to meld university discipline into the Cleaver issue.

The Creation of a Rhetorical Climate

In Stage Two the original issue is transformed so that the structure of authority in the university is itself the target. This is achieved by the following method. The fact that the university rejected the original demands and, even more, the fact that the university disciplined people for rule violations in making those demands are offered as conclusive proof that the university is the real enemy of the forces of truth and justice on the Sacred Topic. Thus, if the original demand was related to the war in Vietnam, the fact that the university disciplined a student for rule violation in making the demand is proof that the university is really working for the war and that it is out to "crush dissent." If, for example, the demonstrations were against Dow Chemical Company recruiters on campus, the fact of university discipline proves that the university is really the handmaiden (or whore) of the military-industrial complex. And the fact that the university refuses to cancel plans for the gym (Columbia) or *does* cancel plans for the Cleaver course (Berkeley) demonstrates that the university is really a racist institution. Why would anybody try to discipline our fellow students and refuse our just demands if they weren't racists, warmongers or dissent-crushers, as the case might be? And, indeed, can't we now see that the university is really just a part of much larger forces of oppression (imperialism, racism) in our American society? In the face of such proof, only the most callous or evil would fail to join us in our struggle to make this a livable university, a place where we can be truly free.

If this attempt to make the university the primary target is successful, the number of people involved in Stage Two will increase enormously. Large numbers of students who will not demonstrate illegally against the war in Vietnam or for free speech will demonstrate illegally if they can demonstrate against someone's being disciplined for illegally demonstrating against the war in Vietnam or for free speech. The original issue is made much more personal, local and "relevant" to their life as students by being redefined, with the university authorities as the main enemy. The war in Vietnam is a long way off, but Grayson Kirk's office is just across the campus. This redefinition of the issue so that the university authorities become the main target is crucial to the success of the entire operation and is the essential characteristic of a successful Stage Two.

Speeches, leaflets, meetings and articles in student papers all serve to create a certain rhetorical climate in which charges that would normally be thought to verge on the preposterous can gain currency and acceptability. Thus, the president of the university is a racist, the board of regents is trying to run the university for its personal profit, the university is fundamentally an agent of the Pentagon and so on. Anyone who remembers the witch hunts of the nineteen-fifties will recognize the distinctive features of this rhetorical atmosphere: the passionate conviction that our side is right and the other side not only wrong but evil, the urgency of the issue, the need for all of us to stand united against the threat (of Communism or the military-industrial complex, depending on your choice of era) and, most important, the burning sincerity of all but the most intelligent.

To accuse a professor of doing secret war research for the Defense Department nowadays has the same delicious impact that accusations of secret Communist party membership did a decade ago. And one even reads the same sort of nervous, apologetic prose on the part of the accused: " 'I was consultant [to the Institute for Defense Analysis] from 1964–67, when I went to meetings and listened and offered comments; however, you will not find my name on the reports,' he said" (The Daily Californian, Tuesday, Nov. 5, 1968, p. 1). The ultimate in such accusations—leaving out such horrendous charges as "He worked for the C.I.A."—are "He's a racist" and "He is in favor of the war." We are, incidentally, going to see a great deal more of this left-McCarthyism in the next few years on college campuses, especially in the United States.

In Stage Two certain new and crucial elements enter the fray—television and the faculty. It sounds odd to describe the jobs television does but here they are: it provides a leader and it dignifies the proceedings. The mechanisms by which television provides the movement with a leader are not generally well understood. It looks like the movement chooses a leader and he addresses the TV cameras on its behalf. But that is rarely what happens; in fact, that almost never happens.

What happens is that among the many speakers who appear at rallies and such, some are more telegenic than others; and the TV reporters and cameramen, who can only use a small amount of footage anyway, are professional experts at picking the one who will make the most interesting news shots. The man they pick then becomes the leader or spokesman or symbol of the movement. Of course, his selection has to be approved by the movement, so any TV selection is subject to ratification by the crowd. If they don't like him, the TV people have to find somebody else, but among the many leaders who are acceptable to the demonstrators, television plays an important role in the eventual success of one or another.

Thus Mario Savio in Berkeley, Daniel Cohn-Bendit in Paris and Mark Rudd at Columbia were people with relatively little leadership position prior to Stage One, but who, as a result of their own qualities and the fact that the television people chose them to present as leaders, were elevated to the status of leaders, at least symbolically. Both Savio and Rudd have complained of this television exaggeration. Actually, Cohn-Bendit is the purest case of mass publicity as a factor in selecting a leader, for Jacques Sauvageot, the leader of the student union, and Alain Geismar, the head of the teachers' union, were both authentic campus leaders and organizers well before Stage One ever got going, but neither is much good on TV, so neither ever attained Cohn-Bendit's symbolic stature. In a sense, the fact that television plays such an important role in the selection of the leader doesn't much matter because it is a feature of this type of political movement that leaders don't lead (they may manipulate, but lots of people who are not "leaders" do that as well); unfortunately it would take me another article to explain why this is so.

In a crazy kind of way, television also dignifies the proceedings. If you are at a demonstration at noon and you can go home and watch yourself on the 6 o'clock news, it suddenly means that the noon behavior is lifted out of the realm of juvenile shenanigans and becomes genuine historical stuff. If you are there on the box it must be pretty serious, an authentic revolutionary event.

This is a McLuhanite generation, raised with a feel for publicity in general and TV in particular. When I was an undergraduate, if you got kicked out of school you went somewhere else and tried to forget about it; nowadays you would immediately call a TV news conference and charge that you did not get due process. As a news medium, television requires the visually exciting, and campus demonstrations are ideal telegenic events; they are dramatic, colorful, often violent, and in slack moments the cameras can rest on the bearded, barefoot hippies or the good-looking, long-haired girls. In return for useful footage, the media men provide the dignity and self-respect that ordinary people derive from mass publicity.

It is very important in Stage Two that a few faculty members side with the demonstrators "on the issues." In general, they will not directly condone rule violations, but by supporting the issues of Stage One they add a stamp of approval to the whole enterprise and thus have the effect of indirectly excusing the rule violations: "It is unfortunate that there should be any disruption of the university, but it really is awful that the administration should kick poor Smith out just for sitting peacefully and nonviolently on the dean's desk for a few hours, especially when Smith was only trying to end racism and the war in Vietnam."

More important, the approval of faculty members provides a source of security and reinforcement of convictions. An undergraduate engaging in a disruption of university operations is not (at least, not yet) engaging in a conventional and established form of political behavior. He feels deeply insecure, and the stridency of his rhetoric should not conceal from us the depth of his insecurity. The apparent passionate convictions of most university demonstrators are in fact terribly fragile, and when away from the crowd many of them are fairly easily talked out of their wildest fantasies. A few faculty members can provide security and reinforcement, and are therefore a great aid in recruiting more student support. Old-fashioned people, Freudians and such, would say that the student needs the faculty member to play the role of an older sibling in his revolt against the administration-parent.

At the end of Stage Two, there is a large-scale demonstration against the university on the issue of Stage One as transformed by the rhetorical impact of Stage Two. In the United States it takes the form of a large sit-in, though this has recently been developing into the seizure ("liberation") of a building, complete with barricaded doors and windows. (In Paris, it was also a matter of building street barricades, but street barricades are a French tradition, not easily exportable, that somehow seems to survive; the survival is aided by the presence of small cars that can be used as building material.) When the sit-in or seizure occurs, the university authorities are strongly inclined to—and usually do—call out the police to arrest the people who are sitting in. When that happens, if all has gone according to the scenario, we enter Stage Three, and we enter it with a vengeance.

The Collapse of Authority

The first characteristic of Stage Three is an enormous and exhilarating feeling of revulsion against the calling of the police. The introduction of hundreds of policemen on the campus is regarded as the ultimate crime that any university administration can commit, and a properly led and well-organized student movement will therefore direct all of its efforts in Stages One and Two to creating a situation in which the authorities feel they have no choice but to call the police. Large numbers of faculty members who have so far watched nervously from the sidelines, vaguely sympathetic with the students' rhetoric but unwilling to condone the rule violations, are suddenly liberated. They are rejuvenated by being able to side with the forces of progress against the forces of authority; the anxieties of Stages One and Two are released in a wonderful surge of exhilaration: we can hate the administration for calling the cops instead of having to tut-tut at the students for their bad behavior. On the students' side, there is a similar euphoria. In Berkeley, the student health service reported in 1964 a sharp decline in the number of students seeking psychological and psychiatric help during Stage Three.

In the transition to Stage Three, the more police brutality you can elicit by baiting and taunting (or the more the police

are able to provide by themselves in the absence of such incitement), the better, but, as any competent leader knows, police brutality is not, strictly speaking, necessary because any
large-scale mass arrest will produce accusations of police brutality no matter what happens.

In the face of the sheer horror of the police on campus,
the opposition to the movement, especially the opposition among
the liberal and moderate students, becomes enfeebled and
usually· collapses altogether. At this point, there is a general
student strike with fairly strong faculty support, and quite often
the campus will be completely shut down.

Furthermore, the original demands of Stage One are now
only a small part of a marvelously escalated series of demands.
Sometimes, as in Paris, the Stage One demands may be pretty
much forgotten. Who, for example, could remember on the
barricades what Cohn-Bendit was agitating for back in Stage
One? A typical list of Stage Three demands would comprise the
following:

The president must be fired (he usually is, in fact).

There must be amnesty for all.

The university must be restructured so as to give the students a
major share in all decision-making.

The administration has to be abolished, or at any rate confined to sweeping sidewalks and such.

The university must cease all cooperation with the Defense
Department and other official agencies in the outside community.

Capitalism must end—now.

Society must be reorganized.

Meanwhile, interesting things are happening in the faculty:
committees are meeting and drafting resolutions, alliances are
being formed and petitions circulated. The faculty government, by tradition a sleepy and ill-attended body that gently
hassles about parking and by-laws, is suddenly packed with
record numbers of passionate and eloquent debaters. There are
endless amendments and fights over the symbolism of a "whereas" clause. Great victories are won and symbolic defeats sustained. Also, in the general unhinging of Stage Three many
faculty members discover all sorts of long-forgotten grievances
they have against the administration. There is simply no end
of good grievances, indeed, in our best universities I believe this
could be one of the conditions of continued employment: if you
can't think up half a dozen really good grievances against the

place you are probably not intelligent enough for continued employment in a university of top caliber.

More important, deep and abiding hostilities and hatreds grow up among various factions in the faculty. Those who are active find that their political role is more important to their standing in the community than their scholarly achievement. No matter what the issues, more energy is expended on hostilities within the faculty than on battle with any nonfaculty foes, and the passionate feelings usually go far beyond those found in the democratic politics of the real world. Like nuns struggling for power in a convent, professors seem to lack the distance and detachment to see Stage Three university politics for the engagingly preposterous affair it usually is.

So now we have come from the halcyon days of Stage One, in which there was "only a small minority with no legitimate grievances," to the full-blown revolutionary ecstasy of Stage Three; the place is shut down, the president is looking for a new job and the *effective* authorities are a handful of fairly scruffy-looking and unplausible-sounding student leaders. How does it work? What is the fuel on which the mechanism functions?

Before I answer that, I need to make the usual academic qualifications about the model: it is intended only as an analytical framework and not a complete empirical generalization. Certainly, not all successful student revolts go through these three stages, and I can think of many counterexamples, and so on. Furthermore, I do not mean to imply that anybody on either side actually plans his behavior with these three stages in mind; I am not suggesting that student leaders sit in cellars asking themselves, "Are we in Stage Two yet?" Furthermore, I am not saying that the demonstrators are either in the right or in the wrong on the demands they make. Student demonstrators, like university administrators, are sometimes right, sometimes wrong; on some occasions, such as the Free Speech Movement in Berkeley, the demonstrators have, in my view, been overwhelmingly in the right. I am just trying to describe a common pattern of events that has recurred in many places and with quite different issues, but it will be obvious from what I have said that I find it at least an *inefficient* method of resolving campus disputes.

Getting back to the question—What makes it work?—the unique feature of the present situation in universities is the pervasive dislike and distrust of authority. Far more students in the Western democracies today—more than, say, 10 years ago—hate their governments, police forces and university administrations (there are complex historical reasons for this, most of which have nothing to do with universities). I can, for example, remember when it was quite common for university presidents to be respected and admired, even on their own campuses. Now it is almost unheard of (except after they have been fired).

The strategy of a successful student movement is to unite this existing mistrust of authority with genuinely idealistic impulses of one of the Sacred Topics in such a way that assaults on university authority become a method of expressing that idealism.[1] Each new exercise of authority then becomes further proof that the administration is an enemy of the idealism, and this serves to undermine authority even more. The transition from each stage to the next, remember, is produced by the exercise of authority, and eventually—with the use of masses of policemen—if all has gone according to plan, campus authority collapses altogether. The strategy, in short, is to pit "the students" (and not "the radicals" or "the small minority") against "the administration" in a fight that appears to concern a Sacred Topic, and then to undermine the administration by provoking exercises of authority that will serve to discredit it. The three stages, then, should be seen as a continuous progression, beginning with the creation of an issue (or issues) and ending with the collapse of authority.

The demonstrators are always puzzled by the hostility they arouse among the liberal intelligentsia outside the university. But what the demonstrators perceive as the highest idealism often looks from the outside like a mixture of vandalism and imbecilic dogmatism. Though they can convince *themselves* that, say, Columbia, Stanford and Berkeley are racist institutions, few on the outside ever accept this view.

When administrations are defeated, they almost invariably go down as a result of technical mistakes, failure to grasp the nature of the struggle they are engaged in and, most important, their own demoralization. A confident administration bent on defending intellectual values, and consequently determined to destroy the power of its essentially anti-intellectual adversary,

[1] In France, because universities are part of the Government, assault on university authority are *eo ipso* assaults on the Government. In that sense, de Gaulle is a university administrator.

can generally win. Victory for the administration requires a readiness to deal with each of the three stages on its own terms and certain over-all strategies involving internal university reforms and the intelligent use of discipline (even including the police when it comes to the crunch). Curiously, many college administrations in America don't yet seem to perceive that they are all in this together. Like buffaloes being shot, they look on with interest when another of their number goes down, without seriously thinking that they may be next.

TO LIVE WITH COMPLEXITY

Franklin L. Ford

Given the plethora of articles about student unrest that leap at us from the pages of daily papers, newsmagazines, Sunday supplements, and journals of opinion, it seems almost brash to venture another written word on the subject. One feature of many (I do not say all) such treatments, however, has come to worry me a good deal. It is the tendency to simplify what are in fact exceedingly complex and differentiated problems of present-day university life. Evidence of this rage to simplify shows up in the ease with which many writers who ought to know better lump all colleges and universities together as though they shared, with only slight variations, the same administrative structures, the same social compositions and—here's where the fun begins—the same faults and weaknesses. All human institutions have their flaws and vulnerabilities, but they are not all the same flaws or uniform vulnerabilities. It does not help anyone's understanding of a given case to assume that the stakes have been the same in French and in Czechoslovakian universities, or that after Berkeley and Columbia, it is clear just what Yale or Chicago or the University of Minnesota is in for. It might be convenient for the editorialists with only limited space if colleges and universities *were* that nearly uniform; but it would also be deadly dull, and in any case, it just isn't so.

Franklin L. Ford, "To Live with Complexity," *Harvard Today* (Autumn 1968), 4–12. Reprinted by permission of the author.

A related and to my mind even more serious case of distortion through simplification afflicts those who are willing to see "student unrest" itself as a single, easily grasped phenomenon, about which we can argue as we might over a cohesive drama or a unified work of architecture. Glib generalizations breed their own species of confusion and misunderstanding. If one deplores, as I most emphatically do, the eagerness of some of our most vocal youth to see the world in terms of emotionally satisfying but intellectually worthless stereotypes— "*the* Establishment," "radical concern versus liberal moral neutrality," "government-university complicity" are only a few such —one must just as firmly deny himself the use of cant terms in talking or thinking about even the young people who rejoice in such language, not to mention the many more young people who do not.

What I propose to do in these few pages is to ask and attempt briefly to answer a series of questions which may at first seem only to complicate the issues but which can in the long run, I believe, help to increase the clarity, the sympathy, the good humor, the firmness, and the sense of shared responsibility, all of which are badly needed as we confront this part of the troubled American scene.

Here are the questions:

(1) If there is no single "student problem," how many different problems, of what orders of magnitude and intensity, need to be recognized within the general pattern of unrest on today's campuses?

(2) What can faculties and their administrations do to meet these problems, without selling out the ideal of educational freedom to the bigotry of zealots, whether from the Right or Left or Underground?

(3) Just how bad *are* things? Once we have sorted out levels and categories of problems, have we any grounds for optimism about the university's ability to deal with any or all of them?

(4) Apart from whatever success may be achieved in avoiding disruption, responding to sensible proposals for change, and maintaining the notion that education is worth more than any riot, how much danger is there that the university and college community will emerge from this time of troubles with its structure and its underlying values twisted or permanently damaged?

(5) And finally, if one finds that there is a danger of such damage, what can he—and here I speak especially to the individual professor—do to help counteract it?

The Circles of Unrest

As to the first point, the structural variety of student unrest, let me suggest a method of analysis that considers such unrest in terms of a series of concentric circles. It is a method that does not assume that all students are unhappy all the time. But it does permit us to perceive differing degrees of diffusion and also of intensity in such unhappiness as does exist. Furthermore, visualizing the circles as concentric helps to explain why students who fall within the inner ones share the discontents felt by all those in the outer, plus some additional aims and impulses *not* shared by everyone in the larger configurations.

The largest circle encompasses those, and they are many, who in one form or another are experiencing the pains of growing up, intellectually, socially, in many cases physically, while in college, a place of challenges, moments of both exhilaration and discouragement, and the competitive tension which no faculty could impose on the young with anything like the rigor youth itself brings to comparative judgments of individuals. At this level, student unrest is nothing new. Is there anyone capable of reading these words who has not felt it, shared in it some time or other? This does not mean that problems of maturing are a negligible factor, but it does mean that they are presumably part of life itself and that to disapprove of their manifold expressions has about as much meaning as would criticism of, say, the Pacific Ocean.

The second circle, which at times, I admit, seems to contain all students in the first, is nevertheless more limited by temporal circumstances. It finds its being in the particular malaise of the 1960's, not exactly a gay decade for anyone, young or old. The thought-benumbing blows of successive assassinations, the equally tragic though more comprehensible crisis of the cities, the growing bitterness of the poor amid the self-congratulations of affluence, the even greater bitterness of black Americans, rich or poor, for whom American society seems to combine legal equality with actual caste discrimination—all of these torments of our day have hit thoughtful young people with peculiar force. This is so not only because youth is a time of extreme vulnerability to grief and frustration, as well as a time of impatient, generous sympathy for the underdog, but also because young people know that they will have to live far longer than

their elders with the results of the assassinations and with the demands of militant (most students appear to believe justly militant) underprivileged groups.

Vietnam Envenoms Criticism

The war in Vietnam deserves a word of separate comment. Though the second circle of unhappiness with the events and conditions of the 1960s would exist even if America were not mired in the jungles of Southeast Asia, I am personally convinced that the war pumps in an element which is simply different in kind from anything else exciting student opposition to things as they are. Without it, we should have criticism of older people and established institutions, criticism much of which would be sharp and some of which would doubtless be raucous; but with the war, we have all of that envenomed by a sense which can only be described as one of horror. It is the war, and I believe the war alone—fought by conscripts and for stated aims its methods seem to mock—which leads so many students to charge America as a whole with the cruelty which might otherwise be attributed to the individual murderers of great men and humble civil rights workers.

To dismiss the depth of student feeling on this issue as a kind of sublimation of unadmitted cowardice makes no sense whatever. If it is foolish to suggest that some genetic miracle has suddenly produced a generation of unprecedented wisdom and moral purity—and that is obviously so foolish that many students who like to needle us with the possibility can scarcely do so without a sheepish grin—it is equally foolish to think that cowardice has broken out in the nation, or to say that "since we had to fight Hitler, why can't they see that they must save America from Ho Chi Minh?" Yet the question of courage would exist for present-day college students, even if their elders all had the good sense not to sneer. It is a question students put to themselves; and I think it not misleading to suggest that some aspects of campus demonstrations, the defiance of authority, the challenge to arrest and prosecution—in short some of the things which are hardest for older Americans to accept—are rooted at least partly in the pressing need many of the demonstrators feel to show themselves, and us, that they are not afraid of danger as such, that they *will* take risks for a cause they think is just. One can in particular cases dispute their judgment and even their definition of justice, but one cannot without imperiling comprehension deny the force of this need.

Dissenters and Militants

A third circle, considerably smaller than the second and very much smaller than the first, really comprises a variety of separate groups of dissenters whose interests occasionally overlap but whose differing complaints are not impossible to sort out. These include the militant black power advocates within universities (whom many other black students do not support but whom almost none of the latter would openly denounce); the more doctrinaire advocates of "student power," as a campaign not just to effect specific reforms but to alter the fundamental distribution of roles and responsibilities in the university; and the most resentful elements among graduate teaching fellows or teaching assistants, who not unnaturally press to have their status as teachers elevated and their status as students de-emphasized.

There are many other militant factions, but these three must suffice for purposes of illustration. Sometimes, as I say, they may attempt to cooperate, but cooperation is not easy. The graduate teaching fellow who seeks to be more honored and better paid as a teacher is scarcely the natural ally of the proponent of student power, and even the most embattled spokesmen of black students at present seem inclined to go it alone. (Last spring I heard one of the latter observe succinctly that "one thing we don't need is a bunch of guilt-ridden suburbanites around our necks.") In any case, it is worth emphasizing that the groups making up this third circle almost without exception stop short of attacking the university in all its aspects. They want to change it, obviously, but just as obviously, its survival as a center of power and influence is essential to their own strivings for advancement.

With the fourth, most restricted circle, we arrive at that segment of the student body whose behavior is most consciously provocative and who provide newspaper and television cameramen and reporters with their most prized material. Even here, I would make one final distinction. This fourth circle, it seems to me, should be restricted to the avowed "wreckers," but it too must provide room for differing motives. In addition to politically doctrinaire revolutionaries, we also confront—and we ought to say so frankly—a scattering of students who seem to be motivated by little more than mischief, a quality some of our most solemn pundits seem to me quite consistently to underestimate. We also confront—and again, this needs to be said clearly, though not without sympathy—the desperate, resentful impulse of a sad handful of individuals who could not make the grade as students and believe they have no recourse but to prove that it is they who've been right all along, the victims of a worthless system.

The politically significant part of the "wreckers' circle" does, however, comprise the few proudly self-identified campus revolutionaries, who have persuaded themselves that American society and government are corrupt beyond saving, so that to destroy a university is simply to hack away a limb of a hopelessly diseased tree. I have been asked from time to time whether I believe any of these students are serious when they call themselves Maoists, as some do. The answer is, of course I believe they are serious. If you wanted to be anti-American, yet felt hostile to the Soviets because the U.S.S.R. is another big Establishment, as well as to Castro because he supposedly failed to stand by Che Guevara, how could you do better than to salute Chairman Mao, who is remote, the enemy of a long list of established powers, and in all other respects just about ideal? This is not to say that many such students know enough about conditions in Red China to have much claim to the name of "Maoist" in any real sense, but no matter.

I have also been asked on occasion if any students "think it is enough just to wreck, not to rebuild." Of course some do, believing that to tear down a bad structure is enough for one generation—let others rebuild. (In taking this position, certain individuals may feel they are following in the tradition of Voltaire, whose *"écrasez l'infâme"* with respect to the eighteenth-century Catholic church admittedly carried with it no constructive suggestions, though I doubt that his latter-day disciples in this regard know, or for that matter care, what a moderate reformer he was in many other respects.)

My series of concentric rings, like any other schematic analysis, is open to any number of modifications and objections on the part of people who would order differently the several elements in the situation. Certainly I do not pretend to have included every such element, let alone every nuance. The important thing, however, seems to me to agree on some recognition that there *are* separate elements. If one does not do at least that much, then he falls into the danger of treating all student dissent, across the board, as though it expressed the aims and the ideology of extreme revolutionaries, who in fact remain a tiny minority. That would be unjust in concept and unhelpful in practice. The other danger of a monolithic approach might be the opposite suggestion, namely, that because a vast majority of dissenting students are not bent on creating general chaos, there are no elements of mischief or nihilism at all in the compound. That too would be both naive and inaccurate, at least in most of the cases about which I know anything.

This breakdown into circles of motives and membership I have developed at some length, for I know it may not be easily accepted by many readers inside or outside the academic community. If the need for some such basis is acknowledged, however, the answers to the other four questions with which I began come rather quickly and can be briefly stated.

What Can Be Done?

Thus, to the query "What can be done about student unrest?" let me reply that we must go on trying to deal with its several sources in several different ways, trying not to overreact but to meet each complaint or demand in terms which our constituents will recognize as neither repressive nor supine, but responsive. To the uneasy young adult of the first, largest circle we must go on offering, and seeking to improve, the advice and help of proctors, of masters and tutors in the residential Houses, of instructors and section men within specific courses, and of more technically trained staff members of the Bureau of Study Counsel. When still more professional attention is required, the University Health Services will as in the past offer their medical, including psychiatric, expertise. The techniques of counseling at all levels are still far from perfect, but in my own 20 years as a college teacher I have seen them win more attention and acquire more sophistication with each passing year. Communication can always be improved, and we must keep working at it; but to say that in a present-day American college or university the student cannot talk to anyone is pure poppycock. It may be easier for him in some institutions and harder in others, but in none known to me is it impossible.

For the second circle, the students most worried by the issues of the day, we can and do offer the chance to discuss those issues in an almost limitless range of situations: in the class-room, in various sponsored group meetings, in wholly informal, and generally nocturnal, bull sessions. Beyond that, I think students have come to realize more and more, especially in just the last few months, that college faculties and administrations do not constitute uncritical pillars of unanimous support for public policies young people want to hear challenged and debated.

As for the third circle, that of specific "interest groups," we must seek, again, to speak to each in its own terms. We shall continue to engage black students in the search for qualified candidates for admission back in their home communities and in the planning of courses, both formal and informal, having to do with the experience of Afro-Americans, including their ancestral roots in Africa itself; but we must reject the notion of guaranteed quotas of black students or staff, as we have resisted past demands for other, essentially negative, ethnic quotas. To the proponents of "student power," we shall continue to offer the chance to make their case for student representation on various faculty committees; but we need not surrender the very concept of differentiation of roles as among governing boards, faculty members, and students. As for disgruntled teaching fellows, we adjust pay scales (as Harvard has just done this fall) when we can be shown the clear need to do so and when we can afford it. For the rest, many departments have shown an increasing sensitivity to the problems of their graduate students who are spending two or three years as apprentice teachers while en route to the Ph.D. Such advanced graduate students can, and I think will, be drawn increasingly into discussions of serious pedagogical matters.

School Will Keep

For what I have portrayed as the narrowest circle, the mis-chief-makers and their solemn fellow-revolutionaries, we have tried to make clear that, like all other students, they have the right to be heard and that we will defend them as individuals against attacks aimed simply at their opinions. On the other hand, without wanting to predict just what action would be taken in any of a long series of hypothetical, and wholly unpredictable, situations, we need to identify at least two kinds of behavior that cannot be tolerated in an educational community.

The first is obstruction of the teaching and learning process itself, whether in classrooms or libraries or laboratories. In short, school is going to keep. The second kind of behavior which must be recognized as egregious, in the most literal sense, is that which violates the civil rights, including the free movement, of other individuals. As I say, it seems unhelpful to elaborate rigid tariffs of crimes and punishments; but on the two central points just noted, it seems to me that the education of the university community should now be complete, and that from here on, no one should expect to violate either of these self-evident rules and still retain his membership in that community.

My third proposed question had to do with the present state of things, seen against a background of visible discontents and corresponding efforts to deal with them as sympathetically as possible and as firmly as necessary. If we can learn any one thing from history, it is that, whether or not one accepts the Greeks' explanation of wrath on Olympus, the uncritically optimistic assertion that things are getting better is all too often the signal for them to get much worse. Nevertheless, there has been so much gloom generated by commentators who either fear student activists in general or distrust everyone who has anything to do with running a college or university, that I feel impelled to report that this year the feeling of rancor and of incipient explosion within Harvard University seems somewhat reduced from the worst levels of 1967–68. (Last year may in fact prove to have been the worst, but very much the worst, of several bad ones for American higher education.) Demands for change and for reform will continue; they may get much louder; but they are not the same as destructive frenzy.

I am not being wholly impressionistic in this, although there is no denying that a university, like any other social organism, has a somewhat different "feel" about it at various times and that numerous people concerned can agree on the general import of that "feel," without being able to explain it precisely. In any event, I can cite three examples to show that if this latest age of student revolution has not wholly yielded to one of student progressivism and reform, there are some restraints detectable in the attitudes of large numbers of students. First, the cycle of violent and genuinely destructive university uprisings, notably those at Columbia, Paris, Berlin, and Mexico City, seems to have left many young people frankly tired of that way of seeking change. I refuse to generalize confidently about this, and

I know that some observers think we are still skidding downhill toward genuine chaos; but what I have been observing in our own institution has been supported by reports from several others, to the effect that most students do want to finish their educations and have now had ample opportunity to see the threat to that aim implicit in mindless violence, regardless of who unleashes it or for what motive.

Second, whatever place Senator Eugene McCarthy ultimately comes to hold in political history, it seems to me that his place in the history of higher education in America is already secure. Admittedly, after the rush back into political participation on the part of college students, triggered by his presidential candidacy and quite predictably interrupted at the Democratic National Convention, many students have lapsed into cynicism once more or have announced themselves as simply "turned off"—for this year anyway. But what impresses me is the very large number who have *not* reacted that way. One of the new student organizations at Harvard is called the Committee for a New Politics and is made up of young people who are determined to go on working within the system, this year supporting specific candidates for the Senate and the House of Representatives whose views they endorse. Thereafter, quite obviously, these students hope to win through the slow, patient processes of the electoral system at its roots what they found they could not achieve by stepping in last winter at its top.

Finally on this count, let me simply point out what I imagine all of us have known at one time or another but may on occasion have forgotten, namely, that most students, most of the time, are skeptical of apodictic statements and apocalyptic visions. They do not believe everything they hear from their parents or from politicians, from professors or from deans, but neither do they believe everything they hear from each other. At their best, they strike me as better able to cut through pompous jargon and unproven claims than are certain of their elders who hover over them in a mixture of apprehension and solicitude.

Are Universities in Danger?

Let me conclude by pulling together the last two questions I asked at the outset. Are there any dangers of long-term damage to the quality of the universities in this country, growing out of recent events and the present atmosphere? And if there are, what can we do right now to reduce that danger? So far as grounds for fear are concerned, I am not sure that there are any I would confidently set against the corresponding chance that out of the turmoil will come some long-term gains. However, I should mention just two possible residues that are worrisome.

One would be the blurring, all across the country, of the recognition by college and university *faculties* of their own absolutely pivotal role in dealing with student unrest. I know of no case of a major blow-up in a university where a fraction of the faculty had not contributed to the trouble by fudging the issues, whether moral, legal or simply rational. Perhaps still more ominous, however, has been the evidence that in some of these cases a somewhat larger part of the faculty involved viewed the crisis as none of its business. Where the line separating "administration" from "the faculty" is very sharp, this danger is particularly acute; where it is less sharp, it seems to me that there has been less trouble. But everywhere, there lingers the possibility that faculty members, who in the last analysis must give corporate sense and continuity to a college, will fall back instead on their right to teach what they please, do their research, and leave the affairs of the institution to those of their younger colleagues who "seem to get along better with the students."

The other possibly damaging hangover would be what I can only identify as a hidden anti-intellectualism, a concern with strong, reputedly visceral moral impulses, which may be admirable in themselves but do not alone qualify anyone to call himself an educated man. It is perfectly obvious that the "intellectual" approach to any topic is not the only possible one, that faith, aesthetic taste, even mysticism and intuition may add to the findings of a disciplined mind. But the intellectual approach *is* the business of colleges and universities, and neither students nor faculty members should fool themselves that they can express contempt for it without repudiating the very interests that presumably brought them together. Words like "concern," "sincerity," "commitment," "bias in favor of good causes," all have a pleasant sound and connotation, but if they were to be put up in opposition to "clarity," "comprehensiveness," and "accuracy of information," then I would wonder what really was left to be discussed in an academic community.

The Curious Reticence

What can we do about our present tensions and our possible dangers? Here, since no one can justly commit his colleagues to what they must do, I can only say what I intend to do. On the one hand, I shall go on encouraging the acceptance of faculty responsibility for the hardest, because most central, decisions we have to take, including when necessary the distasteful business of discipline. Far more important, however, I propose to try to overcome in myself, as I hope many other faculty members will in themselves, the curious reticence which the liberal academic has long shown with respect to the positive values he knows very well are central to his as to many other professions and, indeed, to the survival of any academic community at all. Because academic freedom has tended to be defined primarily in negative terms, as demands and assurances that certain kinds of self-expression will not be interfered with, it is now potentially vulnerable to challenges by some (blessedly few) individuals in the university community who will use it in their own defense but scorn it as a right of everyone else in that community. Even if that were not so, the fact that we have been so much on the defensive in meeting loud, specific demands for action, without regard to that action's implications for freedom, indicates some things have not been getting said as clearly as they should have.

I believe explicitly, and shall say so whenever I am asked, that the university is not only an over-arching institution at one extreme and a collection of thousands of individual human beings at the other but also, and very importantly, a maze of sub-communities—departments, musical and dramatic societies, social and social service clubs, athletic teams, houses and dormitories, faculty committees, student committees, mixed committees—in short that it cannot and must not be turned into a mish-mash, a theoretically undifferentiated horde of people more or less continuously engaged in plebiscites on poorly understood questions.

Even in this age of concern and advocacy, I believe, and shall go on saying, that the *search* for objectivity is an essential part of the search for knowledge; and that while no man can be wholly unbiased, the effort to recognize and then to reduce bias is one of the noblest exercises of the human mind. Noble enough, I might add, so that the soundest and most generous approach even to a "gut issue" cannot be divorced from that effort.

Lastly, I believe firmly and explicitly that there can be no special rules for anyone, whatever his claim to moral superiority and "commitment," at the expense of anyone else. Vehemence is no substitute for equity; and if we yield to demands for special rules, he who now demands them might well one day turn out to be their victim. That's how cards can come up, even— or perhaps especially—from a stacked deck.

THE STUDENT DRIVE TO DESTRUCTION

Louis J. Halle

> " 'We shall destroy because we are a force,' observed Ar-
> kady. . . . 'Yes, a force is not to be called to account.' . . .
> " 'Allow me, though,' began Nikolai Petrovitch. 'You deny
> everything; or, speaking more precisely, you destroy every-
> thing. But one must construct too, you know.'
> " 'That's not our business now. The ground wants clearing
> first.' "
>
> Turgenev, Fathers and Sons

To understand the implications of the students' revolt for the
future of our civilization one should place it in its historical
setting. As a movement of rejection it represents the nihilism
that has been developing for over a century now, to the point
where it is at last becoming the dominant intellectual drive of
our time.

The word "nihilism" was introduced into the common language in 1862, when Turgenev published his *Fathers and Sons,*
a compassionate novel dealing with the gap between the generations. Bazarov, the young nihilist who is its hero, represents the
revolt of the new generation against the old, against its whole
traditional culture.

By the second half of the nineteenth century that traditional

Louis J. Halle, "The Student Drive to Destruction," *The New Republic* (October 19, 1968), 10–13. Reprinted by Permission of *The New
Republic,* © 1968, Harrison-Blaine of New Jersey, Inc.

culture was losing such innate authority as it had once had. It was the possession of a ruling élite, expressed in the affectation of high ideals that took no account either of the findings of science or of the impoverished lives of the great majority of people, on whose labor the élite lived. Nihilism, in these circumstances, was not entirely without point. According to Bazarov's disciple, the student Arkady, "a nihilist is a man who does not bow down before any authority, who does not take any principle on faith, whatever the reverence in which it may be enshrined." Such nihilism stood for a frank recognition of reality, for a society based on science rather than on an obsolete idealism.

Those who affected the culture that the original nihilists opposed took an optimistic view of human nature—that is, they made a polar distinction between their own noble nature, which was soulful, and the nature of the brute beasts. Man, in their view, was essentially divine, created in the image of his maker, and if he had fallen into evil he was still capable of the redemption that they, themselves, pretended to represent. The nihilists, responding to the initial impact of Darwinism, denied this distinction between men and beasts. (Turgenev began writing his great novel just as *The Origin of Species* was published.) For the piously optimistic view of human nature they substituted a new view in the name of scientific realism. Their denial that man was the divine creature he pretended to be took a particularly persuasive form, at last, in the works of Freud and the Freudians, who concluded that men are governed by the destructive forces that represent their basic animal nature, however either sublimation or hypocrisy may cover them up.

Throughout the Victorian Age ladies and gentlemen had pretended to be exempt from the bestial impulses that are, in fact, common to us all. The way new generations were produced was an unmentionable secret, not to be acknowledged—above all, to be kept from the members of the new generation until, inevitably, they at last learned about it in the shame of the wedding night.

With the revolt against Victorianism that followed World War I, Freudianism became a religion among the advanced intellectuals. The zeal with which it was adopted and preached in the 1920's can be understood only if one appreciates the release from former shame and inhibitions that it provided. Those of the new generation who had secretly entertained "wicked thoughts," believing that decent people did not have them, suddenly learned that everyone had them, including their hypocritical elders. The Freudian psychoanalyst, to whom so many of these people now turned, relieved them of the moral burden they had borne. They confessed to him and he took away the shame. The experience was that of an ineffable liberation.

There were other forms of liberation as well, stemming from the thesis that everyone should rid himself of his inhibitions, inhibitions associated with the hypocritical tradition of the Victorian generation. The extreme exponents of this thesis organized free-love camps and nudist communities. For the most part, however, what it produced was greater verbal frankness, together with a more relaxed and informal relationship between the sexes. Women got off the pedestal that had held them at such a distance from men, and by dressing and behaving so as to reduce the differences between the sexes they made possible a camaraderie with men that, a generation earlier, would have been regarded as improper. (They gave themselves a flat-chested appearance by means of the newly invented brassieres, which were simply tight bands; they cut their hair short, and they smoked cigarettes.) All this was the beginning of what we call permissiveness.

These two trends—the disposition to regard man as essentially beastly, and permissiveness—have both continued through the half century since the First World War, until they have at last reached the predominance they are manifesting today. Today, books advancing the thesis that man is a predatory aggressor by nature are welcomed and acclaimed by the intellectual community. At the same time, all censorship and most of the traditional restrictions on sexual indulgence are denounced.

There is a paradox of disastrous implications here. At the same time that man is represented as being an aggressive beast, incapable of moral responsibility, the inhibitions that society has hitherto imposed on his freedom to indulge his nature are to be removed.

Throughout the history of political philosophy, an optimistic view of human nature has been associated with the advocacy of freedom, a pessimistic view with authoritarianism. The pessimistic view that Plato took, in consequence of the disasters that popular rule had just brought upon Athens, was the basis of the authoritarianism advocated in *The Republic*. In ancient China, the optimistic view of human nature led the Mohists to advocate a society based on love rather than force, while the pessimistic view led the Legalists to advocate a police state. Russian authoritarianism, alike under the czars and their successors, is associated with the accepted view that men are destructive creatures who, if only for their own sakes, have got to be held down.

Our own Western tradition of liberalism, which goes back through Thomas Jefferson to John Locke, was justified by the optimistic view of man's nature that prevailed in the eighteenth century. This is also true of the Jacobin tradition, which goes back through Karl Marx to Rousseau. Marx was explicit in his conception of human nature as basically creative rather than destructive. Consequently, he looked forward to the day when, capitalism having been liquidated, the coercive state would wither away, after which men would enjoy in perpetuity perfect freedom for the indulgence of their natural creativity.

IN THE FACE of the logic these cases exemplify, how can one explain the present advocacy of permissiveness by those who regard man as an irremediably greedy, aggressive, and predatory beast? This stands opposed to the logic I have cited, which also takes the form of the principle that men can be free only to the extent that they make a disciplined use of their freedom. It is only where men are prepared to deal tolerantly with the diversity among them, and to abide voluntarily by "the rules of the game," that freedom is possible. Where men will not tolerate the expression of opinions different from their own, and where they refuse to accept decisions reached in accordance with "the rules of the game," the impositions of the police state become unavoidable. Anyone who has raised children knows, from direct experience, that freedom is a function of the capacity for socially responsible and considerate behavior.

It is the tradition of civility in the United States and Britain, expressed in self-restraint, that has hitherto made possible the relative freedom enjoyed by their peoples, and it is the extreme moderation of the Swiss in resolving their internal differences, which are great, that makes possible the freedom they enjoy today. Here we have demonstrations of the fact that human nature, at an advanced stage of civilization, is capable of such self-discipline as a free society requires.

If one looks at the mixed historical record of mankind, or if one consults one's own experience of the people one has known, it is quite impossible to believe that man is either all bad or all good. He may be properly described, it seems to me, as a beast with a soul. Even if I were willing to concede that the evil was predominant in him—in the sense that he was governed by his animal appetites, by a desire to destroy, by a lust for power—

even so, if there is only one spark in the darkness of his nature, there is, in that spark, a basis for unlimited hope. In spite of the fashionable anthropology of our day, which identifies him as a predatory beast, it seems to me clear that man, in his evolution, has already made noticeable progress in rising above the level of his pre-human ancestors.

This is a view for which abundant evidence could be adduced, but it is not a view that can gain a hearing today because it is, for the depressing reasons I have already cited, so unwelcome to those who represent the intellectual fashions of our day. If I should write a book showing that man, like the great carnivores, is predatory by his unchangeable nature, I could be sure that it would be widely read and acclaimed: but if I wrote a book that took an optimistic and teleological view of man's evolution, regarding it as an ascent from the level of the beasts to something ethically and spiritually higher, it would hardly be well received and few would read it. The burden of living up to a high standard is something men can do without. I do not think that this situation will change in what remains of this century, for we seem to be in one of those long periods when civilization, in decline, produces the kind of thinking appropriate to such decline. But if the Phoenix ever rises again, its rise will be accompanied by the general optimism that periods of progress always produce.

Men tend to be what they think they are. If they accept a view of themselves as self-indulgent they will tend to be self-indulgent; if they accept a view of themselves as morally responsible beings they will tend to be morally responsible. I do not think that the widespread denial of social inhibitions on human behavior, which we call permissiveness, is altogether unrelated to the prevalent view of what our human nature really is. Here is a logic that does, in fact, associate the two trends of our time: the hopeless view of our human nature and the assault on social inhibitions. If we are really pigs, rather than fine ladies and gentlemen, then we should not be asked to behave like fine ladies and gentlemen. We should be free to use language regarded as obscene, and there should be no restrictions on theatrical exhibitions of sexual and sadistic practices, no matter how sickening some of them may be. (Whatever may be said in favor of freedom for obscenity, I submit that it is not on the same level of importance as the freedoms guaranteed by the first ten amendments of our Constitution.)

I do not offer this, however, as the primary explanation of

how it is that those who regard man as fundamentally bestial are, nevertheless, the advocates of permissiveness. A further explanation is that they are not really interested in the maintenance or enlargement of a régime of freedom that, on the one hand, they tend to take for granted (having never experienced anything else), and that, on the other, does not in itself cure the intractable problems of our societies. The causes they nominally espouse are not necessarily causes they believe in, but mere pretexts for action that has other ends than their success. Any number of activist students admit in private that when they shout for Marx or Mao or Castro that does not mean they care anything about what these figures stand for. They do not carry intellectual responsibility that far.

SOME OF THE STUDENT leaders have, on occasion, made it clear that what they really want is power for themselves (thereby exemplifying the fashionable anthropological view of human nature). At other times they have not bothered to deny that destruction is, for them, an end in itself—relieving them, as such, of any need to think beyond it. If they invoke causes that are genuinely idealistic and progressive, such as human equality or freedom, they do so for tactical purposes only. They invoke them as pretexts on the basis of which they can confuse men of good will and rally the forces of destruction. When German student leaders led their followers, last September, in a violent physical assault on the Leipzig Book Fair, the reason they gave was that the directors of the Fair had chosen President Senghor of Senegal as the recipient of the Fair's peace prize when they might have chosen, instead, Mr. Stokely Carmichael, the apostle of violence. Here the cynicism is patent.

No one, I gather, doubts the intelligence of these student leaders, however gullible their followers may be. In preferring violence to free speech they know, as the Nazi leaders knew, that its success would spell the end of such free speech as I am exercising in this article. When they deliberately and skillfully provoke a bewildered police force into acts of brutality, and then denounce its "fascism," they know the equivocation in which they are indulging. When they denounce the authorities of New York City as being the rulers of a "police state," and oppose them on that basis, they know that a police state is what their movement, if carried to the lengths they intend, would bring about.

It is no answer to say that there are real and important

matters for grievance. Of course there are! The point is that the proponents of violence are not really acting, as they pretend, to eliminate these matters. Their leaders, at least, know that, if there are stupid professors (a grievance one student offered me as justification for violent demonstrations), destroying the universities is not the way to get intelligent ones. They know that white discrimination against blacks will not be overcome by a course of action that makes votes for Wallace and pushes the American society in the direction already taken by South Africa. The leaders who know these things are acting cynically, however idealistic what they are doing may seem to older intellectuals who think themselves back in 1848.

Violence and destruction for its own sake prepare the way for the police state, as violence and destruction in Germany prepared the way for Hitler's dictatorship. Specifically, they prepare the way for brutal and ignorant leaders to assume the power of a state that, in our case, possesses a nuclear armament with which it could destroy the world. For those who pursue destruction as an end in itself, the possibilities are now unlimited.

One thing that separates my generation from the generation of my children is the experience it has had of the great depression and of the decade during which the tyranny of the fascist police state seemed likely to engulf the world. My generation has vivid knowledge of how easily the structure of civilization can collapse, and of how terrible the consequences can be in terms of human suffering. Our children, on the other hand, have at best read about these experiences in history books. All that most of them have experienced at first hand is full employment, unlimited opportunity to make a living, and the remarkable freedom of speech and behavior that they have enjoyed in an increasingly permissive society. (On the Berkeley campus, a couple of years ago, I saw earnest-looking boys and girls, righteous indignation written on their faces, sitting behind a table marked "Committee for Sexual Libertinism," and I wondered who was preventing them from simply going ahead and engaging in it.)

I cannot imagine that many of those who say they are willing to face the eventuality of a police state, as the consequence of their actions, would not change their minds if ever they found themselves living under one. I have emphasized the element of cynicism in their conduct—but it is accompanied by an innocence of either experience or knowledge that contributes to their moral irresponsibility. (It was Irwin Cobb who said: the trouble with the younger generation is that it hasn't read the minutes of the last meeting.)

I have no doubt that, if mankind is on a long upward path over the millennia, that path will continue to be marked, in the future as in the past, by great crashes of civilization. I cannot quite believe that one of these crashes will spell a final end to the hopes of mankind; but we are now entering a period of human history when new dangers, produced by scientific progress, require us to exercise a greater self-control than ever before. It is not impossible, as a consequence of the breakdown in the discipline of civilization, that Mr. George Wallace or someone like him will become President of the United States in 1973, with responsibility for its international relations and with control over its nuclear armament.

I have talked to students who believe that the basic procedure of democracy is represented by violence in the streets, and that freedom means doing whatever one pleases. To the extent that each generation is responsible for educating the next, my generation must regard itself as a notable failure.

BRINGING
ABOUT CHANGE

Louis J. Halle

When I submitted my article ("The Student Drive to Destruction," October 19) to the editor of *The New Republic,* I said in the covering letter that I would expect it to bring in a storm of dissenting letters. "Some," I wrote, "will misrepresent what I say in it, some will be personal attacks designed to discredit me rather than my arguments, and some will take intelligent issue with the arguments themselves. If the article were to inaugurate a constructive debate in your letter columns it would have to be on the basis of the third category—and I would very much welcome a constructive debate."

The dissenting letters have now come in, and copies of them have been sent me for such rejoinders as I might wish to accompany their publication. However, after writing brief responses to the first five I received, their accumulating volume became so great that I could no longer deal with them individually. My problem, then, was to find in their largely repetitive mass a basis for the constructive debate to which I had looked forward. In this, however, I was to be disappointed, if only because the rules on which constructive debate depend—such as exclusion of personal abuse, of misrepresentation, and of unsupported accusations—do not apply in a situation like this as they do, for example, in a parliamentary assembly.

Louis J. Halle, "Bringing about Change," *The New Republic* (November 23, 1968), 19–22. Reprinted by Permission of *The New Republic,* © 1968, Harrison-Blaine of New Jersey, Inc.

I should observe, here, that I do not know which of the letters the editors will publish, and that I am deliberately refraining from suggesting the choice to be made.

Few of the letters assume that the arguments in my article, even if mistaken, deserve respectful consideration. Presumably on that account, almost none are either thoughtful in their approach or deliberative in their style. Their language is, instead, full of the loose and general terms that serve for rhetorical denunciation rather than reasoned argument.

A curious circumstance is that the great majority of their authors indulge in abuse of me that range from contempt for my mental abilities to insult. I say this is curious because I have no doubt that, in direct conversation with me, most of them would be courteous, however frank in their dissent, and willing to talk in terms of such mutual consideration as might lead to a better understanding of the issues by both parties. Writing for publication, however, they presumably respond to the widespread attitude that prefers what is "hard-hitting" to what is intelligent.

In making my general response to the mass of letters before me, I shall overlook the personal abuse and all the language that represents the level of sneering controversy on a school-playground.

FIRST LET ME DEAL with what appears to represent misunderstanding rather than disagreement.

The commonest basis of misunderstanding between my hostile interlocutors and me is a difference in perspective. As my opening sentence stated, what the article undertook to do was to place "the student drive to destruction" in its historical setting. It proceeded, then, to describe certain aspects of secular evolution over more than a century past. One aspect was the general acceptance, in our culture, of a conception of man that, by contrast with earlier conceptions, emphasized his animal nature. I cited Darwinism, Freudianism, and current writers who hold that man is a predatory aggressor by his basic nature. While I did not disagree with Darwin's conception (which I share), or with Freud's (which seems to me a great mythical vision full of valid insights), I did indicate my doubts about some interpretations that had been put upon them. Today, in any case, we are all brought up to a view of human nature that, by contrast with the view of earlier centuries, emphasizes the animal appetites, including the lust for power, and this is part of the conceptual background of current manifestations against the artificial disciplines imposed by our traditional civilization.

This long view, depending on a degree of detachment, was not comprehended by those of my interlocutors who, standing on the barricades, were not looking beyond the issues of the moment. They therefore interpreted me as saying that the extremist students, reading books by "Robert Ardrey and others," were thereby moved to embark on destructive rampages. In fact, I suppose that most of these students have not read these books.

What I did not bring out in the article as perhaps I should have, is that most people act on a conception of mankind that attributes goodness to themselves and their associates, however great the wickedness of others. Some of my interlocutors took me to task for being blind to the fact that the revolting students had faith in themselves. ("Faith" is one of those words that connotes, however irrationally, some kind of virtue in itself.) But I suppose that Mr. George Wallace and his followers also have faith in themselves.

Another basis of misunderstanding was the view that my article was an attack on the entire younger generation, or on all students, or on all those students who show discontent with the *status quo*. I had thought it clear, however, that the only students to whom it referred were those who had, in the nihilistic tradition, taken destruction as their objective and violence as their means. Since several letters said or implied that such students were largely a product of my own imagination, I here offer, what I had thought unnecessary, evidence to the contrary.

Messrs. Rader and Anderson, who were close to the group that planned and made the insurrection at Columbia, reported in *The New Republic* for May 11 last that the issues on which it was ostensibly based were pretexts designed to enlist the support of those who could be expected to take them in good faith. "The point of the game," they reported, "was power. . . . Everywhere the purpose was to destroy institutions of the American Establishment, in the hope that out of the chaos a better America would emerge." (Note that hope is not a design, and makes no intellectual demands.)

Claire Sterling in *The Reporter* of May 2 last wrote that "a university student striker in Rome was asked what he and his rebels wanted. He replied: 'No demands, no delegations, no deals, no dialogue. The occupation continues. The battle has no objective, it is the objective.' "

I am impressed by the fact that the movement referred to here is distinguished from similar revolts of the past, except those of pure nihilism, by the lack of coherent intellectual content. The old and worn formulations of nineteenth-century radicalism are used to cover up the absence of constructive thought. Surely this is why a student leader can, on one day, advance the anarchists' demand for the permanent elimination of all institutions, and on the next demand a dictatorship of the workers.

A third point of misunderstanding (I call it that because I am here assuming the good faith of all who wrote in) was that I was, at least, indifferent to the great evils in American life, notably the involvement in Vietnam and the plight of black Americans. To use the words of Mr. Dean Acheson when confronted, in the 1950s, with the accusations of McCarthyites, "I accept the humiliation" of defending myself against imputations that I should not have been called upon to answer at all.

I have been consistently against the American involvement in what I have publicly characterized (*N.Y. Times,* March 3, 1968) as "this wrong and calamitous war."

I have been consistently against racism, and have explicitly taken the position that every man should be considered on his own merits, without regard to race. This is a theme of my book *Men and Nations* (Princeton, 1962). It follows that, in so far as the advocates of black power are racist, I do not share their views.

Beside these points of misunderstanding, there are points of genuine disagreement between my interlocutors and me.

I DO NOT AGREE with the position taken by many of them that the state of our universities or the state of our societies is so bad that no alternatives could be worse. There are extremes of exaggeration here that I must suppose to be rhetorical if I am to avoid attributing an implausible degree of ignorance to those of my interlocutors who indulge in them. A number of letters make the claim that there is no real freedom in American society, which is under a ruling establishment that prevents its practice. (I can imagine that President Johnson, the leader of this establishment, may have moments when he wishes he really did have the power to prevent, for example, expressions of dissent from his Vietnamese policy.) Their own views on this and everything else, however, are freely printed and circulated, as those of their counterparts in Russia and China are not. Nor have the students I have seen on American campuses in the last few years seemed to be lacking in freedom.

I agree with M. Jean-Paul Sartre's thesis that the principal moral and psychological burden borne by men today is that of their own freedom. It may be that no generation of students has ever had such a wide range of freedom, both in expressing themselves and in choosing what to make of their lives, as the present generation in the United States. I suspect that it is more than many of them can bear, and that this accounts for the frantic and incoherent elements in their behavior. Some may be genuinely moved, although unconsciously, to use their freedom in order to destroy their freedom.

Although I have been rebelliously inclined toward our higher educational institutions ever since I was an undergraduate, and remain so, I find that the proponents of destruction are generally obscure in their indictments. There is genuine cause for grievance that many professors neglect the students in order to pursue activities not directly related to their educational duties. University administrations are often insensitive or indifferent to student needs. The empty pretentiousness of a good deal that passes for scholarship cries out for the pen of a Voltaire. Many professors have acquired a habit of intellectual arrogance equivalent to that criticized by Socrates when he reported his experience of consulting the sophists. But these evils have always been with us. They represent, in part, the limitations of all organized human enterprise, and even though they have lately been aggravated by the problems of growth they seem inadequate to support the view that no alternative could be worse.

How about the plight of black Americans? Here I must refer my interlocutors to an article by Professor Nathan Glazer in the October *Encounter* entitled "America's Race Paradox: the Gap between Social Progress and Political Despair." Quite devoid of special pleading, this is the most thoughtful and intelligent sociological study I can remember ever reading. It cites evidence that the status of the Negro in America, however unsatisfactory it still is, has been improving rapidly, not only in material terms but also in terms of political enfranchisement and of the consideration with which he is treated by his white compatriots. At the same time, however, the view is coming to be generally accepted that his position in our society could not be worse or more hopeless than it is today.

After Martin Luther King's assassination, which profoundly shocked and grieved the overwhelming majority of white Americans, a former student of mine, writing in a Geneva newspaper, quoted as if it were authoritative the statement that this act was the answer of "white America" to the Negro's demand for equality. Reading it, I thought in the words of Shakespeare's Henry V: "I was never angry until now." For that scurrilous statement identified me, the Editor-in-Chief of *The New Republic,* and all other white Americans as being on the side of the assassin.

In the Book Review section of *The New York Times* last June 2, Mr. James Baldwin wrote: "White America appears to be seriously considering the possibilities of mass extermination." Speaking to a Negro audience last February, Mr. Stokely Carmichael said: "Many of us feel—many of our generation feel—that they are getting ready to commit genocide against us." These statements are equivalent to shouting "Fire!" in a crowded theater where there is no fire. They incite Negroes to desperate acts of violence that tend to bring on the evil they fear, if anything could, thereby putting into play the principle of the self-fulfilling prophecy. Precisely this kind of exaggeration is used by some of my interlocutors to justify the drive to destroy our traditional society.

Let me conclude my remarks on this point by quoting a writer who belongs to a generation older than my own. In the international *Herald-Tribune* of last August 22, Mr. Brooks Atkinson made the following categorical assertion: "Life could not be more ugly or futile than it is in America at the moment." In the very same issue of the very same paper, the banner headline read: "Soviet Bloc Occupying Czechoslovakia."

A final point of disagreement. At least one writer denounces me for comparing today's student practitioners of violence with those who, in Germany, contributed to the rise of Hitler (as ours are contributing to the rise of Wallace). In last July's *Encounter,* M. Raymond Aron wrote: "When, last January, I met the angry students of Berlin, I could not help remembering the angry students of 1930 and 1931, whom I met at a moment when I had just crossed to the other side of the barricades. They, too, as they told me at the time, were necessarily in the right because they represented the future (it bore the name of Hitler). Even then, Professor Marcuse, the *grand-père* of today's angry young men, categorically rejected the existing régime (at that time, the Weimar Republic)." Is it possible that there were some, at the time, who maintained that nothing could be worse than the Weimar Republic? It has been said that those who cannot learn from history are condemned to repeat it.

Having dealt with the prevailing exaggerations and their dangers, let me now say that I agree with those who conceive that the whole tone of our national life is deteriorating. I have publicly expressed my concern at the dominance of "the military-industrial establishment," and at the decline of sensitivity and thoughtfulness in Washington. (See my *The Cold War as History*, New York, 1967, pp. 204 and 316.) There is the ugliness of our cities and suburbs, the despoliation of our countryside, the pollution of our atmosphere, the strident vulgarity of our radio and television programs. There was the miserable choice offered us in the election. Some of the letter-writers say that it is against this degradation in the tone of our national life that the students are rebelling.

Surely there is some truth in this—but it does not apply to the extremists to whom I refer. For one of the most prominent manifestations of the degradation in the tone of our national life is the behavior of these extremists. I take as just one example the assaults of verbal obscenity that students on the Columbia campus last spring made against middle-aged and elderly passers-by who were, for the most part, complete strangers to them. There were cases in which unknown elderly gentlemen were entirely surrounded by students calling them obscene names, and on at least one occasion the assailants spat in the face of an eminent man whom most of us would consider, if not distinguished, at least worthy of respect. Do these students stand for the human dignity that is being demeaned in America? Do they represent a movement to raise the tone of American life?

One final point, and the most important of all for those of us who do genuinely cherish freedom of speech. I have been publishing articles for over thirty years now, and in my experience there has been a spectacular increase, of late, in the mindless and abusive mail they evoke. Even an essentially uncontroversial essay, written in the spirit of a Charles Lamb ("Why I Am for Space Exploration," *New Republic*, April 6), produced a spate of letters that, if they dealt with my arguments at all, did so in terms of *ex-cathedra* contradiction without substantiation; that misrepresented what I had written; and that, for the rest, simply denounced me as a fool or a villain.

Beyond a certain point this kind of thing is inhibiting of free speech. During the McCarthyism of the 1950s public discussion of a wide range of issues (e.g., China policy) was stopped completely by it. Today's conditions have not yet reached anything like this extreme. But the threat is manifest in the experience I have just reported. There are many of us who will, on occasion, prefer to maintain silence if, as the immediate consequence of expressing our opinions, we are going to find ourselves wiping the mud from our faces. The ultimate result might be to leave the field of public debate to the yahoos, of whom the younger generation has as many as any other.

Such degradation of representative democracy has occurred before. Let anyone who doubts it read Thucydides—and then, if only as a supplement, Plato's *Apology*.

THE
PROSPECTS OF
THE ACADEMY

Sidney Hook

I began my college career in the fall of 1919, almost a half century ago. My academic lifetime spans half a dozen revolutions in American education. But have no fear, I am not going to reminisce. I want to stay young, at least in spirit, and I learned from my teacher, John Dewey, whom I observed closely for the last 25 years of his life, what the secret of staying young is, and that is *not* to reminisce about the past. Actually, I never heard John Dewey reminisce until he was in his nineties, and that was as a reluctant response to my deliberate prodding in order to extract biographical data from him.

However, there is a way of talking about the past that is not merely reminiscence or idle reverie. It occurs when we make comparisons of the past and present for the sake of a present purpose or for the sake of finding a new way out of present difficulties.

Fifty years ago when I began my college studies, it would be no exaggeration to say that the belief in academic freedom was regarded as faintly subversive even in many academic circles. The AAUP [American Association of University Professors], organized by two philosophers, Arthur Lovejoy and John Dewey, was in its infancy without influence or authority. Today, except in some of the cultural and political backwaters of the

Sidney Hook, "The Prospects of the Academy," *The New York University Alumni News* (May 1968), 3–4. Reprinted by permission of the author.

U.S., academic freedom, although not free from threats, is firmly established. In some regions it has the support of law.

Fifty years ago, the power of the chief university administrator was almost as unlimited as that of an absolute monarch. Today the administrator is a much harried man with much less power and authority among faculty, and especially students, than his forebears. Today there may be temperamentally happy administrators but their present life is an unhappy one. There seems to be an open season on them, and to such a degree that for the first time in history there is an acute shortage of candidates for the almost 300 vacant administrative posts in institutions of higher learning. When I did my graduate work at Columbia, Nicholas Murray Butler was both the reigning and ruling monarch. I don't believe that in his wildest dreams he could have conceived of the Columbia scene today. The strongest argument I know against the resurrection of the body is that if it were within the realm of possibility, Nicholas Murray Butler would have risen from his grave and would now be storming Morningside Heights.

Having been an administrator in a small way myself, I have learned what an ungrateful job it is, and at the same time how necessary. Without administrative leadership, every institution (especially universities, whose faculties are notoriously reluctant to introduce curricular changes) runs downhill. The greatness of a university consists predominantly in the greatness of its faculty. But faculties, because of reasons too complex to enter into here, do not themselves build great faculties. To build great faculties, administrative leadership is essential. In the affairs of the mind and in the realm of scholarship, the principles of simple majority rule or of "one man, one vote" do not apply. The most "democratically" run institutions of learning are usually the most mediocre. It takes a big man to live comfortably with a still bigger man under him, no less to invite him to cast his shadow over the less gifted.

Targets of Abuse

The paradox today is that as administrative power decreases and becomes more limited, the greater the dissatisfaction with it seems to grow. The memory of favors or requests denied remains much stronger than the memories of requests granted. Faculties are fickle in their allegiance. Overnight the most beloved of administrators can become the target of abuse, a figure of obloquy in the eyes of the very faculty, or a large section of it, which he himself has helped to build. In the very year that Clark Kerr received the Meikeljohn medal for academic freedom, the faculty at the University of California campus at Berkeley panicked in consequence of the events resulting from the *fourth* student sit-in.

In effect it repudiated him by adopting a set of resolutions that made him the scapegoat for the student lawlessness that it conspicuously refused to condemn. The faculty even voted down a motion that would have given the students complete freedom of speech except to urge the commission of *immediate acts* of force and violence. Another example: Vice President Truman of Columbia University was vigorously applauded at Columbia's commencement last June for, among other things, opening new avenues of communication with students. Only a few days ago he was roundly booed by a section of the Columbia faculty.

Why any scholar (and administrators are largely recruited from the ranks of scholars) should want to become a *full-time* administrator has always puzzled me. The duties, sacrifices and risks seem altogether disproportionate to the rewards. In speaking of administrators, one is tempted to characterize them with the words Lecky used in his great history of European morals about the fallen women of Europe . . . "The eternal priestesses of humanity blasted for the sins of their people." Well, university administrators are no longer priests, but whenever a crisis arises they are sure to be damned if they do and damned if they don't.

Synthetic Storms

One thing seems clear. In the crisis situations shaping up throughout the country, administrators are not going to enjoy a peaceful life. Their prospect of weathering the storms that will be synthetically contrived for them depends upon their ability and willingness to win the faculty for whatever plans and proposals they advance in the name of the university. For if they permit students or any other group to drive a wedge between them and the faculty, they will discover the sad fact of academic life that in such rifts the faculty will either play a neutral role or even assume a hostile one.

Not only on good educational grounds, therefore, but on

prudential ones as well, the administration must draw the faculty into the formulation of institutional educational policy. I say this with reluctance because it means the proliferation of committee meetings, the dilution of scholarly interest, and even less time for students. But this is a small price to pay for academic freedom and peace.

In talking about academic freedom, nothing signifies the distance we have come in the space of my lifetime so much as the fact that we now are concerned with the academic freedom of *students*. For historical reasons I cannot now explore, academic freedom in the United States meant *Lehrfreiheit,* freedom to teach. *Lernfreiheit,* freedom to learn, has only recently been stressed. It does not mean the same as it meant under the German university system that presupposed the all-prescribed curriculum of studies of the *Gymnasium*. If academic freedom for students means freedom to learn, then two things should be obvious. There is no academic freedom to learn without *Lehrfreiheit* or academic freedom to teach. Where teachers have no freedom to teach, students have obviously no freedom to learn, although the converse is not true.

Second, students' freedom to learn was never so widely recognized, was never so pervasive in the United States as it is today—whether it be construed as the freedom to attend college or not, or the freedom to select the *kind* of college the student wishes to attend or his freedom of curricular choice *within* the kind of college he selects. Above all, if academic freedom for students means the freedom to doubt, challenge, contest and debate within the context of inquiry, American students are the freest in the world, and far freer than they were when I attended college.

I recall an incident when I was a student in a government class at CCNY. The teacher conducted the class by letting the students give reports on the themes of the course. All he contributed was to say "next" as each student concluded. But when in reporting on the Calhoun-Webster debates, I declared that it seemed to me that Calhoun had the better of the argument, that his logic was better than Webster's although his *cause* was worse, the instructor exploded and stopped me. After emotionally recounting his father's services in the Civil War, he turned wrathfully on me and shouted: "Young man! When you're not preaching sedition, you are preaching secession!" Whereupon he drove me from the class. (The "sedition" was a reference to an earlier report on Beard's economic interpretation

of the Constitution that he had heard with grim disapproval.)
And this was at CCNY in 1920! The incident wasn't typical, but
that it could happen at all marks the profundity of the changes
in attitudes toward students since then. John Dewey's influence
has made itself felt even in the colleges today.

Moral Premise

Of course, there is still a large group of potential college
students who are deprived of freedom to learn because of
poverty or prejudice or the absence of adequate educational
facilities. And as citizens of a democratic society whose moral
premise is that each individual has a right to that education
that will permit him to achieve his maximum growth as a person, our duty is to work for, or support, whatever measures of
reconstruction we deem necessary to remove the social obstacles
to freedom of learning. It is perfectly legitimate to expect the
university to study these problems and propose solutions to
them. All universities worthy of the name already do. This is
one thing. But to therefore conclude that these problems must
become items not only on the agenda of study but for an agenda
of action is quite another.

For it therefore transforms the university into a political action organization and diverts it from its essential task of discovery, teaching, dialogue and criticism. Since there are profound differences about the social means necessary to achieve
a society in which there will be a maximum freedom to learn,
the university would become as partisan and biased as other
political action groups urging their programs on the community.
Its primary educational purpose or mission would be lost. It
would be compelled to silence or misrepresent the position
of those of its faculty who disagreed with its proposals
and campaigns of action. Class and group conflicts would
rend the fabric of the community of scholars in an unceasing
struggle for power completely unrelated to the quest for truth.

Objectivity Imperiled

If the university is conceived as an agency of action to transform society in behalf of a cause, no matter how exalted, it
loses its *relative* autonomy, imperils both its independence and

objectivity, and subjects itself to retaliatory curbs and controls on the part of society on whose support and largesse it ultimately depends.

This is precisely the conception of a university that is basic to the whole strategy and tactics of the so-called Students for a Democratic Society. I say "so-called" because their actions show that they are no more believers in democracy than the leaders of the so-called Student Non-Violent Co-ordinating Committee are believers in non-violence. And indeed the leaders of the SDS make no bones about that fact. In manifesto after manifesto they have declared that they want to use the university as an instrument of revolution. To do so, they must destroy the university as it exists today.

I wish I had time to list some of the clever stratagems they have devised to focus their opposition. On every campus there are always some grievances. Instead of seeking peacefully to resolve them through existing channels of consultation and deliberation, the SDS seeks to inflame them. Where grievances don't exist, they can be created. In one piece of advice to chapter members, they were urged to sign up for certain courses in large numbers, and then denounce the university for its large classes!

Freedom of dissent, speech, protest is never the real issue. They are, of course, always legitimate. But the tactic of the SDS is to give dissent the immediate form of violent action. The measures necessarily adopted to counteract this lawless action then become the main issue, as if the original provocation hadn't occurred. Mario Savio admitted after the Berkeley affair that the issue of "free speech" was a "pretext"—the word was his—to arouse the students against the existing role of the university in society.

Seek to Destroy

One of the leaders of the SDS at Columbia is reported to have said: "As much as we would like to, we are not strong enough as yet to destroy the United States. But we are strong enough to destroy Columbia!" He is wrong about this, too—the only action that would destroy Columbia would be faculty support of the students!—but his intent is clear.

Actually, the only thing these groups, loosely associated with the New Left, are clear about is what they want to destroy, not what they would put in its stead. In a debate with Gore Vidal, Tom Hayden, one of the New Left leaders, was pointedly asked what his revolutionary program was. He replied: "We haven't any. First we will make the revolution, and *then* we will find out what for." This is truly the politics of absurdity.

The usual response present-day academic rebels make to this criticism is that the university today is nothing but an instrument to preserve the status quo, and therefore faithless to the ideals of a community of scholars. Even if this charge were true, even if the universities today were bulwarks of the status quo, this would warrant criticism and protest, not violent and lawless action in behalf of a contrary role, just as foreign to their true function. But it is decidedly *not* true!

There is no institution in the country in which dissent and criticism of official views, of tradition, of the conventional wisdom in all fields, is freer and more prevalent than in the university. The very freedom of dissent that students today enjoy in our universities is in large measure a consequence of the spirit of experiment, openness to new ideas, absence of conformity and readiness to undertake new initiatives found among them.

Arrogant Claim

The first casualty of the strategy of the campus rebels is academic freedom. It is manifest in their bold and arrogant claim that the university drop its research in whatever fields these students deem unfit for academic inquiry and investigation. This note was already sounded in Berkeley. It is focal at Columbia. It is a shameless attempt to usurp powers of decision that the faculty alone should have. After all, it is preposterous for callow and immature adolescents who presumably have come to the university to get an education to set themselves up as authorities on what research by their teachers is educationally permissible.

Unless checked, it will not be long before these students will be presuming to dictate the conclusions their teachers should reach, especially on controversial subjects. This is standard procedure in totalitarian countries in which official student organizations are the political arm of the ruling party. Already there are disquieting signs of this. At Cornell a few weeks ago— *before* the martyrdom of Dr. King—a group of Black Nationalist students invaded the offices of the chairman of the economics department and held him captive in order to get an apology from a teacher whose views on African affairs they disagreed with. Only yesterday, another group at Northwestern demanded that courses in "black literature" and "black art" be taught by teachers approved by the Negro students.

And there are spineless administrators and cowardly members of the faculty who are prepared to yield to this blackmail. Under the slogans of "student rights" and "participatory democracy" the most militant groups of students are moving to weaken and ultimately destroy the academic freedom of those who disagree with them.

Let us not delude ourselves. Even when these militant students fail to achieve their ultimate purpose, they succeed in demoralizing the university by deliberately forcing a confrontation upon the academic community that it is not prepared to face and the costs of which it is fearful of accepting. In forcing the hand of the academic community to meet force with force, the citadel of reason becomes a battlefield. The students glory in it, but the faint of heart among their teachers turn on their own administrative leaders. These militants succeed in sowing distrust among students who do not see through their strategy. They also succeed in dividing the faculties.

Embitter Relations

There is always a small group—a strange mixture of purists and opportunists desirous of ingratiating themselves with students—who will *never* condemn the violence of students but only the violence required to stop it. These students succeed, even when they fail, in embittering relations between the administration and some sections of the faculty. They succeed, even when they fail, in antagonizing the larger community of which the university is a part, and in arousing a vigilante spirit that demands wholesale measures of repression and punishment that educators cannot properly accept.

How is it possible, one asks, for events of this character to happen? There have always been extremist and paranoidal tendencies in academic life, but they have been peripheral—individuals and small groups moving in eccentric intellectual orbits. But not until the last four or five years has the norm of social protest taken the form of direct action, have positions been expressed in such ultimatistic and intransigent terms, have extremist elements been strong enough to shut down great universities even for a limited time.

There are many and complex causes for this. But as I see it, the situation in the university is part of a larger phenomenon, viz., the climate of intellectual life in the country. I do not recall any other period in the last 50 years when intellectuals themselves have been so intolerant of each other, when differences over complex issues have been the occasion for denunciation rather than debate and analysis, when the use of violence— in the right cause, of course!—is taken for granted, when dissent is not distinguished from civil disobedience, and civil disobedience makes common cause with resistance, and readiness for insurrection. A few short years ago, anti-intellectualism was an epithet of derogation. Today it is an expression of revolutionary virility.

Fanaticism Rampant

In the fifties I wrote an essay on "The Ethics of Controversy," trying to suggest guidelines for controversy among principled democrats no matter how widely they differed on substantive issues. Today I would be talking into the wind for all the attention it would get. Fanaticism seems to be in the saddle. That it is a fanaticism of conscience, of self-proclaimed virtue, doesn't make it less dangerous. This past year has presented the spectacle of militant minorities in our colleges from one end of the country to another, preventing or trying to prevent representatives of positions they disapprove of from speaking to their fellow-students wishing to listen to them.

The spectacle shows that we have failed to make our students understand the very rudiments of democracy, that to tolerate active intolerance is to compound it. If we judge commitment by action, the simple truth is that the great body of our students is not firmly committed to democracy or to the liberal spirit without which democracy may become the rule of the mob.

I do not know any sure way or even a new way of combatting the dominant mood of irrationalism, especially among students and even among younger members of the faculty whose political naivete is often cynically exploited by their younger, yet politically more sophisticated, allies. What is of the first importance is to preserve, of course, the absolute intellectual integrity of our classrooms and laboratories, of our teaching and research against any attempt to curb it. We must defend it not only against the traditional enemies, who still exist even when they are dormant, but also against those who think they have the infallible remedies for the world's complex problems, and that all they need is sincerity as patent of authority. Fanatics don't lack sincerity. It is their long suit. They drip with sincerity —and when they have power, with blood—other people's blood.

We need more, however, than a defensive strategy, safeguarding the intellectual integrity of our vocation against those who threaten it. We need—and I know this sounds paradoxical—to counterpose to the revolt of the emotionally committed the revolt of the rationally committed. I do not want to identify this with the revolt of the moderates. There are some things one should not be moderate about. In the long run, the preservation of democracy depends upon a passion for freedom, for the logic and ethics of free discussion and inquiry, upon refusal to countenance the measures of violence that cut short the processes of intelligence upon which the possibility of shared values depends.

These are old truths but they bear repeating whenever they are denied. Even tautologies become important when counterposed to absurdities.

We as teachers must make our students more keenly aware of the centrality of the democratic process to a free society and of the centrality of intelligence to the democratic process. Democracy has our allegiance because of its cumulative fruits, but at any particular time the process is more important than any specific program or product. He who destroys the process because it does not guarantee some particular outcome is as foolish as someone who discards scientific method in medicine or engineering or any other discipline because of its failure to solve altogether or immediately a stubborn problem.

Courage Needed

There is one thing we cannot deny to the intransigent and fanatical enemies of democracy. That is courage. Intelligence is necessary to overcome foolishness. But it is not sufficient to tame fanaticism. Only courage can do that. A handful of men who are prepared to fight, to bleed, to suffer and, if need be, to die, will always triumph in a community where those whose freedom they threaten are afraid to use their *intelligence* to resist and to fight, and ultimately to take the same risks in action as those determined to destroy them.

Yes, there is always the danger that courage *alone* may lead us to actions that will make us similar to those who threaten us. But that is what we have intelligence for—to prevent that from happening! It is this union of courage and intelligence upon which the hope of democratic survival depends.

REVOLUTION DIARY

Melvin J. Lasky

Berlin

I know the *Audimax* on the Garystrasse in Dahlem well, from a dozen formal and stuffy academic meetings: the austere glass-and-concrete modernity of the Ford Hall, the richly gowned *Magnifizenz* and his colleagues, among tastefully placed flower arrangements, facing a quietly seated audience of 1,500 (not a gesture, not a whisper, men in silver ties, women clutching large hand-bags), with a faint acoustical echo as an ensemble from the Philharmonic tones out Beethoven. This old world has now been stood on its head. Nothing is the same. It is as if this incredible scene were taking place in another country, another time. It is a montage by Eisenstein in a setting by Gropius. Four thousand students, shouting, singing, waving red flags, are packed into the hall which seems to tremble with the swaying mass. I stand on a window-sill in a corner, and two students sitting on my shoes help to maintain my balance. The noise and the heat are heady and contagious. When the roaring chant of *"Ho-Ho-Ho Chi Minh"* goes up for the tenth time I find myself drumming the rhythm out with my fingers on the glass pane behind me. (So this is what it was like—that grand primitive rhythmic unity which anthropologists write about! As a boy

Excerpted from Melvin J. Lasky, "Revolution Diary," *Encounter* (August 1968), 81–92. Reprinted by permission of *Encounter* and the author.

one knew only, after the Western at a Saturday film matinee, the joys of screeching *"Ger-on-i-mo!"* I thought of the choral shouts of *"Chay-Doo! Chay-Doo!"* in Silone's *Fontamara*, and of how singularly quiet the effect had been during the war of those 5th Symphony chords, *Da-da-da Dahh!* Did even the Nuremberg Stadium ever ring out with such tribal mind-breaking power as these harmonics from Hanoi? . . .)

I breathed easier when *Ho* gave way to the softer strains of the *Internationale:* it was like moving from Stockhausen to Johann Strauss, and the sentimentalism had its programmatic point. It was all for Herbert Marcuse. He had been acclaimed in Berlin as the Prophet of the Revolution, and he had promised to return (with mixed echoes of Christ and General MacArthur). And now he had come back—back to the city of his birth, where as a young man he had listened to Karl Liebknecht and Rosa Luxemburg and had first sung, with clenched fist, *"Arise, ye wretched of the earth. . . ."* How few lives have such whirling circling unity, a rare thing of Copernican completeness, the reward of devoting a lifetime to the indissolubility of theory and practice. He tore off his jacket, raised his white-shirted right arm, and sang along, *"Hört die Signale. . . ."*

Some signals he seemed to have missed altogether. For all the wild acclamation, there was also a surging undercurrent of dissatisfaction. This is a hep generation, quick and impatient, and Mini-heroes of yesterday may not quite fit into the Maxi-times of an onrushing revolution. Still, they were not ungrateful: for he had taught them much, and probably only he could have supplied that philosophical blessing without which no great movement feels altogether sanctified. They had known only grievances, but he shared with them the nature of grief; they had been hampered by hesitations, and he gave them the words and feelings they needed for absolute faith and commitment.

TWO MAJOR TURNING-POINTS are worth recording since Marcuse's historic appearance in July 1967, in this very auditorium; and I quote the words of a young student, Hermann L., who as it turned out had not read a line in any of the books of *der grosse Philosoph* but who understood him well enough.

"First of all, we were very much worried about Reform. Many many things were wrong with German society, and we wanted to put them right. Should we set about it, as Willy Brandt and all the other socialists tried to tell us, in piece-meal fashion? No, this

was hopeless! Marcuse taught us that it was *the System* that was
wrong, the whole System, all of it. You just simply couldn't
change a bit here and there. *All of it* had to be changed, for it
was all of an organic piece. All of it was evil, and there was
no reform possible, only *Revolution*. . . . Then many among us
were troubled by the so-called virtues of a so-called liberal and
democratic capitalist society. Workers had a right to strike, and
there was freedom of speech, and there seemed to be much
welfare and shared affluence. But this was a misconception, a
false consciousness! It was all a snare and a delusion! The so-
called virtues were the most vicious tricks of all. They were
merely part of the apparatus of Repression and Domination by
which an Out-Dated Society still tried to keep itself in power.
Tolerance? *Quatsch!* It was nothing but Repressive Tolerance,
which reinforced the diseases and prevented true health. Marcuse freed us from all liberal inhibitions. . . ."

GOOD, THEN, WHAT DID the *Theoretiker* now have to say to
the revolutionary convention of Berlin *Praktiker?* They had, in
a series of ingeniously planned demonstrations, toppled both the
Mayor and the Chief of Police. Things were on the march. What
had to be done?

Marcuse's first words were not quite right, and he never re-
covered the old rapport. "Students!" he began, and his white
mane gleamed in the sea of adolescence. *"Genossen heisst das!"*
(Comrades, you mean) came the cry back. They were happier
with Mao and Ho—Herbert was too old and too bourgeois. He
had lost his faith in the revolutionary destiny of the working
class. And if not the Proletariat, who would make the Revolution? He tried to reassure them that there was no loss of faith
in the Revolutionary Future on his part. It would come; they
knew it, and he knew it. But it might come just a little differently from the way Marx predicted. How would it come, say, in
America? "Well," said the Professor (and I quote him directly
here), "a System that is so evil must needs come to an extraordinary end. Some time ago there was a total breakdown of elec-
tric power in New York. It was unbelievable. Everything came
to a halt. Nothing was possible in the black-out except sex, and
in the next year America had the fruits of this creative breakdown. It can happen again, and again. The Revolution will come
in America as a result of a total spontaneous disintegration! . . ."

This was not entirely satisfying to a mass of enthusiastic
activists. "What, then, must we do?" And the boy who was sit-

ting on my left shoe cried out, *"Na klar,* put out all the lights! . . ."

Had the old man been nothing but a Utopian? Now he was no longer talking about Revolution but about—*Transcendence!* And if it was a transcendental Utopia, they had to believe that "today such a Utopia is the *most real* of *all* real possibilities! . . ."

BOOS, PROTESTS, HECKLING began to burst out from all sides of the *Audimax.* They had enough of this old stuff. They knew all about—and didn't need to be told about it again in the midst of a revolutionary situation—how Capitalism was Barbarism, how the Ghettos of the Metropolis would explode, how the Third World would rally to the Cause (led by inspiration from Cuba and China). It was all too much, boring, last year's *Platte.* Points of order were suddenly put from several student leaders. The boy sitting on my right foot knew what was coming, and shouted *"Umfunktionieren!"* The proposed resolution was to "re-function" the meeting and give it new point and purpose. Instead of going on with Professor Marcuse, the evening should be converted to a discussion of strategy and tactics of the forthcoming General Strike.

Marcuse was aghast. The chairman—Professor Hellmut Gollwitzer, a theologian (and he was not unhappy until now about the progress of the not untheological evening)—tried to impress the thousands that after all they simply could not invite a man to come from so far and then simply have him break off in the middle. There were pros and cons. My side of the hall was shouting *"Umfunktionieren!"* and I confess I was with them, not out of any intended discourtesy to an honoured guest, but simply out of the infectious youthful impatience. What was *umfunktionieren* but another name for double-feature billing? On with the next show! But there wasn't quite a majority. Gollwitzer, to noisy disapproval, suggested that "those who wanted to talk about other things should go elsewhere and hold a meeting of their own." Nothing so square had been heard in the University in two years. A Happening or two, spontaneous as befits the form, had been scheduled as part of the historic agenda of the day. Marcuse continued, but he would not succeed completely in repressing the true and inner dynamic of events.

IT WAS CLOSE TO MIDNIGHT when there was some rumbling action high on the platform, half veiled by a huge curtain.

"Ach, nein!" moaned my neighbours on the window-sill, "not
Teufel and Langhans again! . . ." I recognised them, and indeed
they could hardly be mistaken, with their red shirts and yellow
trousers, beards like Marx, coiffure like Struwwelpeter in the
German *Märchen.* They were the leaders of the so-called *Kom-
mune,* a wild extremist fringe group which claimed to know
what authentic liberation was and how truly to attain it. The
orthodox booed the heretics, who began to make away with the
enormous wooden emblem of the Free University which had
hung high over the Auditorium.

I pushed and crawled my way out of the mass, drawn to
where the action was, like a Dostoyevskian gambler in a trance.
On the street the Kommunardists were dancing up and down on
the hated emblem which resisted the first attempts at combus-
tion. Then, burning merrily, it was carried to the Rector's building and finally dismembered into fiery and charred little pieces.
I heard the fire-engines coming in the distance and watched the
police standing quietly on the next street-corner. Some students
began throwing stones at the *Rektorat.* One could still make out
the words on the Emblem in its now-blackened lettering. What
was the hateful inscription—*pro patria mori,* or some other
vicious Fatherlandish sentiment? When the firemen put out the
little blaze one could read: *Veritas, Justitia, Libertas.* . . .

AT ONE IN THE MORNING I keep my rendezvous with Hermann
L. in a *Kneipe* near Thielplatz. He drank his beer with angry
ferocious gulps which did nothing to relieve the grim depression
which had seized him. Surely it was nothing that I had said or
done—for he had promised to be my guide if I committed myself "to keep an open mind, to listen fairly and learn something
new (if possible). . . ." No, it had been Marcuse.

"Für mich ist der Marcuse jetzt tot!" When the words came
they marched out with a funereal finality. "Marcuse is dead for
me now! Dead, finished, through. I'll never listen to him again,
never think about him again. He was once important for us—
last year. We sought him out like a prophet and took over every
formulation. Why, I helped to mimeograph his text and distributed it everywhere! That's how we felt. And now he comes and
talks such utter nonsense. A Revolution is waiting to be made,
and he offers us California metaphysics. Never again with Marcuse! That's all over now. . . ."

No words of mine could cheer or console him. After all, the
old fellow had written a few interesting books. No masterpiece,

to be sure, but that alone doesn't call for burial. Possibly there is still some point to looking at his Hegel volume, and there were at least a few not unoriginal essays among his early contributions to the *Zeitschrift für Sozialforschung*. . . . I sensed the hopelessness and didn't go on. The occasion was too deep for discussion. A little god had failed.

IN THE BEGINNING the search for an explanatory theory was relatively a simple affair. Having to deal with the Californian explosion at Berkeley, it could be persuasively formulated in terms of "American exceptionalism." Here was a uniquely advanced society, affluent as no other, afflicted with a social mobility to the point of almost absolute rootlessness, marked with a liberal permissiveness which led a generation to the edge of personal anarchy. Why should it surprise when "Spock-marked" young, with money in their pockets and a scramble of every idea that ever appeared in paper-back in their heads, rise up and like young Prometheans attack old gods and long for fiery new beginnings? Surely this was a *very* American phenomenon, even if *one day* Europeans who were moving more slowly along the same historic path of development would go and do likewise.

Then Stockholm and Tokyo exploded, and theories had to be revised. But here, too, there were many of the same constituent elements: mass culture, mindless prosperity, etc. Yet the Swedes had a social order of great justice and equality, with none of the outraging miseries of the U.S. Negro ghetto; and how could an Oriental family pattern produce exactly the same dissidence and alienation? Then when the young Germans began to explode, theories began to go out of the window in utter intellectual defenestration. No other land was so lunatically divided, with an iron curtain splitting the nation and a brick wall dividing its capital. True, there was an element of social rootlessness here too (all those refugees from somewhere else), and the German family crisis was deep, and the Teutonic educational establishment cried out for change. But then wasn't there a patriotic ideal which could give emotional coherence to vague dissatisfactions? And wasn't what was wrong with the universities rather that they were old-fashioned and medieval, not (as in Berkeley) mechanical and modern? Surely, what was revolting about *Vater* was not that he was a nice, ineffectual, permissive Big Daddy but that he was still a narrow, authoritarian, stuffy Little Nazi. . . . No, it was all too complicated. And when, one day soon, Paris—and perhaps even Moscow—erupts with youthful *élan,* all sociologists will be ordered back to the drawing board, back to square one. We are floundering in an *embarras de différences.* . . .

THE GENERAL STRIKE is on, and both of the great local institutions of higher learning—the Free University and the Technical University—give the appearance of such complete unanimity that it wasn't even necessary to put up strike pickets. I walk over to the Otto-Suhr Institut which, as the centre for sociology and political science, has become the natural headquarters of the Revolution. There was supposed to be an all-day high-level discussion of the *Notstandsgesetze;* and the day before, at the end of a lecture I had sat in on, a leader of the SDS announced it and went on, "—and we all hope, Herr Professor Löwenthal, that you will be with us and explain how Social Democracy, by favouring such vicious legislation, has once again betrayed the interests of the working class!" Löwenthal smiled, accepted the invitation, but added that what he would say at the Teach-in would be a matter for him to decide. A few laughed at the exchange. It is apparently a running cat-and-mouse game between the Professor and the Cadre. The week before, summing up a long lecture on the Origins of Italian Fascism, Löwenthal had quoted one contemporary revolutionary on the grievous post-war social crisis to the effect that the Status Quo was intolerable, an Establishment was stifling all progress, the Spontaneous Anger of all the Young Forces in the Nation had to rise up and Smash the Old System and release all the pent-up forces of Renewal and Revolution. There was stormy applause from the Cadre. The Professor closed his note-book, and went on only to make the embarassing disclosure that the author had been—Benito Mussolini.

Well, whatever had happened I had missed it. Off again, then, to the *Audimax.* I rubbed my eyes. It couldn't be true: it was a *déjà vu.* There we all were again, four thousand strong, red flags waving. As I come through a side entrance a tiny auto pulls up, packed full of extra-large red flags: a late delivery. I hear the courier rebuked by an organiser on the platform: "If the Revolution is to keep its rendezvous with destiny it had better learn punctuality. . . ." But the nice young man almost makes up for the delinquency by struggling through the portals hectically, finds a sweet little girl waiting in the wings, gives her an extra-small red flag and then takes her by her tiny hand to the podium where for an unscheduled moment she waves it uncertainly and chirps childishly into the microphone, *Ho-ho-ho Chi Minh*. The Happening is on.

THIS IS CALLED by the students their "Smolny Institute," where all the basic revolutionary decisions are taken ("after a full discussion and a fair free vote," I am told again and again, and I see no reason to disbelieve it). Now is the moment for the triumphant report from all the various fronts. The Law Faculty and its student body had indicated some reluctance, but now all pockets of resistance had been overcome and the Strike is complete. Cheers. Good news, too, from Frankfurt where most lectures have been suspended and strike pickets are in complete control. Cheers. Special support from various grammar schools, and hundreds of students from the Goethe and Kant *Gymnasia* will be joining the strikers. More cheers. This evening there will be a special protest in Lankwitz, and among the speakers will be Günter Grass. Boos, then cheers, then a mixed chorus punctuated by something which sounded like a tin drum (could it be Grass himself, on his *Blechtrommel?*). . . .

Someone hands a note to the chairman—a pretty, buxom, blonde German refugee from Rumania called Sigrid Fronius. She has a Problem. The news from the Medical Faculty is not so good. She has just learned that three professors (with laboratory equipment) and several hundred medical students plan to hold their scheduled final lecture in a half hour's time. Loud cries of pain and shame! The lecture is to take place in *this* very building. Shouts of horror! And then, in an instruction which must be unique in the history of revolutionary movements for its cool charm, Fräulein Fronius says, "I think you ought to pay them a little visit. Why don't a few of you over there near the doors simply go upstairs and visit them in *Hörsaal IV-B?* . . ."

IT WAS AS PLEASANT as could be. *Einen kleinen Besuch zu machen.* Nothing sinister about that, and probably only in my foreign ears did it have a formal resemblance to those other and more famous euphemistic constructions: "You need a little protection," or "We're going to take you for a little ride. . . ."

The little visit was fairly uneventful, but doubtless quite what Frl. Fronius had in mind. Some three hundred students or so detached themselves from the outer areas of the "Smolny" and

ambled upstairs. They moved into *Hörsaal IV-B* and took whatever places were still free for medical students who had not yet
arrived. I stood in the corridors with a dozen of the *Mediziner*
(you could tell them apart by their dress—jackets, shirts, and
ties—and a bulging brief-case). "*Ach ja,*" said one, vainly trying to make his way forward, "*noch ein* 'Go-In'. . . ." They were
apparently resigned. In the *Hörsaal* one of the medical professors, in white coat, tried to explain. A few of the *SDS* leaders—
including my friend, Hermann L., who was rushing up and
down, waving his arms, as if he were a laboratory specimen
struggling for freedom—tried to maintain some order. It seems
that these students were taking their final examinations in two
days' time. They had begged the faculty to review some new
material which had not been previously studied and which they
were expected to know. This was the only possible day on which
a special session could be arranged, and that arrangement had
been made weeks before anyone had ever proposed a General
Strike. Even now, they could—and should—do these two hours
together, and then they could go downstairs to the Strike Meeting and participate in the Teach-in.

Nothing doing. He was shouted down by songs and slogans,
and then the cry went up, "*Umfunktionieren!*" A speaker with
a portable microphone and loud-speaker resolved that "this meeting be converted into a discussion of the Emergency Laws and
their fascist implications for the future of democracy in Germany." Approval was roared.

A laboratory assistant, with a great voice and even more
naïveté, suggested that a vote be taken—"but with only the
medical students entitled to vote." Laughter was loud. "That
wouldn't be democratic."

One student leader weakly implored—I was told later his
name was Landsberg, and that after a heart-attack he had resigned his post of elected leadership—"in the name of reason
and tolerance cease and desist from this strategy and tactic."
He was rhetorical and ineffective. "How will it help to deepen
the political consciousness—*die ganze Bewusstseinsbildung*—of
our fellow-students here when you merely force them to do
something by your sheer physical presence? . . ." Enough of that.

THE CADRES WOULDN'T LEAVE, and the medical students
couldn't get in. The technique of *Umfunktionieren* was being
set in motion, and half the *Hörsaal* was already a busy centre
of agitated political discussion. I was frightened, I must confess,

that blows would be exchanged at any moment; but I misread
the temperature of the hostility. There was tension there, but no
anger. One of the professors wearily raised his arm to announce
with a casualness that might have been coolness or might have
been contempt that "in view of the Terror the scheduled *Vorle-
sung* was cancelled. . . ." That was a shade too strong. There
had been nothing that could be called terror, only a little pressure politics, skilfully executed. Except for the tears, for reasons
best known to herself, in the eyes of one of the girl students
nothing especially untoward had happened.

My friend Hermann L. waved across the *Hörsaal* to me and
cracked, "Well, at least one thing is functioning around here—
and that's *das Umfunktionieren!* . . ." One of the laboratory
assistants said to me, almost under his breath, as he carried out
a piece of apparatus, "That's one thing that has always func-
tioned in Germany—except that we used to call it *Gleichschal-
tung*. . . ."

Prague

A Berlin youth group is heading for Czechoslovakia, and I
decide to tag along for a few days. Here are the new heirs of
Karl Marx staging a mighty confrontation of Theory and Reality; and although the plots in this old European Theatre of
Ideology rarely come up with a new twist, it is a Happening
of delicious absurdity. Rudi Dutschke has already been here,
warning the Czech students of their theoretical deficiencies in
Marxian dialectics. He knew better. They must not confound
"liberalisation" (*i.e.*, moving the Czech revolution towards the
bourgeois Right) with genuine "democratisation" which would
be the deepening of the socialist content with anti-authoritarian
(*i.e.*, anti-capitalist) re-structuring. "*Ach so!*" said the Prague
students with mock patient politeness, and wondered what a
young man who was not forced to mouth Marxist-Leninist
phraseology was doing carrying around such mental baggage.

"But then," one young historian at the Charles University tells
me, "we have always had to live with this German arrogance.
They know nothing, but they always know better. Marx purged
Wilhelm Weitling, the only real working-man in the International, because only a German Theoretician understood the proletariat. And he told off Proudhon, that shrewd French peasant,
because only Marx could understand France; and he dismissed

John Stuart Mill, because he knew better that England was heading not for reform but for bloody revolution. . . . The sons of old Karl are chips off the block. Where do they get their arrogance from? They have been wrong—often disastrously and tragically so—on almost every question for over a hundred years now, and they *still* think they know better. Especially here, where for two decades we have had every Marxist-Leninist idea tried out, like in some mad surgeon's operating theatre, on our very bodies—and they now come and tell us about the true nature of Alienation, Exploitation, and Revolution. . . ."

Wasn't this being a little unfair? They were trying to develop their ideas in a different social context and were facing different problems.

"Perhaps so. Then they should declare themselves to be the provincial protestants that they are and not come preaching to us about 'global confrontations.' . . . I found it infuriating to listen to them. What does it mean that the Destruction of Capitalism is the Main Task to Achieve a World without War and Poverty and Exploitation? Here we have had the socialisation of the means of production for twenty years, and there has been plenty of exploitation. As for poverty, we have more than we had before, and certainly more than our prospering neighbours, for even poor little Austria has shown more productive prowess than any society in our Socialist Bloc. How naïve they are! Didn't the U.S.S.R. make a war against Finland and Poland, and isn't there a mortal danger that two socialist countries, Russia and China, can go to war with each other? What about Africa and Asia? Will this ridiculous phraseology explain the economic difficulties of, say, backward Burma, or the murderous hostilities that break out in West Africa among Nigerians and Biafrans? The issues of war and peace—as well as those of prosperity through capital growth—*may* have something to do with Capitalism as Marxists understand it. But how well-educated students on a University level who have not been subjected, as we have been, to a vicious process of intellectual stupefaction, can look out at the world through such simple staring eyes—this is beyond me. Don't they think, read, argue? How can they expect economic aid from the rich developed technologies of Europe if Europeans don't 'exploit' their capital resources more efficiently so as to enable capital to be exported? How are workers going to operate our machine-tool industries in a 'non-Alienating' style? What does it mean to tell us—as Dutschke did a few weeks ago—that we must not interpret 'freedom of the press' so broadly as to allow 'the counter-revolution to have a voice' when every voice which for 20 years differed from that of Big Brother has been condemned as 'counter-revolutionary'? In what world have these fellows been living? Are they so busy marching up and down in demonstrations that they don't have time to read the books in their library? That used to be our fate. Maybe only the Hegelian dialectic can explain this crazy transposition of roles! . . ."

This, surely, was unfairness compounded. I had found much grim studiousness in the new German youth, as I watched the browsing in that astonishing new Revolutionary Bookshop on Olivaerplatz in West Berlin which sells international books and pamphlets that ten years ago (as thirty) it was criminal to peddle. For the Czech students I spoke to, this was small cosmopolitan consolation. Their problem was to move "beyond Communism," and they had little patience for the primitivism with which their contemporaries in the West were struggling to move "beyond Capitalism." I was apparently alone in feeling moved that young persons had committed themselves to "Taking Dreams as Reality." And this, Pavel H. said savagely, "you call an interesting Marcuse-amalgam of Marx and Freud? . . . Sheer nonsense! Freud says: dreams are dreams, and Marx says: reality is reality. And if the twain should ever meet, it won't be—believe me, we know!—because a few charming and energetic juvenile minds have thought up a new slogan to be chalked up on some public wall! . . ."

THE LAST ANGRY WORDS I have ringing in my ears—sternly pronounced in the lobby of the Hotel Alcron where I was shortsighted enough to buy for Karel T. a copy of the *International Herald Tribune* with the latest news of Mark Rudd's liberation of the Low Library on the Columbia University campus—are these:

"I know nothing really about Columbia, or the L.S.E., or the Sorbonne, or any of the institutions of higher learning in the West. But they *must* truly be as bad as your students say they are—for they have apparently produced a youth that is so disoriented and uneducated, so incapable of reading books critically and thinking intelligently, as to be a screaming indictment of themselves. God knows that we have had our tragic illusions about the nature of Capitalism and Socialism. But our students are intellectual giants—and, mind you, educated under the Stalinist terror!—compared to the specimens of pseudo-revolutionaries running around with rocks and petrol rags in your capitalist West! The young generation may well be right to want to destroy the monstrous school system—after all, it produced *them!* I think of it as a kind of Frankensteinian justice. Each society produces the barbarians who then come to sack it. . . ."

Paris

At the Rhine-Main airport, all flights to France were cancelled, and I raced to the Frankfurt *Bahnhof* to catch the train which never departed. At the Hertz office they refused to hire out any cars that would cross the French frontier: "We call it a revolutionary situation," the young manager explained, with chic terminological accuracy. Avis, the hated competition, did actually "try harder," or perhaps they hadn't yet studied the morning's news of Paris strike and riot. I refrained from discussing the headlines and in a few minutes was off in a fully-tanked Opel *Kapitän* towards *la douce France.*

In most of the cities and towns en route there was a significant emptiness, interrupted only by little crowds around factory gates. If the general strike that had been called by the Communists and the *CGT* was the success as reported in the various radio bulletins I could tune into, it appeared through an automobile windshield to be a cool, undemonstrative, and almost normal exercise in industrial relations rather than some excited outburst of revolutionary enthusiasm. The romance was only in Paris, at the Sorbonne. I parked the German car as close to the Latin Quarter as I dared, and strolled through the University buildings. Foolishly enough, I spent most of my time copying out on the backs of envelopes all the slogans I could decipher and some of the verse on the walls and bulletin boards. No point repeating them here, for *Le Monde* has since published a good anthology. My favourites remain: *L'Imagination prend le pouvoir* and *Papa pue.* Easy enough to read in the press dispatches but ah, like brave Crillon, you were not there. I like to think that I will never be the same again for having been on the spot when, for the first time in human history, the Imagination took Power (and Papa stank).

I HAD A CHANCE to talk with Bernard B., who has been one of the Revolutionary Guards for three days and nights now at the Odéon, when he dashed home for a quick bowl of Mama's hot soup and to pick up from Papa his weekly allowance. These are, obviously, the greatest days of his young life, and his enthusiasm is infectious. What spirit, what joy, what talk, what songs will ever compare to this? It appears to be all of a happy harmonic piece, even to the corduroy trousers, short coat, and peaked Muscovite cap. Were all of history's revolutionaries so handsomely outfitted, or do our misty little eyes see everything in Delacroix coloration? Were *sansculottes* beautiful? What did Jack Cade wear?

I am only here for a day, and it is all too bewildering to grasp, but it *must* be very *marvellous.* "Oh yes," says Bernard, a shade too drily, "it is. But, you know, day after day and night after night of continuous discussion is getting to be a trifle boring. None of us is *that* interesting; we just don't have all that much to say. . . ." But then the long longed-for dialogue has never been so free, so uninhibited? "I am not so sure about that either. You see, there are these various *groupuscules* and each of them is absolutely convinced of its theory and strategy. Try and cut across the main line of their tendencies, and you don't get very far. You're shouted down and, in one way or another, you lose *la parole.* . . . It happened to me the other night. I thought we ought to give up the theatre for an evening and let this small dance group hold its scheduled ballet recital. I tried to convince them what a magnificent blow for culture it would be if we withdrew at eight and let them dance—for, after all, dancers are workers too! . . . Then we could come back to reoccupy the place at midnight. Oh, no! As Sartre had put it, this was no time for culture but for revolution. So I mumbled on in a tumult for a few minutes, and then gave up. . . ."

AT LE BOURGET not a plane taking off, and I decide to try and see whether the petrol in the tank will take me as far as the Belgian frontier. I drive along with two youngsters who had marched with the students but now, with heavy heart, were leaving for a long-scheduled holiday at the Club Méditerranée in Tunis. I drove speedily in order to help them catch their re-routed chartered plane in Brussels, but we ran out of gas on the *autoroute* this side of Lille. She was pretty and had been saying how she adored Dany Cohn-Bendit and how there was now, for the first time, hope in the world for a better life. He had been saying that everything around them was evil and corrupt and had to be destroyed. I made him take the walk of ten kilometres to the nearest town for a jerry-can of petrol.

IN BRUSSELS WE LOST our way, drove up and down the clearways looking for a signpost, but the Flemish students had removed the French signs and their own had been removed in turn. The hotel lobby is a scene (or so I imagine) out of 1793 —crowded with "refugees" from Jacobin France, pining for the shores of a Burkean England. At the airport we exchange tidbits of revolutionary gossip, and wonder how long John Bull Jr. will remain cut off on his island.

London

One senses that the heroic days have become legendary, and that the euphoria appears to be dying away on all sides. The strike movement is exhausting itself in the factories; there are ugly rumours of "mercenaries" (*les Katangais*) in the Sorbonne; the mass of students are wearying of the futile spectacle of street-fighting night after night against the brutal special police. "Now watch the press carefully," says Jean-Marie, just over from Paris, "and suddenly you will see a resurgence of the analytical spirit. For weeks there has been scarcely an intelligent word published. How easily does a little tribal excitement dispel all the habits of critical reason! What is it but man's eternal wish to be young, potent, naïve, inexperienced, unburdened by 'the knowledge that bringeth sorrow'? . . ."

He gives me this afternoon's *Le Monde* to add to my clipping collection. In it Claude Roy concludes an article with a phrase of St. Just, "*La question du bonheur est posée en Europe*," and adds only that "since Europe has never given an effective answer Paris has had to pose it again in May 1968." This is the French schoolboy facility which has marked endless generations of Parisian rhetoricians. Has nothing at all been learned since the Jacobins tried to institutionalise happiness and legislate for paradise? Must we always return to 1793?

Or to 1848 and 1871? In the first number of *The Black Dwarf* I note a contribution from that distinguished historian Eric Hobsbawm: "What has happened in France is marvellous and enchanting. . . . For us old members of the fan-club, it proves that Paris still has star quality. . . . It can still put up the barricades, often on the very same spot where they went up in 1848 and in 1944. It is a great moment for sentimental Francophiles. . . ." Could it be that Santayana was wrong? It is not

forgetting the past which makes for tragic recurrence: but remembering it and being condemned to repeat it.

In the 24 May number of the *New Statesman*, the fiery red-
haired editor of that paper writes in the same spirit of Jaco-
binical excitement:

> In the courtyard of the Faculty of Letters, the heart and
> brain of the movement, a thousand flowers not only bloom
> but load the spring air with intellectual incense. . . . This
> jovial young Robespierre [Cohn-Bendit], with his flaming red
> hair and piercing blue eyes, has the true revolutionary's gift
> of combining a philosophy which can be reasoned, slogans
> which can be shouted and a mad-dog taste for taking posi-
> tions by frontal assault. When he speaks, men listen; where
> he leads, they follow. He makes the impossible become pos-
> sible simply by doing it. . . . Once again, the French have
> given birth to a new revolutionary spirit, which will ulti-
> mately enrich the lives of all of us.

What a wonderful thing adolescence is: what a shame to waste
it on jejune journalism. "Paris is on fire," shouts *The Observer*'s
columnist, "yet we still busy ourselves with cultural pastimes.
. . ." On to Piccadilly barricades? "Paris artists," he notes with
that special romantic envy which English Jacobins have always
had for the abandon of their French cousins, "are making common cause with the students and workers. Shall they [*i.e.*, we]
do the same here? A debate on the subject should promptly and
publicly be opened. The need to take sides may be more pressing
than we think."

WHERE SUDDENLY has the great Orwellian tradition gone,
that hard-won intellectual faculty of taking a hard, unsenti-
mental, unromantic look at very mixed events? Here is pre-
Orwellian man, writing from Paris for what used to be the
tough-minded *Guardian*:

> I cannot but be grateful for having lived through at least a
> part of what will certainly be remembered as one of the most
> marvellous moments in the history of Paris. . . . The pre-
> dominant atmosphere was one of youth taking the adult
> world tolerantly in hand and tactfully trying to civilise it.
> The Sorbonne and eventually the whole of the Latin Quarter

became a great forum in the style of ancient Greece. . . .
What we were witnessing was the spectacle of the human
animal as we would always like to see him—the imagination
extended, physical courage, generosity, and optimism tri-
umphing over timidity, fear of insecurity, or just fear of dis-
comfort, which keep our lives moving sluggishly. The fears,
in fact, which cheat us out of part of the experience
of living. One great student slogan summed up the revolutionary attitude: "Take your dreams for reality. . . ."

And, inevitably, a famous English poet (whom I glimpsed the
other afternoon stalking through the Latin Quarter) is, once
again, infatuated with youthful idealists—Oh to offer flowers
again to John Reed in Petersburg or Ralph Fox in Madrid!—
for they can fight with courage and honesty and still live "the
communal life of discussion and mutual considerateness and
disregard for consumer society. . . ."
  But no representative documentation of yet another cliché-
ridden chapter in the history of Intellectuals and Just Causes
can confine itself merely to the banalities of the *bien-pensant*.
There are also twisting complications, and who can quite comprehend the dialectics of the ode which Pier Paolo Pasolini has
just published in Rome? Here that uncompromising Communist
and singular revolutionary spirit in Italian culture writes (according to today's *Corriere della Sera*): "*Simpatizzavo con i
poliziotti perchè i poliziotti sono figli di poveri. . . .*" I have not
yet seen a copy of Moravia's journal in which Pasolini's lines attacking the students appear, but from the various quoted passages they amount, in free translation, to something like this:

> Your faces are those of sons of good families, and I hate
> you as I hate your fathers. The good breeding comes through.
> . . . Yesterday when you had your battle in the Valle Giulia
> with the police, my sympathies were with the police, because
> they are the sons of the poor. . . .

To the students he had only this to say: as bourgeois figures
you had better learn to renounce once and for all any dreams of
power. And to his literary contemporaries: only contempt for
those who are trying to "recover their virginity through the
adulation of adolescence. . . ." Arise, ye prisoners of puberty!
arise, ye wretched of the id! . . .

I STROLL DOWN towards Houghton Street where the Revolutionary Student Federation is preparing its founding conference at the London School of Economics. Tariq Ali has just come out for the abolition of money. "There's no time now to follow the lead of Berlin, New York, and Paris," one student tells me. "But wait till the autumn, and we will be having a revolution all of our own. . . ."

PART IV

Race

THE CONDITION of non-whites in the United States is a national disgrace. Whatever the other achievements and qualities of this nation may be, they are compromised and threatened by this tragedy. Except for the related problem of slavery, there has never been a domestic issue as fraught with danger and despair as this one. The destructive possibilities *for all of us* are awesome; it may even be that the future of American democracy is at stake.

We believe, however, that an understanding of these stark realities is only the beginning of wisdom on this subject, not the end; and we believe that much of the current debate and polemics is a blend of ignorance about the facts, misunderstanding about the processes of social change, blind passion, and a misplaced faith in the efficacy of apocalyptic rhetoric and action. For too long, those who believe both in the equality of man *and* the defensibility of American institutions and ideals have been relatively inconspicuous. The center of the stage has been dominated by racists, white and black, whose languages and prescriptions are negative and destructive. Many young people, in particular, are seldom exposed either orally or visually to anything other than polemics and hysteria on this subject. It is not surprising that frenzy has become confused with dedication, hatred with love, and sloganeering with wisdom.

It is useful to remind ourselves that some gains have been made. It is now fashionable to minimize the significance of the Supreme Court decisions invalidating separate school systems for whites and blacks as well as the many other judicial and administrative decisions in recent years that have established the legal basis for equal rights and opportunities. And it is true that the future direction of Supreme Court decisions on the difficult social and educational problems associated with *de facto* segregation and housing is quite unclear. Two things are abundantly evident however: legally sanctioned segregation is unconstitutional and disappearing; and the primary educational concern of the great majority of both whites and non-whites is the quality of their schools rather than the degree of integration achieved. The second reality may not be as attractive as the earlier preoccupation with integration, but in the face of existing residential patterns and a preponderant sentiment among both black and white against forced bussing over long distances, a period of compromise on earlier ideals would seem inescapable. Meanwhile, wherever practicable, in the light of the racial composition of the school district and its size, integration will remain an objective with as much force and significance as the quality of education, and there is some reason to hope that both will be achieved. It is impossible to speak with much authority about this murky and unresolved issue now, but the rough outline of priorities sketched above seems to have the support of a substantial majority of whites and non-whites and these priorities probably do not contradict any of the essential principles of a democratic society.

Perhaps even more important than the steps that have been taken in the judicial and administrative areas are the measures passed by legislative bodies. Legislators are, after all, ultimately responsible to their constituents in a way that appointed judges, for example, are not. Between 1957 and 1968 Congress passed several important pieces of civil rights legislation. While these various laws are obviously significant in terms of their substance, it could be argued that in the long run they are even more significant as indicators of the popular mood as reflected in the behavior of the people's representatives. There is some evidence that an increasing number of Americans are aware of the plight of the blacks and that they find this condition unacceptable. Polls suggest a significant liberalizing of attitudes on the part of the white community, both North and South, in regard to such matters as desegregated schools, open housing, and equal job opportunities. While it has been a fairly popular pastime over the last several years to predict an extensive white backlash, this backlash, while appearing here and there, has failed to materialize in any really substantial way.

Certain developments in electoral politics also offer hopeful signs. Massachusetts, with a population only 2.2 percent black, elected a black man to the Senate in 1966. Cleveland has elected and re-elected a black mayor and the black population of that city is 28.6 percent. In Los Angeles a black candidate for mayor was defeated but he did receive 47 percent of the votes and the black population is only 13.5 percent.[1] The fact that many white citizens are prepared to cast their votes for a black citizen obviously does not mean that we have reached the millennium in race relations, but it does represent a promising development. (For further evidence along these lines, including positive economic indicators, see the article by Nathan Glazer, pp. 244–262.)

We are not suggesting that "all is for the best in this best of all possible worlds." We are not suggesting that things are getting better as rapidly as is possible or desirable, and such critical matters as the priorities and policies of the Nixon administration on these matters are, at best, uncertain at the present time. What we are suggesting is that an excessive pessimism is as unrealistic and destructive as a false optimism. Recommendations growing out of the former mood are no more likely to be useful than those emerging from the latter.

It is time for fresh perspectives and prescriptions and for a revival of some currently muted themes. The following articles are not offered in the erroneous belief that they say anything definitive or curative. They are neither dogmatic nor especially programmatic. But they do say many things that are as true as they are neglected, and as wise as they are unfashionable. It is our hope that reading them will provide the reader with a realistic perspective from which to continue the long-overdue struggle against second-class citizenship.

[1] These figures are for 1960. Clearly there has been an increase in the black population since that time. However, current projections for Los Angeles, for example, still estimate the black population to be less than 20 percent.

BLACK
AND WHITE
TRAGEDY

James Q. Wilson

More was destroyed here this summer than the lives and
property that fell victim to riots in Detroit, Newark, and elsewhere. The confident generalisations of liberals about what
must be done for the Negro, the hope of some Negroes that
"equal opportunity" alone would change the lives of many, and
the belief of working- and middle-class whites that the government could ensure order whatever happened—all have suffered
a serious blow.

Much of this loss is still referred to only privately, and in
guarded tones. One of the remarkable features of the disturb-
ances of the last few American summers is that they have not
yet shattered the control of the public agenda and the public
rhetoric exercised by the national news media, the Eastern press,
and the liberal professors and politicians whose opinions are
regularly referred to when an oracular statement seems required
by large events. Or to put it more succinctly, what is remarkable
is that there has not yet emerged a McCarthy of race: a figure
with a mass audience (if not a mass following) who would say
boldly and demagogically what millions of people are already
thinking. George Wallace is trying to become that figure, but not
yet with great success.

What they are thinking and whispering, as I understand it, is
that those who resisted residential integration and believed that

James Q. Wilson, "Black and White Tragedy," *Encounter* (October
1967), 63–68. Reprinted by permission of the author.

the Negro was not yet "ready" in the mass (conceding individual exceptions) for full citizenship were right all along, and that those who said that the fact of race was an accidental and irrelevant stigma, unfairly used to the disadvantage of one group, were wrong.

During the last week in July, I found myself in the midst of a minor riot (in Albany, New York), thereby becoming one of the few social scientists who manages to collect more data than he really wants. I was also in the white bars and restaurants of Albany after the disturbance, and in retrospect I am not sure which experience was more frightening. That's not quite true: the riot, being a fact, was more frightening than the talk, which was only a threat. Reasonably prosperous and slightly overweight middle-class whites may talk of buying shot-guns at Sears-Roebuck and of "shooting on sight" Negroes demonstrating or looting near their property, but not many of them, one hopes, are likely to have the inclination or the opportunity to do much along these lines.

The standard explanations of and prescriptions for the riots are being offered in the editorials and in speeches, but even those which I myself fully subscribed to a year ago now have a hollow ring. The concept of "relative deprivation" once struck me as a profound sociological insight; but somehow it is hard to impute to that idea the power to kill forty-three people and destroy 100 million dollars worth of property in Detroit alone. Worse, relative deprivation—the idea that people judge themselves deprived, not absolutely but relative to the lot of people they regard as equivalent—now seems a counsel of despair. Negroes did not riot when they were much worse off than they are today; they are rioting now (so the theory goes) because though they are better off in education and income than twenty or even ten years ago, they are still badly off compared to whites. But if we find some way to increase the rate at which progress is now being made among Negroes, in the short run we are likely only to intensify the feeling of relative deprivation and thus increase the prospect of more riots. Put another way, if the Negro riots are a "revolution of rising expectations," then the more done for them in the name of preventing riots will only further enlarge these expectations and thus (in the short run) stoke the furnaces of revolution.

Nobody should refuse to meliorate adversity or correct injustice on the grounds that it may cause more trouble; at the same time, however, nobody should expect that things done because a riot has forced us to "do something" will in fact prevent a riot. The blunt truth is that nobody has any idea how to prevent a riot, and those that say they have are, in my opinion, substituting hope for facts. This is not to deny the real possibility that unemployment, poor education, bad housing, and inadequate public services are at the root of the matter. But such problems have always been with us; with respect to most of them, things have been getting better in recent years. These "underlying causes" may create the conditions in which riots occur, but they do not explain the crucial question: why *now*, why these riots *today*? The "underlying causes" might explain a generation, or a half century, of rioting, but not two or three summers' worth.

A FEW CLAIM that the proximate explanation is to be found in the seditious statements and activities of black nationalist radicals. The "National Advisory Commission on Civil Disorders" created recently by President Johnson, will probably not be able to accomplish much but it should be able to disprove that theory. Already, it is reliably reported, Mr. J. Edgar Hoover and the FBI are prepared to assert that there is no evidence of any conspiracy, though nobody is confident the FBI has the sources or the information to render it expert in this field. There are, in my opinion, some Negro radicals who are trying to create a conspiracy and who would like nothing better than to cause a riot, but so far they have been unsuccessful—they are in the position of the man chasing the mob shouting that he must follow them because he is their leader. We have conspirators, but as yet no conspiracy.

A more plausible reason why underlying problems are now being converted into civil disorder is that rioting has been made legitimate. Nobody exactly condones it (H. Rap Brown excepted), everybody routinely deplores it, but at the same time everybody—from the Vice-President of the United States on down—has gone around for some time predicting it and saying, in effect, "If I were in their position I would riot, too." Civil rights leaders have regularly and without exception used the prediction of riot as a reason why whatever proposal they were offering at the moment should be accepted—"Do this, or there will be a Long, Hot Summer! . . ." Many of their proposals were eminently worth accepting, but rarely for the reason implied.

Television cameras have given to riots—and more importantly, to rioters—an audience, an immediacy, and a dramatic impact unparalleled in the history of American civil disorders. There have been Irish riots (the Draft Riots of 1863), Jewish riots (the Kosher Meat Riots in New York City), and anti-Negro riots (in Chicago in 1919 and Detroit in 1943), but rarely were they more than sporadic and isolated events—the absence of a pictorial mass media prevented them from being nationalised and thus, in a sense, legitimised. Today, television cameramen and radio announcers on location are at the scene almost before the crowd has become animated, and they rarely need explain to the gathering mob what is expected of them.

One minor riot in a West Coast city last year began *after* TV cameramen in jump suits and crash helmets had set up their equipment in a parking lot on the morning of a Negro school boycott. The youngsters assembled before the cameras; all they lacked was a director to give them their cue. The cues supplied themselves. In the Albany disturbance I witnessed, my car was in Clinton Square next to that of a radio crew broadcasting on a live remote pickup. I heard over my radio what they were saying and saw through my windshield what they were seeing. There was not much relationship between what I saw and what I heard. While Negro kids were still running about, almost aimlessly, and police were circling them without leaving their cars or making an arrest, the radio station—the regular programming of which featured hard rock music and thus was a favourite among young people, white and Negro—was announcing that "Albany has erupted in violence" and a "long, hard night was beginning." As I watched, the nearby saloons disgorged their customers, and cars and pedestrians began arriving to swell the crowds hoping to see the action and, occasionally, to join in. (The newspapers, by contrast, were quite responsible—holding stories of earlier outbreaks as long as possible to avoid putting fuel on the fires and then publishing stories of the conflict in perspective and without sensationalism.)

Bear in mind that, at least in the initial stages, the rioters are young Negro men—many with jobs, others so young that by law they cannot be employed—for whom a display of mass violence has not only become legitimate, but important. Every militant, working-class Negro leader to whom I have spoken (and organizations of such "street men" have begun to spring up in many cities) will say that the younger Negroes are not only ready for violence, but eager for it. In Albany, one working-class civil rights group, calling itself "The Brothers," cooled off a confrontation between the police and young Negroes on a Wednesday night (the incident had arisen from a rumour, later proved false, that a police car had run down a Negro girl). By Thursday night, however, the youngsters had quite plainly decided they had been deprived of a chance to do something they very much wanted to do, and this time the most urgent pleas by the civil rights leaders (who normally are heroes to the kids because many of them have prison records) were to no avail.

In short, we may be facing an irrepressible conflict. Pessimistically, this means that few, if any, Negro ghettos will escape having one major disturbance; optimistically, this means that a self-limiting process may be at work so that few ghettos will have two major riots. The only thing a government can do to prevent a riot is to offer constructive alternatives (jobs, schooling, neighbourhood centres, better housing). But what can government do if the urge for violent self-expression can only be averted by creating a destructive alternative—a moral equivalent for rioting?

ONE WORD THAT IS rarely heard these days is "integration." It was the slogan of the Civil Rights Movement in the 1950s. It is hardly anybody's slogan today. Roy Wilkins' NAACP and Whitney Young's Urban League, both deeply committed to integration, speak as if they realised that to hold their own against Black Power leaders they must emphasise programmes of immediate economic benefit to the ghettos.

But what programmes? There is a spreading disillusionment on the progressive Left as well as on the Right with many "war on poverty" and welfare programmes as being aimless, impossible to administer well (or at all), and irrelevant to the lives of the masses. There is now a good deal more talk of a federal programme of "guaranteed employment"—as Daniel Patrick Moynihan insists, the government should become the employer of last resort—whereby anybody, black or white, literate or illiterate, skilled or unskilled, can walk into a neighbourhood office and be put to work for at least the minimum wage (now $1.40—ten shillings—per hour). This would be a year-round (not a summer only) programme and linked to a large-scale vocational effort. And it would be aimed at males, not females. The furore that followed the release two years ago of the Moynihan Report on the Negro family has begun to die down and a concern for the serious consequences of the matri-focal, fatherless Negro family has now almost become part of the conventional wisdom.

The advantage of a guaranteed employment programme is essentially the same as the virtue Lord Melbourne found in the Order of the Garter—there's no damn merit about it. One doesn't earn it, one *gets* it. The other advantage is that—short of a direct cash handout or "negative income tax," which is politically impossible and may be morally dubious—it is about the only way of ensuring that the beneficiaries of the programme are *the unemployed* and not social workers, university researchers, and local bureaucrats.

The disadvantage of such a programme is that it will not, in my opinion, materially reduce the probability of rioting, at least in the short run. The reason we are having riots at all is that, as Professor Norton Long has put it, one important element of our society has failed to produce a social structure adequate to full participation in the economic system. A combination of unparalleled prosperity and multi-billion dollar welfare and anti-poverty programmes should have brought by now every person but the pathological into full economic citizenship. It has not, and discrimination—especially in the craft unions—is part of the answer but not all of it. It is now quite apparent that a modern economy, however affluent, has great difficulty in doing much for anybody who finds life on the street corner more attractive than life in the factory. This is true of a substantial fraction of Negro men who now operate most of the big-city hustles— pimping, petty gambling, pushing dope, defrauding the tourists (and each other). Ironically, the big-time rackets—machine politics, organised gambling—have been either eliminated or taken away from the Negro, leaving him with only the little hustles. But they are still attractive enough so that many Negroes tell poverty workers that they can keep their $1.40-an-hour jobs. "Duking" on the corner is more stylish, more expressive, and an adequate living.

A recent public service radio advertisement I heard makes the point. The announcer in earnest tones told his listeners that "industry faces a great shortage of unskilled and semi-skilled workers" and that "businessmen needed manpower as never before." Therefore, "if you are physically handicapped," be sure to learn about the many job openings available to you. For reasons we are only beginning to understand, it is easier to place amputees than Negroes in our economy.

The administration in Washington has let it be known there is not going to be much new money for the cities because of the Viet Nam war and the prospective $28 billion budget deficit. Mayors, who once would have applauded such a statement on the grounds that it was fiscally responsible (and anyway federal grants to the cities would only lead to "federal controls"), have now denounced it. Only a small handful of them, I imagine, believe there is any way in the short run that Washington could honourably reduce expenditures in Viet Nam; but a large majority are willing to argue most vociferously that we could well afford to take money away from the space programme (getting "a man on the moon" will cost an estimated $23 billion). In light of what is happening in our cities making a safe manned landing on the moon seems at best ill-timed and at worst frivolous.

THE ADMINISTRATION is looking for low-budget ways of dealing with disorders, and improved police and riot control procedures are obviously going to be one. And there is much to be said for this on grounds other than economy. Whatever else the law is, it is an alternative to private vengeance and right now, for many whites, it is no longer a credible alternative. The government is going to have to make it much clearer than it has so far that it is capable of maintaining order in the cities.

The local police, as they will readily admit, cannot cope with this situation. They are too few in numbers, too thinly deployed, and too lacking in a military command and control structure to be effective against large masses of rioters. Unlike some European countries, American fears of the "military state" and the "garrison city" have led us to combine the constabulary function with the civil order function, and the combination is not working well. Distasteful as it may be, I believe we are going to have to garrison our major metropolitan areas, at least during the summer months, with National Guard units stationed in armouries and available on one hour's notice.

In principle, a military unit has the numbers and the discipline to both isolate a disturbance and suppress it with a minimum of shooting. In practice, the Guard so far, especially in Detroit, has shown itself woefully inadequate to the task. That city, indeed, offered almost a controlled experiment. The National Guard dealt with one half of the riot area, the U.S. Army paratroopers with the other. All the returns are not in yet, but in the opinion of every observer who has so far spoken out, the paratroopers did an incomparably better job—less violence, greater discipline, and more precise and less indiscriminate use of force. President Johnson has already ordered "improved riot control training" made available to the Guard. But how much is this likely to accomplish when the Guard trains only on weekends and for a fortnight during the summer? And even a well-trained Michigan National Guard would have only offered a slight improvement over what happened: it takes so long to mobilise. The early hours of a riot are critical—if it can be contained and looting prevented, then the mass involvement of Negroes and Whites can perhaps be avoided. Once looting starts, it becomes a tragic carnival with prizes for everyone. If two days are necessary to get battalion-size units into a city and on to the streets, the carnival—and the carnage—are inevitable.

An alternative is to stagger the summer training schedule of Guard members so that a few companies train at different periods rather than the whole division assembling at once for field manoeuvres that are well-suited, perhaps, to a European land war but ill-suited to guerrilla warfare in the ghettos. The extra cost would have to be paid by Washington. If the Guard is not going to be used in Viet Nam (and it seems unlikely, especially with a Presidential election next year), then perhaps we ought to make it deliberately and fully into what necessity requires it to be—an organisation that will ensure a minimum of civil order.

Talk of "mobilising the Guard" is as repellent to liberals as talk of "guaranteed jobs" is to conservatives. And I, for one, am not confident that a strong and well-trained Guard will prevent white vigilantism any more than I am confident that a modern Rooseveltian W.P.A. (modern in the sense that it would be coupled with a serious vocational training programme) will prevent Negro rioting. The best that can be said for either proposal is that it will remove the excuse for vigilantism and rioting. And right now, that may be the best we can hope for.

Statement Issued on July 26, 1967 by

Martin Luther King, Jr., A. Philip Randolph, Roy Wilkins, and Whitney M. Young, Jr.

Developments in Newark, Detroit, and other strife-torn cities make it crystal clear that the primary victims of the riots are the Negro citizens. That they have grave grievances of long standing cannot be denied or minimized. That the riots have not contributed in any substantial measure to the eradication of these just complaints is by now obvious to all.

We are confident that the overwhelming majority of the Negro community joins us in opposition to violence in the streets. Who is without the necessities of life when the neighborhood stores are destroyed and looted? Whose children are without milk because deliveries cannot be made? Who loses wages because of a breakdown in transportation or destruction of the place of employment? Who are the dead, the injured and the imprisoned? It is the Negroes who pay and pay and pay, whether or not they are individually involved in the rioting. And for what?

Killing, arson, looting are criminal acts and should be dealt with as such. Equally guilty are those who incite, provoke and call specifically for such action. There is no injustice which justifies the present destruction of the Negro community and its people.

We who have fought so long and so hard to achieve justice for all Americans have consistently opposed violence as a means of redress. Riots have proved ineffective, disruptive and highly damaging to the Negro population, to the civil rights cause and to the entire nation.

We call upon Negro citizens throughout the nation to forego the temptation to disregard the law. This does not mean that we should submit tamely to joblessness, inadequate housing, poor schooling, insult, humiliation and attack. It does require a redoubling of efforts through legitimate means to end these wrongs and disabilities.

We appeal not only to black Americans but also to our fellow white citizens, who are not blameless. The disabilities imposed upon Negro citizens are a century old. They remain because the white citizenry in general supports these restrictions.

The Nineteenth Congress has exhibited an incredible indifference to hardships of the ghetto dwellers. Only last week the House defeated a rat-control bill which would have enabled the cities to get rid of the rats which infest the slums.

And finally, we fully support President Johnson's call "upon all our people (black and white alike) in all our cities to join in a determined program to maintain law and order, to condemn and to combat lawlessness in all its forms, and firmly to show by word and deed that riot, looting and public disorder will just not be tolerated."

No one benefits under mob law. Let's end it now!

AMERICA'S
RACE PARADOX

Nathan Glazer

Something very strange is happening in the racial crisis in the
United States. On the one hand, the concrete situation of Negro
Americans is changing rapidly for the better. This is not only
true when we look at economic measures of all kinds (although
we all know that these are an inadequate measure of group
progress, and that a people that feels oppressed will never be
satisfied by the argument "you never had it so good"); but it is
also true that things are better when we look at measures of
political participation and power. It is even true when we look at
the critical area of police behaviour and police attitudes. There
is no question that police in city after city are becoming more
careful in how they address Negro Americans, more restrained
in the use of force, of fire-arms. The history of the riots alone,
from 1964, demonstrates that.

But on the other hand, the political attitudes of Negroes have
become more extreme and more desperate. The riots are called
"rebellions," and hardly any Negro leader today bothers to deplore them. Militant groups become larger, and their language
and demands more shocking. Cultural nationalism flourishes—
and I think most people think that is good—but political separatism becomes an ever more popular demand, and hardly anyone
can consider that without thinking again. (We all know what

Nathan Glazer, "America's Race Paradox," *Encounter* (October
1968), 63–68. Reprinted by permission of the author.

may happen when a country begins to break up. Look at Nigeria.)

This is an incredible dilemma for social policy. For the fact is that most of us—black and white, liberals and conservatives, socialists and free enterprisers—believe (*1*) that political and social attitudes reflect the concrete economic and social and political situation of people; (*2*) that we can affect those attitudes by changing the concrete conditions; and (*3*) that when things get better people become more satisfied, less violent, the society becomes more stable. When concrete conditions improve and political attitudes become at the same time more extreme and violent, we can resort to two explanations.

There is the well-known "revolution of rising expectations," and the ease with which expectations can outstrip concrete positive changes. And there is the theory of Alexis de Tocqueville, developed in his study of the French Revolution, that the improvement of conditions increases the desire for greater change and for revolutionary change, because people themselves feel stronger and more potent. Both of these processes are undoubtedly taking place, but one's attitude to them must depend on one's attitude to American society. If one looks upon American society as Tocqueville and the French people looked upon their Old Régime, that is, as a conservative, sclerotic, repressive, irrational, and selfish régime which prevented the free development of the people, then one of course will accept favourably the rise of the extreme opinion, and look forward to the crash of the American Old Régime. But if one sees American society and state as fundamentally democratic, as capable of change, as responsive to people's wishes—then one will be deeply concerned whether this society and state can survive. That expectations should rise is good—that they should rise so fast that no policy of any type carried out by anybody can satisfy them, is bad. That people should feel potent and powerful and free to express their resentments and anger is encouraging—that that resentment and anger should serve to overthrow a system that works, that is capable of satisfying their needs and hopes, is deplorable.

A rapid rate of social change has improved the condition of Negro Americans and has gone some way to closing the gaps between the condition of Negro and white Americans, but it has not only *not* moderated the rise of extremism and violence—it has been accompanied by it. At some point one must expect improvement and change to moderate extremism and violence, despite the revolution of rising expectations and the Tocquevillean hypothesis. If there is such a point, it is clear we are not only not arriving at it: we are getting further and further away from it.

There is, of course, another possible explanation of what is happening: that Negro Americans are no longer interested in Integration or even in educational, economic, and political advance within the American social system. They have begun to see themselves as "a subject people" and, as in the case of every such people, only independent political existence can satisfy them. This, in any case, is the direction that militant Negro demands have now begun to take. And if most Negro Americans follow the militant leaders, then all the political skill, ingenuity, and creativity the American nation possesses will be necessary to keep it from being torn apart.

First, let me briefly document the fact that things *are* getting better. We must do this because so many liberal and progressive shapers of opinion, and the vast flock that follows them, are convinced (and *insist*) that the concrete situation of Negro Americans has *not* changed, or has indeed got worse. Sadly enough, social scientists, who should know the facts best, are often among the worst offenders. The writer of that fine study of Negro street-corner men, *Tally's Corner*, for example, states casually that "the number of the poor and their problems have grown steadily since World War II. . . ." Social scientists who contend that the economic situation of Negroes is getting worse will point to the rising *absolute* gap between Negro and white incomes and ignore the fact that Negro incomes have come closer to white incomes as a *percentage* of white incomes. By this logic, if we come to a fortunate time when white median incomes are $10,000 and non-white median incomes are $8,000, it could be argued that Negroes are "worse off" than when whites made $5,000 and Negroes $3,500!

In October 1967, the Bureau of Labor Statistics and the Bureau of the Census put out a compendium of statistics on the *Social and Economic Conditions of Negroes in the United States*. Here are some of the major findings:

Income: In 1966, 23% of non-white families had incomes of more than $7,000, against 53% of white families. Ten years before, using dollars of the same value, only 9% of the non-white families had incomes at this level, against 31% of white families.

If we look at the U.S. outside the South, where the Negro situation on all measures is worst, we find in 1966 38% of non-white families with income above $7,000, against 59% of white families at that level.

Occupation: Between 1960 and 1966, the number of non-whites in the better-paying and more secure occupational categories increased faster than whites: a 50% increase for non-whites in professional, technical and managerial work, against a 13% increase for whites; a 48% increase in clerical occupations, against a 19% increase for whites; a 32% increase in sales workers, against a 7% increase for whites; a 45% increase in craftsmen and foremen, against a 10% increase for whites. And during the same time, the proportions of non-whites working as private household workers and labourers dropped.

Education: In 1960 there was a 1.9 years gap in median years of school completed between non-white and white males over 25; by 1966, there was only a .5 years gap.

In 1960, 3.9% of Negro males had completed college, against 15.7% of white males; in 1966, 7.4% of Negro males had completed college, against 17.9% of white males—a 90% increase among non-white college graduates, against a 14% increase in white college graduates.

Housing: Between 1960 and 1966, there was a 25% drop in the number of substandard housing units occupied by non-whites (from 2,263,000 to 1,691,000 units), and a 44% increase in the number of standard units occupied by non-whites—from 2,881,000 to 4,135,000 units.

If we look at political participation—voting, offices held, in effect, political power—we find an equally striking increase. Thus, Negro voter registration in the South increased from 2,164,000 in March 1964 to 3,072,000 in May 1968, while Negro population remained stable. The National Commission on Civil Disorders surveyed twenty cities to find out the extent of Negro political representation. The cities averaged 16% in Negro population; 10% in proportion of elected Negro political representatives. We have to interpret such a figure in the light of the fact that Negroes of voting age are generally a smaller proportion of the total Negro population in most cities than whites of voting age of the white population, since Negroes in cities have a higher proportion of young families and children, whites a higher proportion of the aged.

Even on that sorest point of black-white relations, the police, the Kerner Commission reports progress in one significant respect: there are now substantial numbers of Negroes on many city police forces—Washington 21% ; Philadelphia 20, Chicago 17, St. Louis 11, Hartford 11, Newark 10, Atlanta 10, Cleveland 7, New York 5, Detroit 5.

These are simply overall measures. When one considers the large number of programmes devoted to getting Negroes into colleges, into graduate and professional schools, into various corporations, to raise their grades in the Federal Civil Service, to moderate police attitudes—and when one considers the incentives to do all these things to be found in riot and threat of riot, boycott and threat of boycott, one cannot help conclude that the situation of Negroes is changing . . . for "the better."

To be sure, all the figures I have quoted can be disputed. Thus, 14% of Negro males as against only 2% of white males (we have recently become aware) never get counted by the census; and if they were counted, they would undoubtedly depress the Negro figures on income, education, occupation, housing. But as against this, it must be pointed out that we have probably not been counting similar proportions of Negro males of working age in earlier censuses; so the change from one census to another represents real change.

It can be argued that the quality of jobs held by Negroes, even if they are in white-collar and skilled labour categories, is worse than that held by whites; and this too is true. But the changes over time are real, and the quality of jobs has certainly not on the whole decreased. Indeed, it has probably improved. Less Negro professionals today are preachers, more are engineers.

It can be argued that the improvement in the economic and educational and housing condition of the Negro is largely an effect of their migration from the South, and from small town and rural areas, to the North and West, and to big cities; if we were to look at Negroes in the North and West alone, we would find such marked changes. But the statistics show improvement in every section.

It has been argued that while these overall measures of improvement truly reflect improvement for the Negro middle-classes, the lower working classes have relatively declined, and have shown no progress. But an unpublished analysis of income statistics by Dr. Albert Wohlstetter (of the University of Chicago) reveals that the *lower* Negro income groups have improved their position relatively to white low-income groups more in recent years than the Negro upper-income groups have improved their position relative to white upper-income groups. In other words, the gap between poor Negroes and poor whites in terms of income is narrower now than in the 1950s. At the same time it is true that other social indicators—*e.g.*, the proportion of broken families and of illegitimacy—continue to reveal worsening conditions.

Finally, one may argue that much of the advance to which I have pointed has taken place since the Viet Nam War expanded in 1965, just as the previous economic advances of the Negro took place during the Korean War, and came to an end when that war came to an end. Between the wars there was relative decline and stagnation.

There is much truth in these last two arguments with the gross statistics of recent improvement. But it is also true that the advances made during wars have not been fully wiped out in the past—it is rather that the rate of change has not kept up. By now the build-up of Negro political power and of national programmes and commitments that guarantee advance is so great and the scale of the advances that have taken place in recent years is so massive, that I cannot believe they will not continue after the war—if, that is, there is not a radical change in the political situation to reverse the social and economic trends of the last eight years.

MORE STRIKING, however, than the advance itself is the fact that on the basis of our present social statistics we can not single out the Negro as a group in the United States which suffers unique deprivation, *i.e.*, as compared to other ethnic and racial groups which suffer from the effects of poor education, depressed rural backgrounds, and recent migration to urban areas. There has been a division among American social scientists as to how to view Negro Americans in the context of the ethnic and racial history of the United States. One tendency is to emphasize everything that is "unique"—and a great deal is unique: the manner of their arrival (by force, and in chains); the conditions under which they lived for two hundred years (slavery); the conditions under which they have lived for the last hundred years (legal inferiority in a good part of the country); finally, the special role of the Negro Americans in American imagination and culture (as central participants in shaping it, and as the subjects of some of its major themes). But it is also possible to see Negro Americans as part of a sequence of ethnic and racial groups that have moved into American society and become a part of it.

A new illusion is now abroad in the land. It asserts that all white ethnic groups have rapidly moved into American society, achieving respectable levels of income, good conditions of living, and political power. All racially distinct groups, suffering from the racism of American society, have been held back; and the Negro American, suffering from the special character of chattel slavery, is furthest back. The truth is nothing like this. Some white ethnic groups—such as the Jews—have shown a rapid economic mobility. Others have been much slower to achieve economically. One of these economically-backward white ethnic groups, the Irish, has been politically gifted, and members of the group are to be found disproportionately among elected officials of every level and in almost every part of the country. Others, such as Italians and Poles, have done poorly both economically *and* politically. Some racially distinct groups —such as the Japanese—have done remarkably well in education and occupation. Most others have done badly.

The range in experience is enormous, and the cause of this difference is not only degree of discrimination and prejudice, though that is an important factor. Equally important is a whole range of elements we vaguely group under the term "culture"—attitudes and behaviour in connection with School, Work, Family. (These have their origin in history and it may well be that the discrimination and prejudice of the past creates the cultural attributes of the present.) Nor is it true that these grossly different patterns of achievement among different groups are to be found in the U.S.A. alone. They are to be found wherever different ethnic and racial groups live together, whether it is Malays, Chinese, and Indians in Malaya, or Indians and Africans in Kenya, or Chinese and Indonesians in Indonesia, or Maharashtrians and Gujaratis and South Indians in Bombay, *etc.* Indeed, it is often the case that when a group is politically favoured in terms of educational and job opportunities—*e.g.,* the Malays in Malaya—these powerful cultural factors prevent the group from taking full advantage of these opportunities; and they remain at a lower educational and economic level. The Negro situation is rather more complex than the gross simplification of having "started at the bottom and staying there." By some measures, the Puerto Ricans do worse in New York, and the Mexican Americans do worse in the South-west. One can indeed contend that the Negro is worst off of the major ethnic and racial groups in this country, but not that much worse off to explain by itself the special quality of despair and hysteria, and the tone of impending violence and doom that now dominates much Negro political discourse.

But of course we must add another factor to the equation: America's obligation as a nation to improve the position of Negroes is much greater than the obligation to groups that emigrated voluntarily. The Negro is aware of this obligation and responsibility, and so the inferiority of his position becomes far more grating than it would be in the case of ordinary immigrants.

The fact is that, regardless of the details of the actual economic and social position of the Negro, an increasingly large part of twenty-two million Negro Americans believes that Americans are "racists," insist on "keeping the Negro down," and will never allow equality, and that the only solution will be some form of separate political existence. One indicator as to how far we have moved is in the use of words. Consider, for example, "genocide." Last February, Stokely Carmichael spoke to a Negro audience in Oakland and felt he had to justify the use of "genocide" to describe the dangers facing Negroes:

> . . . we are not talking about politics tonight, we're not talking about economics tonight, we're talking about the survival of a race of people. . . . Many of us feel—many of our generation feel—that they are getting ready to commit genocide against us. Now many people say that's a horrible thing to say about anybody. But if it's a horrible thing to say, then we should do as Brother Malcolm said, we should examine history.

We have moved far in the course of a year. A leader of the SCLC says "genocide" is a danger. James Baldwin (in the June 2 Book Review section of the *New York Times*) asserts "white America appears to be seriously considering the possibilities of mass extermination." By now even moderate leaders use the term genocide, and feel they have to use it to appeal to young militants and to show they are not "Uncle Toms." By now, of course, white men who want to demonstrate their sympathy for Negroes will not demur from the use of the term; thus, Eliot Fremont-Smith, reviewing John Hersey's *The Algiers Motel Incident* in the *New York Times,* writes that the book, "shows America to be deeply—and unknowingly to most of its citizens —genocidal."

The public opinion polls report fantastically rapid changes of attitude among Negro Americans. A Louis Harris poll conducted *before* the Martin Luther King assassination reported on a measure of "alienation," and concluded that the numbers of Negroes "alienated" had risen from 34% in 1966 to 56% in 1968. The items measuring alienation included: *"Few people really understand how it is to live like I live"* (those agreeing rose from 32 to 66%); *"People running this country don't really care what happens to people like ourselves"* (those agreeing rose from 32 to 52%). The very same poll reports that 73% of the respondents agreed there has been "more racial progress" in recent years than there had been previously.

So the paradox exists in the very consciousness of Negro Americans. They agree there has been more progress, but also feel ignored, stepped upon, and remote from their society. (Whites do too, but in much lesser degree.) The changes in these general attitudes reported by the Harris poll are particularly striking because they are the sort of general question measuring malaise that one would not expect to vary much over time (*viz.,* "Are you happy?"); and yet they have changed rapidly. I speak of attitudes and the use of words. More striking are the realities of action—the riots since 1964, the general expectation of guerrilla warfare, the rise of the so-called Black Panthers in California and elsewhere and their amazing ability to seize the imagination of the Ghetto youth with a programme calling for armed resistance to the police, community control of the ghetto, freeing of black prisoners, and the ultimate hope for some type of national, separate, political existence for blacks.

THERE ARE THREE POSITIONS now current as to what to do about this strange impasse: social improvement and increasing extremism. One is that we must put down extremism, strengthen the police, create riot control forces. A second is that we must increase the rate of material advance more swiftly—eventually it must lead to a harmonious nation. A third is that social improvement is no longer the issue—separate political power and existence for Negro Americans is the only reality that will satisfy.

I think the majority of white Americans reject the first alternative as any full reponse to the crisis, though certainly most believe the maintenance of civil order must be a part of any response.

The second position is the one for which the Kerner Commission has written a brief in its report, and most liberal Americans are likely to accept it. It is almost the only thesis one can put forward if one's conviction is that, on the whole, American society has been a success, that a major sign of its success is that it has incorporated and will continue to incorporate many diverse groups, and that it can handle the complex and frightening problems of an advanced technological society rather better than the varied assortment of Communist authoritarian states or vague utopias that is the rhetorical hope of the New Left. And yet the liberal position—and we can take the Kerner Commission report as expressing it best—has one basic difficulty.

It is that we have *already* carried out and are carrying out social programmes at an ever-increasing scale without, as we have seen, any movement towards the reward of "a united and peaceful nation." Take the figures of the Kerner Commission itself:

> Federal expenditures for manpower development and training have increased from less than $60 million in 1963 to $1.6 billion in 1968. The President has proposed a further increase, $2.1 billion in 1969 . . . to provide work experience, training, and supportive services for 1.3 million men and women . . . [which happens to be more thaṅ twice the number of non-white unemployed].
>
> Federal expenditures for education, training and related services have increased from $4.7 billion in fiscal 1964 to $12.3 billion in fiscal 1969.
>
> Direct Federal expenditures for housing and community development have increased from $600 million in fiscal 1964 to nearly $3 billion in fiscal 1969.

There have been similarly heavy increases in health and welfare expenditures. All these figures are reported in order to criticise the build-up of expenditures as "not rapid enough" and to demand "far more money" in these and other areas. I am left with an uneasy feeling. If these rates of expansion reported by the Kerner Commission have taken place at the same time as the spread of urban riots and political extremism, is it not questionable whether further expansion will stem them? I am *for* the expansion of these programmes because they are the major means we have for achieving equality in occupations, education, housing, *etc.* But I do not think we can count on them to moderate attitudes—for political attitudes and development have a life of their own, and are not simple reflections of economic and social conditions.

There is no question in my mind that the demand for "Black Separatism" will not be easily moderated by new social programmes. Accordingly, we must face up to the demand for separatism in its own terms.

Here one must note that "separatism" seems to mean many different things. Some of them appear to me to be valuable and healthy, both for Negroes and for American society: the emphasis on positive identification with the group, "Black Power" in its sense of greater political impact and representation of Negroes; "Black Capitalism"; "Black history" and art. The chief difficulty presented by Black Separatism arises in the demands for territorial autonomy and "extra-territoriality." These have now been presented in many forms: a group of states to become a black nation; black enclaves in the cities, with certain rights and powers; special legal rights for blacks, as in the "Free Huey" demand and its argument that white judges and juries cannot try blacks (even though there are blacks among them). There is no question that American political leaders (and the great majority of the American people) will resist the demand for territorial autonomy and extra-territoriality. One war has been fought to preserve the Union, and the sense of what all Americans gain from a united nation, and what they might lose from a divided one, is strong enough to ensure that these demands will continue to be resisted. Nor is it clear that any substantial part of Negro Americans at present agrees with the Separatists. But their dynamism is frightening, and they are powerfully supported, in my view, not by the realities of the Negro condition and the hopes they offer of improving it, but by powerful ideologies. In particular, it is the new ideology that Negroes in America are "a Colonial People" and require freedom from colonial status.

IF THE DEMAND for territorial independence succeeds in capturing the minds of Negro Americans, it will be because blacks and whites have not truly understood the relationship between the varying groups that make up American society. Many, in both groups, see the society as far more monolithic and homogeneous than it has ever been. I am afraid that whites will be moved to fight to retain something that has never existed in this country, and the blacks will fight because they have not been convinced of the enormous scope for group diversity the society provides.

Almost every ethnic and racial group that has settled in this country has been "nationalistic" and "separatist," and the laws have permitted a level of separatism for many groups that has not yet been quite reached by American Negroes. Many groups have harboured and supported with money (and sometimes with armed volunteers) nationalist leaders interested in freeing or revolutionising their homelands, even when this was a matter of great embarrassment to the U.S.A. Most groups have maintained schools in their own tongue. Most groups have tried desperately to maintain the original home language, religion, and ethnic customs among their children in America. There has been one limit set on the free development of ethnic and racial groups in this country—territorial autonomy. But short of that, subtle and complex adjustments were made to accommodate a wide variety of differences.

The history of the gross prejudice and discrimination which almost all immigrant and racial groups have faced is well known; but we tend to be less aware of these "American adjustments" to accommodate a mixed population of different ethnic and racial groups. Thus, we have developed a pattern of political recognition, through the parties, in which groups of any substantial number get represented, through appointive and elective office. This system has worked well, without any laws requiring quotas, or specifications of "how much" and "what kind." There has been a pattern of economic integration in which groups have developed bases of economic independence. (Undoubtedly the general freedom this country has given to economic enterprises has aided this development.) Unfortunately, the ability to create such an independent economic base is now considerably limited by, among other things, the host of state and social licensing and regulatory requirements, trade union requirements, federal tax and accounting procedures, all of which today make it much harder for the less literate and sophisticated to become successful in business. We have allowed full freedom to religious organisation, and under the protection of religious organisation a wide range of cultural, social, political activities is carried on. We have given freedom to the creation of independent schools. All this has occurred even though a young patchwork nation has had the difficult task of fashioning a single national identity.

Compared with most countries that have tried to create themselves out of a mixed population, there has been a certain genius in the American style of confronting this problem. The principle has been: no formal recognition of the ethnic and racial groups, but every informal recognition of their right and desire to self-development, assimilation or integration at their own chosen rate, to an independent economic base, independent social, religious, and political institutions, and political recognition as part of a united country. The principle has often been broken: laws have been erected against certain groups—most massively in the case of Negroes, but also in the case of American Indians and Orientals; and we have often restricted the free and spontaneous development of various groups through movements of "Americanisation" and forced patriotism. But the most massive and inhumane breaks in these principles have in the end been recognised as "un-American," and wrong: slavery for the Negroes; "separate but equal" facilities for Negroes; public discrimination against Negroes; separate schools for the Chinese; land laws restricting the right of purchase by Japanese; the forced relocation of the Japanese and their loss of property; the immigration laws establishing quotas for peoples and races; attempts of states to ban private schooling. All these have in the end been overcome by courts and legislatures, and the basic principle—no public recognition of race or ethnicity; every private consideration of its reality and meaningfulness—has, in the end, prevailed.

UNDOUBTEDLY, TO ARGUE that the Negroes, who stand at the very heart of American civilisation as a cruelly harmed people, can be (and, indeed, have been in large measure) incorporated into this pattern, will appear to many an act of Pollyanna-ish refusal to face up to the evil in American society. Professor Robert Blauner (of the University of California at Berkeley) has argued forcefully that there are certain "colonised" peoples in the United States who do not fit the ethnic pattern I have described; and these are the Negroes, the American Indians, and the Mexican Americans. According to this thesis, the ethnic pattern that permitted a self-granted rate of integration into American life prevailed only for the European immigrant groups; and to a much more modest degree, it prevails for the Chinese and Japanese. But there was a different pattern for those peoples who were conquered or brought here as slaves. They have been "colonised," made inferior to the "settlers" in every part of life (political, economic, social, cultural), deprived of their power and "manhood"; and for them only the colonial pattern of rebellion, resistance, and forceful overthrow of settler dominance is meaningful. Thus Frantz Fanon's passionate argument for the significance of violence against the settlers in recreating the colonised as a people (in his *Wretched of the Earth*) speaks to American Negroes as it speaks to the colonised everywhere.

If Professor Blauner is right, then all that remains for us "non-colonised," as settlers, is to figure out how, when the colonised are so scattered among the settlers, we may give them the independence that will make them whole—or, if we refuse, wait for them to take it, or destroy the Union in the effort.

But I think he is wrong, and for one basic reason: whatever the relevance of the "colonisation hypothesis" to the past—when the Negroes lived as agricultural workers in the South, the Mexican Americans in villages in the Southwest, the American Indians on the reservation—it is scarcely relevant today when three-quarters of American Negroes have moved to cities to become not only workers and servants but skilled workers, foremen, civil servants, professionals, white-collar workers of all types; when (at a slower rate) the same thing is happening to Mexican Americans; and when even Indians can free themselves from any politically inferior status by giving up the reservation and moving to the city (as more and more are doing). These moves are voluntary—or if involuntary to some extent, no more so than the migration of many other groups escaping political persecution and economic misery. They lead to the creation of a voluntary community of self-help institutions. They lead to a largely self-regulated rate at which group cultural patterns are given up and new ones adopted. It is all quite comparable to what happened to the European immigrant groups. Statistics which show the wide range of outcomes that we find in all groups, whether European immigrant, racial immigrant, or the so-called "colonised," are strong evidence for the similarity.

Undoubtedly all these groups still face prejudice and discrimination; but this still does not make the "colonial" analogy fit. Prejudice and discrimination, it seems, are endemic wherever different groups socially interact. Are the Algerian workers of the slum settlements around Paris now "colonised"? Are the Spanish and Turkish immigrant workers of Europe "colonised"? Or are they not, rather, immigrant workers facing the prejudice and discrimination and inferior living conditions strangers so often do? Nor are prejudice and discrimination insuperable obstacles to economic advancement and political power. If we were to have to wait for "the end of prejudice and discrimination" before we could say the Negro was truly a part of American society, we would have to wait forever. The issue is: what is the *level* of prejudice and discrimination, how is it formulated in *harmful policies,* what *official assistance* does it get, and to what extent (on the other hand) *does the state act against its private manifestations.* If we apply these tests, I believe, we will find that the "colonial analogy" as applied to the American Negro is meaningless. For there has been a steady decline in all forms of expressed prejudice against Negroes, as indicated in public opinion polls and in everyday behaviour, and there has been stronger and stronger state action, outside the South (and even in some parts of the South) against manifestations of prejudice. Even the recent riots (as far as we can tell from the evidence) have led to no increase in prejudice or white antagonism.

The "colonial pattern" makes sense if one of two conditions prevails: there is a *legal* inferiority of the colonised, in which the settlers are given greater rights and prerogatives; or, even if there is a *formal* equality, in fact only tiny proportions of the colonised can reach high status in society. But this is not true of the Negro Americans, nor will it be true shortly of the Mexican Americans, and, if they so choose, of American Indians. The fact is that instead of keeping these groups out of privileged status most public policy and the programmes of most large private U.S. institutions is to bring them in larger and larger numbers into privileged status. What else is the meaning of the work of the Federal civil service in continually upgrading minority employees, of the colleges in recruiting them beyond the numbers that could normally qualify, of the various corporation programmes for training minority group executives and franchise holders? The scale of some of this is much too small; but the point is that its aim is to speed up a process of incorporating these groups into the mixed American society, rather than slowing it down.

THE ISSUE OF WHETHER Negro Americans are "colonised" or not is not to be settled by arguments between professors: it will be settled by Negro Americans themselves. If they view themselves as colonised, as suffering unbearable repression, as prevented from leading that degree of national and separate existence that they wish within the present prevailing American pattern, then they will do everything to break that pattern; and it will be up to all Americans to decide whether the awful suffering of wars of national unity is to be preferred to the dangers of separatism. No one who has thought deeply about the American Civil War (or what is happening in Nigeria now) will be able to give a pat answer to this question.

The issue, I think, is not yet settled, despite the extravagance of Negro militant rhetoric. Three factors still argue against the victory of the "colonial analogy" among Negroes.

1. The substantial numbers of Negroes who *are* integrated into American society—the civil servants, the white-collar workers, the union members, the political party members, the elected and appointed officials. They are truly in a tragic situation, and no one can say whether they will choose to identify with those who insist on seeing them as "colonised," or whether they will argue for integration into American life, along the pattern that I have described.

2. The second is the possibility that moderate and available social change can still pacify the militants. While making large separatist demands, they would perhaps be satisfied with more jobs, better jobs, more Negro appointed and elected officials, better schools, better housing, a more integrated and respectful police force, and that degree of separate institutional identity and control which the American pattern can tolerate. Certainly we have done too little in all these areas; but we have done a good deal, and we must do more, hoping that in effect the separatists are not really as intransigent as they sound.

3. The enormous difficulty of any territorial solution to the demand for separatism, and the difficulty of devising any alternative.

But there are indeed factors which argue for the success of the "colonial analogy" and the victory of separatism.

One is the enormous impact on Negro experience of past and present experience in the South, where Negroes were held captive and colonised indeed, and where there still remains the most unrelenting and sophisticated resistance to Negro equality in whole states and in large sections of the population. The colonial imagery of the South has been transported to East and West and to the great cities which are largely free of colonialism. There it struggles against the immigrant analogy—and, on the whole, it is losing. They shout, "We are still slaves" and "We want freedom" in the North, where the issue is neither slavery nor freedom.

The second is our failure to adopt rapidly enough new approaches to achieving effective equality for the Negro. While the immigrant analogy is still, to my mind, in large measure valid, it is not fully valid. Negro business must be created, subsidised, sustained, advised; job programmes must become better and more meaningful; the colleges must learn new techniques for incorporating large numbers of minority students, and the urban schools must undergo a transformation (though its nature is hard to define) in becoming effective with minority students. But all this is enormously demanding, so demanding indeed that we may not succeed. Mayor Lindsay, speaking to businessmen in New York—and he was perhaps the dominant liberal member of the Kerner Commission—has described what businessmen must do to make the hard-core unemployed effective:

> You've got to literally adopt this kind of employee, be responsible for his total condition 24 hours a day, seven days a week. . . . Adopt their families, a piece of the block where they live, a chunk of the city and its future. Know where they live, their economic condition, how their children are, whether there's a police problem, what the neighbourhood pressures are. If it's a woman, you have to know whether there's a male in the house and what her problems are. . . .
> The businessman who does hire the hard-core unemployed is going to be confronted with absenteeism, poor working habits, deficiencies in reading and writing, negative attitudes. . . .

If this is truly what businessmen and perhaps teachers must do effectively to employ or educate a substantial part of the minority population, we may simply not have the required degree of compassion, commitment, and capacity to succeed.

The third is the inability of both black and white to comprehend the character of the American pattern of group incorporation which has already had so many successes. On the white side, there is widespread fear of Negro separatism and Negro power, and it is a fear which, as I have suggested, fails to understand that every group has gone through (and some have retained) a substantial degree of separatism, and all have demanded (and many have obtained) political representation in appointive and elective office, and control over pieces of the political action. As long as the nation does not succumb to a society of rigid compartments and fixed quotas and reserved seats, Americans can go some distance in meeting separatist demands. If suburban towns can have their own school systems and police forces, then, to my mind, there is no reason why certain parts of the larger city should not have separate school systems and police forces. In any case, when the authority of teachers and the police have been destroyed—and they have been, in large measure, destroyed in the ghetto areas—there is no alternative to some pragmatic adjustment, to the creation of new social forms.

ON THE BLACK SIDE—and here blacks are joined of course by many whites, both liberal and progressive—there is an equal failure to comprehend the relationships of groups to the larger American society. There is a failure to understand that even while prejudice and discrimination exist, groups and individuals can achieve their ends and a satisfying and respected place in the American social structure. There is a failure to understand that groups vary in their cultural characteristics and in the area and character of their achievements, and that the owlish insistence on some total equality of representation is to deny the significance of special achievements and characteristics. There will come a time when the special gifts of Negro Americans may mean massive representation in politics, or in the arts, even if today it tends to mean over-representation only in such areas as professional sport. But the special character of American group life—its acceptance of individual merit and capacity and its calculated arrangements for group character and pride —should not be destroyed by a demand for fixed quotas and their incorporation into legal and semi-legal arrangements.

After all, I believe, there is a failure to understand, on the part of black militants and their too-complaisant white allies, that there *is* an American society with a tremendous power to incorporate and make part of itself new groups, to their advantage and not to the advantage of the larger society, and that this is not a *white* society. I find nothing so sad as hearing universities denounced as white racist enclaves, corporations denounced as white racist enterprises, the government denounced as a white racist establishment. A hundred years ago, it could have been easily said these were all "English institutions," and yet Germans and Irish became part of them. Fifty years ago it could have been said these were all "Christian institutions," and yet Jews became part of them. Today, it is contended that they are white institutions—and yet this too is not true. They will become and remain white institutions only if Negro Americans insist on some total separateness as a nation, only if they decide that the American pattern of group life cannot include them.

ARE <u>YOU</u> GUILTY OF MURDERING MARTIN LUTHER KING?

Michael J. Halberstam

Guilt boomed out of the loudspeakers and oozed from the pores of the true believers one lovely day in April in a Georgetown park as assorted members of the New Left rallied to discuss "Why Washington Burned." The guest speakers, Dick Gregory and Thomas Hayden among them, scourged their white listeners for their guilt and their racism and their violence and the faithful murmured, "Amen." But among the unconvinced, the ones like myself who had come to hear something new, there seemed to be no mass confession of sin. The unconvinced applauded when the war was denounced and the President attacked, but they sat silent when Hayden told them that they belonged to "the most violent nation in the world"—and told them to feel guilty and angry because of the assassination of Martin Luther King.

I listened to Hayden and felt angry (I wanted to punch him in the nose), but no matter how often I brought myself back to the awful fact of the assassination and the riots, I could feel no guilt. The cries of "guilty" continue to ring out from pulpits and professors and letter writers, and yet the nation itself seems reluctant to come to the sinners' bench. Hiroshima, Leipzig, the Navaho Long March, genocide, assassination, the threat of a Nuremberg in which the prosecutors will be Oriental, all these

Michael J. Halberstam, "Are *You* Guilty of Murdering Martin Luther King?", *The New York Times Magazine* (June 9, 1968), 27–29 plus. © 1968 by the New York Times Company. Reprinted by permission.

are hurled at us, and yet we continue to play golf on Sunday and watch the Dean Martin show. Am I without conscience if I cannot agree with those who call me guilty? Are we a nation without a conscience?

THE ANSWER TO THE QUESTION above is: "No." Nations are not guilty as nations, and America, to its great credit, realizes this well. What is more troublesome than the simple refutation of national guilt is the pathopsychology and political theory of those who, heaping guilt upon themselves, insist on including the rest of us in their ritual. For not only is the concept of national guilt a dubious one, but it is ultimately a self-defeating one.

I am angry at the accusers, not because I am susceptible to their arguments or feel they are hitting close to home, but because people I know, friends and patients, in the early morning weakness of their souls, are susceptible and suffer for it. As a physician, I would protest if one of my patients constantly reproached his wife for the death of their child. As a physician, I can see communal depression and communal confusion, and I must protest against those who cry communal guilt. I must also work to remedy the real situation which provoked the accusations, but we must remember that guilt has little to do with reality situations.

The truth of this is evident when one considers that the person who is moved to help the Negro by guilt feelings will continue to do this work until he feels better—not until the Negro is better. Guilt is self-directed and self-terminated. What is worse, in terms of guilt as a force for effective social reform, is that the guilty person smells of guilt, and the odor is easily recognized. The Negro adolescent, wary, experienced, cynical, can smell this guilt a block away. Of all the people who have offered him help or interest, the black youth is most contemptuous of the guilt-stricken white.

The reason the young Negro—and almost everyone else who is not a psychiatrist—avoids the guilt-ridden human is that guilt inevitably implies a sense of self-abasement. Freud felt that patients who showed inappropriate guilt behavior such as compulsive door-opening or hand-washing were warding off an incompletely resolved Oedipal complex. The normal human being, confronted with a compulsive hand-washer, working out his Oedipal complex, feels impelled to look the other way. Things may be bad for the ghetto youth, but not so bad that he welcomes the attentions of a horde of psychic cripples.

A LITTLE GUILT IS, of course, inevitable and desirable in the development of human conscience. When the child transgresses the accepted standards of behavior in his community, he must be made aware of his transgression. A sense of guilt is part of our Western heritage, so inescapable a part, in fact, that most physicians and psychiatrists would agree that it hardly needs to be encouraged further.

Inappropriate guilt manifests itself in a pervasive depression which leads to a sense of complete futility. If we are all guilty, damned and unworthy, what of good can we possibly accomplish? The religious person confronts this dilemma with hope of salvation through belief, but a secularist has no escape. Michael Harrington points out that the attack on poverty in America requires among other things "a spirit, an élan, that communicates itself to the entire society." It is this kind of spirit which is incompatible with a sense of guilt.

In talking to patients and friends about the racial situation in America, I have been very much struck by the fact that those who feel guiltiest about it are doing the least to change it. One young woman who worked for the poverty program told me, "I feel terribly guilty about what we do to Negroes in this country. It's all so awful. I just don't see what we can do about it." Her own evenings are spent in rather aimless conversation and moviegoing. Two years ago she did volunteer work for a settlement house, but gradually drifted away from it.

One can only guess why she no longer has any direct contact with the poor or with Negroes, but certainly it is true that it is impossible to have a healthy relationship with anyone toward whom one constantly feels guilty. The relationship is prefigured, and what every human wants—to be treated and respected as an individual—is impossible. Perhaps the young people with whom this woman worked sensed that she regarded them not as individuals, but as representatives of a whole group of people toward whom she felt guilty. They would hardly be inclined to treat her with respect, and one would expect that her interest and enthusiasm would soon vanish.

Conversely, Jack Gonzales, a consultant to the Head Start program and a veteran of the civil-rights movement, reacted angrily when I asked him if he felt guilty about the assassination of Dr. King and the ensuing riots. "Of course I don't feel guilty," he said, adding: "For the past couple of weeks anytime we have a Head Start meeting and get together with people who have a common goal and who've known one another for a number of years, we get bogged down in recriminations about 'white racism' and 'white guilt' and we don't get anything done for the kids. It's poisoning the atmosphere."

White liberals who admit to guilt feelings about the racial situation usually pick out specific instances in which they did not back up their ideals completely with action. Furthermore, they frequently told me, they "feel guilty—but only a bit." Thus one young woman said that she regretted not having followed up a friendship with several Negro classmates more vigorously. June Siena, wife of a Washington lawyer and the mother of three children in the District's public schools, said, "I had a sudden wave of guilt at the all-District music festival. My boy was singing there in a chorus which was mostly Negro and the other kids were singing so well and so fervently, and then they all started 'America the Beautiful' and I knew the Negro kids meant it—and I wondered how they would feel in five or 10 years. Maybe it wasn't exactly guilt—more a certain sadness."

SOME WHITES REJECT the concept of guilt angrily, others sardonically. One card-burning member of the New Left told me, "I don't feel guilty, because in this society, except for a very few in the power élite, we're all niggers. The black ones just stand out more."

If many white liberals reject the idea of racial guilt, why should one bother to argue with those who are promoting it? For one thing, a good many white Americans, especially the young, feel guilty because they don't feel guilty. "I know I should feel guilty about Dr. King," one young man told me, "but I just can't. I was horrified by his death, but I didn't feel as though I had any part in it. There must be something the matter with me." Youth today probably has enough problems without despising itself for insufficient guilt.

Dr. Jack Katzow, a Washington psychiatrist who has worked with several poverty and slum programs, says, "I don't feel guilty and as a psychiatrist I'm concerned with all the talk about guilt. Sure, some people have done bad things and should feel guilty. But for a lot of people talking about their own guilt and including everyone else in, the racial situation is just the outer layer in a personality which is ridden with guilt at the

HALBERSTAM **267**

very core. You might be able to get some effective work out of people motivated by guilt, but only for a brief time. The line between honest concern for other people and masochism is hard to define, but I think most people by instinct can tell where it is—and a lot of what's being said and done today is just masochism."

WHEN LIBERALS FEEL GUILTY enough, they appear to abandon their better judgment and good sense in a way which damages everything they touch. We find that white students who two years ago were memorizing Staughton Lynd's casebook of non-violence are now as graduate students arguing for revolutionary violence. They gave nonviolence two years and it didn't work. Without passing on the philosophic validity of either violence or nonviolence (I have always liked the idea of selective retaliatory violence), I find the abrupt shift from one to another explicable only in terms of emotions—particularly guilt. Guilt prompts whites and moderate or middle-class Negroes who otherwise know better to swing maniacally from one extreme to another in order to be in tune with what's happening. Unfortunately, what's happening this year may not be what's happening next year. Perhaps next year Northwestern Negro students who petitioned for a separate black dorm will be calling it the "Black Hole" and denouncing the university for giving in to their demands. The white administrators who wrote an abject confession of racism in May of this year will be wondering why their confession wasn't enough.

It wasn't enough because it was promoted by guilt (and perhaps by fear). The university administration did not apparently bother to consult the alumni, trustees or student body before declaring on their behalf that "throughout its history it has been a university of the white establishment." After a condescending nod to those faculty and students who fought to right racial evils, the administration went on to confess responsibility for the "continuance over many past years of these racist attitudes." Presumably one of these "racist" attitudes was the desire some years ago to end dormitory segregation. Now Negro militants want it back. Those Northwestern white liberals who worked with Negroes to end dormitory segregation some years ago might well resent their efforts being labeled "racist." True, right now integrated housing may not be relevant to what some Negroes want, but it was achieved by whites working with the Negro militants of 10 years ago. "Passé," perhaps; "racist," no.

THIS ABANDONMENT of intellectual candor for the moment's surge of guilt is not likely to do either whites or Negroes much long-range good. As Ernest Papanek of the Wiltwyck School has written, "Guilt feelings and social anxiety do not always repress or sublimate aggressiveness; they sometimes arouse it." Whites who are made or urged to feel guilty about Negroes are possibly the most likely candidates for future explosions of violence against them.

IF I, LIKE MANY AMERICAN white liberals, refuse to accept personal guilt for riots and assassinations, am I not implicated in our collective guilt as a nation? No, thank you—I won't wear this one, either. I was introduced to the concept of collective guilt at the age of 5 when I was told that some people didn't like Jews because they thought the Jews had killed Jesus. I considered the idea ridiculous at the time and I still do. Even during World War II my parents, to their credit, cautioned my brother and me not to hate the Germans, but to hate Hitler and those who started the war and persecuted the Jews.

After the war we learned of Dachau, and the temptation to hate Germans—all Germans—grew. For a time I felt flawed, almost guilty, because of my inability to hate the Germans. Dwight MacDonald's essay, "The Responsibility of Nations," articulated my unease and, in demonstrating the weakness of all humans faced with a war machine, helped remind me of the very human frailties which lie behind such mass accusations.

MacDonald showed that the attribution of human qualities to nations is a denial of what is unique about man. To speak of the "heroism" of London in the blitz or the "guilt" of Germany in the holocaust is to ignore the fact that neither the Londoners nor the Berliners had much choice about their roles. In addition, since not all Londoners were heroes and since many Germans resisted the Nazis at the cost of their lives, the real responses of real people become meaningless when collective labels are awarded. On practical grounds, MacDonald objected to the attribution of guilt to all Germans since this not only "ignored the deep cleavage between the Nazis and the people, but also cemented these cracks up again."

The idea of collective guilt is a delusion. As I listened in Georgetown to Dick Gregory drone on about the real conspiracy which had culminated in Dr. King's assasination ("How come that little tree in front of the motel just happened to be cut down a day before he got shot?"), I suddenly remembered a news story I had just read.

Pushing the teaching of more "Negro history" in the schools, a black group had pointed out that Negro soldiers had played an important part in the winning of the West and had "helped chase the Sioux into Canada." Perhaps some Sioux militant, recognizing that the Negroes had been instrumental in the "genocide" of his people, had decided to take revenge on the most prominent of those oppressors. On the other hand, from a consistently paranoid view, the Christians were ultimately responsible for the genocide of the Jews (and that *was* a genocide) with Germans only the handy agents—in this paranoid view they did what others schemed to do—and since Dr. King was indubitably a Christian, perhaps some wild-eyed rabbinical student with long sideburns and a steady hand had decided to make concrete his idea on collective guilt. . . .

ONCE THE IDEA of collective guilt is accepted, any number can play, and the permutations are endless. There is no need, however, to accept the challenge, since collective guilt is not a new or sophisticated concept, but rather a phenomenon of primitive cultures, less and less viable as we become more sophisticated. Primitive man, knowing little of weather, conception and other natural cycles, tended to see all events as related to the sum of his group's morality.

Western civilization, particularly Christianity with its emphasis on individual salvation, has for many reasons been wary of the concept of collective guilt. The residuals of "scapegoat" theology were renounced specifically by the Vatican. Rationalist man searches for rational causes of disaster or of triumph—the more precisely identified through historical research, the more convincing.

The idea of collective guilt has some persistence among the followers of Carl Jung. Though he differed with Jung, Freud, too, believed in a variant of the collective unconscious. The Jews, thought Freud, are haunted by excessive consciousness of guilt because their ancestors killed the founder of their race, Moses. Blamed by Christians for killing Jesus and by Freud for killing Moses, the Jews would seem to have refuge in neither religion nor psychiatry.

Black and white racial relationships have also been analyzed in the context of historic, unconscious guilt. The ambivalent attitude of the first European explorers of the New World toward the Indians, whom they idealized as a "new and gentle race" and then feared as the embodiment of savagery, repeats itself in dozens of psychoanalytic forays into American race relations. The critic Leslie Fiedler has found in classic American novels a haunting theme of idealized love of a white man for a dark man —"idealized," because to develop it openly would unleash the twin taboos of homosexuality and miscegenation.

Frantz Fanon, who wrote from the very clearly delineated view of a black Antillean psychiatrist educated in France (he differentiates not only between the psyche of the "French Negro" and the American Negro but between the Antillean and the Senegalese), rejected the idea of the collective unconscious as responsible for white-black tension. Although he felt that part of the tension between white Europeans and African blacks developed because "the Negro is the genital," representing primitive sexuality, Fanon did not believe that this was innate, but rather "cultural, which means acquired."

UNCONSCIOUS COLLECTIVE RACE TENSIONS may, in fact, exist, if merely by the mechanism of a child's first striking awareness of a child of another color, in which the new child becomes the personification of The Other. But if some such tension is inherent, it is certainly less important than learned attitudes. The "myth of Negro sexuality," invoked by many interpreters of race relationships as a source of white anxiety, is hardly universal. We do perhaps spin fantasies about the sexuality of The Other, but the black is not always The Other. In New England towns Protestant boys fantasize about Catholic girls and vice versa. And as I remember the sexual mythmaking of my childhood and youth, the attitudes of the grocer's daughter were much more likely to be a source of speculation than any group potency. Like many white Northerners, I was introduced to the "myth of Negro sexuality" by anthropology reading in college.

If then, as a certified white liberal who admits freely to his whiteness and his liberalness, I can summon neither conscious nor unconscious, individual nor collective guilt feelings toward the Negro, am I without compassion or sensibility? Should I be tried at some future Nuremberg? I would say no, for though I reject the idea that white America must feel guilt en masse, I welcome the distinctions among guilt, shame and responsibility.

In the monograph, "Shame and Guilt," the psychiatrist Dr.

Gerhart Piers drew a useful distinction between the two. Guilt, he felt, results from a conflict between the ego and the super-ego and develops whenever we violate a taboo set by the super-ego. Shame, on the other hand, stems from tension between the ego and the ego-ideal and occurs whenever a goal presented by the ego-ideal is not reached. "Guilt anxiety accompanies trans-gression; shame, failure."

Seen in this light (which is not unlike the theologic differen-tiation between sins of omission and commission), the inability of many white Americans to feel guilty about black America is clear. The white liberals have not murdered leaders, bombed schoolhouses, voted against poverty programs. If, after preach-ing racial equality, they covertly fought to prevent a Negro from moving into their neighborhood, then they indeed were briefly guilty (they violated their own beliefs) and should briefly rec-ognize it. But the emotion which best fits the despairing mo-ments of our recent racial history is shame, for it is clear, using Piers's schema, that we have failed to live up to our ideals.

SHOULD WHITE AMERICA then be transfixed by a sense of shame? Even here one should not be too quick to assume a label. If we feel collective shame at the death of Dr. King, should we feel collective pride when Bill Russell becomes coach of the Celtics? I think, perhaps, that we do, but we should not dwell on either—"we" did not become coach of the Celtics, we did not pull the trigger. We should not become overly infatu-ated with either collective shame or collective pride, but rather concentrate on our individual responses to particular problems.

Is this merely quibbling? I think not. Mass guilt and those who preach it should be rejected by the nonguilty. When James Baldwin told white reporters after the assassination of Malcolm X, "You did it . . . whoever did it was formed in the crucible of the Western world, of the American Republic," was he telling us about Malcolm X, the American Republic or James Baldwin? When the New Leftists accuse every suburban housewife of "white racism," must we fall down and agonize?

FANON HIMSELF RECOGNIZED that mature human relation-ships could not develop from a sense of guilt. "I as a man of color do not have the right to hope that in the white man there will be a crystalization of guilt toward the past of my race. . . . There is no Negro mission; there is no white burden. Am I going to ask the contemporary white man to answer for the slave ships of the 17th century; am I going to try by every possible means to cause guilt to be born in minds?" Fanon answered no, and, passionate that humans should encounter each other as individuals, not symbols, wrote, "I am not the slave of the slavery that dehumanized my ancestors."

Fanon knew that guilt damages those who manipulate it to their advantage just as much as it does those manipulated. The Negro militant who exploits or promotes white guilt may gain temporary support for his programs, but only at the expense of learning that he too can be a cynical schemer. The long-term loss in self-esteem is rarely going to be worth the temporary advantage. The wife who plays on her husband's guilt feelings to obtain a new fur coat is not going to like her husband, herself, or the coat.

Guilt, therefore, is an inevitable but rarely therapeutic emotion. It is so much a part of Western civilization that it rarely has to be fanned. Yet we should note that its role and importance vary from group to group. Neither my father nor my grandfather was particularly religious, but they descended from a dynasty of Hasidic rabbis. The Hasidim are still my kind of people—they sought the goodness of God everywhere, and thus found it everywhere. They danced, sang, drank and prayed, and the dancing was part praying and the praying was part dancing. Though they believed in sin and atonement for sin, the Hasidic rabbis worried very little about guilt. The word and the concept rarely appear in Martin Buber's two-volume "Tales of the Hasidim," for the masters were too busy teaching their disciples how to live a good life and reach God.

But Rabbi Yitzak of Ger once preached a sermon on guilt, saying, "He who has done ill and talks about it and thinks about it all the time does not cast the base thing he did out of his thoughts, and whatever one thinks, therein one is; one's soul is wholly and utterly in what one thinks, and so such a man dwells in baseness he will certainly not be able to turn, for his spirit will grow coarse and his heart stubborn and in addition to this he may be overcome by gloom. What would you? Rake the muck this way, rack the muck that way—it is still muck. Have I sinned or have I not sinned? What does Heaven get out of it? In the time I am brooding over it, I could be stringing pearls for the delight of Heaven. That is why it is written: 'Depart from evil and do good'—turn wholly away from evil, do not dwell on it, and do good. You have done wrong? Then counteract it by doing right."

THE LESSON does not fade. Perhaps in an Existentialist or Calvinist sense, we are all assassins—but we are not all Calvinists or Existentialists. Nor is the nation debating theology or psychoanalytic theory. We are trying to relieve immediate social injustice—children robbed of childhood, adults shorn of adulthood. We need Black Pride and White Pride and neither can flourish in an atmosphere of guilt and recrimination.

White America need not accept a burden of collective guilt, but, dominating the nation politically and economically, it cannot evade collective responsibility. One can be responsible for great works as well as for evil deeds. The opportunities for such works are limitless, and they begin with individual effort. Those Americans—white and black—who have been guilty of racism themselves will hardly be reached by sermonizing. Those Americans—white and black—who have fought racism in the past should in their pride, increase their efforts. Those Americans—white and black—who have stayed outside the fight are welcome to join. The rabbi of Ger would approve.

PART V

The Political System

A FEW YEARS ago, the American political system was under severe attack only by the radical Right and a traditionally ineffectual and frustrated band of academic reformers. The war in Vietnam and the black revolt have changed the mood in this country drastically and it has now become commonplace to denounce nearly every aspect of the nation's political institutions, practices and traditions.

National crises are bound to induce disaffection and challenges to existing institutions, but the present alienation is unusually widespread. Whether it is also more than superficial remains to be seen. Calls for drastic reform or revolution in this country generally lose their strength as the specific evils that spawned them are eliminated or controlled.

As much of the preceding part of this book suggests, we believe that most of the critics of the American political system betray a lack of political sophistication and historical perspective. We do not, of course, endorse every aspect of traditional American political practice. There is always room for improvement and reform proposals should be judged on their merits. But we do believe that on balance our constitutional system of government and many of the customs and traditions surrounding it have served this nation well for nearly 200 years and should not be lightly tossed aside in the vain hope that something better might turn up.

The first two articles discuss two of the most criticized elements: political parties and presidential nominating conventions. Our major parties and the two-party system have been under severe attack and conventions have become a favorite whipping boy. If a sound defense can be made for the conventions and the two-party system then perhaps there is something to be said for the system as a whole. The articles below by two distinguished political scientists forcefully put the case for their defense. The essay by William Gerberding synthesizes an analysis of the politics of the radical Left with a vindication of the American system.

It is interesting to note, by the way, that Professor Banfield's article was originally published in 1964, yet it deals with most of the criticisms currently in vogue. Each generation of reformers is inclined to believe that it is raising the "fundamental questions" for the first time. It may or may not comfort the current critics to discover that most of these issues have been debated for years.

The last article does not fit neatly into any of our five Parts, but it does say a number of important things about the problems addressed in this book and is most appropriately included at this point. Eric Sevareid, like his topic, is not easily categorized.

IN DEFENSE OF
THE AMERICAN
PARTY SYSTEM

Edward C.
Banfield

The American party system has been criticized on four main grounds: (1) The parties do not offer the electorate a choice in terms of fundamental principles; their platforms are very similar and mean next to nothing; (2) they cannot discipline those whom they elect, and therefore they cannot carry their platforms into effect; (3) they are held together and motivated less by political principle than by desire for personal, often material, gain, and by sectional and ethnic loyalties; consequently party politics is personal and parochial; and (4) their structure is such that they cannot correctly represent the opinion of the electorate; in much of the country there is in effect only one party, and everywhere large contributors and special interests exercise undue influence within the party.[1]

[1] These criticisms are made, for example, by the French political scientist, Maurice Duverger, in *Political Parties* (New York: Wiley, 1954). For similar criticisms by Americans, see especially Committee on Political Parties of the American Political Science Association, *Toward a More Responsible Two-Party System* (New York: Rinehart, 1950), and E. E. Shattschneider, *Party Government* (New York: Farrar & Rinehart, 1942). Criticisms of American parties are summarized and analyzed in Austin Ranney, *The Doctrine of Re-*

These criticisms may be summarized by saying that the structure and operation of the parties do not accord with the theory of democracy or, more precisely, with that theory of it which says that everyone should have a vote, that every vote should be given exactly the same weight, and that the majority should rule.

"It is a serious matter," says Maurice Duverger, a French political scientist who considers American party organization "archaic" and "undemocratic," "that the greatest nation in the world, which is assuming responsibilities on a world-wide scale, should be based on a party system entirely directed towards very narrow local horizons."[2] He and other critics of the American party system do not, however, base their criticisms on the performance of the American government. They are concerned about procedures, not results. They ask whether the structure and operation of the parties is consistent with the logic of democracy, not whether the party system produces—and maintains —a good society, meaning, among other things, one in which desirable human types flourish, the rights of individuals are respected, and matters affecting the common good are decided, as nearly as possible, by reasonable discussion. [3]

If they were to evaluate the party system on the basis of results, they would have to conclude that on the whole it is a good one. It has played an important part (no one can say how important, of course, for innumerable causal forces have been at work along with it) in the production of a society which, despite all its faults, is as near to being a good one as any and nearer by far than most; it has provided governments which, by the standards appropriate to apply to governments, have been humane and, in some crises, bold and enterprising; it has done relatively little to impede economic growth and in some ways

---

sponsible Party Government (Urbana: University of Illinois Press, 1954). Defenses of the American party system include A. Lawrence Lowell, *Essays on Government* (Boston: Houghton Mifflin, 1889), Chs. I, II; Arthur N. Holcombe, *The Political Parties of Today* (New York: Harper, 1925); and *Our More Perfect Union* (Cambridge: Harvard University Press, 1950); Pendleton Herring, *The Politics of Democracy* (New York: Norton, 1940); and Herbert Agar, *The Price of Union* (Boston: Houghton Mifflin, 1950).

[2] *Op. cit.*, p. 53.

[3] The report of the Committee on Parties of the American Political Science Association, cited above, discusses the "effectiveness" of parties entirely in terms of procedure. Duverger does the same.

has facilitated it; except for the Civil War, when it was, as Henry Jones Ford said, "the last bond of union to give way,"[4] it has tended to check violence, moderate conflict, and narrow the cleavages within the society; it has never produced, or very seriously threatened to produce, either mob rule or tyranny, and it has shown a marvelous ability to adapt to changing circumstances.

Not only has the American party system produced good results, it has produced better ones than have ever been produced almost anywhere else by other systems. Anyone who reflects on recent history must be struck by the following paradox: those party systems that have been most democratic in structure and procedure have proved least able to maintain democracy; those that have been most undemocratic in structure and procedure— conspicuously those of the United States and Britain—have proved to be the bulwarks of democracy and of civilization.

This paper explores this paradox. It maintains that there is an inherent antagonism between "democracy of procedure" and "production of, and maintenance of, a good society"; that some defects of procedure are indispensable conditions of success from the standpoint of results, and that what the critics call the "archaic" character of the American party system is a very small price to pay for government that can be relied upon to balance satisfactorily the several conflicting ends that must be served.

Difficulties in Planning Change

Before entering into these matters, it may be well to remind the reader how difficult is the problem of planning social change.

Social relationships constitute systems: they are mutually related in such a manner that a change in one tends to produce changes in all of the others. If we change the party system in one respect, even a seemingly trivial one, we are likely to set in motion a succession of changes which will not come to an end until the whole system has been changed. The party system, moreover, is an element of a larger political system and of a social system. A small change in the structure or operation of parties may have important consequences for, say, the family, religion, or the business firm.

The changes that we intend when making a reform, if they

4 Henry Jones Ford, *The Rise and Growth of American Politics* (New York: Macmillan, 1900), p. 303.

occur at all, are always accompanied by others that we do not intend. These others may occur at points in the system far removed from the one where the change was initiated and be apparently unrelated to it. Commonly changes produced indirectly and unintentionally turn out to be much more important than the ones that were sought. This is a fact that is seldom fully taken into account. Those who support a particular reform are often indifferent to its consequences for values that they either do not share or consider subordinate. Even those who feel obligated to take a wide range of values into account do not usually try very hard to anticipate the indirect consequences of reforms—often for a very good reason: the complexity of the social system makes the attempt implausible. Usually we take it on faith that the consequences we get by intention justify the risk we take of incurring others that we do not intend or want. Since these others are seldom recognized as consequences of our action at all (they either go unnoticed or seem to have "just happened"), the basis of our faith is not called into question.

No doubt it is a great help to the practical reformer to have tunnel vision. But those who are concerned with the welfare of society as a whole must take the widest perspective possible. They must try to identify all of the consequences that will follow from a reform—the unintended ones no less than the intended, the remote, contingent, and imponderable no less than the immediate, certain, the specifiable. And they must evaluate all of these consequences in the light of a comprehensive system of values.

Those who devise "improvements" to a social system can rarely hope to attain all of their ends; usually they must be prepared to sacrifice some of them to achieve others. This is so because resources are usually limited and also because there are often incompatibilities among ends such that a gain in terms of some necessarily involves a loss in terms of others. The reformer must therefore economize. He must be able to assign priorities to all ends in such a way that he can tell how much of each to sacrifice for how much of others, on various assumptions as to "supply."

The critics of the party system tend to value democratic procedure for its own sake, that is, apart from the results it produces. There is no reason why they should not do so. But they are in error when they do not recognize that other values of equal or greater importance are often in conflict with democratic procedure, and that when they are, some sacrifice of it is essential in order to serve the other values adequately. If they faced up to the necessity of assigning priorities among all of the relevant ends, they would not, it is safe to say, put "democratic procedure" first. Probably they, and most Americans, would order the ends as follows:

1. The party system must above all else provide governments having the will and capacity to preserve the society and to protect its members. Any sacrifice in other ends ought to be accepted if it is indispensable to securing this end.

2. The party system must insure periodic opportunity to change the government by free elections. Any sacrifice of other ends (except the one above) ought to be accepted if it is indispensable to securing this one.

3. The party system should promote the welfare of the people. By "welfare" is meant some combination of two kinds of values: "principles," what is thought to be good for the society, described in rather general terms, and "interests," the ends individuals and groups seek to attain for their own good, as distinguished from that of the society. The party system should produce governments that assert the supremacy of principles over interests in some matters; in others it should allow interests to prevail and should facilitate the competitive exercise of influence.

4. The party system should moderate and restrain such conflict as would threaten the good health of the society. Other conflict it should not discourage.

5. The party system should promote and exemplify democracy, meaning reasonable discussion of matters affecting the common good in which every voice is heard.

These ends have been listed in what most Americans would probably consider a descending order of importance. In devising a party system, we ought not to try to serve fully each higher end before serving the one below it at all. The first two ends are exceptions to this rule, however: each of them must be attained even if the others are not served at all. With respect to the remaining three, the problem is to achieve a proper balance— one such that no reallocation from one end to another would add to the sum of value.

Finally, we must realize that we can rarely make important social changes by intention. The most we can do is to make such minor changes as may be consistent with, and more or less implied by, the fixed features of the situation in which we are placed. Even to make minor changes in an institution like a political party requires influence of a kind and amount that no group of reformers is likely to have or to be able to acquire. It is idle to propose reforms that are merely desirable. There must also be some possibility of showing, if only in a rough and conjectural way, that they might be carried into effect.

With respect to the American party system, it seems obvious that the crucial features of the situation are all fixed. The size of our country, the class and cultural heterogeneity of our people, the number and variety of their interests, the constitutionally-given fragmentation of formal authority, the wide distribution of power which follows from it, the inveterate taste of Americans for participation in the day-to-day conduct of government when their interests are directly at stake—these are all unalterable features of the situation. Taken together, they mean that the party system can be reformed only within very narrow limits.

A Model Party System

Let us imagine a system free of the alleged defects of ours. In this model system, every citizen is motivated—highly so—by political principles, not subsidiary ones, but ones having to do with the very basis of the society. (In France and Italy, Duverger says approvingly, political warfare "is not concerned with subsidiary principles but with the very foundations of the state and the nature of the regime."[5]) The electoral system, moreover, is such as to give every side on every issue exactly the weight that its numbers in the population warrant; no group or interest is over- or under-represented. ("One's thoughts turn," Duverger says, "to the possibility of a truly scientific democracy, in which parliament would be made up of a true sample of the citizens reproducing on a reduced scale the exact composition of the nation, made up, that is, according to the very methods that are used as a basis for public opinion surveys like the Gallup polls."[6])

Assuming that the society is divided by the usual number of cleavages (e.g., haves versus have-nots, segregationists versus anti-segregationists, isolationists versus internationalists, etc.), the following would result:

1. There would be a great many parties, for no citizen would support a party with which he did not agree fully.

[5] *Op. cit.*, p. 419.
[6] *Ibid.*, p. 158.

2. The parties would tend to be single-issue ones. If logically unrelated issues (for instance, segregation and isolationism) were linked together in a party program, only those voters would support the party who chanced to be on the same side of all of the linked issues. The number of these voters would decrease as the number of issues so linked increased.

3. Parties would be short-lived. They would come into and pass out of existence with the single issues they were organized to fight.

4. In their election campaigns and propaganda, parties would emphasize their single defining principles. This would tend to widen the cleavages along which the parties were formed.

5. Ideological issues, not practical problems, would constitute the substance of politics.[7]

6. The number of such issues pressing for settlement at any one time (but being incapable of settlement because of their ideological character) would always be more than the system could accommodate.[8]

7. Coalitions of parties would seldom form, and such as did form would be highly unstable. Party leaders would find compromise almost impossible because it would lead to loss of highly principled supporters.

8. Coalitions of parties being unstable, governments would also be unstable and therefore lacking in power and decision.

9. Those selected for positions of political leadership would tend to be ideologues skilled in party dialectics and symbolizing the party and its positions. Practical men, especially those with a talent for compromise and those symbolizing qualities common to the whole society, would be excluded from politics.

10. Matters having no ideological significance (a category that includes most local issues) would either be endowed with a spurious one or else would be left outside the sphere of politics altogether.[9]

---

[7] In France, according to Siegfried, "every argument becomes a matter of principle; the practical results are relegated to second place." André Siegfried, "Stable Instability in France," *Foreign Affairs*, XXXIV (April 1956), 395.

[8] According to Siegfried: "The difficulty is that too many questions of fundamental importance on which the various parties have cause to disagree have come up for decision at one time." *Ibid.*, p. 399.

[9] In France, Luethy says, "politics," which deals with ideological matters, and the "state," i.e., the bureaucracy, which deals with practical ones, function "in watertight compartments" with the con-

These points should suffice to show that a system with a perfectly democratic structure would not produce results acceptable in terms of the criteria listed above.

Now let us introduce into the model system one of the alleged defects which the critics find most objectionable in the American party system. Let us suppose that at least half of the electorate is prevailed upon to exchange its vote in matters of fundamental principle for advantages that have nothing to do with principle, especially private profit, sectional gain, and nationality "recognition."

One effect of this would be to reduce greatly the intensity of ideological conflict and to make political life more stable and conservative. This, in fact, seems to be what happened when American parties first came into being. John Adams tells in his diary how in 1794 "ten thousand people in the streets of Philadelphia, day after day, threatened to drag Washington out of his house and effect a revolution in the government, or compel it to declare war in favor of the French Revolution and against England."[10] After parties had been organized, however, patronage took the place of ideological fervor. "The clubs of the social revolutionists which had sprung up in the cities, blazing with incendiary ideas caught from the French Revolution," Henry Jones Ford says, "were converted into party workers, and their behavior was moderated by considerations of party interest."[11]

Another effect would be to encourage the formation of a few (probably two) stable parties. These might begin as alliances among the profit-minded, the sectional-minded, and the nationality-minded, but to attract support from principled voters the parties would have to seem to stand for something—indeed, for anything and everything. Since no faction of them could hope to win an election by itself, principled voters would attach themselves to those parties that they found least objectionable. The parties would develop corporate identities and mystiques; principled voters would then subordinate their differences out

---

sequence that French democracy is an amalgam of absolutist administration on the one hand and of anarchy, tumultuous or latent, on the other. Herbert Luethy, *France Against Herself* (New York: Meridian Books, 1957), p. 61. On this see also Siegfried, *op. cit.* p. 399.

[10] Quoted by Henry Jones Ford, *op. cit.*, p. 125.

[11] *Ibid.*, p. 144.

of "loyalty" to the party and in response to its demands for "regularity." Competition for middle-of-the-road support would cause the parties to offer very similar programs. This competition might lead to there being only two parties, but this result would probably be insured by introducing another supposed defect into the system: a principle of representation (single-member districts and plurality voting) which, by letting the winner take all, would force small parties to join larger ones in order to have some chance of winning.

In one way or another, the "defects" of the system would tend to produce these consequences—consequences which have in fact been produced in the United States:

1. A strong and stable government would be possible. The country would be governed by the party that won the election, or (given the particular complexities of the American system) by two closely similar parties engaged in give-and-take and, therefore, in a sense constituting one party under two names.

2. There would be a high degree of continuity between administrations elected from different parties. Elections would not shake the nation to its foundations because the competing parties would be fundamentally in agreement. Agreement would be so built in by countless compromises within the parties (each of which would be under the necessity of attracting middle-of-the-road support) that a change of party would seldom entail complete reversal of policy in an important matter.

3. There would exist many substructures of power that would be largely or wholly impervious to the influence of political principle or ideology. "Machines"—party organizations of the profit-minded, the sectional-minded, and the nationality-minded —would not be inclined to offer pie in the sky or to stir the emotions of the masses because they could count upon getting their votes in other ways. These essentially apolitical centers of power would therefore exert a stabilizing and conservative influence throughout the political system. By making business-like deals with the leaders of the "machines," the President could sometimes buy freedom to do as he thought best in matters of principle.

4. The diversity of the principles and the multiplicity of the interests within the party would be another source of strength to the leader elected from it. He could afford to offend some elements of the party on any particular question because there would be enough other elements unaffected (or even gratified)

to assure his position. The more fragmented his part, the less attention he would have to pay to any one fragment of it.

5. The assertion of interests (as distinguished from principles) would be encouraged. The profit-minded, the sectional-minded, and the nationality-minded would in effect give up representation on matters of principle in order to get it on matters involving their interests. Thus two different systems of representation would work simultaneously. The party leader would act as a trustee, disregarding interests in favor of principles ("Congress represents locality, the President represents the nation," Ford wrote in 1898.[12]) Meanwhile legislators dependent on machines and, in general, on profit-minded, sectional-minded, and nationality-minded voters would act as agents of interests. The trustee of principles (the President) and the agents of interests (Congressmen) would of necessity bargain with each other; by allowing the agents of interests some successes—but only in this way—the trustee of principles could win their support in the matters he considered most important. Thus, there would be achieved that balancing of interests and of interests against principles (the most important principles usually being vindicated) that a good party system should produce.

6. The formation of deep cleavages would nevertheless be discouraged. The competition of the parties for the middle-of-the-road vote; their tendency to select practical men of wide popular appeal, rather than ideologues, for positions of leadership; and the definition of the politicians' task as being that of finding the terms on which people who disagree will work together, rather than that of sharpening ideological points— these would all be unifying tendencies.

Some critics of the American party system have attributed its alleged defects to the absence of class consciousness in our society. No doubt there is some truth in this. But causality may run the other way also. We may be lacking in class consciousness because our politicians are prevented by the nature of the party system from popularizing the rhetoric of the class struggle; the party system actually induces the voter to forgo the allurements of principle and ideology by offering him things he

---

[12] *Ibid.*, p. 187. For a recent brilliant account of how the two systems of representation work, see Willmoore Kendall, "The Two Majorities," *Midwest Journal of Political Science*, IV, No. 4 (November 1960), 317–345.

values more: e.g., personal profit, sectional advantage, and nationality "recognition."[13]

In those countries where the voter expresses at the polls his ideology rather than his interests, he may do so not from choice but because the party system leaves him no alternative. In such countries, class warfare may be the principal subject-matter of politics simply because matters of greater importance to the voters are not at stake.

Experience in the underdeveloped areas seems to bear out the claim that certain "defects" in a party system may be essential to good government. The transplanted "defects" of the American party system are among the factors that have made the Philippines the most democratic country in Southeast Asia. According to Professor Lucian W. Pye:

. . . the image of leadership that evolved in the Philippines was clearly that of the politician who looked after the particular interests of voters. Elsewhere the pattern of the Western impact under colonialism gave emphasis to the role of the rational administrator who apparently operated according to the principles of efficiency and who was not supposed to be influenced by political pressures within the society. Consequently, when the politicians emerged in these societies, they tended to become the champions of nationalistic ideologies and even the enemies of the rational administrators.[14]

In the Philippines, as at home, our party system has had the

[13] ". . . in coordinating the various elements of the populations for political purposes," Ford says, "party organization tends at the same time to fuse them into one mass of citizenship, pervaded by a common order of ideas and sentiments, and actuated by the same class of motives. This is probably the secret of the powerful solvent influence which American civilization exerts upon the enormous deposits of alien population thrown upon this country by the torrent of emigration. Radical and religious antipathies, which present the most threatening problems to countries governed upon parliamentary principles, melt with amazing rapidity in the warm flow of a party spirit which is constantly demanding, and is able to reward the subordination of local and particular interests to national purposes." (*Op. cit.*, pp. 306–307.)

[14] Lucian W. Pye, "The Politics of Southeast Asia," in G. Almond and J. Coleman (eds.), *The Politics of the Developing Areas* (Princeton, N.J.: Princeton University Press, 1960), p. 97. Copyright © 1960 by Princeton University Press.

defects of its virtues—and the virtues of its defects. On the one hand, Pye says, the Philippines have never had an efficient administrative machinery, and the demand for higher standards of personal integrity among their public officials is reminiscent of the muckraking era of American politics; on the other hand, "the Philippine electorate seems to recognize that the most fundamental question in politics is who is going to control the government, and thus, while the parties have not had to expend much effort in trying to distinguish themselves ideologically from each other, the expenditures of money on political campaigns in the Philippines are probably the highest in proportion to per capita income of any country in the world."[15]

Making Parties "Responsible"

Some think that the American party system can be reformed without changing its nature essentially. Several years ago, a Committee on Parties of the American Political Science Association proposed making certain "readjustments" in the structure and operation of the party system to eliminate its "defects." These readjustments, the Committee said, would give the electorate "a proper range of choice between alternatives" in the form of programs to which the parties would be committed and which they would have sufficient internal cohesion to carry into effect. Thus, the two-party system would be made more "responsible."[16]

What this means is not at all clear. "Responsibility" here seems to be a synonym for accountability, that is, the condition of being subject to being called to account and made to take corrective action in response to criticism. In the case of a party, this can mean nothing except going before an electorate, and in this sense all parties are by definition responsible. "Responsibility" can have no other meaning in this context; as William Graham Sumner remarked, "a party is an abstraction; it cannot be held responsible or punished; if it is deprived of power it fades into thin air and the men who composed it, especially those who did the mischief and needed discipline, quickly reappear in the new majority."[17]

---

[15] *Ibid.*, pp. 123 and 126.

[16] See the Committee Report, *op. cit.*, pp. 1 and 85.

[17] William Graham Summer, *The Challenge of Facts* (New Haven, Conn.: Yale University Press, 1914), pp. 271–272.

Leaving aside both the question of what "responsibility" means when applied to a party and the more important one of whether as a matter of practical politics such "readjustments" could be made, let us consider how the political system would probably be affected by the changes proposed.

The hope that the two-party system might be made to offer a choice between distinct alternatives is illusory for at least two reasons. One is that a party which does not move to the middle of the road to compete for votes condemns itself to defeat and eventually, if it does not change its ways, to destruction. But even if this were not the case, the parties could not present the electorate with what reformers think of as "a valid choice." The reason is that the issues in our national life are such that there does not exist any one grand principle by which the electorate could be divided into two camps such that every voter in each camp would be on the "same" side of all issues. The idea of "left" and "right" is as close as we come to having such a grand principle, and it has little or no application to many issues.[18] The logic of "left" and "right" does not, for example, imply opposite or even different positions on (for example) foreign policy, civil liberties, or farm subsidies. Without a grand principle which will make unities—opposed unities—of the party programs, the electorate cannot be offered "a valid choice." A choice between two market baskets, each of which contains an assortment of unrelated items, some of which are liked and some of which are disliked, is not a "valid" choice in the same sense that a choice between two market baskets, each of which contains items that "belong together" is a "valid" one. In the American party system, most items are logically unrelated. This being so, "valid" choice would become possible only if the number of parties was increased to allow each party to stand for items that *were* logically related, if one issue became important to the exclusion of all the others, or if, by the elaboration of myth and ideology, pseudo-logical relations were established among items.

The hope that the parties might commit themselves to carry

[18] One can imagine a set of symbols connected with a diffuse ideology dividing the society into two camps, and to a certain extent this exists. But it is hard to see in what sense this would present the electorate with "a valid choice." In other words, the existence of a body of nonsense which is treated as if it were a grand principle ought not to be regarded by reasonable critics of the party system as equivalent to the grand principle itself.

out their programs is also illusory. A party could do this only if its leaders were able to tell the President and the party members in Congress what to do, and could discipline them if they failed to do it. Therefore, unless, like the Russians, we were to have two sets of national leaders, one in governmental office and another much more important one in party office, it would be necessary for our elected leaders—in effect, the President, since only he and the Vice President are elected by the whole nation—to control the Congressmen and Senators of their party. This would be possible only if the President could deny re-election to members of Congress who did not support the party program. Thus, instead of merely bringing forward and electing candidates, as they do now, "responsible" parties would have to govern the country. We would have a parliamentary system with the President in a position somewhat like that of the British Prime Minister, except (a very important difference) that, not being a part of the legislature, he could not use it as a vehicle through which to exert his leadership.[19] The legislature would in fact have no function at all.

This great shift of power to the President would remedy another "defect" in the party system: its receptivity to the demands of interest groups.[20] With the President in full control of Congress, logrolling would cease or virtually cease. It would do so because no one could any longer make the President pay a price for assistance in getting legislation passed; the traders who now sell their bits and pieces of power to the highest bidders would have to lower their prices and would probably go out of business. With their opportunities for exercising influence vastly reduced, interest groups would be less enterprising both in their efforts to anticipate the effects of governmental action and in bringing their views to the attention of the policy makers.

The making of policy would thus pass largely into the hands

[19] The Prime Minister is the leader of his party outside as well as inside Parliament. Party leaders who are not also members of Parliament take no part in the running of the government, as the late Professor Harold Laski discovered when, as a leader of the Labour Party, he presumed to give advice to Prime Minister Atlee. The party leaders discipline their followers by threatening to deprive them of renomination; accordingly most members of the House are "backbenchers" who participate in its affairs only as audience, and the function of the House as a whole is to criticize and advise the leaders of the majority party.

[20] Cf. Report of the Committee on Parties, *op. cit.*, pp. 19–20.

of technical experts within the majority party, the White House, and the executive departments. These would be mindful of principles and impatient of interests. They would endeavor to make "coherent" policies, meaning, presumably, policies not based on compromise.[21] In all important matters, however, "the public interest" would prove an insufficient guide; the experts, when confronted with the necessity of choosing between alternatives that were equally in the public interest—that is, when no authoritative, ultimate criterion of choice existed for them to apply —would by the very necessities of the case have to balance the competing values as best they could, which means that they would have to fall back upon their personal tastes or professional biases.[22] Thus they would do badly (but in the name of "impartial administration") what is now done reasonably well by the political process.

The destruction of political traders and of local centers of power would mean also that the President's power would derive from somewhat different sources than at present. Instead of relying upon logrolling and patronage to get the votes he would need in Congress, he would have to rely upon direct appeals to the electorate. To some extent he might manipulate the electorate by charm and personality; TV and the arts of Madison Avenue would become more important in politics. But in order to get elected he would have to depend also, and to a greater extent, upon appeals to political principle or ideology. Whereas the political trader maintains his control by giving and withholding favors to individuals (a circumstance which makes his control both dependable in its operation and cheap), the President would have to maintain *his* by the uncertain and costly expedient of offering to whole classes of people—the farmer, the aged, the home owner, and so on—advantages that they would have only at each other's expense. If charm and the promise of "something for everybody" did not yield the amount of power he required to govern the country, the President might find it necessary to exploit whatever antagonisms within the society might be made to yield more power. Class and ethnic differences might in this event serve somewhat the same function as logrolling and patronage do now. Mayor LaGuardia, for example, depended for power upon direct, personal appeal to the

21 *Ibid.*, p. 19.

22 This argument is developed in E. C. Banfield, *Political Influence* (Glencoe, Ill.: Free Press, 1961), Ch. 12.

voters rather than upon organization. His charm and his support of "liberal" programs are well remembered. But it should not be forgotten that he depended also upon exploitation of ethnic loyalties and antipathies. According to Robert Moses,

It must be admitted that in exploiting racial and religious prejudices LaGuardia could run circles around the bosses he despised and derided. When it came to raking ashes of Old World hates, warming ancient grudges, waving the bloody shirt, tuning the ear to ancestral voices, he could easily out-demagogue the demagogues. And for what purpose? To redress old wrongs abroad? To combat foreign levy or malice domestic? To produce peace on the Danube, the Nile, the Jordan? Not on your tintype. Fiorello LaGuardia knew better. He knew that the aim of the rabble rousers is simply to shoo into office for entirely extraneous, illogical and even silly reasons the municipal officials who clean city streets, teach in schools, protect, house and keep healthy, strong and happy millions of people crowded together here.[23]

That a President might rely more upon appeals to political principle does not at all mean that better judgments or results would follow. For the discussion of principles would probably not be *serious;* it would be for the purpose of securing popular interest and consent, not of finding a wise or right course of action. As long ago as 1886, Sir Henry Sumner Maine observed that democracy was tending toward government by salesmanship. Party and corruption had in the past always been relied upon to bring men under civil discipline, he said, but now a third expedient had been discovered:

This is generalization, the trick of rapidly framing, and confidently uttering, general propositions on political subjects. . . . General formulas, which can be seen on examination to have been arrived at by attending only to particulars few, trivial or irrelevant, are turned out in as much profusion as if they dropped from an intellectual machine; and debates in the House of Commons may be constantly read, which consisted wholly in the exchange of weak generalities and strong personalities. On a pure Democracy this class of gen-

[23] Robert Moses, *LaGuardia: A Salute and a Memoir* (New York: Simon & Schuster, 1957), pp. 37–38. Copyright © 1957 by Simon & Schuster.

eral formulas has a prodigious effect. Crowds of men can be got to assent to general statements, clothed in striking language, but unverified and perhaps incapable of verification; and thus there is formed a sort of sham and pretence of concurrent opinion. There has been a loose acquiescence in a vague proposition, and then the People, whose voice is the voice of God, is assumed to have spoken.[24]

Efforts to create "levity of assent," as Maine called it, will become more important in our politics to the extent that other means of bringing men under civil discipline are given up or lost.

The Danger of Meddling

A political system is an accident. It is an accumulation of habits, customs, prejudices, and principles that have survived a long process of trial and error and of ceaseless response to changing circumstance. If the system works well on the whole, it is a lucky accident—the luckiest, indeed, that can befall a society, for all of the institutions of the society, and thus its entire character and that of the human types formed within it, depend ultimately upon the government and the political order.

To meddle with the structure and operation of a successful political system is therefore the greatest foolishness that men are capable of. Because the system is intricate beyond comprehension, the chance of improving it in the ways intended is slight, whereas the danger of disturbing its working and of setting off a succession of unwanted effects that will extend throughout the whole society is great.

Democracy must always meddle, however. An immanent logic impels it to self-reform, and if other forces do not prevent, it must sooner or later reform itself out of existence.[25]

The logic of this is as follows. The ideal of democracy legitimates only such power as arises out of reasonable discussion about the common good in which all participate. Power that comes into being in any other way (e.g., by corruption, logrolling, appeals to sentiment or prejudice, the exercise of charm

[24] Sir Henry Sumner Maine, *Popular Government* (New York: Henry Holt, 1886), pp. 106–108.

[25] For data and analysis pertinent to the discussion that follows, see James Q. Wilson, *The Amateur Democrat* (Chicago: University of Chicago Press, 1962).

or charisma, "hasty generalization," terror, etc.) is radically un-democratic, and people inspired by the democratic ideal will therefore endeavor to eliminate it by destroying, or reforming, whatever practices or institutions give rise to it.

No society, however, can be governed *solely* by reasonable discussion about the common good; even in a society of angels there might be disagreement about what the common good requires in the concrete case.[26] In most societies, far more power is needed to maintain civil discipline and protect the society from its enemies than can be got simply by reasonable discussion about the common good. Therefore the logical culmination of democratic reform, viz., the elimination of all undemocratic sources of power, would render government—and therefore the preservation of the society—impossible. Democratic reform can never reach this point, of course, because, before reaching it, democracy itself would be destroyed and the impetus to further reform removed.

So far as it does succeed, however, the tendency of demo-cratic reform is to reduce the power available for government. Such loss of power as occurs from the elimination of undemo-cratic sources of it will seldom be offset by increases in power of the kind that arises from reasonable discussion about the common good. Since there is a point beyond which no increase in democratic power is possible (the capacity of a society to en-gage in reasonable discussion about the common good being limited), reform, if carried far enough, must finally reduce the quantity of power.

There is, then, a danger that reform will chip away the foun-dations of power upon which the society rests. But this is not the only danger. A greater one, probably, is that in making some forms of undemocratic power less plentiful, reform may make others more plentiful, and by so doing set off changes that will ramify throughout the political system, changing its char-acter completely. If, for example, politicians cannot get power by the methods of the machine (corruption, favor-giving, and patronage), they may get it by other methods, such as charm, salesmanship, and "hasty generalization." The new methods may be better than the old by most standards (they cannot, of course, be better by the standard of democracy, according to which *all* power not arising from reasonable discussion about the common good is absolutely illegitimate); but even if they are better, the

[26] See Yves R. Simon, *The Philosophy of Democratic Government* (Chicago: University of Chicago Press, 1951), Ch. 1.

new methods may not serve as well as the old, or may not serve at all, in maintaining an effective political system and a good society.

Reform is, of course, far from being the only force at work. Compared to the other forces, some of which tend to produce competing changes and others of which tend to check all change, reform may be of slight effect. This is certainly true in general of such reform as is sought through formal organizations by people called "reformers." It is much less true of reform in the broader sense of the general view and disposition of "the great body of right-thinking people." This kind of reform is likely to be of pervasive importance in the long run, although its effects are seldom what anyone intended.

Jefferson may have been right in saying that democracy cannot exist without a wide diffusion of knowledge throughout the society. But it may be right also to say that it cannot exist *with* it. For as we become a better and more democratic society, our very goodness and democracy may lead us to destroy goodness and democracy in the effort to increase and perfect them.

ARE POLITICAL CONVENTIONS UNDEMOCRATIC?

Herbert McClosky

No feature of American politics has so aroused the disdain of political purists as our Presidential nominating conventions. Raucous, windy, tumultuous, festive, noisy—to the casual observer they seem as rowdy as a Tammany saloon, as stylized as a Kabuki drama, as ritualized as a professional wrestling match. Overripe in their rhetoric, inelegant in their proceedings, a combination Mardi Gras and clambake, they suggest a carnival rather than a deliberative body charged with the momentous task of nominating a Presidential candidate and shaping a party program. Some observers consider them an offense against dignity, reflection and sensibility. Others, wearied by their interminable talk, find them irksome and boring.

The standard description of the convention's decision-making process is scarcely more flattering: In back rooms and hotel suites, candidates, delegation leaders, functionaries and "bosses" meet clandestinely to arrange the convention's business and to work out agreements and accommodations favorable to their mutual interests; "deals" are made, bargains are struck, principles are compromised and beliefs are sacrificed to expediency.

Herbert McClosky, "Are Political Conventions Undemocratic?", *The New York Times Magazine* (August 4, 1968), 10–11 plus. © 1968 by the New York Times Company. Reprinted by permission. In view of the events in Chicago in August 1968, Professor McClosky offered to write a postscript to the original article. It appears at the end. We are grateful to him for doing so.

This description, however widely voiced, is caricature. Like most caricature, it contains elements of truth, but it is far from being either generous or entirely accurate. This year such comments on our Presidential nominating process have increased, and there have been urgent calls by many prominent in public affairs for the abolition of the national convention. These doubtless reflect the unparalleled events of the past five years: the assassination of three of our most-gifted and venerated public men; the horror, dashed hopes and frustrations caused by Vietnam; dramatic and disconcerting changes in the ecology of our cities; uprisings and disorder in the ghettos and universities; the reversion in many quarters to "confrontation" politics in place of democratic civility and mutual accommodation. All these matters have profoundly shaken the national consensus, provoked what some regard as a crisis of legitimacy, and brought into question many of our institutions, including, of course, our procedures for nominating the nation's Chief Executive.

EVENTS SPECIFIC to the present campaign have increased the misgivings many voters feel not only about the national convention as an institution but about the particular two conventions being held this month. Some have even been led to the conviction that the electoral process has miscarried this year and has deprived many voters—especially young people—of an effective voice in the shaping of their own and the nation's, affairs.

Notable among these events were: (1) President Johnson's decision to remove himself from the race (itself a response to the profound cleavage he sensed among the national electorate), which left his critics without a major target for venting their anger about Vietnam; (2) the withdrawal of Romney and Rockefeller from the primaries, which for a time deprived Republicans of a liberal alternative; (3) Nixon's easy sweep (partly for that reason) of every state primary he entered, and (4) the paralyzing and embittering effect of Senator Kennedy's death on many blacks, young people and intellectuals, who have withdrawn into political apathy.

By far the most exasperated voters are the McCarthy supporters. They see a fundamental flaw of our prenominating system in the fact that Humphrey has succeeded in acquiring strong delegate support without having participated in the primaries (he was unable to enter before most deadlines for filing, owing to the timing of the President's withdrawal), while McCarthy, although losing most of the contested primaries, made an unexpectedly strong showing in some of them and, like Humphrey, has scored well in the polls. McCarthyites believe that their man should be rewarded for having first challenged Johnson for the Democratic nomination and for having helped force a change in our Vietnam policy.

They complain further that McCarthy has received a smaller share of the delegates from some of the state organizations than his popular support warrants; that the combined McCarthy and Kennedy vote in the primaries signified a rejection of Administration policies; and that the convention machinery will be used in an effort to exclude from the platform an adequate expression of McCarthy's views on Vietnam and other issues. They allege, in short, that the convention is not being kept "open" and that the popular will is about to be denied by the men who command the party organization.

Some of these changes, of course, are typical of the complaints voiced in political campaigns by the "outs" against the "ins." Nevertheless, one must concede that the existing method of nominating Presidential candidates is, from the point of view of democratic theory, less than ideal. Some of its deficiencies are inherent in all complex forms of political organization, while some are peculiar to the party system as it evolved under American conditions.

One consequence, for example, of combining a Presidential form of government with a Federal two-party system is that it puts the parties under severe pressure to bring together a coalition of state delegations large enough to nominate the one nationwide candidate who will represent the party in the general election. In contrast to multiparty, cabinet systems of government, more emphasis is put on attaining a majority than on calling attention to the diverse views within the electorate. Little effort is made in party conventions to expose, much less heighten, the cleavages that divide the country; instead, the emphasis is on unity and on the search for a candidate who can reconcile the often conflicting interests of party members and voters from different parts of the society.

The warning sounded by critics that each of this month's conventions may seek in its proceedings to minimize the national conflicts over Vietnam, the cities, law and order, etc., is a realistic expectation. In the face of crisis, and the bitter election struggle it is likely to evoke, party leaders will be especially concerned to soften existing differences, or at least to keep them from being paraded before the eyes of millions of television viewers and newspaper readers. The American parties are loose confederations of state parties, and this not only reduces their motivation to publicly debate divisive national questions, but also affects the degree to which party members across the nation are adequately represented. Whether a state's delegates are chosen by a primary, state convention, caucus, state central combination of these, no special effort is made to represent the state's party membership in proportion to their beliefs or preferences.

PRIMARIES, IN FACT, sometimes turn out to be the least representative, since they assign the entire state's delegations to the Presidential candidate who gets a plurality. Certain state parties are strongly dominated by the governor or some other official, and these leaders are often more concerned with the strength and unity of the organization than with its representativeness.

Once a majority forms at a convention, or is on the way to becoming a reality, its usual impulse is to take command. It may stop short of actually trampling on the minority, but considerable forbearance is required for it to refrain from exploiting its strength to enlarge its advantage. The candidates who appear to be running behind in the delegate count are at a disadvantage, for they are less likely to win the close ones.

When a group of party leaders sense that they have, or are likely to have, a majority at the convention, some of them will surely try to force the appearance of unity upon the party by shutting out the minority in any way they can—the more so if they happen to perceive the minority as dissident or disloyal. Thus, in the present contest for the Democratic nomination, a number of factors may conspire to place the McCarthy forces at an even greater disadvantage than they would suffer from the mere fact of having attracted a smaller number of delegates, to begin with.

The entire drama, however, need not go in this direction, for there are counteracting considerations which lead one to believe that the conventions are, or may be, less tightly dominated than one might suppose. The incentive of the majority to command, for example, is to some extent counteracted by a commitment Americans share about the "rules of the game." These include the sense of fair play and the respect for minority rights.

Then, too, while the party leaders of key states can, if they combine, move large numbers of key delegates, it is an oversimplification to assume that the convention delegates are mere pawns in a political chess game played out by masters. Not all delegations are dominated by a leader or unified in their preferences. Some delegations are the handiwork not of a single "machine" but of competing machines. Some contain dissident factions that challenge the leaders at every turn. Nor is the influence in one direction only, for even strong political leaders can retain their power only if they know when to bend to the wishes of the delegation.

WE WOULD ALSO BE mistaken to assume that the convention leaders always see eye to eye. Some are rivals or even enemies. They are not a syndicate or a clearly defined oligarchy, but rather a loose, unstable coalition, volatile and, except for a few of its members, surprisingly uncool. Behind the formal structure, especially among Democrats, one discovers a bewildering assortment of factional, class, geographic, ethnic and ideological interests—the state of affairs that led Will Rogers to his famous comment that he belonged to no organized party, for he was a Democrat.

While some leaders or delegates have more power than others, one ought not to conclude that *more* power equals *absolute* power, or that *less* power equals *no* power. Like all men who are eager to win, they are weakened by their ambitions. Their desire, for example, to avoid a bloody public squabble may lead them to make concessions (these may involve changes in the platform, opportunities for certain individuals to address the convention, the seating of contested delegations, or in extreme cases, the Vice-Presidential nomination). Few party professionals want to drive the minority out of the party. The predominant motivation is to achieve unity, and it is this, rather than oligarchic usurpation, that most often leads to "deals" and accommodations.

It should be noted that the minority plays the same game as the majority, but enjoys the advantage, as a minority, of appearing the more virtuous. McCarthy supporters, for example, have been no less active than Humphrey's in trying to line up the support of party leaders and delegates. For Humphrey, there is no way to emerge unscathed: if he is nominated on the first ballot, he (or the "organization") will be said to have rigged the convention beforehand; if he wins only after several ballots, he (or the "organization") will be said to have successfully manipulated the convention in Humphrey's favor; and if he loses the nomination to McCarthy or some other candidate, he (or the "organization") will be said to have been overturned by an uprising of the "people."

In short, the degree to which partisans favor or oppose the nominating convention notoriously reflects the vicissitudes of the political contest. It is not uncommon for the losers in a political struggle to propose the structural reforms of the institution which denies them victory.

THE CIRCUMSTANCES of the Republican contest differ from those of the Democratic, but similarities can be detected. The Rockefeller camp, aware that Nixon enjoys a considerable initial edge in delegate strength, points to the national opinion polls to prove its claim that Rockefeller is the preferred candidate of the voters. Owing to Rockefeller's fumbling and indecision in first withdrawing from the race, and his re-entry when it was too late to compete in the primaries, his associates cannot complain about the inappropriateness of the convention system or extol the superiority of a national Presidential primary. Nevertheless, they too have sought to circumvent the convention as an instrument of decision-making by asking, in effect, for a national plebiscite to be officially conducted by the Republican party, the results of which would presumably guide if not actually bind the delegates at Miami Beach.

The assumption behind both objections to the convention system is that the selection of the Presidential candidates ought properly to be lodged with the voters themselves, and not with a body of party practitioners. A national primary, its proponents claim, would correct the deficiencies that now attend the Presidential nominating procedure. It would not only be democratic, allowing all party supporters to participate in the choice, but would also draw on the people's wisdom, remove the party from the hands of the political bosses and mountebanks and return it to the governed, restore a sense of individual participation in the shaping of one's destiny, awaken voter interest, and permit the electorate to register its preferences for urgently desired changes.

The recommendation is well-meaning; it is also, however, misguided, for many of its assumptions are false, and the cure would, in any event, be worse than the disease.

The *mystique* that surrounds elections in a democracy has been carried over by the proponents of the Presidential primary to bolster their claim for its superior wisdom. If the assumption

of *vox populi, vox dei* holds for general elections, why should it
not also hold for primaries?

One difficulty with this assumption, however, is that voters
often differ sharply in their views, and unless God speaks in
many and conflicting tongues, their claim to superior wisdom
becomes difficult to sustain on this ground. Nor do voters always
exhibit sagacity in their choice of rulers, for they have elected
men of malignant as well as benevolent aspect. Nothing in the
electoral process insures that wise, just, prudent and compassionate men will be preferred to stupid, cruel and irresponsible
ones. Voters have elected despots and democrats, Fascists and
Communists, totalitarians and libertarians, liberals and conservatives, the virtuous and the vicious, men of honor and integrity
as well as liars and cheats.

ON WHAT GROUNDS, then, should we expect the electorate to
exhibit greater insight when it participates in a Presidential
primary? Indeed, since a primary removes party differences and
other familiar guides that are ordinarily available to the voter
in a general election, the danger is increased that he will fall
victim to demagogues and crowd-pleasers, matinee idols and
publicity seekers, familiar names and celebrities. Primaries are,
to an even greater degree than general elections, popularity
contests. Men of minor talent who, by ostentatious display, are
able to call attention to themselves, enjoy an unusual advantage
in the primaries over men of greater gifts, but of more sober
demeanor.

No DEFENDER of the convention system needs to apologize for
the over-all quality of the men who have been nominated for
the Presidency. During the present century, the conventions have
turned up, among others, Woodrow Wilson, William Jennings
Bryan, Theodore Roosevelt, William Howard Taft, Charles Evans
Hughes, Franklin Roosevelt, Herbert Hoover, John F. Kennedy,
Harry Truman, Thomas Dewey, Richard Nixon, Wendell Willkie
and Adlai Stevenson. A few of the nominees may have fallen
short of Presidential caliber, but the list on the whole is an
impressive one.

Nor does the historical record show that the men chosen by
the conventions were less able and deserving than the men they
rejected. How many distinguished and supremely qualified men
can one name who would have been nominated by a national
Presidential primary but who were passed over by the conven-

tions? In some instances conventions have turned up men of extraordinary quality and distinction who were not widely known to the electorate and who would certainly have been unable to win a national Presidential primary. Woodrow Wilson is one example, and Adlai Stevenson is another. It was the "organization" and the convention system that discovered Stevenson, recognized his brilliance, integrity and highmindedness, and nominated and renominated him for the nation's highest office.

The delegates' ability to recognize and nominate superior candidates is not fortuitous. Through comparative research on the characteristics of party leaders and voters, we have learned that convention delegates are much better prepared than ordinary voters to assess the attributes of candidates. They are more interested, aware, and concerned about political outcomes. Ideologically they are far more sophisticated and mature than the average voter. Despite their differences, the delegates to the two conventions constitute, to a far greater extent than their rank-and-file supporters, communities of cobelievers. Not only does each of the party delegations tend to converge around identifiable belief systems, but they also tend to diverge from each other along liberal-conservative lines. Their respective followers, however, tend to look alike.

Thus, it is not the delegates of the two parties but the mass of their supporters who can more appropriately be described as Tweedledum and Tweedledee. Whereas the delegates are prone to search out and select candidates who embody the party's values, the mass of Democratic and Republican voters, participating in a national Presidential primary, would be likely to select candidates who are ideological twins. Nomination by primary, in short, might well afford the electorate less of a choice than nomination by convention.

WE HAVE GROWN so accustomed to the stereotype of convention delegates as Babbitts who wear funny hats and engage in juvenile hijinks that we often overlook the fact that they are a relatively sophisticated group of people. Most of them are above average in education, have participated in politics for many years, have usually held public or party office, are active in their local communities, and associate with the men who lead and manage affairs in almost every segment of society.

Our stereotypes of politicians and convention delegates have done them (and us) the disservice of misleading us about the pride many of them feel about the political vocation. Like physicians, journalists, professors or carpenters, most of them are concerned to do a good job and to uphold acceptable standards. No matter how drastically the political vocation changes, we persist in imagining the delegates as city-hall hacks and self-servers, ignorant and coarse.

Convention delegates actually are found to be not only less cynical politically than the average voter, but they have higher political standards and make greater demands on the performance of their colleagues. Many of the delegates who pursue politics mainly as an avocation hold important positions elsewhere in society. They are trade-union leaders, businessmen, editors, physicians, writers, civil-rights leaders, lawyers, professors, engineers, or have other jobs that require education or the ability to perform effectively in organizational roles. Many are conscientious citizens who belong to good-government groups, foreign-policy associations, organizations of women voters, and other voluntary bodies concerned with the public welfare. In sum, it is difficult to see by what logic or evidence convention delegates can be derided as morally shabby and intellectually inferior to the voters who participate in primaries, or as less qualified to assess the claims of the would-be candidates.

Consider also that the convention delegates often know the candidates personally, or have had opportunity to observe them at close quarters. The average primary voter, by contrast, has only superficial and indirect knowledge of the candidates, is poorly informed about even the simpler issues, has little special information concerning who in the party has worked industriously, shown originality or proved himself trustworthy, intelligent or responsible. His concern with politics and with the party's welfare is marginal, and he generally lacks the motivation and knowledge to relate his opinions to a larger belief system.

The depths of misinformation among primary voters is sometimes astonishing. Surveys conducted in this year's Oregon primary, for example, confirmed that more than three-fourths of the voters who favored Kennedy or McCarthy were either unable to identify, or completely misidentified, the Vietnam views of the two men, although for many weeks the campaign had been fought over this very issue.

One must not, on the other hand, overstate the qualifications and wisdom of convention delegates. Not all of them meet the standards demanded of a society of philosophers, astrophysicists or the League of Women Voters. But if the delegates fall short of the ideal, how much greater is the distance between the ideal and the average primary voter. The contrast holds not only for their knowledge of candidates, but also for their understanding of the requirements and deeper meanings of political democracy. The delegates are ahead of the average voter in this respect as well. What is even more startling is that they prefer, to a greater extent than the voters do, parties that divide by ideology, that stand for something, and that distinguish themselves from each other.

ONE ALSO HEARS that conventions are inherently "conservative" and designed to defend the status quo, while direct primaries are "progressive" and open the system to new ideas. Even a moment's reflection, however, will confirm that conventions have nominated a large number of imaginative and forward-looking men (as well as some conservatives), and that the electorate has nominated and elected numerous conservatives and reactionaries (as well as many liberals).

Nothing about the primary process gives it an inherent advantage over the convention process in opening candidates to new ideas. Indeed, as much research bears out, one is more likely to find tendencies toward innovation and experimentation among active party members and leaders than among voters. On many questions, notably civil rights, tolerance, constitutional liberties, openness to "change," conformity and conventionality in opinions and life-styles, the delegates of the two parties are usually more enlightened than the ordinary citizen. What determines "progressiveness" is less the formal nominating device than the purposes to which it is addressed and the manner in which it is employed. To insist otherwise is to value appearance over substance.

Although the conventions tend to select candidates who represent the party's dominant ideological position and thus afford the voters a genuine choice, they are, oddly enough, less likely to confront the electorate with political extremists. There is no contradiction in observing that a convention will choose a candidate who can be ideologically differentiated from the opposition while maintaining that he is unlikely to be an extremist. Forces toward convergence and divergence are simultaneously at work in the conventions. The usual outcome is that one of the conventions (the Democratic) selects candidates who are somewhat left of center but not radical extremists; while the other convention (the Republican) chooses candidates who are some-what right of center but not reactionary extremists.

One observes in the convention the pull of ideology in the one direction, and a desire to win, and therefore to attract the middle range of voters, in the other. Some people argue that the desire to win is so overwhelming that everything is sacrificed to that objective, and that the pull toward the center invariably prevails. But these observers overlook the genuine political convictions of the party activists. The delegates want to win, of course, but they hope to do so on something resembling their own intellectual terms. Strongly held beliefs are not the sole motivation for active political involvement, but neither are they entirely absent from the political activity of thoughtful men.

The nomination of candidates is for most voters only a small matter. They read, talk and reflect upon politics much less often than the delegates do, and most voters see elections as having little relevance to their daily lives. The extent of their indiffer-ence is evident from the size of primary turnouts. It is not unusual for primaries to involve as few as 25 to 40 per cent of the electorate. Since the election of Governors, Senators and other important officials is frequently at stake, one may doubt that a national Presidential primary would activate many of the voters who now neglect to participate.

ONE OF THE MOST SERIOUS drawbacks of a national Presidential primary, however, is the damaging effect it would have on the operation of our political parties. Primaries are profoundly antagonistic to the achievement of a responsible party system, for they deprive the party of its most important functions, the right to select candidates and to formulate programs on which those candidates are to stand.

Candidates selected by primary rather than party have won their positions by plebiscite, and have little reason to feel obligated to any organization. They can refuse to support the party's candidates, and even flirt with the opposition, without fear of being disciplined.

A party that consists of totally autonomous individuals, none of whom bears any ideological or fraternal relationship to any other, is the equivalent of no party system at all. It is extremely difficult to derive from such an arrangement a coherent, integrated set of policies. Without a responsible party, every representative works only for himself, thinks only of his own political safety and advantage, and cannot be depended upon to behave in predictable ways.

In such a system, not only is a legislative program difficult to attain, but the voters are left in confusion. Party labels mean little. Under such conditions when voters choose someone who calls himself a Democrat or Republican, they have no idea what policies he is likely to follow. Thus, what seems on its face to be a more democratic and representative arrangement turns out in the end to be less representative, because more capricious and less predictable, than is possible under a more orderly, responsible system of party organization. In modern societies, with their vast and complex problems, the need for responsible political parties is greater than ever before.

MANY POLITICAL OBSERVERS believe that the American parties are already too diffuse and too weak to impose discipline on their members or hold them to a political line. Even now, each survives as a party by the sheerest good fortune, with 50 state party units and no effective national office, no continually functioning executive committees, no clear criteria for membership, not even regular national newspapers or magazines to communicate with the rank and file, and no effective power to punish or reward members.

The parties can scarcely afford further impediments to their ability to function as national organizations. What holds them together now is in some measure a common set of beliefs, a sense of fraternity, informal personal and organizational ties and, perhaps most of all, a big, splashy, quadrennial meeting in which each tries to work out a common program, select national leaders, heal divisions and unite in a common effort to elect party candidates. A national Presidential primary would be a step in the wrong direction: it would seriously weaken the chances of producing a strengthened, more responsible, more meaningful party system.

DESPITE ALL THE FLIMFLAM about national primaries, the charge that bosses "put over" their own hand-picked candidates in disregard of the popular will, and that the "true" party leaders are seldom chosen, the two candidates most likely to emerge victorious from the Democratic and Republican conventions (Humphrey and Nixon) are by almost every criterion the leaders of their respective parties, who, if they win the nomination, will have earned it.

Both Humphrey and Nixon embody rather closely the ideological tendencies (liberal the one case, conservative in the other) of their parties. Both have the largest followings among party activists throughout the nation. Both have devoted themselves to their respective parties. Both are among the most experienced leaders of their parties, having served for more than two decades in party and Government offices. Both have been Senators and Vice Presidents, and have gained extensive experience in national and international politics beyond that of most (perhaps all) other contestants for the nomination. Both have expended much energy and time in raising funds and promoting their parties' causes and candidates. Both are men of unusual intelligence and political savvy. Both are energetic, active, lively and effective politicians. Both have long been recognized as high among the highest-ranking leaders of their parties, and have long been thought of as qualified Presidential candidates. Even Rockefeller, who comes closest of all the other candidates to having comparable experience, does not have better credentials for the nomination than Nixon or Humphrey.

It is ironic, in light of their considerable achievements and records, that the convention system should now be challenged on the grounds that Humphrey and Nixon are likely to be the nominees. What would one say about the effectiveness of a party system which excluded or by-passed men of their qualifications?

THE RECOMMENDATION to eliminate the national convention and to nominate Presidential candidates by direct popular primary is a manifestation of that misplaced democratic zeal that has led to such absurdities as the election of sheriffs, dog-catchers, assessors and coroners. Nothing about democracy requires that every official be elected. Like most virtues, democratic participation can be carried to excess and perverted by the very ubiquity or capriciousness with which it is employed. To elect certain officials in a large representative democracy is essential, but to subject every office to election is to impose impossible demands upon the electorate's ability to judge wisely. We would all be kept so busy with politics that we would have no time to read books, enjoy music, watch baseball or make love.

A few state primaries in the course of a national campaign might conceivably be useful as warm-ups or to help candidates to estimate the effectiveness of various appeals. But the costs of these and other benefits are excessive.

The use of primaries lengthens the course of the campaign,

and may serve, in the end, to diminish rather than increase voter interest. Primaries also add enormously to the cost of campaigns, and permit men of large fortunes an even greater advantage than they enjoy in general elections (the Rockefeller campaign this year—expensive, flamboyant and lavish beyond belief—affords a dramatic example of the power of wealth to return a candidate from relative obscurity to the forefront of the political arena).

In discussing these and other shortcomings of Presidential primaries, Nelson Polsby and Aaron Wildavsky ("Presidential Elections") have observed that a national primary would invite the candidacy not merely of two or three participants, but of many, perhaps 10 to 12, with none coming close to a majority. This would necessitate a second or "run-off" primary which would add further to the length and expense of a campaign procedure that is already absurdly grueling and expensive.

SOME OF THE ARGUMENTS against primaries can, of course, be made against elections as well. One deludes himself in thinking that elections are in any sense ideal devices for the selection of rulers; they are simply the least bad of all the devices we have been able to think of so far. If we knew a way to recognize and appoint philosopher-kings, it would be mere fetishism on our part to continue to elect public officials. But we are, alas, fallible, and no method of appointment has so far been discovered that assures the selection of political leaders who are noble, fair, just, honorable, generous, compassionate, beneficent, strong, courageous, sensible, refined, prudent and wise.

None of the alternative methods so far employed to select political leaders—hereditary title, oligarchic selection, military conquest, seniority, appointment by co-optation, charismatic revelation, ruthlessness and the ability to climb over and eliminate rivals, etc.—have demonstrated a systematic capacity for producing leaders of superior virtue and solicitude for the governed. We use free elections because they offer us an opportunity to hold leaders responsible. When rulers govern without opposition or fear of removal, the temptation to oppress their subjects, to destroy rivals, to usurp power and aggrandize themselves is too great for most of them to resist.

But if elections are essential to democracy, national Presidential primaries are not. Conventions are not only an acceptable but superior alternative, entirely in keeping with the democratic idea. Doubtless they could be improved. They could be made smaller, more deliberative, less chaotic, more representative and less oratorical.

It is not clear, however, that either the parties or voters want the conventions reformed.

Postscript (July 1969)

Because of the demonstrations in downtown Chicago and the angry jockeying for advantage among the contending delegations within the Amphitheater, the Democratic National Convention of 1968 has come to be regarded in some quarters as final proof of the unsuitability of the Convention system. In reality, however, that Convention was remarkable for its many innovations and solid achievements as well as for its turbulence. An informed and high-minded debate on alternative approaches to Vietnam took place both on the Convention floor and in the Platform Committee. The Convention drafted and adopted a domestic platform universally acknowledged to be among the most liberal in the Party's history, one that fully embodied and amplified the Party's dominant political philosophy. (It supported, among other things, the implementation of the Kerner Commission recommendations on civil rights, the broadening of programs for Equal Employment Opportunity, Medicare, Social Security, public housing, open housing, and tax reform and redistribution.) In the contests over credentials, the Convention took the momentous step of refusing to seat the regular Mississippi delegation because of its segregationist cast and of replacing it with a racially integrated loyalist delegation. In the case of Georgia, it seated an integrated liberal delegation of insurgents along with the regular delegation, and divided the state's votes between them. From the Credentials Committee, the Rules Committee, the Special Equal Rights Committee, and the Convention delegates as a body, there emerged important recommendations that aimed to abolish the unit rule at all levels of Party organization, to eliminate all racial discrimination in the selection of delegates, to propose reforms that would further democratize and broaden participation in the procedures for selecting delegates, to assure that delegates will be chosen at appropriate points in time when issues are actively before the public, and to reapportion the votes of the delegations to achieve equal representation. Particularly significant was the establishment of a special Rules Commission to consider and recommend major reforms on all matters appropriate to pre-Convention and Convention procedures. Finally, the 1968 Democratic Convention nominated as its Presidential candidate one of its most brilliant and experienced leaders, generally regarded as the leading spokesman for the Party's liberal philosophy, and the candidate shown by most of the polls to be most widely favored by rank-and-file Democratic voters. As its Vice-Presidential candidate, the Convention selected an exceptionally wise, able, enlightened and dignified man, entirely competent, from all appearances, to assume the Presidency if the need arose.

THE POLITICS OF THE ALIENATED LEFT: AN ASSESSMENT

William P. Gerberding

The politics of the Alienated Left, like all politics, should be judged with respect to both its purposes and its techniques, its ends and its means. The means employed by the Alienated Left include nonviolent civil disobedience, disruption of political and educational processes, coercion, and violence. The last three have generally been regarded by democrats as unacceptable in a democratic society that provides for freedom of speech and accessible means for effecting change.

There has been less agreement about the status of nonviolent disobedience. My own view is that it can be condoned in this country only as a last resort in answer to intolerable conditions. Each situation must be judged separately. This approach implies neither a militant nor a moderate, neither a liberal nor a conservative, set of political perspectives. Such perspectives manifest themselves in specific circumstances as the question arises whether nonviolent civil disobedience should be resorted to or not. My own tendencies on this issue, for example, range from moderate (on non-racial issues) to militant (on some racial matters).

Most of the Alienated acknowledge that many of their means would be unacceptable in a "genuinely democratic" society. They take the position that their more severe means are necessary and appropriate techniques for destroying all or substantial parts of the American political system *because that system is undemocratic and illegitimate.* They refuse to abide by the "rules of the game" because they do not approve of the "game" and they want to create a new one. They contend that their ends—fundamentally reordering the American political system and its social, economic and educational underpinnings—justify their means.

Their conviction that means (actions, techniques) must be judged to a considerable extent in terms of the ends they serve is a sound one. Coercion, violence, revolution and even civil war can be condoned under certain circumstances. It follows, therefore, that a general denunciation of illegal, coercive, and violent behavior is not a satisfactory response to their behavior and beliefs. It must be shown that their purposes do not justify these drastic means, that their remedies are disproportionately, and therefore improperly, related to the alleged evils, and that their means will create even greater evils than those they are determined to eliminate.

Whether a political system is adjudged to be "legitimate" depends on what criteria are invoked and what degree of fulfillment of those criteria is regarded as sufficient. If one requires that the political system guarantee that the foreign policies pursued by the government will always (or even nearly always) be wise or noncontroversial; that it generate policies which insure fair treatment for racial minorities; that it insure direct public participation in all major decisions; and above all, that existing political institutions—parties, legislatures, bureaucracies, courts, and so forth—conform to idealized conceptions of self-government, then the American system decidedly fails the test.

But such criteria cannot reasonably be invoked regarding any nation, and particularly a nation as vast, diverse, and complex as this one. Yet these criteria are being invoked by the Alienated Left. Many of these people are, like most political radicals, believers in the millennium. They are confused and ill-informed about politics, whether democratic or undemocratic. They are recklessly ignorant of both its limitations as a method for changing behavior and its unlimited potential for genuine savagery. In their pursuit of the millennium, they see neither the virtues of the system they denounce nor the possibility that their actions will exacerbate the problems they sometimes correctly identify and, in addition, create even worse ones.

It is incumbent on the responsible critic of American society to invoke different criteria, to raise politically mature questions which take into account human history and human nature and are grounded in reality, not an obsession with lifeless utopias. The questions which should be asked about a political system

are of the following kinds (and roughly in the following order):
(1) To what extent are political, cultural, and religious freedoms honored and protected? (2) To what extent is the political
system responsive to the wishes of the citizens? (3) Given this
level of responsiveness, to what extent does this result in laws
and policies, both foreign and domestic, that, *on balance*
and given the frailty of human intelligence and judgment, can
reasonably be called prudent and rooted in genuine concern for
justice?[1] (4) Specifically, to what extent have all citizens been
guaranteed the equal protection of the law and equal access to
educational and economic opportunities? (5) To what extent
has the economic system, as fostered and protected by the political system, provided the necessary goods and services for the
citizenry?[2]

Freedom in America

Without attempting to offer a satisfactory definition of such
terms as "freedom" and "free men," I merely suggest that a free
man is one who enjoys such rights as freedom of religion, freedom of speech, freedom of assembly, freedom to petition his

[1] It is recognized that prudence and a concern for justice do not
always coexist comfortably, and may indeed often be incompatible.
This will be discussed below.

[2] Only questions 3 and 4 will be discussed extensively in this
essay. Questions 1 and 2 will be treated fairly briefly.

Question 5 will not be discussed at all. The American economy
is indisputably a remarkably productive one, and the simple answer
to question 5 is "abundantly." Aside from fundamental questions
about its capitalistic character—and I approve of the kind of "mixed
economy" we currently have in the United States—the most important issue is not its productivity, but the distribution among the
citizenry of its goods and services, especially the continuing existence of poverty. This is, of course, an important matter; I have
merely chosen to concentrate on other problems.

Any such list of "key questions" is bound to be selective and controversial. One could do worse than simply to use, instead, the words
of the Preamble to the Constitution and ask: To what extent does
the American political system "establish justice, insure domestic
tranquility, provide for the common defense, promote the general
welfare, and secure the blessings of liberty to ourselves and our
posterity"?

government for a redress of grievances, freedom to run for public office, freedom to vote for whom he chooses, freedom to move around as he pleases, and freedom to quit his job. Since "freedom" is so laden with positive connotations, it has sometimes been used as a virtual synonym for such related concepts as justice and equality. This usage confuses many important matters and is regrettable.

The American political system is committed to and protective of individual freedom; American citizens, with a few and dwindling exceptions, are free men. In these distracted and hypercritical times, it is unfashionable to assert the reality of American freedom; unfashionable but true. Moreover, there is nothing —except the provision of the bare physical necessities of life— more important about a political system than the extent to which it affords its citizens freedom.

It should be emphasized in this regard that cultural, religious and political freedom are more often denied than honored in human affairs, past and present. Yet in this country, despite a recent past marked by wars, depression and a good deal of political turmoil, our liberties have been protected and even expanded. This is a remarkable and vital fact.

It may be that our liberties are now so ingrained that our citizenry can take them for granted; one hopes that this is so. But if it is true, it represents an unusual achievement. Most human beings, both now and in the past, have experienced only a political environment anything but free.

It is true, of course, that freedom is not self-evidently the highest or nearly the highest political value. Many people quite obviously prefer security or discipline or political power or social justice to freedom. It is by no means obvious that many of the Alienated Left attach much importance to freedom. Their view tends to be ambivalent and they have adopted two distinct positions. One is a candid declaration that freedom is a "bourgeois" concept and therefore not worthy of respect. Some, in the ancient tradition of political repression, have made it clear that only "correct" views ought to be published or spoken. They reject the democratic virtues of tolerance and diversity. They know what is best for everyone and there is, therefore, nothing to be gained from endless argument, debate, compromise, accommodation.

A rather more subtle assault on American freedoms holds that they are essentially fraudulent. One cannot really be free unless one "knows the truth" or is "liberated." And since Americans are, it is claimed, the unwitting dupes of the mass media, "the Establishment," the government, and assorted other villains, they cannot be genuinely free. Since only the Alienated possess the truth, they alone are free. For reasons which should be readily apparent, this perverse argument is far from persuasive in the abstract and bears little or no relationship to conditions in the United States.

The Public Will

To what extent is the political system responsive to the wishes of the citizens? Anyone familiar with the hazards of trying to get an unambiguous sense of public sentiment on major public issues is likely to find this question impossibly naive. And so it is, if anyone expects to discover anything like unanimity or constancy in public opinion. But the New Left and others do raise this broad issue of responsiveness and in some form or another those concerned with the substance of democracy must grapple with it. Those who chant "All Power to the People" may not understand the irony of their plea—if "the people" were to exercise their power *vis-à-vis* the chanters, unchecked by the safeguards provided by the hated "system" in this country, then vigilantism or other kinds of suppression could easily result— but they do raise an important question.

The first thing that must be said about this problem, as suggested parenthetically above, is that many of the Alienated have confused their own voices with those of "the people." Having done so, they then compound their mistake by insisting that the government adopt their policies, as if governments had no other responsibility than the pursuance of policies insisted upon at any given moment by "the people."

Their presumption was never more visible than over the tragic issue of Vietnam during the Johnson years. They and the non-alienated dissidents who joined them on this issue were never a majority, nor did they represent that fictional monolith, "the people."[3] Yet they repeatedly declared that the failure of the

[3] This is, to be sure, a complicated issue and one widely misunderstood. Obviously, popular support for the war declined sharply between 1965 and the election year of 1968. Frustration was the dominant mood and there was a widespread demand for new leadership. Specifically, the polls showed the public moving steadily away

Johnson administration to accept their prescriptions was conclusive proof of the undemocratic nature of the American political system. If reminded that they were not in fact a majority, they would shift the basis of their claim to political power by claiming that they were right. Perhaps they were—I believe they were more right than the government—but a democracy is based on the belief that policies should be made, for the most part, by majorities and their representatives, not minorities; and that while minorities may sometimes be wiser or more just than majorities, over the long run the best form of government is one that, with certain individual rights remaining inviolable, grants authority to majorities, not minorities.

---

from the view that the decision to commit combat troops was correct. By the summer of 1968, a majority of the population (53 percent) had come to believe that this decision had been a mistake. (Gallup Poll, *Los Angeles Times*, August 25, 1968.) But nothing like a majority ever supported any of the various prescriptions of the critics, even the comparatively mild—and subsequently adopted—ones such as a bombing halt or acceptance of a coalition government in which the Viet Cong would have a role. The proportion favoring the more drastic solution of a unilateral American withdrawal never reached as high as 20 percent.

The claim that "the people" supported the critics' view of American policy in Vietnam did not, therefore, rest on the evidence of the polls. Instead, it depended primarily on the impressive primary election successes of Senators Eugene J. McCarthy and Robert F. Kennedy. Elections, however, bring a large number of issues into play, and policy orientation is by no means the most significant. A Louis Harris poll published in the *Los Angeles Times* on August 22, 1968, continued the following information: "When asked directly who would do a 'better job in handling the war in Vietnam,' the American people prefer Vice President Hubert Humphrey to McCarthy by 47 to 29%. Among Democrats, Humphrey is preferred to McCarthy on the war issue by an even larger 55 to 24%. . . .

"The real key to popular support for the McCarthy candidacy, despite all the speculation to the contrary, does not rest on the substance of the Vietnamese war issue alone. Rather, the senator has caught fire with sizable majorities of the American people for his personal political courage and his new style of politics, whether or not they agree with his positions on Vietnam. . . . Democrats who support McCarthy are actually opposed to a halt in bombing of North Vietnam by 55 to 29%. This is somewhat lower than the figure for the nation as a whole, which opposed a bombing halt by 61 to 24%, but it is still almost 2 to 1."

As intimated above, however, the problem is even more complex because it is by no means clear that democratic governments have a duty to accept even genuine—as distinguished from imaginary—majority opinions. In a nation of 200 million people, there is a good deal to be said for "representative government," as distinguished from "direct democracy" or direct expressions of opinion. In the former, elected officials make policy and are subject to reelection or rejection in free elections. In the latter, means are designed—such as polls, referendums, or plebiscites—to discover "public opinion" on each and every significant issue, with that opinion automatically becoming public policy. The advantages of the former system are compelling, especially when it is borne in mind that elected officials in this country are ordinarily extremely sensitive to the opinions of the many publics. There should be, in other words, room in our political system for governmental discretion and independence of judgment, as well as a powerful role for the views and attitudes of the governed. And this is, in fact, the case.

Among the ironies associated with the claim that President Johnson was undemocratic and unresponsive regarding his Vietnam policy is the fact that in the final analysis both he and his policies were undermined by the minority of the citizenry who disagreed with his policies. This may have been a happy development, but it does raise some uncomfortable problems for those who insist so loudly and undiscriminatingly that "the people" must prevail. The simple fact is that the Alienated Left is not much interested in whether "the people" approve of their favored policies. They seem to understand instinctively that public sentiment does get thoroughly aired in this self-conscious, self-critical political system and that, for the most part, government is, if anything, *too* responsive to public opinion. Indeed, in their more candid moments, their contempt for "the people" is readily apparent and it could scarcely be otherwise, given their perfervid rejection of the primarily "bourgeois" ethos of the American people. It is one thing to pose as spokesman for "the people"; it is another to accept the rather accurate representation of those people that our political system insures.

What the Alienated really care about is not whether the policies of "the people" or the majority are being implemented; for the most part, that is the case. Instead, they care deeply about whether, by one means or another, they—the bearers of Political Truth, the self-appointed, non-elected "representatives" of the American people—get their way.

Vietnam and American Democracy

Given this (high) level of responsiveness, to what extent does this result in laws and policies, both foreign and domestic, that, *on balance* and given the frailty of human intelligence and judgment, can reasonably be called prudent and rooted in a genuine concern for justice?

As suggested above, the concepts "prudence" and "justice" do not always coexist comfortably. Perhaps, indeed, the Alienated would accept only "just policies" and not merely "prudent policies" as an appropriate standard for judgment. The word "prudent" was inserted primarily because this selective discussion is focussed on the crucial and vulnerable issue of foreign policy, and very few reasonable people would insist that the only criterion for American foreign policy ought to be whether it is "just." Nearly everyone, that is, concedes that in an unstructured and dangerous area such as foreign affairs, governments ought to be prudent first (about such matters as, for example, national security) and then as "just" as prudence will permit.

Has United States foreign policy, on balance, been prudent and just? The Alienated Left believes that it has seldom been either and that in Vietnam appalling and *inevitable* depths of imprudence and injustice have been reached. That our intervention in Vietnam was imprudent is a proposition that most Americans, including this one, would accept. But the moral status of our performance there is, in my judgment, rather more complicated. The original intervention, though ill-conceived strategically, was motivated by honorable sentiments and was aimed at defensible ends. If we had been able to intervene quickly, discriminatingly, and successfully, there would have been much to commend such an action from a moral standpoint. As the war dragged on, however, and as the means employed there bore less and less of a necessary and proportionate relationship to our ends, the moral status of our policies became badly frayed and, in the minds of some, entirely undermined.

It is beyond the scope of this essay to argue these propositions. Serious moral assessments rest on complex calculations of relative good and relative evil, likely consequences of the pursuit of various policy options, and other often obscure matters. What I mean to suggest includes the following: the political objective in South Vietnam sought by the leadership of the Viet Cong (and North Vietnam) was (and is) the establishment of another dreary, totalitarian, Communist regime, like the one in North Vietnam and worse, therefore, than the one "governing" South Vietnam; the United States had become heavily committed to the preservation of a non-Communist Vietnam, and the credibility of our international commitments is not something that moral men ought lightly to dismiss in this dangerous world; and it was, therefore—for both of the above reasons—morally supportable to help the South Vietnamese resist this fate *provided the means employed and the attendant consequences of such support bore some reasonable, proportionate relationship to the end sought.* A quick, discriminating, and successful application of force might very well have been a reasonable, proportionate response. As it turned out, no such option existed.

The crux of the claim of the Alienated, however, is not that our policy in Vietnam was imprudent and morally indefensible; it is that this outcome was *inevitable,* or nearly so. This assertion raises the tough question. Presumably even the idealized government envisaged by the Alienated would occasionally err; so far as I can tell, they have not pretended, like the Bolsheviks, that they are infallible riders of the waves of history. The question, then, is whether Vietnam was an aberration or whether it was part of a pattern that was foreordained by our society, economy and political institutions; or whether it was something in between. The Alienated Left claims that the Vietnam involvement was part of an unavoidable pattern. I contend it was somewhere in between an aberration and an inevitable pattern, and much closer to the former than the latter; and, most importantly, not likely to be repeated. It was, I would argue, a tragic mistake, made by fallible men of limited vision, doing what they thought was best for their country and the broader interests of mankind.

There is a dazzling diversity of viewpoints about the purposes and consequences of recent American foreign policy. Much of the critical writing and argument is reflective of discerning and coherent intelligences. Much of it, however, is not, and this includes many of the basic propositions put forward by the Alienated Left.

There are a number of central and interrelated themes at the root of the critique of the Alienated. Essentially, the argument comes down to this: the United States was primarily responsible for the onset of the Cold War; the United States has been the major initiator of Cold War confrontations and tensions; and, in the process, the United States has become an aggressive, imperialist power. This is not the place to analyze and assess these arguments. They are, in my judgment, grotesque distortions of history and their growing popularity and superficial plausibility are some of the many costly consequences of the disaster in Vietnam.

It has been necessary to develop "explanations" for this transformation of the United States from an isolationist lamb to an aggressive interventionist lion, and many have been offered. Some of these "explanations," while they do not really support the extreme positions mentioned above, are nonetheless perceptive. It is charged, for example, that the dominant mood in both major political parties—as well as in the public at large— has been obsessively and undiscriminatingly anti-Communist and that the so-called "Lesson of Munich"—that any appeasement of aggressors only invites greater disasters later on—has been crudely applied. There is truth in these charges; they begin to explain the excesses and errors in postwar American foreign policy, especially in Vietnam. They do not by themselves, however, demonstrate the validity of the critical themes cited above; they merely impart to such themes a superficial plausibility.

In order for these themes to carry much conviction it is necessary to uncover darker, more sinister causes than a mere misreading of events. Four such "causes" have been most prominently adduced: a frantic pursuit of individual and national economic advantage; bureaucratic inertia and self-gratification; a cowardly, myth-protecting mass media; and an alleged addiction to violence for its own sake.

There is some truth in these alleged "causes" of United States "militarism, interventionism, and aggression." We *do* individually and collectively as a nation manifest a notable fondness for economic well-being; we are a society that, among other things, values highly material possessions. It is also true that our "National Security Bureaucracy"—the military and its allies within the federal bureaucracy—has a vested interest in the Cold War, in high defense budgets, and perhaps even in occasional "experimental" wars. And when these vested interests combine—even if they don't conspire—with those considerable elements of the corporate and political worlds that have a stake in the same kinds of things, they do indeed constitute a "Military-Industrial Complex." It is true, moreover, that the mass media tend to reflect the values of a predominantly middle-class society and are not eager to criticize the basic institutions or values of that society. And unquestionably, the United States, by comparison with other Western democracies, is abnormally plagued by violence.

Still, as "explanations" for our allegedly primary responsibility for the Cold War or our allegedly inescapable drive toward intervention and empire, these arguments are unpersuasive. Let us look at each of them against the most incriminating test of all: Vietnam.

Few people would contend that we went to war in Vietnam for traditional economic reasons: to protect investments, or to maintain access for purposes of trade or because of certain precious minerals or products. Such a contention would be absurd. Insofar as the "economic" argument has any plausibility at all regarding Vietnam, it has to do with the undeniably substantial profits being made by corporate contractors and the alleged dependence of the economy on vast defense budgets. With some companies exclusively or primarily dependent upon Department of Defense contracts for their survival and many others realizing substantial profits in the same way, it would be foolish to deny that many persons have developed a stake in defense budgets and, therefore, to some extent a stake in such things as the perpetuation of the Cold War—if not with Russia, then with China—and perhaps even occasional "limited wars." It may even be true that many such persons and firms have little sense of public responsibility and will follow the imperatives of the profit motive blindly, selfishly, and without any mature sense of their own or anyone else's longrange interests.

But this proves nothing about their *influence*. One of the wonders of a free society is that through such means as published memoirs and the daily outpouring of an aggressive press corps, there is little that an attentive citizen cannot learn about how and why major decisions are made by our government. Our Vietnam decisions have been subjected to constant scrutiny and criticism in the press and many former Kennedy and Johnson officials have gone into private life and published exposes, confessions and more prosaic accounts. Anyone who has read much or all of this material and who still believes that economic considerations of *any* kind played a role in our decisions regarding Vietnam must believe, also, that there is a vast conspiracy of silence about this. The simple fact is that no such evidence exists.

A more serious issue is posed by the "National Security Bureaucracy" and its political allies. Bureaucrats and generals do develop vested interests and, too often, inflexible and illusory patterns and habits of thought. Regarding Vietnam, it appears to be the case that most of the career officials—civilian and military—took an orthodox, almost blindly simple-minded view of what was happening there and of our security interests. Moreover, the top political leadership was predisposed in the same direction and there was apparently little serious dissent and questioning within the bureaucracy.

None of this, however, should surprise anyone familiar with bureaucracies. The choice would seem to be between abolishing bureaucracies or somehow trying to contend with their inadequacies. The latter is the only serious possibility. The question, then, is whether bureaucratic orthodoxies and vested interests can be managed successfully, so that the broader national interests will be served. The answer would seem to be that, with difficulty, they can be managed, adjusted, rearranged, redirected. Once again, Vietnam is a crucial test.

President Johnson was misled—albeit unintentionally—by his bureaucratic and political advisers. But the ultimate responsibility was his, not theirs. He, not they, made the basic decisions; and he, therefore, must bear the responsibility. It is fair to blame the "National Security Bureaucracy" for its inadequacies; it is not fair to blame it for our national policies.

Admittedly, however, and unlike those with economic interests in our defense policy, these bureaucrats and political appointees do have great influence on a President; therefore, they do and will influence foreign policy. But we come back to the original question: Is their influence inevitably on the side of intervention, of "military solutions," of an "activist, aggressive" foreign policy? No, it is not and it has, as a matter of fact, often been on the side of caution, of nonintervention. In 1954, for example, the chiefs of staff of the military services were unanimously opposed to American intervention in Indochina when President Eisenhower was being pressed to intervene by many of his civilian advisers, including then Vice President Nixon and Secretary of State Dulles.

As for the future, it is unimaginable that either the civilian or military elements of the "National Security Bureaucracy" have not, like the country as a whole, been sobered and deeply affected by the tragedy of Vietnam. There is nothing at all inevitable about our future policies, and very little likelihood that the strategic errors and moral miscalculations that characterized our intervention in Vietnam will be repeated. Indeed, a better case can be made for the reverse proposition, namely, that fingers so badly burned will stay so far away from the fire that it might get out of control. But that is another matter.

The central points being argued here are that (a) the "National Security Bureaucracy" is influential but not in control, and (b) it is subject to changes in orientation and mood, just like the public. If the Supreme Court "follows the election returns," so too does the "National Security Bureaucracy."

The role of the mass media can be disposed of more readily regarding Vietnam. It did not lead the trend toward dissent, but anyone who believes that it did not report it, exaggerate it and, perhaps unwittingly, foster it must have been living in another country. Two illustrations should suffice: television's coverage of the war, whatever the purposes of the network officials may have been, was a powerful factor in the growing public distaste for the war. Very little of the horror of war was kept off the screens; the effects were as dramatic as they were predictable. Secondly, the most influential newspapers in this country were filled with stories, columns and editorials which implicitly and explicitly challenged the assumptions upon which our policies were based, as well as the policies themselves.

We turn now to the last-mentioned "cause" of our involvement in Vietnam: an alleged addiction to violence for its own sake. Much depends on how one defines this issue; and however it is defined, convincing evidence is hard to come by. There is the crude version which holds that we intervened in Vietnam because President Johnson and those around him were starved for a bit of gun-play. I suppose it is conceivable that in Lyndon Johnson's unconscious lay a passion for war, but I doubt it very much and, for better or for worse, we'll probably never know. Even if this were true, however, it would hardly be evidence for anything much beyond the psychological condition of one man.

There is, however, a more troublesome version of the "violence explanation." As an active participant in international politics, the United States is comparatively inexperienced and has been abnormally successful. Therefore, the argument runs, we lack a sense of tragedy and a sophisticated appreciation of the limited utility of power, especially military power, in international affairs. As a youthful, optimistic, energetic, and relatively unscarred nation in an increasingly complex and intractable world, the United States is bound to be terribly frustrated. Instead of accepting disappointment gracefully and with a sense of the ephemeral and uncertain nature of life, it is argued, the

United States attempts to retrieve its diplomatic setbacks by the use of its immense military capability. We turn, in other words, too readily to organized violence as a means of relieving our anxieties, insecurities and frustrations.

There is a good deal to be said for this view and in this sense we may be more violence-prone than most countries; at least recent evidence tends to support the view that our swords are rather easily unsheathed. If this is true, however, it raises a number of interesting problems, none of them especially comforting to the seekers of a lost innocence and middle-aged celebrators of the cult of youth. It does, after all, suggest that violence—for nations as well as individuals—is more often associated with inexperience and immaturity than with their opposites. Crime statistics reinforce this melancholy impression: violent crimes are committed in a vastly disproportionate number of cases by persons under thirty. It may not be fair to jump to any conclusions about who, therefore, should be more trusted than whom—and our foreign policy has undeniably been made by men over thirty—but at least the fashionable version of the cliche does not acquire much support from this kind of focus on violence.

Another ironic and troubling aspect of this problem is that if the Europeans have a better record in this regard, it is of rather recent vintage. Could it be that they are less violence-prone only because they are simply exhausted after generations of slaughtering each other and colonizing "less advanced" peoples? If so, the prospects for a diminished American propensity for violence may be less hopeful—and in some ways even less attractive—than might otherwise seem to be the case. Or perhaps, conversely, the agony and tragedy of Vietnam may prove to have been an immunizing experience, teaching us the bitter lessons of living too readily by the sword.

Who knows? Surely not the Alienated, who neither have a program for removing the virus from our veins nor themselves abjure the use—indeed, even the adulation—of violence when it suits their own purposes.

What I have been arguing comes down to this: the sweeping case of the Alienated against American foreign policy is a weak one. The intellectual and moral errors responsible for our foreign policy mistakes were neither inevitable within the framework of our present economy, society and political system, nor were they the result of avarice or narrow selfishness. Taking even the disaster of Vietnam as the test, these were the mistakes of honorable and decent men, trying to do what they thought was best for their country and for democratic values generally. They were, in my judgment, tragically mistaken; they were not evil, nor is "the system" that produced them.

What I have not explicitly argued, but which also needs to be said from time to time in this fractious and self-important age, is this: the United States has on the whole pursued honorable and prudent policies in this difficult post-war period, and it has done so on behalf not only of its own security—a legitimate goal —but also on behalf of other peoples and democratic values. Our self-righteous rhetoric, our errors of judgment, and even our selective cooperation with elements of reaction abroad do not gainsay this: in the difficult and dangerous post-World War II period, this inexperienced nation has successfully defended itself, its allies and others, while incurring grave risks and sometimes great costs, and it has done this with considerable skill. It has, moreover, sought accommodations with those who chose to be its adversaries, been generous with its friends and allies and, to a lesser degree, with the sometimes hostile, usually difficult "non-aligned" nations. Many of the undiscriminating and reckless critics of recent American foreign policy are talented people, and some of them are honorable and well-intentioned as well. But the day that their grotesque distortions and partial truths are widely accepted will be a sad one for truth.[4]

Race in America

The most difficult challenge of all to a generally positive assessment of the American political system issues from the question "to what extent all citizens have been guaranteed the equal protection of the laws and equal access to educational and economic opportunities?" Following the example of the preced-

[4] I would like to make it unmistakably clear that I do *not* mean to include among "the undiscriminating and reckless critics of recent American foreign policy" such non-alienated (as I have used the term) and often constructive critics as, for example, Theodore Draper, Senators J. William Fulbright and Eugene J. McCarthy, and Ronald Steel.

It should also go without saying that I have nothing but respect and admiration for such generally dissenting (regarding Vietnam and many other matters) individuals as, for example, Hans Morgenthau and George F. Kennan. They speak and write, as they have for many years, in the highest traditions of critical scholarship.

ing discussion, I shall restrict myself to discussing the most difficult of the issues raised: in this case, of course, race. And the answer must be that American performance has fallen far short of even minimally acceptable standards. The treatment accorded non-white minorities in this country has been and remains a national disgrace.

Is the present political system incapable of drastically improving on this sorry performance? To put it another way, should black Americans embrace revolutionary rhetoric and prescriptions? Are not pleas for "moderation" and "reason" merely disguises for an essentially reactionary and racist position? In this treacherous and murky area, where the susceptibility to self-deception *for blacks and whites* is considerable, one ought to tread with caution; but I believe that a convincing argument can be made—from a non-racist, humane and democratic standpoint—for a negative answer to this question. An increasingly large minority of blacks would not agree, but a majority are still willing to test the effectiveness of democratic means.

The argument has two parts. The first and weakest is that halting but nonetheless hopeful developments are taking place. The second part of the argument—a stronger but less positive one—is that a resort to "revolutionary means," especially violence, for a redress of these grievances is as destructive as it is superficially attractive.

There have been hopeful developments in the last fifteen years or so.[5] Anyone who denies these advances either does not understand the facts or is anxious to suppress them. And beyond the generally favorable statistics and the developments in law is the related and in some ways more significant fact that blacks in this country today are experiencing the excitement of participation in a noble cause. In the process, they have developed a saving sense of pride and purpose.

Obviously, however, these developments do not dispose of the problem. How much progress has there been? How much remains to be accomplished? Is it not true that this progress, such as it is, has been extracted from a reluctant and racist white population primarily by coercion and violence? Does this not suggest that the best thing for black Americans to do is to maintain and perhaps increase this kind of pressure?

The answer to the first question (How much progress?) is,

[5] They are discussed in Nathan Glazer's "America's Race Paradox," pp. 244–262.

of course, complex and various, depending upon the area of the country and the issue. But everywhere the movement away from second-class citizenship is much too slow and in many places and circumstances scarcely detectable at all. The great stain of racism on the fabric of American life would not wash away easily even with the best intentions in all sections of American society; and that latter condition quite obviously does not obtain. The Wallace candidacy did not exhaust or even fully plumb the depths of resistance to equality in this country. The struggle is promisingly underway, but it is a long way from being over and, tragically, it is conceivable that reaction may turn the clock back again.

Therefore, the call for "revolutionary violence" (or "the destruction of the system" or whatever it's called) has a good deal to commend it. The status of the blacks *is* intolerable, the movement toward equality and justice *is* too slow, and fear of violence *has* helped to induce racial reform in recent years. Viewed exclusively from the standpoint of black Americans, it might appear that only more coercion, and more violence will improve their lot.

But the argument is deceptive and, ultimately, fallacious. If it were only the currently anathematized "white liberal" that the blacks had to contend with, then one *might* agree that the best way to advance toward equality and justice would be to employ coercive and violent tactics.[6] But the fact is that permissive, sympathetic "white liberals," to say nothing of white radicals, do not constitute a majority of the nation's population. Relatedly, they do not always control governmental policies, to say nothing of social mores. Those who prescribe coercion and violence seem to operate on the assumption that the much-hated "Establishment" is necessarily liberal and defenseless and can, therefore, be easily seduced or coerced into ameliorative action. But the "Establishment" in this democratic society changes over time and there is no guarantee that the sometimes ineffectual but essentially libertarian and humane elites that have generally ruled this country will always do so.

Some of the harsher truths about race relations in this coun-

[6] The reason why I use the word "might" rather than "would" is that even in this hypothetical situation I'm not sure that either the whites or the blacks would be happy with the conditions obtaining in the aftermath of an equality and a justice achieved by such methods. It might be largely a formal victory, lived out in a largely bitter and hostile environment.

try are overlooked—or at least minimized—by many sentimental white liberals and violence-prone militants alike. Surely
the most important of these is the existence of many millions of
white Americans who regard their material goods, their social
status and often their very lives as threatened by the black revolt.
These people are difficult to categorize neatly. Some of the more
evocative terms that are used to label them are "lower middle
class," and "ethnics" and "the forgotten Americans." Whatever
one calls them, two facts about them should be borne clearly in
mind: they are genuinely frightened and there are *many* more
of them than there are blacks and white radicals. Their fears
may be exaggerated and ignoble, but they are real. And those
fears are, in this responsive political system, becoming increasingly consequential in American political life. Some of the more
fanciful of the Alienated may regard themselves as waiting in
the wings, but the more serious contenders for political power
in the country are the George Wallaces and the Sam Yortys.

What black Americans are confronted with, in other words,
is a predominantly white nation composed of diverse and conflicting elements, many of them sympathetic to racial progress,
some of them not. To believe that the whites are either all
racists or all liberals is to make a fateful mistake. Black Americans share at least this with white Americans and all other
citizens of democratic societies: they live in a complex, vari-
egated environment which they will influence to their advantage
or disadvantage by their words and deeds. What strategies and
tactics they employ, therefore, are matters of cardinal importance.

The first ingredient of a successful strategy is a large dose of
truth. It may be that many of the concessions and improvements have been induced by fear of violence and civil insurrec-
tions. It is difficult to measure such things, but it seems likely
that the gains in the legislative arena have been primarily due
to black militancy of a non-violent kind and to feelings of outrage and shame at the lawless and brutal behavior of some
whites. But even if it were true that most of these gains were
dependent upon white fear of black violence, it does not follow
that such an indulgent, positive response is permanently assured. For one thing, the issues change. It is one thing to insure
that blacks have the right to vote; it is quite another to award
them compensatory cash grants, or to guarantee annual incomes for blacks—or, for that matter, for whites—or to turn
over law enforcement responsibilities or public schools to black

sections of a city. Moreover, there is a point of diminishing returns in matters of this kind. Original responses to coercion and violence may be relatively indulgent and yielding; over time, however, patience wears thin and repression replaces concession. These are the grim realities for black and white alike.

It should also be noted that I have been discussing primarily the political arena: how one gets favorable legislation enacted, progressive mayors elected, and so forth. But the political arena is not the only important one for black or white Americans. Beyond it, though assuredly deeply affected by it, is the workaday world in which whites and blacks must live and work together.[7] The quality and tone of these interrelations depend in the long run on some minimal sense of community, some minimal agreement about each other's essential decency and dignity and rights. A strategy of coercion and violence could only inject more poison into the atmosphere.

In sum, I am arguing that even if it can be shown—and I doubt it—that coercion and violence have paid off in the short run, there is a point beyond which they will have reverse effects; and generally speaking, I believe if such a point ever existed, we are well past it. The overwhelming weight of the evidence of public opinion polls and, more importantly, elections is that coercion and violence of any kind—whether individual or concerted, for private or for political ends—are regarded by the vast majority of the population—including most blacks—as intolerable. The burden of proof, therefore, is on those who contend that these methods can be curative in contemporary America.

What methods do offer hope? All the traditional techniques employed by minority groups in this country are available: the development of political strength within the major political parties, the use of pressure group tactics in the governmental and economic spheres, and full utilization of existing laws and the courts. In addition, moreover, there is the tactic of nonviolent protest which black Americans have used with greater effectiveness than anyone else in American history. When this

[7] Obviously, there is a considerable difference in the extent to which they do these things *together* in this country today. Whites and blacks increasingly work together and the trend is for more and more integration. As for living together, however, there is precious little of that and most integrated neighborhoods don't stay that way for long.

tactic did not bring about the millennium, it became unfashionable and, for many, discredited. It deserves a better fate than
that, both because of its many successes and because the "more
aggressive" tactics are so destructive.

It is obviously true that even the most intensive employment
of all these techniques is not likely to alter reality with revolutionary speed. It is equally true that black Americans face
barriers that did not obstruct the paths of earlier aspirant groups
in this country. These are sad realities, and techniques must be
chosen with care to insure that they take on a happier rather
than a still sadder face.

But I come back to the original theme: there is improvement,
there is change, there is hope. It is quite obvious we are not
going to be a genuinely integrated, color-blind society tomorrow
or the day after tomorrow. But that does not mean that blacks
cannot live meaningful, proud and dignified lives in this country, or that it would be better to destroy the society in the vain
hope that something better might turn up. The problem of
racism is not peculiarly American; it exists all over the world.
In this tormented land, we are beginning to get a grip on it.
With enough intelligence and good will, we will reduce it to
manageable, tolerable proportions. There is no other way, no
other hope.

Campus Disorders

The current wave of disorders in American higher education
is, of course, one of the more spectacular symptoms of contemporary alienation. Whatever its ultimate consequences may
be, its immediate consequences warrant some comment in an
essay on the politics of alienation.

For the most part, the university militants find their academic
targets an easy prey: faculties and administrations that are slow
to respond, sympathetic, guilt-ridden, and, in many cases, cowardly. But the larger community beyond the campus is a very
different group of people, and especially but not exclusively at
public institutions, the day of reckoning approaches, or has
already arrived. In the University of California, for example, the
student militants have received mixed but generally sympathetic
and compliant reaction from administrators and faculty. The
public, however, has become outraged by campus disorders and
associated forays into the outside community. Two results,

among many, make my point with force: the voters recently resoundingly defeated a bond issue for higher education, thereby reversing a long tradition of support; and Governor Ronald Reagan—an almost perfect symbol and instrument of the public's outrage, who was elected and will quite probably be reelected in good measure because of the "law and order" issue in general and the University issue in particular—now has a University Board of Regents that sees the problems as he sees them. The radicals on the faculties and among the students are furious, of course, but few of them have discovered that they have been and will continue to be greatly responsible for creating the very conditions they abhor. One abiding characteristic of most political radicals—and one that makes them at once so irritating and so irresponsible—is that they refuse to make any distinctions, save between themselves and everyone else. They gleefully assisted in the dispatching of Governor Pat Brown and were then shocked to discover that Ronald Reagan really exists, really does appoint University Regents, and really is different from friendly Pat Brown.

The hard core extremists, of course, were not surprised. They operate on the basis of the naive and disastrous notion that "things will never get better until they get much worse." Whether this view is based on misanthropic attitudes or simple naivety is an open question, but its consequences are painfully clear.

Every generation of college students believes that it has shed the prejudices and irrationalities of its predecessors. What distinguishes the situation today from most past manifestations of this age-old conflict is (a) the extent to which student rebels, both black and white, are willing to resort to coercive methods to achieve their objectives, (b) the extent to which they have unnerved their elders, and, relatedly, (c) the extent to which they have found allies within the older generation who not only support their vaguely revolutionary objectives but who share their mood of outrage and endorse their often coercive and sometimes violent methods. This minority element is no longer numerically insignificant and, partly because of the inept and sometimes repressive responses of "the system," its influence with the vast majority of students who are moderate seems to be growing.

Each case, each "confrontation," must be judged on its merits and some of the grievances are genuine. But a number of things, beyond those mentioned above, need to be said to and about these young rebels and their older associates. There is a quality of fanaticism, of spilled religion, about their behavior which ought to give more of them pause. Their contempt for "reason" and "traditional academic pursuits and concerns" and their millenarian rhetoric and aspirations are deeply troubling phenomena. Romanticism in politics is a heady brew and it has often served as the justification among the romantics for their own ruthlessness, cruelty, and repression. Many great political crimes have been committed in the name of some grand ideal. Moreover, as stressed above, to inflame political debate and action to high levels of intensity and passion is to invite equally passionate responses from others.

What do these young rebels, predominantly the adolescent products of comfortable middle-class homes, know about *real* political repression, *real* fascism, *real* totalitarianism? What do they know about mankind's—including, therefore, their own—capacity for *real* bestiality? Have they read about what life was like in Nazi Germany or Stalinist Russia? Have they wondered about the connection between political fanaticism and political barbarism?

It is a measure of their confusion and naivety that they assume either that such things are impossible here—in which case they are free to be as irresponsible in word and deed as they choose, with no fear of disastrous consequences—or that the United States today is already a fascist state, committing hideous crimes at home and abroad. But both assumptions are reckless and thoughtless. America is neither that good nor that bad.

Concluding Remarks

I have been arguing that with all of its imperfections the American political system is defensible and legitimate; that it protects our individual freedoms, is responsive to the wishes of the citizenry, and promulgates laws and pursues policies that are on balance both prudent and rooted in a genuine concern for justice; and that its greatest single shortcoming—the treatment accorded non-white minorities—relates to an ancient problem that the nation is finally beginning to grapple with.

What is the alternative offered by the Alienated Left? Since they are not an organized cohesive political movement, it is impossible to spell this out in a simple and representative way.

Some would socialize part or all of American industry, some would not. Some are pacifists regarding international affairs, some are not. Some would increase governmental authority, some would sharply decrease it. They say they want a society without poor people; where either racial integration is complete or, alternatively, where blacks control their own affairs; where war as an instrument of policy is abolished and defense budgets are either eliminated or drastically reduced; and where a "sense of community" replaces our present "alienation" from each other and from our work. They want, finally, an allegedly new kind of government, a "participatory democracy" wherein more citizens play an active role in making the decisions which affect their lives.

Many of these conditions would presumably be welcomed by most decent, non-radicalized, non-alienated Americans; some are more arguable. But even where there is agreement on goals or ideals, there remain the basic differences about how we get from here to there, and when. And if their present performance is suggestive of the kind of society they are aiming for, then it is unacceptable to libertarians, democrats, and any other respectors of a civilized and tolerant political system.

But the issue that is probably at the root of their alienation has not yet been mentioned: the quality of American life, or the "life style" of most Americans. Much of their rhetoric and action being symbolic and, at best, non-rational in the sense of not being goal-oriented, much of the preceding argument does not really touch their basic concern. That is, even if they could be convinced of the formal adequacy or validity of the preceding argument, their rage and alienation would not be affected in any decisive manner. They do not like the kind of people they think we have become: acquisitive, materialistic, impersonal, vulgar, self-righteous and hypocritical.

At this point, the argument between the Alienated and the rest of the population becomes, like the issues raised, terribly murky and slippery; and, as usual, as the precision and certainty recede, the rhetoric and intensity accelerate. Where they see predominantly "the rat race" (acquisitiveness, materialism), others, including this writer, see predominantly hard-working people, bent on enjoying an earned higher standard of living. A concern for material prosperity is generally an object of scorn only among those who are fairly well off and expect to remain so.

Where they see impersonality, I see an inevitable aspect of

industrialization and urbanization; and while I, too, would like a "softer," more "personal" society, I am willing to accept its sharpness and angularity as a price worth paying for the compensations associated with modernity. Moreover, the sense of community ascribed to earlier, more simple times is both sentimentalized and irretrievable. I also value privacy highly, and it is a concept closely akin to impersonality. Finally, friendships and intimacies *do* flourish in this society and everyone from the Hippies to the chairmen of the board is free to cultivate warmer relations with his fellow man. Freedom involves the freedom to be gregarious or aloof, warm or cold.

The vulgarity of contemporary American civilization is undeniable. The defacing of the continent's beauty, the garishness of much of the outer face of contemporary urban America, the sickening mediocrity (and worse) of television, and the reckless pollution of our environment are serious indictments of "the American way of life."

But it is also true that *any* nation of 200 million free human beings, most of whom have money to spend on items beyond the bare necessities, will have a substantial element of vulgarity in its public and private life. The word "vulgar" refers to characteristics of "the common people." It may be that one or two free countries may achieve great affluence—and therefore great visibility and outlets for "the masses" as well as "the cultured"—and avoid vulgarity; Great Britain may manage it, for example. But I doubt it very much. "The man on the street" prefers television soap operas to Shakespeare and in an affluent, free, and democratic society, he will get what he wants. There are more people like him than there are esthetes and artists. The United States is a country where the tastes of "the man on the street" are most conspicuous; to the extent that this is the price of freedom and affluence, so be it. And there is, of course, much beauty and sophistication available to those who want it in this country. We have great symphony orchestras as well as untalented and noisy rock groups.[8]

Self-righteous? Hypocritical? These charges generally issue

---

[8] This suggests another issue: the vitality, creativity, and beauty of parts of "the popular culture." It is not by accident that the Beatles and Frank Sinatra and Simon and Garfunkel—to name a few—grew out of the free and competitive environments of the Western world. What can one say about the popular culture in the "People's Democracies," where political elites decide what shall be seen and heard and done?

from sources *at least* as self-righteous and hypocritical as the objects of their censure. Suffice it to say that there is much truth in the allegations and an even greater lack of perspective, self-awareness, and sense of humor in the conclusions drawn therefrom.

An open mind is not disturbed by differing "life styles" and differing hierarchies of values; our culture is enriched by this extensive and typically American diversity. As noted above, contemporary popular music is often inspired and the current explosion of color in art and clothing is delightful. Are such beautiful, sensitive, exciting developments evidence of widespread rebellion or simply one more manifestation of the endless creativity and dynamism of American (and Western) society? When the current mood of self-laceration and alienation recedes, it will be obvious that the answer is: "Both, and that's one of the secrets of our vitality."

It is easy to dismiss this essay, this argument, as one more version of a tired old act, the American Celebration. In its essence, it is just that. But if one is able to rise above fashionable cynicism and sophomoric utopianism, one may see that, after all, there is much to celebrate as well as much to change.

THE WORLD STILL MOVES OUR WAY

Eric Sevareid

There are those who say the dream is dead or dying, poisoned by self-interest, rotted by surfeit and indifference, maimed by violence. The great aspiration is ended, they tell us, and America is now only another crowded nation, not even able to maintain order; a Power, but not a society, not a culture. We have gone, almost directly, they would have us believe, from primitiveness to decadence, a far poorer record than that of Rome.

The fireworks of this July 4—which may well illuminate the scene again, of whole urban blocks consumed by flames, from the Molotov cocktail, not the holiday sparkler—will give further force to this cry of the Cassandras.

But the cry is as old as the nation. It was sounded in Jefferson's time, when the states seemed ready to drift apart; in Lincoln's time, when they split apart; in Roosevelt's time, when, by the millions, husbands shuffled in soup lines; in Truman's time, when the Russians and Chinese were supposedly reordering the earth and Communist traitors were supposedly infesting the Government.

But this is not It—this is not our Armageddon, not the great day of judgment on America. For America is change, and the changes have come, often enough, in convulsive spasms. This

Eric Sevareid, "The World Still Moves Our Way," *Look* (July 9, 1968), 27–28. Copyright 1968 by Eric Sevareid. Reprinted by permission of Harold Matson Company, Inc.

country is the vast experimental laboratory in human relations for the twentieth century; it is, in a sense, defining and creating the twentieth century for much of the world.

Unless it is seen in this light, America cannot be understood at all. If many of our contemporary intellectuals, especially those communing with one another in New York City, almost a separate nation in spirit, do not understand it, this is partly because they do not understand themselves. As they attest in innumerable books, they do not know who they are. It may be news to them that the overwhelming majority of Americans *do* know who they are, do *not* feel alienated from their country or their generation.

This is not a "sick society." It is a deeply unsettled and bewildered society, and the reason is not merely the extraordinary changes in this last generation but the speed of these changes. It is the *rate* of change that is new. The life of Americans today resembles that of, say, Grant's time, less than life in Grant's time resembled life in ancient China. The nation is not overpopulated, but the population has shifted out of balance. In the last 20 years alone, 18 million people, including, of course, the Negroes, have moved into the urban centers. This second industrial-scientific revolution has jammed us together, polluted much of our air and waters, smeared ugliness over much of our countryside, obliged us to work within greater economic units and increased the tensions of daily living.

Two other revolutions have been taking place in concert with the new industrial-scientific revolution. One is the communications revolution, which brings every social evil, every human tragedy and conflict immediately and intimately within everyone's ken. The other is the educational revolution, which adds millions every year to the ranks of those moved to add their investigation, articulation or actions to the processes of problem-solving and problem-creating.

We are not becoming less democratic but more democratic. It is not our individual freedom that is in jeopardy, in the first instance, but our public order. It could be argued that we are moving away from representative government, in the direction, at least, of direct democracy, by no means an unmixed blessing. For the immediate future, the problem is not only the indifference or "apathy" of the much-abused middle class or any other group. It is also the problem of too many untrained cooks in the kitchen.

Many current phenomena to the contrary notwithstanding,

Americans are the most natural workers-together in the world. We say we live by the system of individual enterprise, while we are the supreme cooperative society. Totalitarian countries say they are cooperative societies, while their regimes must coerce their people to work. It is absurd to believe that the races of men who turned an empty, forbidding continent into the most efficient engine of production and distribution ever seen, who created the first *mass* democracy with essential order and essential freedom will not solve the problems of crowding, poverty, pollution and ugliness. The solutions will create new problems, after which there will be new solutions, then new problems, and so our life will go on. Time is life. Were human problems ever totally solved, change would come to a stop, and we would begin to die.

American cynics and Cassandras see neither their own history nor the rest of the world with clarity. Violence? We have *always* had a high tolerance level for violence. Abraham Lincoln worried about what he called "the increasing disregard for law which pervades the country; the growing disposition to substitute the wild and furious passions, in lieu of the sober judgment of courts; and the worse than savage mobs, for the executive ministers of justice."

It is even to be doubted that crime is more prevalent than it was in the nineteenth century. Historian Arthur Schlesinger, Jr., reminds us that a century ago, every tenth person in New York City had a police record.

Alienated and irreverent youth? To a degree, youth is always alienated and to a degree ought to be. More that 2,000 years ago, Plato wrote that in a democracy, the father "accustoms himself to become like his child and to fear his sons. . . . The schoolmaster fears and flatters his pupils . . . the young act like their seniors, and compete with them in speech and action, while the old men condescend to the young. . . ." This happens because democratic life carries the in-built impulse to wish to please and accommodate to others.

The alarm over drug-taking is also exaggerated. There is far less use of dangerous drugs today than a half century ago, before narcotics control, when about one American in every four hundred was an addict of some harmful drug, ten times the present rate.

Americans, of course, are not spiritually geared to the past but to the future. It is a reflection of what John Steinbeck, speaking of the onpushing, haggard "Okies" in the dust-bowl years, called the "terrible faith," that we are constantly seized with concern for our children more than for ourselves. Yet it is not possible to see our society in perspective without these backward glances to what we once were, with the consequent realization that we are using different scales of measuring well-being today.

At the turn of the century, a newborn could expect to live about to the age of 50; today, the expectancy is about 70. Once, a mother had sound reason to fear giving birth; today, death in childbirth is regarded as intolerable. Once, a full high school education was the best achievement of a minority; today, it is the barest minimum for decent employment and self-respect. Once, the timber and mining barons stripped away the forests and topsoil wholesale; today, these companies are confronted by their communities at every other move.

One could cite hundreds of similar examples of how our standards of expectancy have risen, as they should, along with our standard of life. The truth is that we Americans are perfectionists, which simply means that we were not, are not and never will be satisfied either with the quantities or the qualities in our life.

By the year 2000, we will look back upon these present years not only as one of America's periodic convulsions but as a rather backward period. By then, the typical American family will have an income of around $20,000 a year or more; a typical American adult will have had at least two years of college, with far broader intellectual and aesthetic horizons. By then, the old urban centers will have been rebuilt, and many millions will live in satellite "new cities," part-urban, part-rural. The incurable diseases like cancer and arthritis will be under far better control.

The present explosion in books, theater, music and art will have transformed tastes and comprehension to an enormous degree. And already, according to the Englishman C. P. Snow, something like 80 percent of the advanced study of science in the Western world is going on in the United States of America. This is the heart reason for the "brain drain" from abroad to the U.S., not merely the higher pay. The facilities, the action, the creative excitement are increasingly here. None of this guarantees a single new Shakespeare, Rembrandt, Beethoven or Einstein, because genius is not developed (though even this may occur one day through selective breeding and cell transplant).

What it does guarantee is a great lifting of the massive center, of the "ordinary" people. This is the premise and the point about America—ours is the first organized dedication to *massive* improvement, to the development of a *mass* culture, the first attempt to educate *everyone* to the limit of his capacities. We have known for a long time that this can be done only through the chemistry of individual freedom. Soviet Russia is just now beginning to discover this for itself. I am unable to understand the thrust of the sufferings and strivings of Western man over the last thousand years save in terms of this kind of achievement.

The popular passion of Americans is not politics, baseball, money or material things. It is education. Education is now our biggest industry, involving more people even than national defense. The percentage of children in kindergarten has doubled in a rather short period; the percentage of youth in college climbs steeply upward. Today, even a Negro boy in the South has a better statistical chance of getting into college than an English youth. And there are about 44 million full- and part-time *adult* students pursuing some kind of formalized learning on their own!

Intelligent foreigners nearly everywhere understand the mountainous meaning of all this for the world as well as for America. They know that much of the world will be transformed in the American image, culturally if not politically. They know that struggle is really all over—it is the Western way of living and doing, our way and the way of Europe combined, that the world wants. It is North America and West Europe that make up the "in" world; Russia and China are still the outsiders trying to enter.

Communism already appears irrelevant, essentially passé. The more the Communist regimes educate their people, the more complex their life will become. They will struggle with the complexities the Western world confronts already, and they will discover that authoritarian direction from the top cannot cope with them. Only the essentially liberal society can manage twentieth-century life, even in practical terms. They will learn, as we have always known, that the effective, the lasting revolution lies in the West, particularly in America.

Why, then, are we in such a state of uproar in this year of Our Lord, and why is much of the world upset about the America of today? Because, as a philosopher once said, "nothing that is vast enters into the life of mortals without a curse," and America is struggling to rid itself of one old curse and one new one. The old curse is the Negro slavery Europeans fastened upon this land long ago, which continues in a hundred psychological, social and economic, if not legal forms. The Negro Passion of today is a revolution within the continuing American revolution, and the one absolute certainty about it is that it is going to succeed, however long and distracting the agony for everyone. It will succeed not only because it has justice with it (justice has been suppresed before) but because there is a deep evangelical streak in the American people, a true collective conscience, and it has been aroused.

RACISM EXISTS in almost all societies on this globe, virulently so, incidentally, in Black Africa. It may be that race prejudice—the psychologists' "stranger hatred"—is an instinct tracing from our animal origins, and therefore ineradicable. Yet man is the only animal *aware* of his instincts; the only animal, therefore, capable of controlling, if not eliminating, his instincts. New law, enforced, compels new behavior. Behavior repeated daily comes to seem normal, and attitudes change. Illusions tend to vanish. The idea that a difference in skin color is an essential difference is an illusion. I am struck by an observation of McGeorge Bundy of the Ford Foundation. He said discrimination will end, partly because this college generation regards racial equality as natural, whereas the older generation regards it only as logical.

The twentieth-century war over radical injustice is now in its virulent stage. The nineteenth-century war in its virulent stage lasted four years. This one will last much longer because it is fought on a thousand narrow fronts, like guerrilla war, and because no grand climacteric is possible. But it is not going to "tear this country apart" or "burn America down" or anything of the sort. A tiny percentage of extremists among only 12 percent of the American population can do much, but they cannot do that.

The new curse has come with America's new military power. A form of Parkinson's Law operates here. The greater the power, the more the men who associate with it, extoll it and find needs, real or sophistical, for its use. The use of available, flexible force becomes easier than hard thought; and the worst aspect of the curse is the gradual, almost unconscious identification of power with virtue. John Adams said, "Power always thinks it has a great soul and vast views beyond the comprehension of the weak. . . ."

We have fallen ino this trap with the Vietnam intervention. For the first time, we have misused our power on a massive scale. But it does not mean that we are a "Fascist" or aggressive people, any more than the racial mess means that we are a hating or oppressive people. Vietnam is not typical; it is a mistake, now recognized as such by most serious thinkers in this country. If millions of people in Europe (every province of which is soaked in blood) stand aghast at what we have done and reproach us bitterly, one unarticulated reason is that they *expect* the United States to act with humaneness and common sense. They do not shout advice to Russia and China, whatever their misdeeds, for the same reason that the crowd in the bullring does not shout advice to the bull but to the bullfighter.

The reassuring thing is not merely that we will get out of this trap and undo the damage as best we can but that we will do so because our own people demand it, not because the enemy is too strong, not because of foreign criticism. We could, if we would, lay North Vietnam totally waste. The American conscience will not permit it. We may not win a military victory in Vietnam, but we will win a victory in our own soul.

No—the humaneness of the American people is still there. The new problems have piled up too rapidly for our brains and our institutions to cope with at anything like the same rate, but the will for justice is as strong as ever—stronger, in my own belief, because thought and expression are freer today than ever before. This is why the Negro revolution has come now— not because conditions of life became worse, save for some, but because of a climate of free expression. In just such periods of great intellectual freedom have nearly all revolutions been generated.

It is a remarkable fact that great numbers of very ordinary people in distant lands understand all this about America better than some of our own intellectuals. If, by some magic, all barriers to emigration and immigration around the world were lifted tomorrow, by far the single biggest human caravan would start moving in one direction—our way.

One day recently, I asked a Cuban refugee why most Cubans like himself wanted to come to the United States rather than go to Latin American countries with the same language and the same general culture. Was it just the thought of greater economic opportunity?

"No," he said, "many of us would have an easier time, economically, in a Latin country. It's just that we feel better here. We can feel like a human being. There seems to be something universal about this country."

This is living testimony, not abstract argument, from men who know the meaning of America in their bones and marrow. Of course, it is the truth. Of course, the dream lives on.

Let those who wish compare America with Rome. Rome lasted around a thousand years.

ALIENATION AND THE AMERICAN DREAM

Duane E. Smith

IF IT is true that a contented nation is a nation gone Tory, as David Lloyd George once claimed, there would seem to be no immediate danger of the United States' lapsing into that condition. There is, doubtless, a large number of American people who are sleek and contented, convinced that theirs is the best of all possible worlds, but this enclave of self-satisfaction continues to shrink. While they enjoy a high degree of material prosperity and a demonstrated capacity for resolving their outstanding problems, the fact remains that the American people are a people beset by doubt, troubled and uncertain. The causes of this uncertainty are the obvious shortcomings of American society, shortcomings so manifestly apparent that it is possible for only the most obtuse to ignore them; this uncertainty is deepened by the large corps of critics and dissenters intent upon bringing these faults to the public's attention. Seldom has any country possessed so many people bent on performing the role of the Socratic gadfly: social critics, political analysts, essayists, journalists, and dissenters, determined to sting the conscience of the nation and to stir it to action. A country blessed with William Buckley and Gore Vidal, Russell Kirk and Tom Hayden, James Kilpatrick and Stokely Carmichael, to name but a few of the more notorious, is not a society likely to drift off into satisfied slumber, even if it wishes to do so.

There are some people, among whom the most prominent are the advocates of the New Left and the New Politics, who suggest that this outburst of criticism and dissent represents a new development in American life. Indeed, the labels themselves convey the impression of novelty and departure from established ways. The fact is, however, that in spite of a popular notion that the United States has been a nation enveloped in a miasma of self-satisfied tranquility, it has had, during most of its history, its share of native critics. Virtually from the beginning, Americans have been given to self-examination, a self-examination sometimes marked by anxiety, sometimes characterized by a more reflective mood. This analysis has occasionally involved a comparison, not always favorable, of American society and culture with that of Europe. More frequently, Americans have been given to evaluating the present state of American society in terms of the promises of the past, of the extent to which the American Dream has in fact been fulfilled.

The existence of a tradition of criticism and dissent clearly indicates vitality. A nation whose institutions and practices are not subjected to continuing analysis and constant criticism is, in all probability, a nation in stagnation. Perfection is reserved for the gods, and perhaps for art. Political life and institutions, human practices, and social arrangements are not, alas, capable of such perfection. Consequently, the institutions by which men are governed and the manner in which the relationships between the members of a given society are ordered are never above criticism or beyond the possibility of improvement. Since this is so, the current critics ought to be viewed not only as manifestations of the profound disorders afflicting American society, but also as indications that the nation still has the vitality to confront those disorders, that it has not drifted off into the false tranquility of an illusory perfection.

To admit the desirability, indeed, the necessity of criticism, is not to say that criticism itself is beyond critical analysis. Some criticisms are better than others. Contrary to the protestations of intellectual egalitarians, the ideal of equality does not apply when we turn to an examination of the claims and prescriptions made by various critics. Such an examination reveals that the most fashionable criticisms are often the most vacuous.

The most modish among the current critics of American society are to be found among those who are associated with the New Left and the New Politics. The causes for the fairly widespread acceptance, especially among intellectuals and liberals, of the observations and arguments of these critics must remain in the realm of speculation, although one is tempted to observe that even intellectuals are not immune to the famous American passion for the latest models—whether in automobiles, fashions, or political and social criticism. Some, of course, would argue that this acceptance is necessitated by the bankruptcy of traditional liberalism, that the circumstances are so desperate that only the most desperate recommendations are relevant.

One need not question the urgency of the problems facing contemporary American society to retain a degree of skepticism regarding the analyses of these "new" critics and dissenters. Indeed, it is precisely this urgency that demands such skepticism. Behavior resulting from anxiety, no matter how justified that anxiety may be, is not likely to be productive behavior, whether we are speaking of an individual or of a society. Consequently, an examination of certain characteristics of these critics and their arguments is in order and does not constitute a denial of the existence of all the problems to which they have addressed themselves.

In one respect the new dissenters are typically American: they are given to invoking the spirit of at least some of the figures in the American pantheon of political, social, and cultural heroes. It is not inappropriate, therefore, to compare these dissenters with one of the folk-heroes of American history. This comparison will make it possible to evaluate the analyses of the "new" critics in light of those of one of the "old," and to shed some light on the central, and, it seems to me, weakest feature of the criticism of the past ten years.

2

"It is not an era of repose. We have used up all our inherited freedoms. If we would save our lives, we must fight for them."[1] These words, which might have been uttered by a contemporary critic of the United States, are, in fact, the words of Henry David Thoreau. Thoreau enjoys a certain popularity among the advocates of radical politics, particularly in connection with the doctrine of civil disobedience. One suspects that this popularity is the result of a highly selective reading of his works. A

[1] *The Writings of Henry David Thoreau* (Boston, 1894), IV, p. 407.

more complete reading of Thoreau's political philosophy reveals attitudes which those who are given to invoking his name tend to ignore.

There are three aspects of Thoreau's work which are especially relevant to the present discussion: his rejection of politics, his extreme individualism, and his utter detachment and lack of resentment and alienation.

One influential interpretation of the American experience argues that the dominant school of political thought in the United States is derived from the premises of John Locke.[2] Surprisingly enough, Thoreau is very much a part of this tradition. Among other things, Locke maintained that government should perform relatively limited functions, the most important of which is the provision of security for the citizens and their property.[3] This minimization of the role of government clearly represents a suspicion of, if not actually a hostility to, the exercise of power by the political institutions of society. And this suspicion in turn results from Locke's individualistic bias, a bias revealed by the fact that the state of nature in which men exist as atomistic individuals, held together by the most tenuous ties of self-interest, may be said to provide the model for Locke's ideal political system. The purpose of the political order is, in short, to protect the rights of these individuals. It does not transform them into a community, and its function is not to create the conditions for love, direct and intimate human relationships, and an escape from loneliness, to borrow some of the language of the New Left.[4]

Although Thoreau firmly rejected certain prominent features of the society in which he lived, and was a dissenter—a dissenter who was when the occasion demanded prepared to go to jail for his beliefs—when he wrote on political matters, he seldom strayed from the Lockian framework. To the extent that

[2] Louis Hartz, *The Liberal Tradition in America* (New York, 1955).

[3] John Locke, *Two Treatises of Government,* ed. Peter Laslett (Cambridge, 1960), p. 368.

[4] "The Commonwealth seems to me to be a society of men constituted only for the procuring, preserving, and advancing their civil interests.

Civil interests I call life, liberty, health, and indolency of body; and the possession of outward things, such as money, lands, houses, furniture, the like." John Locke, *Treatise of Civil Government and a Letter Concerning Toleration,* ed. Charles L. Sherman (New York, 1937), p. 172.

there are anarchistic premises implicit in Lockianism, it was Thoreau who made these premises explicit. His general attitude toward politics is revealed in the passage, "What is called politics is comparatively something so superficial and inhuman, that practically I have never recognized that it concerns me at all."[5] The activities performed by governments "are, it is true, vital functions of human society, but should be unconsciously performed, like the corresponding function of the physical body."[6] He heartily concurred with the motto: "That government is best which governs least."[7] He went on to say, however, "But to speak practically and as a citizen, unlike those who call themselves no-government men, I ask for, not at once no government, but *at once* a better government."[8] And his concept of the function which would be performed by a better government was made clear when he declared that "government is an expedient by which men would fain succeed in letting one another alone; and, as has been said, when it is most expedient, the governed are most let alone by it."[9]

These several passages reveal that Thoreau, in spite of his reservations about various aspects of American society, shared a typically American skepticism regarding politics and government. And his conviction that "government is an expedient by which men would fain succeed in letting one another alone" was a manifestation of yet another aspect of his thought which was also characteristically American: his individualism and his belief in the virtues of self-reliance. Thoreau's singular manner of living sustained his conviction that each man can elevate himself by his own conscious effort and that the attainment of one's goals had little, if anything, to do with society. Indeed, since society can only interfere with the real business at hand, each man must free himself to the utmost from the claims of that society. At the same time, one has no right to make any claim upon that social order except, of course, the claim to be left alone.

Thoreau's extreme individualism led to what is, for this discussion, the most significant element of his thought: his utter detachment, complemented by a total absence of alienation. "Perhaps," he wrote, "I am more than usually jealous with re-

5 Thoreau, IV, p. 480.
6 *Ibid.*, IV, p. 481.
7 *Ibid.*, IV, p. 356.
8 *Ibid.*, IV, p. 357.
9 *Ibid.*, IV, p. 357.

spect to my freedom. I feel that my connection with and obligations to society are still very slight and transient."[10]

The most notable event in Thoreau's life was his sojourn at Walden Pond. This act of physical detachment from the town of Concord may have been largely symbolic, but nevertheless, it epitomizes Thoreau's attitude. The real business of a man's life should be pursued apart from society. A man must make his own life, alone. Solitude and isolation should be pursued rather than avoided, for they provide the conditions in which a man's true humanity is to be found. Thus Thoreau indicated his commitment to the private quest for self: "it is time to look after the *res-privata*. . . ."[11]

While Thoreau rejected the demands of the state and society, he did not rail against them. When he was released from jail after his refusal to pay his taxes, he proceeded on his way to the huckleberry patch toward which he had been headed at the time of his arrest. There, he calmly remarked, "the state was nowhere to be seen."[12] It is this mild, indeed, bland dismissal of society and its institutions which is one of the most appealing aspects of Thoreau's thought. The anger and resentment of the alienated man simply were not a part of his character. He was a critic of American society, he sought to escape from at least some aspects of that society, and yet paradoxically, in his search for isolation, he was very much a part of the society of which he was one of the most eloquent critics. For the search for isolation, for independence, whether it involved going to Walden Pond or to the western frontier, was a central feature of the American Dream. That dream can be described as an attempt to recapture the total freedom and isolation of the state of nature. The communitarian impulse has not been completely absent from American life, but it has, until recently, been relatively rare. Although Brook Farm, the Oneida Community, and various other utopian experiments were manifestations of that impulse, it remains true that for most Americans, the ideal has been an asocial, apolitical one, in which each man is essentially alone.

Thoreau was not an isolated case. He was, to the contrary, the archetypal American in this regard, as can be seen if one considers, even briefly, various American folk heroes. Huck Finn, floating down the Mississippi, was making his escape from

[10] *Ibid.*, IV, p. 460.
[11] *Ibid.*, IV, p. 476.
[12] *Ibid.*, IV, p. 380.

SMITH **351**

society—and not, it should be noted, sneering at it, as his modern counterpart, Holden Caulfield, was to do. One of the most characteristic of American heroes is the detective—Sam Spade, Phillip Marlowe, and the other characters of the novels of Dashiell Hammett and Raymond Chandler. They are men essentially outside of society—loners—without lasting attachments of any sort, slightly cynical perhaps, but possessed of a certain tough integrity. Marlowe is described on the cover of the paper edition of *The Lady in the Lake* as "just an ordinary guy [who] wants to make a fairly honest buck and *live in peace*"[13] (italics mine). In *The Simple Art of Murder*, he says of himself, "It is quite true that I wasn't doing anything that morning except looking at a blank sheet of paper in my typewriter and thinking of writing a letter. It is also quite true that I don't have a great deal to do any morning. But that is no reason why I should have to go out hunting for old Mrs. Penruddock's pearl necklace. I don't happen to be a policeman."[14] Marlowe, like Thoreau, would prefer to be left alone, but society and its Mrs. Penruddocks continue to make their unwelcome demands. Still, the desire to escape, the desire for isolation remains. Similarly, the hero of Cooper's *Leatherstocking Tales* was also a man alone, essentially in the state of nature. And the litany would not be complete, obviously, without a passing reference to the Gary Coopers, the John Waynes, and the various other heroes of that peculiarly American genre, the "Western," a genre which might be described as the final Americanization of the Lockian state of nature.

3

Dreams by their nature do not last, and sometimes they become nightmares. The American Dream is no exception. The ideal of the personal pursuit of happiness, of the private quest for self, of the challenge of an invigorating isolation, appears to have gone sour. America has discovered society and in the process has also discovered, paradoxically, alienation. It is this discovery which may constitute America's lost innocence.

[13] Raymond Chandler, *The Lady in the Lake*, Pocket Book ed. (New York, 1946).
[14] Raymond Chandler, *The Simple Art of Murder*, Pocket Book ed. (New York, 1952), p. 3.

The new American hero desperately attempts to escape from isolation, driven by an obsessive fear of being alone. As a result, we read of Saul Bellow's Herzog, madly writing letters to the living and the dead in an insane attempt to establish contact with another soul. John Updike's Couples are described as indiscriminately coupling in a desperate effort to touch one another and reassure themselves of their own existence. In Edward Albee's Zoo Story, the effort to escape from loneliness, ultimately from one's self, ends on the point of a knife. Instead of sharing the delightful insouciance of Huckleberry Finn, we are subjected to the whining of Holden Caulfield. In place of Thoreau's calm pursuit of isolation, we have Portnoy's interminable complaints.

Alienation is now among the most common of American preoccupations. Psychologists describe it, sociologists analyze it, political scientists discuss its impact on the political life of the nation, the young (and not so young) revel in it, and novelists and playwrights use it as their principal theme. Virtually everyone, particularly those who wish to be regarded as sensitive and intelligent, claims with anguish that he too is to be numbered among the alienated, although the anguish is often rendered suspect by the undercurrent of pleasure which one sometimes detects in such confessions. In short, alienation is extremely chic, both as a concept and a condition, and one is tempted to observe that it has, perhaps, replaced original sin as the object of horrified fascination for a people who remain Puritan at heart, but have lost their faith.

What actually does it mean to be alienated? The concept was originally a European one and has been used to refer to a variety of phenomena. It did not, for example, mean the same thing for Marx as it did for Kierkegaard, and its modern usage has connotations somewhat different from those found in either of these writers. In general, it may be said that in contemporary literature there are usually two conditions associated with alienation: estrangement and resentment. Sometimes one of these is stressed, sometimes the other, and we frequently find both of them emphasized.

One of the classic examples of estrangement is the hero of Camus' novel The Stranger. Here was a man who, while in this world and more specifically and importantly, in a particular society, was not of it. His was a condition of total unrelatedness. His relationships with people were infected with an atmosphere of unreality. The Mediterranean sun, the sea, physical and sensual pleasures, constituted the primary reality—his sole connection with the world. He was, as the title suggests, literally a stranger and unable to overcome that condition. Indeed, in spite of a vague recognition that he ought to overcome it, he had no real desire to do so.

The other condition, resentment, is exemplified by Holden Caulfield. While American adolescence is commonly a stage of development characterized by resentment, this response to the world is also to be found among various categories of adults. This reaction emerges from a feeling that in some way the world doesn't quite measure up, that society has not fulfilled one's expectations, that one's hopes have been dashed by an uncomprehending reality. It is this feeling which gives to the expression of resentment its most characteristic tone: a combination of the accusation and the whine.

The quality of resentment and its source can perhaps best be captured by a quotation from John Ruskin: "I am no misanthrope, only a disappointed philanthropist—a much more difficult kind of person to deal with."[15] The most prominent examples of those people beyond adolescence whose alienation includes this mood of resentment are artists and intellectuals. Of the former, Albert Camus tells us that they see themselves as "solitary creators, who are obstinate rivals of a God they condemn."[16] They see their task as "not only . . . to create a world or to exalt beauty for its own sake, but also to define an attitude. Thus the artist becomes a model and offers himself as an example. . . ."[17] It is clear that much of what Camus said of the artist is equally applicable to the intellectual. And the refusal of those to whom the artist or the intellectual offers himself as a model and an example to accept him in these roles is, doubtless, a critical factor in the resentment with which these men confront society. The disappointed, rejected philanthropist is, as Ruskin reminded us, a very difficult kind of person to deal with.

Estrangement and resentment have been discussed and indeed can exist separately. However, as suggested, they are often found in combination, and it is probable that they feed on each other, estrangement leading to greater resentment and vice versa.

Finally, let us consider the relationship of alienation to iso-

15 *The Works of John Ruskin,* ed., E. T. Cook and Alexander Wedderburn, Library Edition (London, 1903–1912), XVII, p. xi.

16 Albert Camus, *The Rebel,* trans. Anthony Bower (New York, 1958), p. 53.

17 *Ibid.,* p. 53.

lation and loneliness. Isolation is not a condition that is necessarily associated with alienation. Robinson Crusoe was isolated,
but he was not alienated. Holden Caulfield, on the other hand,
was surrounded by the masses of the city, and, as he frequently
reminds us, was a very alienated little fellow. Indeed, in light
of the fact that alienation is a response to society, either in
terms of estrangement or resentment, it may be said that the
man who is physically separated from a society is not alienated
unless he sought such isolation as a result of his estrangement
or resentment.

Psychic isolation, however, presents a different problem. A
man may be surrounded by people, he may even be acquainted
for that matter friendly with some, and yet be essentially isolated, that is to say, alone. For some men, this condition is not
an undesirable one; it may be consciously sought, as it was by
Thoreau. For others, however, it is painful, a condition to be
avoided at any cost, and these are the lonely men. One of the
most poignant descriptions of loneliness is to be found in E. E.
Cummings' *The Enormous Room:* "In the case of Surplice, to
be the butt of everyone's ridicule could not be called precisely
suffering: inasmuch as Surplice, being unspeakably lonely, enjoyed any and all insults for the simple reason that they constituted or at least implied a recognition of his existence. To
be made a fool of was, to this otherwise completely neglected
individual, a mark of distinction; something to take pleasure in;
to be proud of." It meant, in short, "I, Surplice, am a very necessary creature after all."[18]

There are various possible responses to loneliness, of which
alienation is one. What is more reasonable, after all, than to
resent that society which ignores one, which leaves one in the
psychic squalor of the loneliness which is the source of fear
and dread?

4

What has all of this to do with the New Left, the New Poli-
tics, and student and adult dissent in modern American society?
The answer is that the most characteristic feature of the radical
Left is the blatant alienation of its advocates and this alienation

[18] E. E. Cummings, *The Enormous Room*, Modern Library ed.
(New York, 1934), p. 262.

has set the general tone of the social and political criticism of the past ten years.

This criticism can be discussed in three ways: (1) from the point of view of the posture which the critics have assumed toward that society against which their criticisms are directed; (2) from the perspective of the issues raised; (3) from the angle of the solutions proposed.

The first of these is the most important. The characteristic stance which the advocates of the New Left and the New Politics take toward American society clearly is one of alienation, an alienation compounded of estrangement and resentment. This alienation, in turn, is a reaction to what is perceived as the impersonality of modern American society and its institutions. Three passages from one of the classic statements from the New Left, "The Port Huron Statement," suggest that this is the case. Here it is stated: "We regard *men* as infinitely precious and possessed of unfulfilled capacities for reason, freedom, and love. . . . We oppose the depersonalization that reduces human beings to the status of things. . . ."[19] And further: "The real campus, the familiar campus, is a place of private people, engaged in their notorious 'inner migration.' "[20] Finally, we are told, "Loneliness, estrangement, isolation describe the vast difference between man and man today."[21]

Alienation has moved out of the novel, it has come down from the stage, and it has entered into the realm of American political and social criticism with results which shall be elaborated below.

To claim that all of the issues around which the dissenters have gathered are reflections, direct or indirect, of their alienation would be inaccurate. One of the first was, of course, America's racial tragedy. The hollowness of the promises of American democracy in the face of the determined, systematic, and brutal exclusion of black people from even the most elementary participation in its benefits, material and otherwise, has long been viewed as an affliction on the American body politic. Only the most insensitive, the most morally obtuse can fail to see it as such. The war in Vietnam and, more generally, America's role in the world, particularly *vis-à-vis* the developing countries, was also a problem about which many not identified with the New

[19] Paul Jacobs and Saul Lanlow, *The New Radicals* (New York, 1966), p. 154.

[20] *Ibid.*, p. 157.

[21] *Ibid.*, p. 155.

Left or the New Politics have demanded a re-examination. One need not be alienated to have serious doubts about the wisdom of our Vietnam policy. A third issue has involved the university, and, once again, one may have questions regarding the extent to which it is performing appropriate functions successfully without being numbered among the alienated. And finally, the political system itself has come under attack, but reservations about the success with which the institutions of the United States facilitate the full attainment of the democratic ideal are hardly unique to the dissenters.

Consequently, it is not the issues themselves which distinguish the new critics from their liberal opponents. (And, alas, it is liberalism which is viewed as the enemy.) After all, concern regarding such matters as racial injustice, a dubious foreign policy, the problems posed by the multiversity, and the effective functioning of the government in terms of meeting the needs of the people can hardly be taken as manifestations of alienation.

The evidence of alienation is most clearly seen in the tone of the criticism and the nature of the solutions offered. The cases of the university and American political institutions are the most instructive.

The university is denounced by the disaffected as "a place of private people."[22] While many of the criticisms of the university are directed at the alleged irrelevance of its curriculum and toward its complicity with the notorious Establishment and the many crimes it is said to be guilty of perpetrating, the criticism in the main comes down to the fundamental charge that the university is "a place of private people." For example, take the charge of irrelevance. Relevance is essentially a personal matter, a matter to be determined by the private person alone. The appeal for greater relevance can be seen, then, as a plea for an escape from privacy, from the lonely task of determining for one's self what is relevant and how. Similarly, the reaction against the multiversity, its bureaucracy, and its impersonalism: it is within such an institution that privacy, or loneliness, is most intensified, and it was precisely the desire to escape from this loneliness which gave rise to the Luddite tantrums of Mario Savio and those he inspired. "There is a time," Savio announced, "when the operations of the machine become so odious, make you so sick at heart, that you can't take part. And you've got to put your bodies upon the gears and upon the wheels, upon the

22 *Ibid.*, p. 157.

levers, upon all the apparatus, and you've got to make it stop. And you've got to indicate to the people who run it, to the people who own it, that unless you're free the machine will be prevented from working at all."[23]

One of the Free Speech Movement symbols at Berkeley was an IBM card labeled: "STUDENT AT UC: DO NOT BEND, FOLD, OR MUTILATE." The significance, clearly, was not in the words but the symbol itself. The student is regarded by the bureaucracy as a number, a coded IBM card, and not as a person. (One might point out that there are certain advantages in being regarded as a number, of which privacy is the most obvious. The symbol of the IBM card is not necessarily as devastating as it is sometimes thought to be. Anonymity, like virtue, has its rewards.) Consequently, the complaint against professors is not only that they do not do a good job of teaching, a complaint with a distressing degree of validity. It is also that professors are not willing to breach the privacy of the students and are not in turn prepared to permit the students to invade their privacy, that they are not, in short, prepared to enter into personal relationships, providing students with the coziness of an ersatz family. In sum, the revulsion against the university in large measure comes down exactly to this: it is not a community, it does not provide a warm environment within which one can escape from the essential isolation of the intellectual endeavor.

Turning to the criticisms of the political system, one theme is constantly reiterated: participation, or more popularly, participatory democracy. Political parties are attacked because they do not provide the means for greater participation by the masses of the people in those decisions having major impact upon the quality and direction of their lives. Various forms of community organizations are romanticized because, presumably, they do facilitate such participation. Of course, there are many reasons why participation in political life is desirable. For one thing, it tends to encourage a greater degree of responsibility on the part of those charged with the task of making decisions on behalf of the community. Interestingly enough, this is rarely the reason brought forward by those people devoted to more intense forms of participation. Rather, participation is seen as a path offering an escape from loneliness, from isolation.

Participation has become a means of transforming those no-

23 *Ibid.,* p. 61.

torious private people into public people, outward rather than inward facing. There is little if any tolerance for those who would cultivate their own gardens, who, like Thoreau, would go to Walden, or like Phillip Marlowe, would prefer to live in peace. Tom Hayden proclaimed, "we seek the establishment of a democracy of individual participation, governed by two central aims: that the individual share in those social decisions determining the quality and direction of his life; that society be organized to encourage independence in men and provide media for their common participation."[24] The possibility that for some men the quest for independence is along other paths is not entertained.

The accounts given by various young people who have participated in the activities of SDS, and more generally, in The Movement, suggest that the emphasis on participation is not seen primarily in terms of the development of beneficial public policies. What is stressed is the development of authentic human relationships, the attainment of a sense of community, the escape from loneliness. "To be in The Movement is to search for a psychic community, in which one's identity can be defined, social and personal relationships based on love can be established and can grow."[25] Further, we read, "For many members and leaders SDS is more than an organization; it is a community of friends. . . . Personal relationships are often inseparable from political life. . . ."[26]

Even the public policies which are pursued are frequently described in terms of personal relationships, of destroying the alienation which is seen as one of the most decadent features of modern society. One of the goals of The Movement, we are told, "is expressed by the desire to change the way we, as individuals, actually live and deal with other people. We speak of the desire to achieve 'community,' to reach levels of intimacy and directness with others unencumbered by the conventional barriers of race, status, class, etc."[27]

One has the sense that the game was given away by an account of the sit-in at the Palace Hotel in San Francisco, a sit-in the purpose of which was to obtain more jobs for blacks. One participant wrote that "the lobby was filled, the lobby and the long corridors on either side, and we each realized, scanning

24 *Ibid.*, p. 155.
25 *Ibid.*, p. 4.
26 *Ibid.*, p. 29.
27 *Ibid.*, p. 163.

the mass of a thousand faces, that *we were not alone* . . . when it was over we were no longer strangers to one another. For twenty-four hours we were a community."[28]

5

To assert that people are satisfying deep personal needs through their participation in political activity is to rob that activity of neither its nobility nor its validity. Quite clearly, the motives which lie behind any human action are of varying degrees of complexity, and this is especially true of those which lead men to participate in politics. However, some of the more questionable characteristics of the New Left and the New Politics can best be understood as responses to alienation, an alienation which emerges from the psychic void felt by the man who is alone and does not like his condition.

One of the most striking and in some ways most disturbing features of this political style is its resurrection of a kind of Sorelian commitment to action. (One is tempted to describe it as a kinetic theory of politics.) Stated in its simplest terms, action is good, inaction bad. Indeed, two sympathetic observers of the young tell us, "These young people believe that they must make something happen. . . ."[29] And one cannot but notice the frequency with which the participants in various aspects of the radical Left, whether it be civil rights, SDS, or what have you, describe themselves as a part of "The Movement," the term itself suggesting action, motion, and excitement. This reflexive activism, this view of politics as a "happening," this passion for merging one's self in The Movement, is, I suggest, an attempt to escape from isolation, from loneliness, from alienation. *"We were not alone. . . ."*

The activist impulse, the passion for movement, is closely allied to yet another disturbing feature of the radical Left: its anti-intellectualism. There is a marked tendency to elevate emotion over reason and this devotion to emotion is the result of a conviction that reason often tends to delay, temporarily if not quite indefinitely, action. "We are . . . disgusted with the liberal's rhetoric, agnosticism, and incapacity for political action,"[30] it is

[28] *Ibid.*, p. 213.
[29] *Ibid.*, p. 3.
[30] *Ibid.*, p. 99.

asserted. But, one might point out that agnosticism—i.e., the absence of an unreasoning commitment—is often the result of a devotion to a reasoned examination of the problems, an examination which leads to a fuller appreciation of the complexity of these problems, an appreciation which minimizes the possibility of total commitment. The result should be not an incapacity for political action, but an increase in the probabilities that such action will lead to the desired outcome.

Moreover, one detects a resurgence of the cult of feeling, and more specifically the cult of love, of which Erich Fromm was once the high priest. The present leaders have ensconced themselves in emotional gardens far more intense and dramatic than Fromm's, and in some instances infinitely more bizarre: the land of psychedelia, the territories of folk and rock music, and the monasteries of various arcane Eastern religions.

This emphasis upon feeling, emotion, and especially love, is obviously an aspect of the anti-intellectual revolt against the rationalism of liberalism. One can hardly miss the frequency with which love is made a part of the political platforms offered by the spokesmen of the radical Left. And it does not require a great deal of psychological sophistication to see this too as an attempted escape from loneliness, a flight to the warmth of community where intimacy and directness are protected from the abrasive intrusions of reason—examining, questioning, doubting, and worst of all, fault-finding reason. Thoreau would simply cringe.

6

Thomas Hobbes wrote: "The *vain-glory* which consisteth in the feigning or supposing of abilities in ourselves, which we know are not, is most incident to young men, and nourished by the histories, or fictions of gallant persons; and is corrected oftentimes by age, and employment."[31] The new radicalism is largely the product of youth and one is tempted to dismiss their claims and ambitions as Hobbesian vain-glory and to pray that this condition will be corrected by age and employment. While this would almost certainly be a mistake it is equally misguided to stand on the sidelines, applauding every action, approving

[31] Thomas Hobbes, *Leviathan,* ed. Michael Oakeshott (Oxford, 1957), p. 36.

every claim, and seconding every demand. The young are praised for their sincerity and honesty. Leaving aside the fact that sincerity and honesty are probably overvalued in the current ethical marketplace, it can be pointed out that the young are always sincere. In fact, the younger you are, the more sincere you are likely to be, and the average three year old child is sincere beyond belief. Clearly, sincerity alone is not enough to warrant a claim to attention and respect.

In addition, one must guard against the American obsession with youth in evaluating the political convictions and activities of the young. There is a tendency among those over thirty to attempt to recapture their lost youth through a pathetic capitulation before every claim of the young. This tendency should be resisted and to those for whom the process of growing old is a problem we ought, perhaps, to prescribe a program of physical exercises.

At the same time, it is equally clear that some (by no means all) of the issues which disturb young people are among the most serious confronting the American society. These include, among others, the problems of poverty and of minorities; the quality of education in the schools and universities; and responsive and responsible political institutions. We ought, of course, to be paying attention to those problems, not because the young talk about them, but because they are problems for all of us. The American political system must prove its capacity to solve these various problems at the same time that it affirms its commitments to individual freedom, reasoned and civilised political action, and detached and skeptical political inquiry.

We must, however, continue to question the dictates of the young and the demands of those who would abandon their individuality in an orgy of togetherness. One of the ironies in the present circumstances is that the young are frequently praised for their independent spirit, their adventurousness. Yet one of their most marked tendencies is a fear, indeed a hostility to isolation, aloneness. The middle-age whining of Herzog, as he surveys the wreckage of his life, makes some kind of sense. But it makes no sense when one encounters it in the young, particularly among those who are given to invoking the spirit of Thoreau. There is, perhaps, more to be learned from Thoreau than has yet been learned; aloneness, isolation, and detachment are not necessarily conditions to be feared and avoided. Rather, they are to be embraced, since it is precisely when a man is alone that he is most free. This is not to advocate an irresponsible individualism in which one ignores the ills of the world. Phillip Marlowe did go out and find old Mrs. Penruddock's pearl necklace and Thoreau did refuse to pay his taxes.

Consequently, to those compulsive seekers of community in the lobby and corridors of the Palace Hotel, to those who believe that intimacy, directness, and love constitute all that is worthy in human life, the reply must be: "When the springs dry up, the fish are all together on dry land. They will moisten each other with their dampness and keep each other wet with their slime. But this is not to be compared with their forgetting each other in a river or a lake."[32]

Just as there is a time for living and a time for dying, so there is a time for remembering and a time for forgetting, as well as a time for being remembered and a time for being forgotten.

[32] *Ibid.*, p. lxvi.

CONTRIBUTORS

Renata Adler has been a contributor to *The New Yorker* and reviewed films for *The New York Times.*

Edward C. Banfield is Professor of Government at Harvard University. Among his books are *The Moral Basis of a Backward Society, Political Influence,* and *Big City Politics.*

Midge Decter is an editor of *Harper's Magazine.* She has also contributed to *Commentary* and *The Atlantic.*

Franklin L. Ford was formerly the Dean of the Faculty of Harvard University where he is now Professor of History. He is the author of *Robe and Sword* and *Strasbaury in Transition.*

William P. Gerberding is Associate Professor of Political Science at the University of California, Los Angeles. He is the author of *United States Foreign Policy: Perspectives and Analysis.*

Nathan Glazer is Professor of Education and Social Structure, Graduate School of Education, Harvard University. Among his books are *The Social Basis of American Communism, The Lonely Crowd* (with David Riesman and Reuel Denney), and *Beyond the Melting Pot* (with Daniel P. Moynihan).

Michael J. Halberstam is a physician.

Louis J. Halle is a professor at the Graduate Institute of International Studies in Geneva. Among his books are *Dream and Reality* and *The Cold War as History.*

Sidney Hook is Emeritus Professor of Philosophy at New York University. He wrote, among many other books, *Heresy, Yes—Conspiracy, No; The Ambiguous Legacy: Marx and the Marxists;* and *The Paradoxes of Freedom.* He was an organizer of the Congress for Cultural Freedom.

Irving Howe has taught at Brandeis, Stanford, and Hunter College. He is the author of several books, including *Politics and the Novel.* He is the editor of *Dissent.*

Irving Kristol was an editor of *Encounter* and is a co-editor of *The Public Interest.* He has been a contributor to *Foreign Affairs, Fortune, The New York Times Magazine,* and *Harper's Magazine.*

Melvin J. Lasky is a co-editor of *Encounter.*

Herbert McClosky is Professor of Political Science at the University of California, Berkeley. He is the co-author of *The Soviet Dictatorship* and a contributor to various professional journals.

John Osborne is the author of *The Entertainer, Epitaph for George Dilon, Look Back in Anger, Luther, A Patriot for Me,* and other plays.

John R. Searle is Professor of Philosophy at the University of California, Berkeley. He wrote *Speech Acts.*

Eric Sevareid has been with CBS since 1939.

Edward Shils is Professor of Social Thought and Sociology at the University of Chicago. Among his books are *The Torment of Secrecy* and *Political Development in the New States.*

Duane E. Smith is Assistant Professor of Political Science at the University of California, Los Angeles.

Tibor Szamuely is Lecturer in Politics at the Univeristy of Reading (England) and a regular contributor to *Spectator* and other British journals.

The late Robert Waelder was a psychoanalyst. He was the author of *Basic Theory of Psychoanalysis* and *Progress and Revolution.*

James Q. Wilson is Professor of Government at Harvard University. Among his books are *Negro Politics, The Amateur Democrat,* and *Varieties of Police Behavior.*

ABCDEFGHIJ- R -765432l0